Anna D. Havinga
Invisibilising Austrian German

Lingua Historica Germanica

Studien und Quellen zur Geschichte
der deutschen Sprache und Literatur

Herausgegeben von
Stephan Müller, Jörg Riecke,
Claudia Wich-Reif und Arne Ziegler

Band 18

 GGSG Gesellschaft für germanistische Sprachgeschichte e.V.

Anna D. Havinga

Invisibilising Austrian German

On the effect of linguistic prescriptions and educational
reforms on writing practices in 18th-century Austria

DE GRUYTER

Printed and published with the assistance of the
Association for German Studies in Great Britain and Ireland.

ISBN 978-3-11-054629-3
e-ISBN (PDF) 978-3-11-054704-7
e-ISBN (EPUB) 978-3-11-054649-1
ISSN 2363-7951

Library of Congress Cataloging-in-Publication Data
A CIP catalog record for this book has been applied for at the Library of Congress.

Bibliografische Information der Deutschen Nationalbibliothek
Die Deutsche Nationalbibliothek verzeichnet diese Publikation in der Deutschen
Nationalbibliografie; detaillierte bibliografische Daten sind im Internet über
http://dnb.dnb.de abrufbar.

© 2018 Walter de Gruyter GmbH, Berlin/Boston
Druck und Bindung: CPI books GmbH, Leck
♾ Gedruckt auf säurefreiem Papier
Printed in Germany

www.degruyter.com

Fürn Papa und de Mama

Acknowledgements

This monograph was presented as a doctoral thesis to the University of Bristol in March 2016. My research was generously supported by the University of Bristol as well as the *Association for German Studies in Great Britain and Ireland* (*AGS*) and the *Deutscher Akademischer Austauschdienst* (*DAAD*), for which I am very grateful. I also wish to express my gratitude to the helpful employees of the *Austrian State Archives* (Vienna), the *Styrian Provincial Archives* (Graz), the *Archives of Upper Austria* (Linz), the schoolbook collection of the *Austrian Federal Ministry of Education* (Vienna), and the *School Museum Bad Leonfelden*.

Special thanks go to my main supervisor Prof. Nils Langer, who encouraged me throughout my PhD, provided very constructive feedback on my research as well as on growing tomatoes, and always had time for a chat. I also thank my second supervisor Dr Steffan Davies for his useful advice and his help with the translation of historical terms.

Furthermore, I wish to express my gratitude to my examiners, Prof. Robert Vilain (Bristol) and Prof. Paul Rössler (Regensburg), as well as to various academics for their helpful suggestions and advice: Prof. Martin Durrell (Manchester), Prof. Stephan Elspaß (Salzburg), Dr James Hawkey (Bristol), Prof. Rudolf Muhr (Graz), Dr Simon Pickl (Salzburg), Dr Stefaniya Ptashnyk (Heidelberg), Dr Raf van Rooy (Leuven), Dr Wendelin Sroka (Essen), Prof. José del Valle (New York), Prof. Peter Wiesinger (Vienna). I also thank the *Historical Sociolinguistic Network* (*HiSoN*) for bringing specialists in the field of historical sociolinguistics together, which led to very fruitful discussions.

Last but certainly not least, my thanks goes to everybody who supported and encouraged me throughout my PhD and the book publishing process: my wonderful husband Adam, my parents Edith & David, my sister Laura and her boyfriend Mike, my brother Michi and his wife Beth, my former housemates Fiona and Markus, and many more friends/relatives, who showed interest in my research, in particular Helfried, Kathi, Kerstin, Sara, Barbara & Warren, Claire, Hodi, Nic, Gesine, and Sean & his family. I am particularly grateful for the contribution of Bernhard and Claudia. A big thank you also goes to all the members of the German Department/School of Modern Languages at the University of Bristol, who have made me feel at home in Bristol (Annette, Christophe & Tim, Debbie, Edith, Evi, Hannah, Jonas, Margit, Mark, Ruth, Stephan & Tobi).

Anna D. Havinga
Bristol, 2017

Contents

List of Figures

List of Tables

Abbreviations and notes on presentation

acc.	accusative
act.	active
BMB	*Bundesministerium für Bildung (Austrian Federal Ministry of Education)*
c.	circa
CG	Central German
comm.	communication
dat.	dative
decl.	declension
ECG	East Central German
ENHG	Early New High German
EUG	East Upper German
fem.	feminine
Fig.	Figure
gen.	genitive
ind.	indicative
MHG	Middle High German
NG	North German
nom.	nominative
OOLA	*Oberösterreichisches Landesarchiv*
p.	page
part.	participle
pers.	person
pl.	plural
pres.	present
sg.	singular
STLA	*Landesarchiv Steiermark*
subj.	subjunctive
Tab.	Table
UG	Upper German
vs	versus
WUG	West Upper German

The original spelling is generally kept in direct quotations as well as in the titles and transcription of primary sources. However, the long *s* (ſ) is replaced by *s* since it is an allograph of *s* and its use is solely dependent on the position in a word (word-initial and within words). Furthermore, umlauts are spelled with dots (e.g. *ü*) instead of superscript *e* (e.g. *ů*). Words given as examples in direct quotations are printed in italics to ease the reading and comprehension of the text. All translations from German into English are my own.

1 Introduction

In their ambition to provide a comprehensive account of the history of language use, historical sociolinguists face a number of practical challenges in their work: as historians they must rely on what evidence survives from the past. However, with regard to preservation of historical language use, three principal problems arise: not everything that was language use was written down, not everything that was written down was considered worthy of preservation at the time of writing and not everything that was meant to be preserved was retained to the present-day. Historical linguists need to make do with what survives but historical sociolinguists are also tasked with trying to work out what did not survive or was never written down in the first place. My research addresses this issue by providing an account of the disappearance of Austrian German from the written domain and demonstrates how certain top-down language policies in the eighteenth century can be *shown* to change writing practices in Austria in contemporary and subsequent generations.

Whilst recognising that spoken data from historical times prior to the invention of audio recording cannot be analysed, the surviving text types from, say, the 18th century, represent different degrees of orality, with legal texts displaying a language use that is much more formal and 'scribal' than, for example, private letters from lesser-educated writers. However, historical material that is conceptually closer to spoken language (cf. Koch & Oesterreicher 1985, 1994) is often difficult to find and rarely preserved in archives or libraries. This means that varieties and variants that were only used in spoken discourse remain 'invisible' to modern-day researchers since they are not recorded in written texts. In this context, the term 'invisibilisation' has been suggested to refer to a process of implicit or explicit stigmatisation, which prevents the use of certain variants or varieties in writing (cf. Havinga & Langer 2015).[1]

In this monograph, the case of the decrease of Upper German (UG) variants in 18th-century Austrian German texts is discussed to show how a particular variety became increasingly invisible in writing, even though it continued to be used and passed on to future generations in speech. This invisibilisation can be linked to language ideologies, to the normative works of 18th-century grammarians, and to the introduction of Empress Maria Theresa's educational reforms in the second half of

---

1 The term 'invisibilisation' is more forceful than 'disappearance' and implies a degree of deliberate agency, i.e. a particular variant or variety is no longer written down for a reason, not accidentally. Skutnabb-Kangas's (2000) wider use of 'invisibilisation' corresponds with this understanding of the term. In her discussion of the suppression or marginalisation of minority languages, cultures, and peoples, she refers to cases where languages are not acknowledged, are not granted the label 'languages' or regarded as small parts of the majority language. Thus minority languages and cultures are stigmatised and made invisible by those in power (Skutnabb-Kangas 2000: 662).

DOI 10.1515/9783110547047-001

the 18th century. While the norms prescribed by 18th-century grammarians and the ideologies behind the language reform are well-understood (cf. Rössler 1997 and Wiesinger 1995, 1997, 2000), a comprehensive study of how these norms were actually implemented, i.e. how the language reform actively changed *language use* and thus invisibilised Austrian German in the 18th century, has not yet been undertaken.

The key area for the success of the language reform was the domain of education, more specifically the requirement for everyone to attend school and the practices of teachers to disseminate a certain type of language use when teaching basic literacy and writing. Despite the generally acknowledged importance of education for the standardisation of languages (cf. Deumert & Vandenbussche 2003), in particular for the dissemination of norms, relatively little is known about how precisely teachers functioned as norm transmitters or norm makers in the past (cf. Davies & Langer 2014 on the role of teachers in modern Germany).[2]

The standardisation of a language goes hand in hand with the stigmatisation of certain varieties and variants. By selecting and implementing particular language norms, varieties deviating from this norm are stigmatised. These stigmatised varieties and variants are then usually avoided, especially in writing, since they are perceived as 'bad', 'wrong' or 'lower class'. However, the exclusion of these varieties and variants from writing does not necessarily lead to the complete disappearance of the stigmatised forms. They may remain to be used in spoken and informal contexts but are invisible in formal written sources.

This is certainly the case for the majority of features I analysed: *e*-apocope in nouns, the absence of the prefix *ge-* in past participles, and alternative forms of *wir/sie sind*. The UG forms are still common in spoken and informal contexts but are not used in formal writing in Austria today. My research examines how this process of invisibilisation advanced in 18th- and early 19th-century Austria, focusing on the role of grammarians and of school reforms introduced by Empress Maria Theresa (1740–1780).

1.1 Theoretical background

My research is set in the field of historical sociolinguistics, a discipline which has slowly been establishing itself for the last thirty years (cf. Nevalainen & Raumolin-Brunberg 2012). Historical sociolinguistics can be best described as the study of the influence of language on society and vice versa in the past, stretching to the present. There are a number of practical and ideological challenges associated with conduct-

---

2 With regard to the Swiss situation, Messerli (2002) and Büttner (2015) investigated how and why reading and writing was taught in the 18th and 19th centuries. Since the research presented here focuses on 18th-century Austria and specifically on the transmission of language norms (rather than literacy in general) Büttner's and Messerli's work will not be discussed in detail.

ing research in this discipline. In the following sections I will highlight some key concerns which bear direct relevance to my research, namely the uniformitarian principle and the framework of language history 'from below' (Elspaß 2005), which is closely linked to Koch & Oesterreicher's (1985, 1994) model of conceptually written versus spoken language. Furthermore, previous research on the topics, corpora, and features discussed in this monograph is summarised in sections 1.1.4, 1.1.5, and 1.1.6.

1.1.1 The principle of uniformitarianism

The 'principle of uniformitarianism' postulates that current processes are not any different in kind from processes happening in the past (Joseph 2012: 70). Assuming that language varies and changes in the same ways today as it did in the past, current sociolinguistic mechanisms can be used to explain language changes in the past, and vice versa (Nevalainen & Raumolin-Brunberg 2012: 24f.). The uniformitarian principle underpins the work by, amongst others, Labov (1994), Romaine (1988), or Joseph (2012), who explain instances of language change with recourse to modern and historical case studies.

Of course, the 'uniformitarian principle' can equally be applied to the case of Austria. The present-day situation in Austria can be described as a 'two-competence model', i.e. two language varieties coexist independently: a standard German and a dialect variety, with speakers usually being able to switch consciously from one variety to the other depending on the context (Moosmüller 1995: 259f.). By investigating how these dialect varieties differ from today's standard language we are able to determine features (such as *e*-apocope in nouns) that became invisible in writing but did not disappear from actual language use.

Applying the 'uniformitarian principle', i.e. looking at what is happening today, allows researchers to fill gaps they encounter in the historical data available to them. As Joseph (2012: 70) points out, historical data is "simply not as complete as data collected in a contemporary investigation can be". Indeed, the absence of crucial data can lead to overstated claims for change. As an example, Joseph (2012: 71f.) discusses the case of acronymic coinage, which may be viewed as a new phenomenon due to its obvious presence in the modern world. The establishment of many modern institutions and the invention of modern technology in current times may have provided more opportunity for coining acronyms (such as *FAA* for *Federal Aviation Service* or *CPU* for *central processing unit*) but the word-formation process itself, which appears, for example, in Latin, is certainly not a new type of change (ibid.). By applying the 'uniformitarian principle', we can assume that processes of change remain the same, i.e. developments today are parallel to those in earlier years, with differences being a matter of degree rather than kind (ibid.).

The 'uniformitarian principle' offers one way of dealing with 'imperfect data' (Janda & Joseph 2003: 14), following Labov's (1994: 11) approach of 'making the most of bad data'. The terms 'imperfect' or 'bad data' refer, on the one hand, to the fact that all of the available material is written (see above). On the other hand, they allude to problems regarding the preservation of old documents, with informal texts from 'semi-literate writers' (Elspaß 2012: 158) often not deemed important enough to be preserved in archives. Why these texts are particularly interesting to historical linguists is explained in the following sections.

1.1.2 Language history 'from below'

Traditional linguistic historiography, which is still dominant in many university textbooks, tends to focus unduly on literary, often printed, and formal texts from higher social classes, while handwritten texts from 'non-professional writers' were excluded (Elspaß 2012: 156). The main reason for this exclusion is that literary texts were seen as *the* representation of language use in the past (thus confirming a standard-language bias in such historiographies), while other forms of language were regarded as regional or local varieties and, therefore, non-influential in the development of a standard language.

Naturally, the exclusion of handwritten texts from 'semi-literate writers' has left gaps in the study of the history of language since "a complete account of language history, viewed from the perspective of its agents, can only be achieved if we attempt to consider as many text sources from as many different times, varieties, regions, domains, and text types as possible" (Elspaß 2012: 156). In recent years, an increasing number of linguists working on a wide range of languages (such as Elspaß 2005, Fairman 1999, 2003 & 2007, Graser & Tlusty 2012, Langer 2012, Lodge 2004, Mihm 1998, Nobels 2013, Schiegg 2015, Topalović 2003, Vandenbussche 1999 & 2007) have begun to compile these various text sources and analyse them with a view 'from below', i.e. with a focus on texts from people belonging to lower social classes, who were less educated than the wealthy upper and middle classes. The ultimate aim of these studies is to present 'alternative histories' (Watts & Trudgill 2002) by researching texts that are as close to spoken everyday language use in the past as possible. Handwritten texts such as diaries and private letters are particularly suitable for achieving this aim. This is explained in more detail in the following sections.

1.1.3 Redefining spoken and written language

Since 'performance data' (Schneider 2002: 67), i.e. the 'actual' use of language in specific situations, normally constitutes the basis for the study of language variation and change, and since speech is considered primary to writing, historical linguists, working on a period before speech recorders were invented, try to find text sources which are close to spoken language (Elspaß 2012: 157). A model by Koch & Oesterreicher (1985, 1994) categorizes text sources which are closer to spoken language than others by distinguishing between 'language of proximity' (*Sprache der Nähe*) and 'language of distance' (*Sprache der Distanz*). As shown in the figure below, Koch & Oesterreicher (1994: 587f.) not only differentiate the medium of language (spoken versus written), but also, more importantly, its 'conception': By placing various text sources on a continuum between 'language of proximity' and 'language of distance', a private letter, for example, can be identified as 'conceptually' closer to spoken (everyday) language than a sermon, despite the fact that the latter is spoken. Consequently, text sources which are on the 'language of proximity' end of the continuum, i.e. texts which are spontaneous, private, informal etc., are most suitable for studies on language history 'from below' (Elspaß 2012: 157f.).

a = talk with family	f = sermon
b = phone call/talk between friends	g = scientific lecture
c = private letter	h = editorial article
d = job interview	i = legal text
e = newspaper interview	

Language of proximity:
- dialogue
- spontaneity
- private
- face-to-face interaction
- familiarity between comm. partners etc.

graphic

c   e   h   i

⬅——————————➡

a   b   d   f   g

phonic

Language of distance:
- monologue
- plannedness
- public
- spatiotemporal separation
- non-familiarity between comm. partners etc.

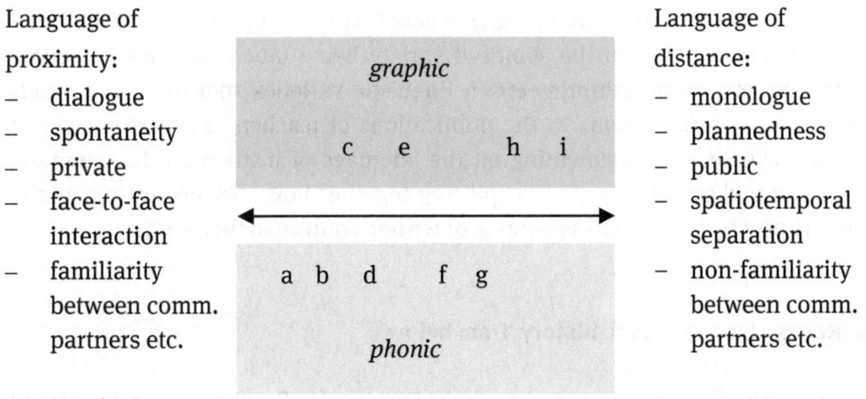

Fig. 1: 'Language of proximity' – 'language of distance' model adapted from Koch & Oesterreicher (1994: 588)

Ágel & Hennig (2006), who focus on historical texts, further develop the model illustrated above by specifying parameters typical of 'language of proximity' and their relation to each other. At the basis of Ágel & Hennig's complex system, which aims at improving the process of determining how 'conceptually oral' a text is, lies the assumption that 'conceptually oral' texts are generally characterised by an open sender-receiver relationship, i.e. the sender and receiver of information can switch their roles at any time (2006b: 18). Based on this assumption and a hierarchy of parameters, texts can be analysed and their percentage of 'language of proximity' can be calculated (Ágel & Hennig 2006c: 35). This calculation allows for a greater comparability between different text types. Ágel & Hennig (2006a: XI) state that the historical texts that are closest to the 'language of proximity' pole are interrogation records of witch trials, accounts of lives of 'ordinary' people as well as a variety of correspondences.

Elspaß (2012: 158) specifically categorizes private letters and diaries as being the closest to actual speech of all written text sources. Furthermore, these private letters and diaries should ideally be written by 'lesser educated' rather than highly educated or professional writers as "their writing can be assumed to be the least influenced, and, still less, dominated by traditions of a 'writing of distance', so that their private texts can be regarded as the most 'oral' written sources in language history" (Elspaß 2012: 158).

As previously mentioned, it is difficult, though not impossible, from a practical point of view to find such private letters and diaries by semi-literate writers, particularly in times before the introduction of basic compulsory schooling when a high percentage of people remained illiterate. Historical linguists may, therefore, have to expand this rather limited range of text sources. Besides letters and memoirs, Langer (2012: 88–102) lists a variety of sources which can help establish how certain linguistic varieties were used in the past: School textbooks might mention the existence of varieties other than the standard variety being taught in schools, school inspection reports might address certain linguistic varieties spoken by the pupils and teachers, and discussions in the publications of teachers' associations might also prove revealing by commenting on the language of instruction. In summary, linguists can make some progress in piecing together how varieties were actually used in the past by incorporating a range of written sources in their research.

1.1.4 Research on language history 'from below'

The framework of a language history 'from below' was first advocated by Elspaß (2002, 2005) and aims to fill the 'blank areas' (or 'witte vlekken' as van der Wal (2006) puts it) in language histories. By focusing on language use of larger sections of the population, especially the lower social classes, the perspective is changed from a 'bird's eye' to a 'worm's eye' view (Elspaß 2007: 4). The investigation of sources that are as close to speech as possible not only provides a "different starting point of the description and explanation of language history" (ibid. 5), it also leads to a more complete and accurate representation of language use in the past. In order to exemplify this point, three research projects are discussed in this section.

Elspaß (2005) analysed 19th-century handwritten letters by Germans who emigrated to North America and wrote to their relatives back home. He focused on 648 documents out of approximately 7,000 of these letters (collected by the historian Wolfgang Helbich) and produced a comprehensive linguistic analysis: grammatical features, lexis, orthography as well as the use of formulaic language were investigated.

Elspaß (2005: 461) concludes that these documents represent conceptually spoken language to a significant extent and that they are characterized by pragmatic requirements, writing traditions as well as influences of spoken language. People wrote to achieve their communicative aim, i.e. mainly to maintain contact with their relatives and to provide information on their circumstances (ibid.). Formulaic language was frequently used as a kind of *Formulierungshilfe* (an aid to formulate sentences and whole texts) and appeared to be old-fashioned as well as repetitive compared to the 19th-century literary language (ibid. 462). With regard to the grammar, distinctive features between the written everyday and literary language were identified: For example, the finite verb in a subordinate clause introduced by *weil* (*because*) was frequently placed in the second position in the letters, whereas only verb-final position was accepted in the literary language (ibid. 463). Generally, everyday written language was characterized by directed variation and syntactic flexibility, with a view to reducing grammatical marking and an increase of analytical forms (ibid. 464). The letters also exhibited diversity in lexis and orthography (ibid. 465–467). This shows that considerable variation remained in everyday written language in the 19th century, despite the standardisation efforts of grammarians as well as teachers (ibid. 468), and hence offers insights into the effectiveness of language authorities in influencing language use. Elspaß (ibid. 468f.) stresses that this variation was not arbitrary but depended on what the writer sought to achieve (e.g. clear handwriting rather than grammatical correctness) as well as conventions that existed 'below' the prescriptive norms and were common in everyday written language.

Elspaß's (2005) findings are particularly relevant for my research as they indicate that variation in language use was still common in the 18th and 19th centuries, i.e. the period under investigation in this monograph. By using text sources that had been ignored in traditional language history, Elspaß provided a more accurate picture of which variants and varieties were used by whom during a particular period of time, challenging the widely held belief amongst linguists that the standardisation of German was ultimately concluded in the 19th century (Elspaß 2005: 470).[3]

---

3 Elspaß (2005: 470) adopts Haugen's (1994) definition of standard language, which suggests that a language is standardised only if it has a unitary written norm which is accepted by the language participants.

Since Elspaß's (2002, 2005) work on private letters of 'ordinary people', the framework of language history 'from below' has been applied to a variety of languages (cf. Elspaß et al. 2007). Nobels (2013), for example, analysed a corpus[4] of handwritten Dutch 'sailing letters'. Similar to Elspaß (2005), Nobels (2013: 261) identifies a significant amount of morphological and syntactic variation in her corpus, which leads to the conclusion that Dutch was not fully standardised by the 17th century, contrary to what traditional language histories claim. Furthermore, a link between social class and gender was identified: With regard to the distribution of forms of address, negation, and diminutive suffixes, female letter writers generally behaved similarly to lower class writers, while male writers were generally similar to upper class writers (ibid. 263). This link is not surprising given that men from the upper social class usually not only obtained better education than women and members from the lower classes, but were also more experienced in writing (ibid.). This indicates that the influence of social class and gender variables on the distribution of specific linguistic features can be indirect: The main influence on this distribution can be a writer's level of education and experience in writing, which, in turn, is determined by the social class and gender of the writer to a certain extent (ibid.).

While my corpora do not allow for a distinction between gender and social classes since the writers of the majority of sources remain unknown, it is important to stress that similar differences may have existed in 18th- and early 19th-century Austria. In other words, the corpora I used are not – and do not aim to be – a 'true' representation of how language was used by different people at a certain point in time. Instead, the focus lies on more general differences between writing practices. Indeed, as Schiegg (2015) demonstrates, the same person may have used different linguistic varieties and registers in different circumstances. Schiegg's corpus consists of 19th- and early 20th-century letters written by patients, who were admitted into two southern German mental hospitals (Irsee and Kaufbeuren). A number of these patients sent formal as well as informal letters to different recipients. The comparison between these letters reveals that writers adjusted their style as well as their language to the intended addressees, with informal letters containing more regional features. Written at a time when the printed texts from the areas contained no or hardly any southern or Bavarian features, Schiegg's evidence from his private-letter corpus 'visibilises' the spoken language of the time. The style-shifts of these letter writers indicate that speakers of German in the past – as is the case today – had more than one linguistic variety in their repertoire and used them according to circumstances. The instances of explicit code-switching between dialect and stand-

---

4 Nobels' (2013: 51) corpus consists of 595 letters by 441 writers taken from the so-called *Letters as Loot* corpus, which comprises more than 38,000 letters from the second half of the 17th to the early 19th centuries and is described in more detail online: http://www.hum.leiden.edu/research/letters-as-loot/ [accessed 26.04.2017].

ard German, which Schiegg (2016) found in a number of letters, provide strong evidence for this. This, in turn, reveals the limitations of the corpora I compiled: They only present the language used by individual writers in one particular (formal) situation. The following section explains why these corpora are – despite their limitations – worth investigating.

1.1.5 Research on reading primers, newspapers, and petitionary letters

An important problem in assessing language use is the identification of what constitutes contemporary language use. In historical sociolinguistics, the principal method is to compile a corpus of a particular text type. I use three corpora of language use (reading primers, newspaper issues, and petitionary letters) to reveal differences in writing practices in 18th- and early 19th-century Austria.[5] While these three text types have been studied separately (with newspapers being afforded the most attention), the differences in language use between these sources have not yet been investigated.

A particularly noticeable gap in historical linguistic research constitutes the role of schooling in the standardisation of languages. Deumert & Vandenbussche (2003: 459) state that education has "so far received only sporadic and unsystematic attention in standardisation studies".[6] Indeed, the role of reading primers in the standardisation process of German has not been researched in detail yet. While the history, literary and ideological content of reading primers has been studied by various researchers[7], the language used in these books has not formed part of major linguistic analysis. With regard to Austrian reading primers, Sroka (2013) presents a small-scale study on the stigmatisation of Upper German lexical items in four reading primers, printed in 1788, 1813, 1825, and 1844. These textbooks contain several footnotes declaring one variant as 'correct', while stigmatising the Austrian variant as 'wrong', e.g. "Man sagt Käse, nicht Kas. Milchrahm st. Obers. [...]" ("One says *Käse*, not *Kas. Milchrahm* instead of *Obers.*") (ibid. 13). In this way, one variant was propagated, which – in a number of cases – may have led to the exclusion of the Austrian variant from modern standard German as codified in dictionaries. Indeed, the orthographic *Duden* (2006: 566), i.e. the main reference work with regard to

---

5 See section 4.1 for a detailed description of these three corpora.

6 Cf. Messerli (2002) and Büttner (2015) for accounts on how literacy was taught in the Swiss context in the 18th and 19th centuries. Furthermore, Bob Schoemaker (University of Leiden) and Magali Boemer (University of Namur) try to fill parts of this research gap with their studies on language-in-education policies.

7 Cf. the International Society for Historical and Systematic Research on Textbooks and Educational Media (https://www.philso.uni-augsburg.de/de/lehrstuehle/paedagogik/igschub/fibeln/) and their Reading Primers International (RPI) Newsletter.

German spelling, does not mention the Austrian variant at all in its entry for *cheese* but includes the item *Kässpätzle* with the following note: "südd., österr. für *Käsespätzle*" ("south German, Austrian for *Käsespätzle*"), which implies that it is the form with -*e* that is 'more standard'. The 42nd edition of the *Österreichisches Wörterbuch* (*ÖWB, Austrian Dictionary*) (2012), on the other hand, marks *Kas* as colloquial, while the controversial[8] 35th edition (1979: 218) lists *Käs* without any markers under the item *Käse*. The noun *Obers*, on the other hand, is listed separately in the *Duden* (2006: 741) explaining that this word is the East Austrian term for *Sahne* ("ostösterr. für *Sahne*"). The 42nd edition of the *ÖWB* (2012: 507), in contrast to the 35th edition, marks it as "esp. eastern Austrian". *Obers* is also one of the 23 words specified in the 1994 EU law, Protocol No 10, entitled *On the use of specific Austrian terms of the German language*. Even though *Obers* was stigmatised as 'incorrect' in 18th- and 19th-century reading primers and despite its use being restricted to the eastern part of modern-day Austria, it received European constitutional status in 1994. Sroka (2013: 16) provides a list of another eleven Austrian variants[9] that are stigmatised in footnotes of the four reading primers and their fate in modern standard German. He concludes that language learning is more than a mere product of schooling and standard-based instruction, since not all of the stigmatised variants were replaced by their propagated equivalents. Nevertheless, reading primers – "as tools for the transmission of language norms" (ibid.) – deserve a more detailed inspection.

Considerably more research has been undertaken on newspapers, which are frequently compiled or included in major historical corpora, such as the *Zurich English Newspaper Corpus* (*ZEN*)[10], spanning the period from 1661 to 1791 and comprising a total of 1.6 million words, or the *Mannheim Corpus of Historical Newspapers and Magazines* (*MKHZ*, 18th and 19th century, more than 4.1 million words).[11] Newspapers also formed part of the *GerManC* corpus (1650–1800, approximately 900,000 words).[12] This corpus, which was collected and annotated by Martin Durrell et al. (Manchester), formed the basis for research on the role of newspapers in the standardisation process of German in the 17th and 18th centuries.[13] Durrell et al. (2008)

---

8 Cf. Ammon 2003, who explains that this edition was heavily criticised for its inclusion of variants that were considered 'dialect'.

9 These are: *Anten, der Butter, Fürtuch, Hendl, Knödel, Königlhasen, Kuchel, Ribissel(n), Weinbeere, Zuspeise,* and *Zwespe(n)*.

10 Cf. http://www.es.uzh.ch/en/Subsites/Projects/zencorpus.html [accessed 26.04.2017], compiled by Fries et al. (2004).

11 http://repos.ids-mannheim.de/fedora/objects/clarin-ids:mkhz1.00000/datastreams/CMDI/content [accessed 26.04.2017].

12 Cf. http://www.llc.manchester.ac.uk/research/projects/germanc/ [accessed 26.04.2017].

13 The texts of the *GerManC* corpus are categorized into three periods (1650–1700, 1700–1750, 1750–1800), five regions within the German-speaking countries (North, West Central, East Central,

illustrate how the printers of newspapers assisted the development of standard German by adapting to the supra-regional language of the newspaper correspondents. In the second half of the 18th century it was still common practice to print the news in the form it was reported from the correspondents and agents from around Europe (ibid. 265). Consequently, the varieties used in newspapers were primarily those of the correspondents and, therefore, not dependent on the written language of the places where the newspapers were printed (ibid.). Durrell et al. point out that the identity, origin and level of education of these correspondents cannot be determined for certain. What can be ascertained is that they wrote for a supra-regional readership, rather than a certain town or region, since they sent their reports to various newspapers. Thus it appears that early newspapers transmitted a model of supra-regional language (ibid.). Since none of the originally handwritten letters from the correspondents have been preserved, it cannot be established whether the printers revised the language in these letters before printing them in the newspapers. Researchers are only able, therefore, to study the final product as depicted in newspapers without knowing how much – if any – editing took place. The results of Durrell's et al. analysis of a number of phonological/orthographical, morphological, and lexical features in the newspaper part of the *GerManC* corpus (approximately 100,000 words) indicate that the norms prescribed by contemporary grammarians were not necessarily the decisive factor for the selection of a particular variant that became the standard later on. Also the developing norms used (but not prescribed!) by newspaper correspondents certainly played a role in this selection, leading to the dissemination of particular variants (ibid. 275). In this way, newspapers of the late 17th and early 18th century contributed to the standardisation of the German language (ibid.).[14]

Acknowledging that newspapers are usually taken to represent formal, written language, Hosokawa (2014) tested this claim by examining 19th-century newspapers with regards to evidence of linguistic orality. He investigated six newspapers[15] published in 1850/51, which were categorized into regional versus supra-regional as

West Upper, East Upper) and eight genres (drama, humanities, legal texts, letters, narrative prose, newspapers, scientific texts, sermons) (cf. *GerManC* documentation, which can be downloaded from http://www.llc.manchester.ac.uk/research/projects/germanc/files/ [accessed 26.04.2017]). Three text passages of 2,000 words were chosen for each genre, period, and region, which amounts to about 900,000 words in total (Durrell 2016: 214).

14 Recent research by Durrell (forthcoming) suggests, however, that newspapers did not lead the trend towards certain variants. The language in newspapers did not differ from texts written by professional and educated writers and the same frequency of regional features was observed in a variety of text types.

15 These six newspapers are: *Neue Freiburger Zeitung*; *Leipzig Illustrirte Zeitung*; *Wiener allgemeine Zeitung für Theater, Musik, Kunst, Literatur, geselliges Leben, Conversation und Mode*; *Morgenblatt für gebildete Leser*; *Correspondenzblatt und Kieler Tageblatt*; and *Deutsche Reform: Politische Zeitung für das constitutionelle Deutschland* (Hosokawa 2014: 31–34).

well as newspapers for the mass-market versus a restricted readership/specifically political newspapers. His analysis of syntactic, lexical and morphological features that can be associated with orality (e.g. short sentences, deictic expression, and apocopes) revealed that these features only rarely occurred and that the language used in newspapers closely resembled that of classic German authors (such as Goethe and Schiller). However, differences between regional and supra-regional newspapers were detected, with shorter sentences and deictic expressions being used more frequently in the local newspapers (ibid. 136, 266). The newspapers designed for the mass-market, on the other hand, appeared as the ones closest to the literary language (ibid. 266). In general, it can be argued that journalists aimed at writing articles corresponding to the contemporary language norms. Through their use in newspapers, these language norms were disseminated to the majority of the population – also to lower social classes in rural areas, who were reading newspapers from (at least) the mid-19th century onwards (ibid. 42, 267).

Similarly, Barton & Hall (1999: 5) challenge the perception that newspapers contain a single language style of formal, written language. They argue that newspaper articles contain elements of letter-writing since they arose from letters written by correspondents. While this is certainly a historical fact, it is difficult to recognise similarities between 18th-century newspapers and contemporary private letters, such as the correspondence of the Mozart family (Reiffenstein 2005) or the petitionary letters that form part of the language use corpus compiled for my research. Parts of these petitions seem closer to prayers than to any other text genre (cf. Karweick 1989: 31f.). Indeed, many of the petitionary letters are highly formulaic, as section 4.1.3 will illustrate. Grosse (1989: 13) points out that the formulaic language used in petitionary letters stood in stark contrast to spoken language. However, this does not necessarily mean that petitions do not contain any features of orality. As Fairman (1999, 2003, 2007) shows with evidence from English, paupers' applications for the relief of the poor often contained features associated with orality, depending on the authors' level of literacy. In other words, the pauper letters analysed by Fairman contain features that are invisible in printed texts.

It should be pointed out that it is often difficult to establish who the writer of a letter was since the applicant's name signed at the end of the letter did not necessarily correspond to the author of the application (Fairman 1999: 64). Many applicants were 'orate', i.e. for them, language only existed as sound but not as visible marks, and they asked other people to write a paupers' letter for them (ibid.). Often these writers would not be professional scribes but friends, relatives or neighbours of the applicant, who did not demand any money for their services (Karweick 1989: 18). If these possibilities failed, the applicant had to write the letter him-/herself – thus "even unschooled or little-schooled writers functioned effectively [...] as letter writers" (Barton & Hall 1999:9). Paupers' and petitionary letters, therefore, constitute a valuable source within the framework of language history 'from below'.

Within the three corpora of language use (i.e. reading primers, newspaper issues, and petitionary letters), the occurrence of a number of morphological variants that can be ascribed to the Upper German (UG) language area is analysed, both quantitatively and qualitatively. The following section provides information on these features and summarises previous findings.

1.1.6 Research on Upper German variants

In order to test the effectiveness of prescriptions by 18th-century grammarians and the 1774 school reform on changing written language use, my research focuses on the following morphological features: *e*-apocope in nouns (e.g. pl. *Fisch* vs *Fische*), the formation of past participles without the prefix *ge-* (e.g. *kocht* vs *gekocht*) and with the ending *-t* (e.g. *geschickt* vs *geschicket*), and alternative forms of *wir/sie sind* (*wir/sie sein/seyn/seind/seynd/seint/seynt*). These features find explicit discussion in 18th-century metalinguistic discourse, were noted in schoolbooks at the time, and are found in the three historical corpora of language use that I compiled. Importantly, however, the features selected for analyses continue to be highly salient in Austrian German today, with *e*-apocope being one of the most noticed features of the variety. This is significant as it shows that the stigmatisation of these features in the 18th century and their subsequent disappearance in writing did *not* affect the spoken language anywhere to the same degree.

Previous linguistic findings allow for a comparison of the results gained from the analyses carried out in my research project. Of particular relevance is Rössler's (2005) research on graphematics and morphology in Austrian and Bavarian printed texts from the 16th to 18th century, which formed the starting point for the selection of features. In a 437,279-word-corpus, compiled of texts printed in Austrian and Bavarian cities between 1528 and 1774, Rössler analyses 24 graphematic and morphological features, which were categorized into features associated with East Central German (ECG, i.e. the variety used in Saxony and in the adjacent parts of Thuringia and Saxony-Anhalt) or Upper German (UG, i.e. the variety used in the south of the German-speaking area, including Austria).[16] Thus Rössler aimed at determining if and when certain variants obtained the function of a shibboleth, i.e. of a (here) regional group marker. The analysis of the corpus, which included religious texts (such as

---

16 It is, as Rössler (2005: 360) points out, important to note that there is no definite dichotomy between ECG and UG graphemes in terms of an isogloss. Rather, the line between ECG and UG is blurred, i.e. features of each variety are possible in texts of each language region.

sermons, necrologies) as well as secular texts (reports, legal texts, biographies etc.), led to the following findings[17] (Rössler 2005: 19–29, 358f.):

Tab. 1: Findings by Rössler (2005: 359): Trends in the development of the variation of graphematic and morphological features in East Upper German texts printed between 1530 and 1765

Trends in the development of variation of graphematic and morphological features in East Upper German texts printed between 1530 and 1765 (Rössler 2005: 359)

	Influence from ECG ▼	UG ▼	1530	1565	1600	1630	1660	1690	1720	1765
1	*ei*	*ai*	□	◈	○	↑	↓	●		
2	*ein*	*ain*	◈	↓	●					
3	*u, ü*	*uo, üe*	□	◈	○	↑	↓	●		
4	*u*	*ů*	○	↓		●				
5	*ie*	*i*	□						↓	●
6	*o* in front of nasal	*u* in front of nasal	◈	○	●					
7	*k, ck*	*kh, ckh*	○	↓	●					
8	initial *b*	initial *p*	○	↓	●					
9	*nicht*	*nit*	□				◈			↓●
10	*-nis*	*-nus*	■							↓●
11	*wir/sie sind*	*wir/sie sein/d/t*	□							↓○
12	dat. pron. *ihm*	dat. pron. *ihme*	○	◈	◈	↑	↓	◈		↓○
13	*dem*	*deme*	●			↑	↓	●		
14	final *-e* in nouns	*e*-apocope in nouns	□							↓○
15	weak inflection of attributive adj., sg. (*der junge Herr*)	strong inflection of attributive adj., sg. (*der junger Herr*)	□	◈	●					

---

17 The key to these findings is provided below Rössler's (2005: 359) table. The symbols in the table show changes in the trends, with empty spaces indicating that the trend illustrated by the symbol in the preceding space (i.e. to the left) continues.

Trends in the development of variation of graphematic and morphological features in East Upper German texts printed between 1530 and 1765 (Rössler 2005: 359)

			1530	1565	1600	1630	1660	1690	1720	1765
16	weak inflection of attributive adj., pl. (*die besten Freunde*)	strong inflection of attributive adj., pl. (*die beste Freunde*)	◈							O
17	superlative with -*st*-	superlative with -*ist*-/-*est*-	◈			↑	◈	↓O		↓●
18	past part. -*et*	past part. -*t*	□				◈	↑	↓	O
19	past part. with *ge*-	past part. without *ge*-	O	◈		↑□	□	↓		O
20	verb: 3ʳᵈ sg. pres. ind. ending in -*et*	verb: 3ʳᵈ sg. pres. ind. ending in -*t*	O			◈			□	↓◈
21	verb: 1ˢᵗ sg. pres. ind. ending in -*e*	verb: 1ˢᵗ sg. pres. ind. ending in -Ø	□	◈	◈		O			●
22	subj. II: *stünde*	subj. II: *stünd*	□	◈	O	●				
23	past ind.: *sahe*	past ind.: *sah*	■		□	↑	↑		●	◈
24	imp. sg.: *rede!*	imp. sg.: *red!*	□	◈	O					
		Time ▶	1530	1565	1600	1630	1660	1690	1720	1765

Tab. 2: Key to Rössler's (2005: 358f.) findings

- ■ ... (almost) exclusive use of UG variants (ca. 95–100 %)
- □ ... dominance of UG variants (ca. 60–95 %)
- ◈ ... balanced use between UG and ECG variants (ca. 40–60 %)
- O ... dominance of ECG variants (ca. 60–95 %)
- ● ... (almost) exclusive use of ECG variants (ca. 95–100 %)
- ↓ ... beginning of strong decrease of UG variants (= increase of ECG variants)
- ↑ ... beginning of strong increase of UG variants (= decrease of ECG variants)

From the morphological variables listed by Rössler (9–24 in the figure above), numbers 11 (*wir/sie sind* vs *sein/d/t*), 14 (ending -*e* vs *e*-apocope in nouns), 18 (past participle ending -*et* vs -*t*), and 19 (past participle with vs without *ge*-) display particularly striking developments, which were not fully completed by 1765. What these four variables have in common is that the ECG variants were dominant by 1765 but the UG variants had not been completely eradicated. It can, therefore, be assumed that both variants of each variable occur in texts printed and written between 1744 and at least 1774 and that this period thus constitutes a key transitional period. For this reason, the analyses presented in this monograph focus on this time period and follow the development into the 19th century (until 1834) to reveal to what extent these variants continued to be used.

In this context, Durrell's (2016) work on the language of a variety of text types provides important evidence and supplements Rössler's findings. The findings of both research projects are summarised in the following sections.

1.1.6.1 *e*-apocope in UG texts

With regard to *e*-apocope in nouns, Rössler (2005: 241) explains that from Old High German onwards the stress in nouns became fixed, which led to a reduction of the now unstressed syllables in polysyllabic nouns. In the Central German area, this process was less common until the 16th century and thereafter never gained the same significance as in the UG region (Solms & Wegera 1993: 165). Furthermore, the presence of word-final -*e* was associated with Martin Luther (hence the term 'Lutheran -*e*') and the ECG language area.[18]

According to Rössler (2005: 241), *e*-apocope occurred in the following types of nouns:

- nouns of feminine gender in their singular form, e.g. *Frag/e*
- weak masculine nouns, e.g. *Hirt/e*
- mixed-declension neuter nouns, e.g. *Aug/e*
- strong masculine and neuter nouns in the dative singular form, e.g. *am Tag/e*
- nouns of all genders in their plural form in the nominative, genitive and accusative case, e.g. *Fisch/e*.[19]

Variation between *e*-apocope and presence of final -*e* in these nouns was observed in the texts analysed by Rössler from the 16th to the second half of the 18th century (ibid. 242f.). However, certain authors, typesetters and printers had a tendency to either decide for or against the use of the ending -*e*, i.e. in Rössler's corpus there was little variation within one text (ibid. 242). In the first half of the 18th century, the *e*-apocope was still dominant at 68 % in the texts analysed by Rössler, whereas it was

---

18 Martin Luther's greatest influence was in the Central and Northern German area, hence the association of a regional linguistic feature from there with Protestantism. Cf. also Macha (2014) on the interrelationship between linguistic features and religious affiliation. Cf. von Polenz (1994) and Habermann (1997) on a critical discussion of the term 'Lutheran -*e*'.

19 In other words, the *e*-apocope occurred in most types of nouns, which results in a high frequency of this variable in the three corpora. In mixed-declension masculine nouns (e.g. *Nam/e*), too, the *e*-apocope appears. The frequency of mixed-declension and weak masculine nouns as well as strong neuter nouns was, however, too low to gain reliable results across the three corpora. Consequently, only feminine nouns, strong masculine and neuter nouns in the dative singular case, and nouns in plural were investigated.

less common (37 %) than using the *e*-ending after about 1750. Nevertheless, both variants continued to appear in the texts (Rössler 2005: 244f.).

Rössler (2005: 247) also notes that the usage of the ending -*e* depends on the text genre. A sermon published in the UG region usually contains more instances of *e*-apocope than other text types, such as reports or legislative texts, since it is always addressing an audience (ibid.). It is, therefore, conceptually closer to speech. Rössler (ibid.) argues that the *e*-apocope may have been used intentionally in sermons in order to create closeness to the audience. Another motive for the use of *e*-apocope in Catholic sermons is to signal distance from ECG Protestant texts (ibid.). Rössler explains that it cannot be ascertained which of these two motives led to the relative frequency of *e*-apocope in religious texts (in comparison to secular texts). The more important observation made by Rössler is the clear trend away from the *e*-apocope around the mid-18th century, which correlates with the increasing dissemination of ECG norms and the influence of Johann Christoph Gottsched – a literary scholar and grammarian hailing from East Prussia (Juditten) and later working in Saxony (Leipzig) – in Austria at that time (ibid. 245). Therefore, analysing this feature will be particularly revealing.

Durrell (2016) discusses the occurrence of *e*-apocope in a range of text types from across the German-speaking areas. Durrell (2016: 215) states that *e*-apocope is recorded from the 13th century onwards, with occurrences first appearing in the Bavarian language area, from where it spread across most of the German-speaking area, apart from East Central German. Later, the ending -*e* was restored in many cases, partly due to its morphological function (e.g. as a plural marker in nouns) but also in contexts without any morphological function (e.g. at the end of feminine nouns).

Durrell's (2016) results, based on evidence from the *GerManC* corpus, generally indicate that the trend away from the *e*-apocope between 1650 and 1800 differed in regions and text genres, with instances of *e*-apocope mainly occurring in the Upper German area between 1650 and 1750. This area clearly adjusted its use of *e*-apocope to the North and East Central German area between 1701 and 1800, with the *e*-apocope becoming increasingly invisible.[20] With regard to the text genres, it is striking that the *e*-apocope is more common in drama, legal texts, and sermons than in other text genres (particularly in comparison to letters, newspapers, and scientific texts) in the East Upper German area. Durrell (2016: 228, 230) explains that the higher frequency of *e*-apocope in drama and sermons may be attributed to the spoken nature of these texts. This would imply that the variants without final -*e* were acceptable in spoken language and that they did not raise any communication prob-

---

20 A notable exception is the use of dative -*e*, which slightly decreases between the first two periods (1650–1700 and 1701–1750) of the *GerManC* corpus in the East Upper German texts (Durrell 2016: 225).

lems for the audience. Regarding the high frequency of *e*-apocope in legal texts, it can be argued that these texts are linguistically rather conservative, which may partly be due to their reliance on older model texts (ibid. 231). By contrast, the most significant increase of dative *-e* in the East Upper German area between 1750 and 1800 can be observed in newspapers (from 14 % in 1701–1750 to 71 % in 1750–1800) (ibid. 227). Durrell (2016: 228f.) points out that these findings in newspapers suggest that newspapers followed, rather than led the trend away from the *e*-apocope, as a significantly higher percentage of dative *-e* occurs in East Upper German scientific texts between 1701 and 1750 (48 %).

In summary, Durrell's findings illustrate that there are text-specific as well as regional differences in the development of *e*-apocope, with variation occurring in the Upper German area for a longer period of time. It can, therefore, be assumed that variation with regard to *e*-apocope will still appear between at least 1750 and 1800 but the development might vary between different types of texts.

1.1.6.2 Past participles in UG texts

With regard to the prefix *ge-* in past participles, Rössler (2005: 303) points out that only a small number of past participles can be formed without the prefix *ge-*. The tendency of re-occurring lexemes which can be formed without *ge-* results in a greater likelihood that the spelling of these few lexemes becomes fixed (ibid.). In other words, the absence of *ge-* only occurs in a limited number of past participles. Rössler (2005: 303–305) categorises possible variants (with/without *ge-*) into four smaller groups:

– Variants due to phonetics, such as *ge-/Ø-geben, ge-/Ø-kauft*: The prefix *ge-* is often deleted in participles that begin with a *g-* or *k-*.
– Variants due to morphology, such as *nachge-/Ø-kommen, überge-/Ø-blieben*: The prefix *ge-* is often deleted in separable verbs.
– Variation in past participles due to perfective meaning, such as *ge-/Ø-worden, ge-/Ø-troffen*: As the semantic of these verbs includes a sense of completion, the *ge-* is often absent.
– Variation in past participles which have lost their prefix, such as *ge-/Ø-blieben* (from MHG *belîben*, 16th century *be-leiben*): As the past participle of verbs with prefixes like *be-* and *er-* are formed without *ge-*, past participles that used to have these prefixes can be formed without *ge-* in UG varieties.

For the morphology of Early New High German (ENHG), Solms & Wegera (1993: 238) report that the consistent use of the prefix *ge-* in these cases seems to have started in the late 16th century. Apart from the groups of verbs listed above, other past participles without the prefix *ge-* can be found in ENHG, particularly for the verbs *brauchen, brennen, heissen, offenbaren, schneiden, trinken*, and *ziehen* (ibid.).

Rössler (2005: 306) encounters variation in UG texts during the entire time period under investigation (1530–1765). While past participles with the *ge-* prefix were dominant around 1530 (the prefix *ge-* is used in 72 % of all cases), there is a rise in past participles without *ge-* in the 17th century (around 1660, the *ge-* prefix was not used in 89 % of all cases). The number of instances of this variant decreased again at the end of the 17th and the beginning of the 18th century until the past participle with *ge-* begins to be dominant again from the mid-18th century onwards (being used in 86 % of all cases in 1765). Rössler (2005: 307) considers the increasing grammaticalization as well as the rising influence of grammarians as the two factors for the decrease of the variant without *ge-*.

Whereas the absence of the prefix *ge-* in past participles can be regarded an UG feature, the regular past participle suffixes *-et* and *-t* appear to distinguish written from spoken language more generally. Rössler (2005: 299) assumes that the ending *-t* was more common in spoken language, while the ending *-et* was used to signal a sophisticated style in both written and – to a lesser extent – spoken language. This means that both suffixes were used in the UG as well as the ECG area and mark different styles rather than different regional varieties (ibid.). In Rössler's analysis (2005: 297–299), the suffix *-t* is dominant in the 16th century, with 91 % around 1530 and 83 % around 1565. In the 17th century, the *-et* suffix generally becomes more common (34 % around 1600, 38 % around 1690) and is used more frequently than *-t* in the 18th century, with 69 % of *-et* around 1720 and 79 % around 1765. Rössler's (2005: 298f.) findings reveal that the *-et* suffix was not frequently used in the UG area before the 18th century. According to Rössler (ibid. 299), the increase of the ending *-et* was motivated by the prescription of 18th-century grammarians as well as by the usage of *-et* for a more elegant style.[21] Rössler further states that it was only with Johann Christoph Adelung's grammar *Deutsche Sprachlehre* (1781), which prescribes the *-t* suffix in the indicative active[22] (in verbs not ending in a dental stop[23]), that the *-t* form came to be regarded as equivalent to the *-et* suffix again. It is, therefore, unlikely that the establishment of one form will have been completed by the beginning of the 19th century. Consequently, my analysis of texts printed and written

---

21 The prescription for the *-et* variant by Gottsched, whose norms were based on an ECG variety of German (see section 3.3) and the dominance of *-t* in the UG area in the 16th century might justify Rössler's classification as *-et* being a feature associated with the ECG region. However, given that both variants were used in both regions, this classification remains problematic.

22 Cf. section 3.6.2 for Adelung's conjugation of the verb *loben*, which indicates that he uses the ending *-t* for regular past participles in active indicative forms while prescribing the ending *-et* for active subjunctive as well as all passive and infinitive forms.

23 The suffix *-t* was replaced by *-et* in verbs that ended in a dental consonant, such as *redt > redet*, since the mid-17th century. Therefore, there are very few instances of the ending *-t* in these verbs in the 18th-century texts analysed by Rössler (2005: 302).

at the end of the 18th and beginning of the 19th century in chapter 4 will be particularly revealing with regard to this feature.

1.1.6.3 Alternative forms of *wir/sie sind* in UG texts

Solms & Wegera (1993: 310) state that there were two variants for the 1st pers. pl. ind. pres. in ENHG: *sîn* and *sint*, with *sîn* being mainly preserved in the East Upper German area while *sint* was – in some parts – already the more common variant in the 14th century. Apart from *sîn* and *sint*, the UG variant *sei* was used. In the 3rd pers. pl. ind. pres., the form *sein* appeared besides the variant *sint*, especially in the UG language area, where it was partly used more frequently than *sint* in the 16th and 17th centuries (ibid.). In other words, variants with diphthong (*sei*, *sein*) are mostly used in the UG language area, while the form with monophthong and final -*t* (*sint*) was used more frequently in other areas in ENHG.[24]

Rössler (2005: 213) identifies eight variants that he associates with the UG language area: *seyndt*, *seynt*, *seynd*, *seindt*, *seint*, *seind*, *seyn* and *sein*. Rössler's (ibid. 211–222) findings illustrate that the UG variants *wir/sie seynd*, *seind*, *seyn*, and *sein* are the dominant variants in printed UG texts of the 16th to mid-18th century, with *seynd* being the most popular variant.[25] However, after about 1750 there seems to be a radical shift towards the ECG variants *sind* in the printed texts analysed by Rössler. Rössler (2005: 221f.) regards the language reform during the reign of Empress Maria Theresa as the cause for this rapid development towards the ECG variants. By about 1765, the number of UG variants is significantly lower (26 %) than around 1720 (99 %). These results suggest that this radical change from the UG to the ECG variant happened around 1750, i.e. in the period that I investigate here, with the UG variant disappearing quickly from printed texts.

Rössler's (2005) findings indicate that the development of the features selected for analysis had not been completed by the second half of the 18th century. The occurrence of these features in the three corpora of language use mentioned above will be compared to the prescriptions of 18th-century grammarians in order to address the research objectives outlined below.

1.2 Objectives

The main objective of my research is to examine the discrepancy between spoken and written Austrian German. In this context, I will focus on what appears to be a

---

24 Solms & Wegera (1993: 310) do not specify in which areas the variant *sint* was particularly common.

25 The variant *sein* is the least common and the other variants are preferred in order to distinguish the verb from the possessive pronoun *his* (Rössler 2005: 214).

crucial time period for this difference, namely the second half of the 18th century. During this period, ideas of Enlightenment and linguistic ideologies triggered the urge for linguistic and educational reforms, which were advocated by Empress Maria Theresa (chapter 2). A number of 18th-century grammars, which prescribed the use of particular language norms and implicitly or explicitly stigmatised the use of other variants, seemed to be instrumental in this language reform. In order to assess how effective this language reform was in the suppression of UG variants from written domains, I will contrast the language prescriptions of 18th-century grammarians with language use. The corpus of texts representing the language prescription and the introduction of northern norms consists of five grammars written by Johann Balthasar von Antesperg (1747), Johann Christoph Gottsched (1748), Johann Siegmund Valentin Popowitsch (1754), Johann Ignaz von Felbiger (1775), and Johann Christoph Adelung (1781) (chapter 3). Data representing language use was collected from three sub-corpora, namely reading primers, newspaper issues, and petitionary letters (section 4.1). The language use in these three corpora, which represent educational texts, public media texts, and non-public handwritten texts respectively, is compared to the prescriptions of grammarians, focusing on features which are known to be salient even in Modern Austria (see above and chapter 4). A comparison between the three sub-corpora will also reveal any differences in the language use between these text types (section 4.6).

The analysis of language use in these three diachronic corpora and the comparison to the language norm prescriptions by 18th-century grammarians will show if language planning 'from above' can ever truly affect language use. In the case of written Austrian German, it indeed appears that the language reform resulted in a process of invisibilisation, i.e. a disappearance of certain features in writing through stigmatisation, which increased the gap between written and spoken language use.

2 Language, Enlightenment and education in 18th-century Austria

This section first provides a brief outline of the general development of German as a literary language. It then focuses on the language situation in 18th-century Austria and presents reasons for the move away from the Upper German (UG) variety.[26] For administrative and official written discourse, an UG linguistic variety based on the chancery language of Emperor Maximilian I had been used until the mid-18th century (Wiesinger 2008: 253f.). This poses the question why this variety was dismissed as inappropriate in the written domain and why the literary language based on East Central German (ECG) norms was introduced instead.[27] Furthermore, this chapter discusses the role of education in the language reform.

2.1 The standardisation of German

The creation or emergence of standard varieties appears to take place in very similar ways in different languages. Einar Haugen's model (1966) consisting of four stages (selection, codification, implementation, elaboration) is generally accepted as a particularly suitable theoretical framework (cf. the use of Haugen's model in the accounts of the standardisation histories of all Germanic languages in Deumert & Vandenbussche (2003)).[28] Haugen's four stages are plausible and have been attested for many languages, even though there is, of course, some variation. Haugen (1966: 931f.) argued that first, a norm is selected, which is then codified in grammars and dictionaries with the aim of minimal variation in form. In the third stage, the function of this norm is elaborated, i.e. the norm is implemented across as many functions as possible (ibid.). Finally, the selected and codified language has to be accepted by the community in order to be regarded standardised in Haugen's definition. Not all scholars have used this model, however. For German, Besch (1987: 39) categorizes the development of the literary or standard language into three phases: a phase of laying the foundations in the 16th century, a phase of exten-

---

26 The Upper German language area, which can be divided into Alemannic, East Franconian, and Bavarian-Austrian (König 1978: 138), spans across the south of the German-speaking area. The primary texts I analysed (see chapter 4) all originate from the Bavarian-Austrian area, also known as East Upper German (EUG).

27 The term East Central German comprises the linguistic varieties used south east of the Benrath line, i.e. Upper Saxon, Thuringian, and Silesian (cf. König 1978: 138).

28 This is not to say that Haugen's model fits every Germanic language. It serves, however, as a "useful and pragmatic basic structure" (Deumert & Vandenbussche 2003: 464f.), allowing for new directions in the study of language standardisation.

DOI 10.1515/9783110547047-002

sion and dissemination, and finally, a phase of purification in the 18th century with major influence from ECG. While this may imply that the standardisation of German was completed by the end of the 18th century, recent research (Elspaß 2002, 2005) has shown that written German had not been completely standardised by the 19th century, as a considerable amount of variation can be found in 19th-century text sources.[29] Nevertheless, a movement towards a more unified language can be observed from the Early Modern period onwards, when particular features become stigmatised as being 'wrong' or 'bad', while the language use of certain groups is endorsed as 'right' (Salmons 2012: 264). This process did not immediately or automatically replace local dialects but rather added other, artificial layers to the pool of language varieties available (ibid.).

Mattheier (2003: 213f.) identifies four regional written dialects, which developed from a process of unification and variant reduction in the 15th century: East Upper German (EUG) (centres: Augsburg and Nuremberg), West Upper German (WUG) (centres: Strasbourg, Basle, and Zurich), East Central German (ECG) (also known as 'Meißnisches Deutsch' – 'Meißen German'), and West Central German (WCG) (centres: Cologne, Mainz, and Frankfurt). Mattheier points out that some of the constructions used in these regional written dialects were distinct from spoken language, i.e. the written language began to increasingly diverge from the spoken varieties. Out of these four regional written dialects, the EUG variety emerged as the supra-regional, proto-standard variety from the mid-15th century onwards, mainly due to the influence of the economic centres of Augsburg and Nuremberg and of the Imperial Chancellery of Maximilian I (ibid. 215). Contemporaries referred to this variety as 'gemeines Deutsch' (Mattheier 1991). This 'common German' was first used alongside but soon also in place of the regional written language in the Low German and WCG area (Mattheier 2003: 215f.). In the ECG area, by contrast, a process of gradual diffusion of EUG variants into the ECG variety can be observed, while the regional character of the written language was maintained in the WUG area (ibid. 216).

From 1500 onwards, i.e. about 50 years after the invention of printing, three regional print languages emerged through processes of diffusion and levelling: the southern German print language (Augsburg, Nuremberg, Vienna), the WCG print language (Cologne, Mainz, Frankfurt), and the ECG print language (Wittenberg, Jena, Leipzig) (ibid.). Due to its status as 'common German', the EUG written and print language influenced or replaced other print languages at the beginning of the 16th century (ibid.). This development was, however, interrupted by Martin Luther (1483–1564) and the Reformation (ibid. 217). Luther's writings, which acted as a linguistic model from the 1520s onwards, were based on the ECG written norm,

---

29 Several scholars (for example, Besch 1983 and Mattheier 1988) consider a standardisation process completed when the majority of the population have access to the written as well as spoken standard (Elspaß 2002: 43).

which gained in prestige and was disseminated through printing, particularly in the Protestant territories (ibid.). The Catholic parts of the German-speaking area, such as Austria, on the other hand, continued to use 'common German', which was influenced by the UG variety (ibid.). Thus two proto-standard varieties – '*Lutherdeutsch*' (based on ECG varieties) and '*gemeines Deutsch*' (based on UG varieties) – co-existed from the 16th century onwards. In the 17th century, two discourses arose from this situation, and they continued in the 18th century: a) what is the 'correct' or 'good' variety and b) which norms should be described and codified in grammars? (ibid. 219).

Von Polenz (1994: 135) describes the language policy movement of the 17th and 18th century as a shift from a comprehensible to a correct language. 17th- and 18th-century grammarians and literary scholars believed that a correct, noble German language with cultural prestige was needed, which exceeded the practical need of a general comprehensible language in German-speaking areas (ibid.). This ideology of a correct language (*Sprachrichtigkeitsideologie*) also led to a decrease in the tolerance for and richness of Early New High German variants (ibid. 136). Von Polenz, however, stresses that in principle, single grammarians or lexicographers did not 'set' the language norms prescriptively, nor were language ideologies invented arbitrarily. Rather, they were part of an evolutionary development of late German Humanism, during which the reflection on the value and improvements of the German language went hand in hand with the publication of linguistic descriptions and justifications of 'ideal' German language use (ibid.).

In the discourse about German language norms in the 17th and 18th centuries, this 'ideal' language was associated with stylistic qualities, such as 'purity', 'richness', and 'clarity' (Leweling 2005, Faulstich 2008). These terms were used in different ways by the participants (grammarians, lexicographers, literary scholars etc.) in the discourse about language norms. The term 'purity', for example, had a number of meanings: it could refer to a) an unchanged language, free of foreign influence, b) a clear and precise language without superfluous stylistic additions, c) the current 'improved' and correct state of a language, or d) a beautiful language (Faulstich 2008: 510f.). In order to achieve this 'purity' one should, according to 18th-century grammarians, avoid loan words, variants used by lower-class people and archaic expressions (ibid. 511–514).

While the language debate at the beginning of the 17th century was mainly concerned with the preference of German over other languages (particularly Latin), the issue of which kind of German was the 'correct' variety became more central around the mid-17th century (Langer 2001: 114f.). This issue was mainly discussed in language societies (*Sprachgesellschaften*), such as the *Fruchtbringende Gesellschaft* (*Fruitbearing Society*) founded in 1617, which advocated the cultivation and purification of the German language (Mattheier 2003: 224). The language discourse in these societies influenced 17th-century codifiers (e.g. Martin Opitz, Justus Georg Schottelius, and Kasper Stieler) in their effort to describe the 'correct' German language (ibid.). While the discourse about 'correct' German was well under way in the central and northern German regions in the 17th century, the southern regions only started to participate in this discourse in the 18th century. With regard to Austria, Wiesinger (2008: 255) states that it was only after 1730 that an interest in the German language awoke. According to Wiesinger, this new interest in language was, firstly, due to the criticism by well-educated Protestants from the UG language area regarding the linguistic differences between the UG-Catholics and the CG-Protestants. The dominance of Jesuits in Austria's education and literature, too, was criticised. It was, in particular, Georg Lizel (1694–1761), a Protestant philologist and theologian from Ulm (a town in the WUG area), who began to condemn the linguistic, literary, and educational situation in the Catholic southern German areas (ibid.). In 1731, he published his criticism in *Der Undeutsche Catholik Oder Historischer Bericht Von der allzugroßen Nachläßigkeit der Römisch-Catholischen, insonderheit unter der Clerisey der Jesuiten, In Verbesserung der deutschen Sprache und Poesie* (*The un-German Catholic or a historical report of the Roman-Catholics' negligence, particularly under the clergy of the Jesuits, in the improvement of the German language and poetry*). In his writings, Lizel criticised the inadequate command of the German language among educated people, which was, in his opinion, mainly due to the Jesuits, who consciously neglected the German language in order to stop any intrusion of literature from the Protestant countries (Wiesinger 2008: 256). Lizel also made suggestions for improving the linguistic and educational situation in the German-speaking areas, including the following (ibid. 256f.):

1) to transfer the academic eagerness to learn Latin and French to learning German
2) to train German teachers in written and oral language use thoroughly in order to fulfill suggestion one (since speaking German does not necessarily mean that one can teach German adequately)
3) to produce linguistically 'pure' schoolbooks, which illustrate German orthography and grammar clearly, and to print them faultlessly
4) to read many good books in 'pure' German in order to acquire a good way to express oneself
5) to found an imperial German language academy for the establishment of universal norms and language maintenance.

These points can be categorized into two main objectives: While Lizel wants to promote the German language (instead of Latin and French) in all domains, including religion and science (see point one), he also implicitly argues for a 'verticalisation' (Reichmann 1988), i.e. a hierarchical structure of German varieties. Points two to five suggest that, for Lizel, there is a German variety that is 'pure' and, therefore, 'better' than others. The following quotations reveal that Lizel regards the variety used in Saxony as being at the top of this hierarchical structure, while he describes the variety used by the Catholic community, which was most prominent in the EUG area[30], as 'bad' German:

> Nachdem ich nun eine Zeitlang von den Jesuiten ins besondere geredet, [...] will ich nun jezo von den Catholiken insgemein, sie mögen geistlich oder weltlich seyn, in meiner Rede fortfahren, und zwar anfänglichen die Ursachen anzeigen, theils warum sie so übel Deutsch reden und schreiben, theils auch, warum sie fast keine oder doch so schlechte Verse machen. Das erstere belangend, halte ich davor, daß der Fehler steke so wol in der Auferziehung, als in dem eigenen Fleiß, oder vielmehr Unfleiß. Die Catholiken sind darinnen unglücklich, daß sie meistentheils in solchen Landschaften gezeuget werden, worinnen eine rauhe Sprache im Gebrauch ist. (Lizel 1731: 68)

> After talking about the Jesuits for some time, I will now continue with the Catholics, may they be clerical or secular, in my address, namely firstly showing the reasons for why they speak and write such bad German on the one hand, and also why they produce hardly any, and then such poor verses. With regard to the first point, I reckon the mistake lies in the upbringing as well as in their diligence, or rather their lack of diligence. The Catholics are unfortunate in that they are mostly sired in such areas in which a rough language is used.

Catholics, according to Lizel, speak 'bad' German, which is connected to their upbringing and their lack of diligence but also to the area they are living in, i.e. mainly the southern parts of the German-speaking area. In order to improve their German, Catholics should interact with Saxons:

> Den Catholiken würde es nicht schaden, wenn sie viel mit Leuten umgehen würden, die gut Deutsch reden. Sie dörfen nur in Sachsen reisen, wo man davor hält, daß eine gute Mundart vor andern Kreisen Deutschlands im Gebrauch sey. Dieser Meinung ist selbsten der oben gedachte Spanier, Laurentius Villavincentius, nicht abhold, und scheinet, als ob er zuvor gesehen, daß ich seinen Religions=Verwannten, in seinem Namen, diesen Rath zu geben nöthig habe: *Puritatem patrii sermonis*, schreibet er, *non haurias, nisi vel ex familiari convictu eorum, qui tersissime & nitidissime illum sonant; vel ex libris commendatissima dialecto editis: qualis multorum judicio censetur in Germania dialectus Misnensis.* Woraus folget, daß er einem deutschen Catholiken rathet, man müsse die Reinigkeit der Muttersprache lernen, entweder durch den täglichen Umgang mit den Sachsen, und fürnemlich mit den Meisnern, oder durch Lesung solcher Schriften, die nach einer netten Mundart geschrieben sind: Dergleichen nicht nur in Meissen, sondern auch in andern Evangelischen Landschaften angetroffen werden. (Lizel 1731: 103)

> It would not do any harm if the Catholics interacted a lot with people who spoke good German. They just have to go to Saxony, where it is believed that a good vernacular, before other areas of Germany, is used. Even the Spaniard mentioned above, Laurentius Villavincentius, is not adverse to this opinion, and it seems as if he had seen that I am required to give this advice to

---

30 Wiesinger (2008: 243) explains that large parts of Upper and Lower Austria, Styria and Carinthia were re-catholicised – mainly due to the Jesuits and Emperor Ferdinand II – in the first half of the 17th century. Protestantism only survived in the Alpine regions of the south of Upper Austria, in Upper Styria and in Upper Carinthia as well as in the Archbishopric of Salzburg.

his religious supporters in his name: *The purity of the native speech*, he writes, *you may not draw if not either from the familiar community of those who let it sound the cleanest and keenest, or from the books, which are published in the most recommended dialect: such as the dialect of Meissen is believed to be in the opinion of many in Germania.* From which follows that he advises a German Catholic to learn the purity of the mother tongue, either by daily interaction with Saxons, and in particular with the people from Meissen, or by reading texts which are written in a nice vernacular: The like are not only found in Meissen but also in other Protestant areas.

Thus a clear hierarchy of German varieties is presented, with the Saxon variety at the top and the variety used by the Catholics, i.e. mainly UG, at the bottom. That the Saxon variety is placed at the top of the hierarchy by a Protestant theologian is not surprising, given that Martin Luther was from Saxony and that his Bible translation was based on an ECG variety. Lizel (1731: 22f.) highlights the importance of Luther for the German language and presents Luther's German as the best variety:

> Wenn ich sage, daß unser Luther der erste gewesen, welcher die Deutschen Deutsch gelehret, glaube ich nicht, daß ich von jemand einen vernünftigen Widerspruch zu gewarten habe. [...] Vor ihm [Luther] hat keiner so gut geredet und geschrieben [...]. (Lizel 1731: 22f.)

> I don't think that I have to expect any reasonable objections from anyone when I say that our Luther was the first who taught German to the Germans. [...] Nobody before him [Luther] had spoken and written so well [...].

Lizel (1731: 26) even places Luther's German Bible translation as instruction of how to speak and write 'good' German above any German grammars:

> Unsre deutsche Bibel ist besser als tausend Grammatiken: Du findest darinnen mehr, als tausend Sprachmeister dir nicht sagen können: Sie zeiget dir, wie du gut Deutsch reden und schreiben solt [sic] [...]. (Lizel 1731: 26)

> Our German Bible is better than a thousand grammars: You find more in it than a thousand grammarians can tell you: It shows you how you should speak and write good German [...].

While it does not seem as if he advocated the publishing of grammars, Lizel (1731: 103f.) proposes the foundation of a German language academy, similar to the Académie Française, which should examine existing grammars, draft an exhaustive reference work for orthography, produce an adequate dictionary, and endeavour to set everything that may serve to improve German in good order and in general use. Even though Lizel mentions both spoken and written language use in the quotation above, he indicates that the universal norms, which the German language academy should agree on, can only apply to writing:

> Ich rede vom Schreiben. Denn, wie es im Reden ein schweres Begehren seyn würde, daß alle angeborne Mundarten solten in der Aussprache sich nach einer allein verändern; wie es auch, des unterschiedenen Geschmackes wegen, ein unausgemachter Streit werden würde: ob, zum Exempel, die Aussprache eines Schlesiers, oder eines Holsteiners, der Hochteutsch redet,

angenehmer sey? So ist dennoch nicht zu läugnen, daß, so wohl der Niedersachse, als der Schlesier, wenn sie eine gute Feder führen, in der Orthographie und in denen Grund=Sätzen der Sprache einander gleich kommen werden. (Lizel 1731: 109)

I talk about writing. Because, as regards speaking, it would be a difficult demand that all native vernaculars should change in their pronunciation according to one only, and it would also become an undecided argument because of different tastes: if, for example, the pronunciation of a Silesian or a Holsteiner, who speaks High German[31], would be more pleasant? Nevertheless, it cannot be denied that the Lower Saxon as well as the Silesian, if they write well, will be equally good in orthography and in the principles of language.

According to Lizel, it is implausible to choose one German pronunciation as the norm, partly because of the subjective nature of taste. Interestingly, the examples that Lizel provides in the quotation above mention the pronunciation of German speakers from the north of the German-speaking area, which are both described as 'pleasant', while the pronunciation of speakers from the UG area is not mentioned. It could be inferred that UG speakers do not have a 'pleasant' pronunciation but Lizel does not state this explicitly. Indeed, Lizel never uses the term 'Upper German' but instead links language use to religious denomination.

By contrast, Johann Christoph Gottsched (1700–1766), a literary scholar and grammarian from Leipzig, whose fame was also recognized by Austrians, stigmatises UG features explicitly while also propagating the Upper Saxon variety used by higher social classes.[32] Wiesinger (2008: 255, 257) sees Gottsched as the second, but certainly stronger, catalyst for the awakening of interest in the German language. Gottsched's weekly periodicals *Die vernünftigen Tadlerinnen* (1725–1726) and *Der Biedermann* (1727–1729), in which he advocates clear linguistic expressions and the banning of French loan words, helped to renew the *Deutsche Gesellschaft*, a language society concerned with the promotion of good literary practices (ibid. 257). The ideas and ideologies held by this German Society found their expression in their *Beyträge zur Critischen Historie der Deutschen Sprache, Poesie und Beredtsamkeit* (*Contributions to the critical history of the German language, poetry and eloquence*), which were published from 1732 to 1744 in eight volumes (ibid.). Finally, Gottsched published his own grammar entitled *Grundlegung einer Deutschen Sprachkunst* (*Foundation of a German Grammar*) in 1748, which pursued the following goals (ibid. 257f.):

- to establish German as a national language in all domains, especially in the aristocracy (replacing French) as well as in university and in the academic sciences (replacing Latin), and to suppress loan words
- to create an obligatory written norm, namely 'High German', based on the variety used by the best literary scholars from Saxony (i.e. the ECG region, which was

---

31 As opposed to Low German.
32 See chapter 3 for specific quotations.

considered the geographical centre of the German language area) and from the northern German area
– to eradicate regional differences in the use of written language by implementing the 'High German' language norm in all German regions
– to develop a clear and intelligible linguistic way of expressing oneself through clear and simple syntax and a plain style.

By aiming to eradicate regional differences and establish a single written norm, Gottsched's activities also had an implicit effect on the linguistic landscape of Austria. Wiesinger (2008: 259) claims that the highest social classes ("der Adel und das Großbürgertum") in Saxony used a kind of sophisticated ("gehobene") vernacular, which closely approximated to the written language, from the 17th century onwards and that the use of 'dialect' was restricted to lower social classes in Saxony.[33] By contrast, the use of 'dialect' dominated everyday life – also for the highest social classes – in the southern parts of the German-speaking areas, according to Wiesinger. This, however, neither meant that 'dialect' was the only existing language variety in 18th-century Austria, nor that there was only one Austrian 'dialect'. In his description of Upper Austria, Matthias Höfer (1800, as cited in Wiesinger 2008: 259), a Benedictine monk from Kremsmünster with an interest in language, distinguishes between three varieties in Austria:

> Die Sprache an sich selbst betrachtet, richtet sich nach der Verschiedenheit des Standes. Gleichwie die Art, sich zu kleiden, nach dem Ausdrucke des Pöbels, dreyfach ist: 1) städterisch oder herrisch; 2) markisch, wie es unter gemeinen Bürgern in den Marktflecken üblich ist; und 3) bäuerisch. Eben so verhält es sich auch mit der Art und Weise, im Reden sich auszudrücken. (Höfer 1800: 56, as cited in Wiesinger 2008: 259)

> The language itself conforms to the different social estates. It is, as is the case for the way people dress, according to popular perceptions, threefold: 1) urban or noble; 2) *markisch*, i.e. the way people commonly dress in small towns [so-called *Märkte*]; and 3) rustic. The same distinction is true for the way people express themselves when speaking.

---

33 While it is true that the language use of lower social classes was stigmatised, also the higher social classes in Central and Northern Germany did not exclusively use a sophisticated, supra-regional variety. As von Polenz (1994: 225) points out, sophisticated, supra-regional speech was only used by a small, educated group of people, who belonged to the highest social class (*Oberschicht*), until the 19th century. However, this supra-regional variety was only used in certain communicative situations, e.g. in public and in professional discourse, which implies that also the higher social classes in Central and Northern Germany used 'dialect' in private settings. Therefore, Wiesinger's (2008: 259) claim that 'dialect' was restricted to lower social classes in Saxony has to be questioned. It could, however, be argued that the use of regional varieties was more common in public settings for high social classes in the UG language area.

This threefold distinction of co-existing varieties in Austria is based on a social as well as an urban/rural distinction. Since no detailed descriptions of any of these varieties exist, we have to rely on meta-linguistic comments in order to get an insight into their linguistic appearance. A particularly interesting example of such comments can be found in the *Teutsches Namen oder Lehrbüchl*, printed in Vienna around 1750 (see figure and transcription below).

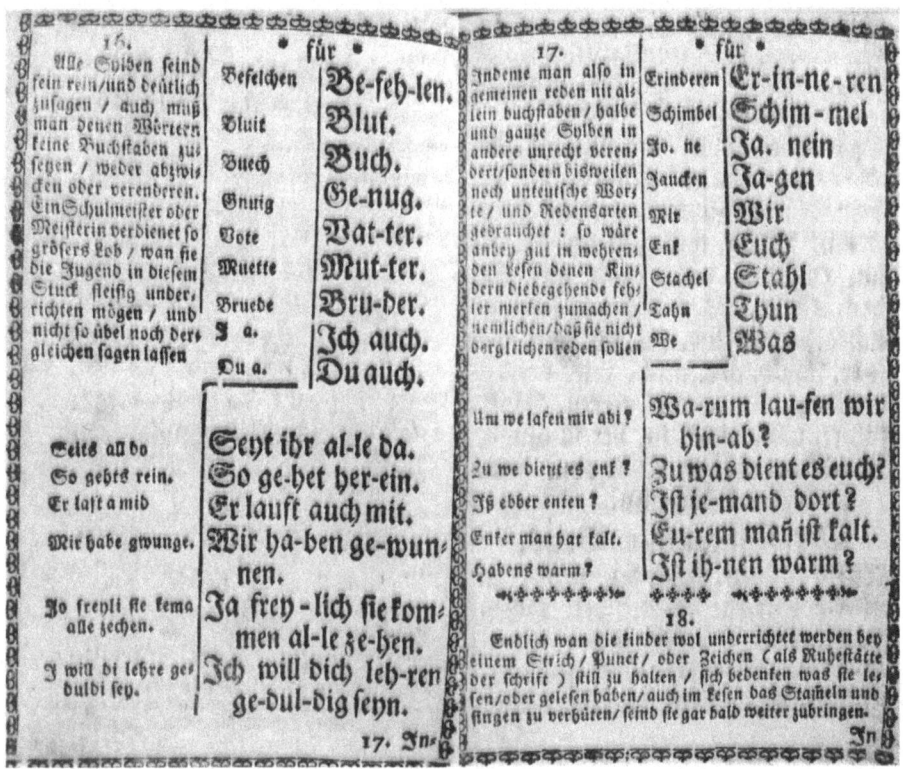

Fig. 2: Examples of regional variants in the *Teutsches Namen oder Lehrbüchl* (c. 1750)

This reading primer intended to teach how to read and pronounce words 'correctly'. At the beginning, the alphabet is listed, followed by individual syllables and words. These lists include comments for the teacher on the side. After pointing out the importance of 'correct' pronunciation in order to distinguish words (e.g. *Hütte* vs *Hüte* – huts vs hats), two pages of this reading primer present examples of what would probably fall into Höfer's 'rustic' or 'markisch' category on the left, with their equivalents in literary German (in larger font) on the right hand side (see figure above and transcription below).

16.	*für*		17.	*für*	
Alle Sylben seind fein rein/und deutlich zusagen / auch muß man denen Wörtern keine Buchstaben zu=setzen / weder abzwi=cken oder verenderen. Ein Schulmeister oder Meisterin verdienet so grösers Lob / wan sie die Jugend in diesem Stuck fleisig under=richten mögen / und nicht so übel noch der=gleichen sagen lassen	Befelchen Bluit Buech Gnuig Vote Muette Bruede I a. Du a.	Be-feh-len. Blut. Buch. Ge-nug. Vat-ter. Mut-ter. Bru-der. Ich auch. Du auch.	Indeme man also in gemeinen reden nit al=lein buchstaben / halbe und ganze Sylben in andere unrecht veren=dert/sondern bisweilen noch unteutsche Wor=te / und Redensarten gebrauchet : so wäre anbey gut in wehren=den Lesen denen Kin=dern die begehende feh=ler merken zumachen / nemlichen/daß sie nicht dergleichen reden sollen	Erinderen Schimbel Jo. ne Jaucken Mir Enk Stachel Tahn We	Er-in-ne-ren Schim-mel Ja. nein Ja-gen Wir Euch Stahl Thun Was
Seits all do So gehts rein. Er laft a mid Mir habe gwunge. Jo freyli sie kema alle zechen. I will di lehre ge=duldi sey.	Seyt ihr al-le da. So ge-het her-ein. Er lauft auch mit. Wir ha-ben ge-wun=nen. Ja frey-lich sie kom=men al-le ze-hen. Ich will dich leh-ren ge-dul-dig seyn.		Um we lafen mir abi? Zu we dient es enk? Iß ebber enten? Enker man hat kalt. Habens warm?	Wa-rum lau-fen wir hin-ab? Zu was dient es euch? Ist je-mand dort? Eu-rem mañ ist kalt. Ist ih-nen warm?	

18.

Endlich wan die kinder wol underrichtet werden bey einem Strich / Punct / oder Zeichen (als Ruhestätte der schrift) still zu halten / sich bedenken was sie le=sen/oder gelesen haben/auch im Lesen das Stañeln und singen zu verhüten/seind sie gar bald weiter zubringen.

17. In=   In

Fig. 3: Transcription of examples of regional variants in the *Teutsches Namen oder Lehrbüchl* (c. 1750: 30f.)

From the examples depicted above, the pronunciation of certain words, and even phrases, can be deduced: *Bluit, Buech,* and *gnuig* were pronounced with a diph-thong but spelled with a monophthong in 'correct' literary German (see right hand side) and in the phrase *Er laft a mid* the diphthong in *laufen* is pronounced as a monophthong, the *auch* is reduced to *a*, and there is a lenition of *t* in *mid*. Of course, these pronunciations could also be deduced from present-day regional Bavarian (which include Austrian) varieties. However, some of the examples given may seem unusual to a speaker of a contemporary Bavarian variety, such as *erinderen* for *erinnern*, *Stachel* for *Stahl*, and *we* for *was*. Also the use of *haben* instead of *sein* in the phrases *Enker man hat kalt* and *Habens warm?* is relatively uncommon nowadays but still in use in South Bavarian varieties, i.e. the Tyrol, East as well as South Tyrol and Carinthia. The fact that this textbook was printed in Vienna poses the question of whether the author of this primer was from the South Bavarian area, whether this kind of construction was more widely used in 18th-century Austria, or whether the author chose variants from different regions (Havinga 2015: 273f.).

While the examples provide an indication of how particular spellings might[34] have been pronounced, the key point is that the regional variants given on the left hand side were considered 'bad', 'wrong' or even 'un-German', as the text below section 17 suggests:

> Indeme man also in gemeinen reden nit allein buchstaben / halbe und ganze Sylben in andere unrecht verendert / sondern bisweilen noch **unteutsche** Worte / und Redensarten gebrauchet : so wäre anbey gut in wehrenden Lesen denen Kindern die begehende fehler merken zumachen / nemlichen / daß sie nicht dergleichen reden sollen [...]. (*Teutsches Namen- oder Lehrbüchl* c. 1750: 31, my emphasis)

> By not only wrongly changing letters, half or whole syllables to others in common speech, but also by even using **'un-German'** words and expressions: therefore, when reading, it would be good to make the children aware of their mistakes, namely that they should not speak in the following way [...]. (*Teutsches Namen- oder Lehrbüchl* c. 1750: 31, my emphasis)

This reading primer clearly advocates the pronunciation of words as they are written in literary German, while stigmatising regional Bavarian varieties. Many 18th-century grammarians take a similar judgemental and prescriptive stance. As mentioned before and as von Polenz (1994: 160) states, Gottsched made disparaging comments on regional varieties, especially those of the south[35], and of the "Pöbelsprache", i.e. the language of the lower classes. According to Gottsched, 'dialect' and everyday language use by uneducated people is something corrupted (ibid.). He, therefore, based his norms on written language, particularly the language use of established authors.[36] By contrast, Johann Christoph Adelung (1732–1806) – the most famous German language authority after Gottsched, born in Spantekow (Prussia), whose *Deutsche Sprachlehre* (*German Grammar*) (1781) became *the* reference work in the

---

34 This reading primer might not supply a very accurate representation of the actual pronunciation, e.g. the letter *e* could stand for an [ɛ] or [ə] sound.

35 See section 3.3 for examples of such comments.

36 See section 3.3 for a selection of these authors.

late 18th century according to Rössler (1997: 86f.) – also focuses on spoken language and describes the pronunciation of the two main varieties of German ('Upper' and Low German/Low Saxon)[37] in more detail, be it in rather vague and non-linguistic terms (1781: 17f.):

> [D]ie Oberdeutsche unterscheidet sich durch ihre hohe Sprache, durch ihren vollen Mund, durch ihren Hang zu hauchenden blasenden und zischenden Mitlauten, zu den breiten und tiefen Selbstlauten und zu rauhen Doppellauten, durch ihre Härten, durch ein weitläufiges Wort= und Sylbengepränge, durch weitschweiffige Ausdrücke, Überfüllungen und hohe Figuren. Sie ist dabey reich an Wörtern und Ausdrücken, fast alle Begriffe mit allen ihren Schattirungen oder Graden der Stärke auszudrucken, und verräth dadurch ihre frühe und lange Cultur, aber einer Cultur ohne Geschmack und feines Gefühl. (Adelung 1781: 17, § 30)

> 'Upper German' distinguishes itself [from Low German/Low Saxon] by its high language, by its full mouth, by its disposition to aspirated blowing and hissing consonants, to broad and deep vowels and to rough diphthongs, by its hardness, by an extensive word- and syllable-pomp, by circuitous expressions, by inundation of high figures. It is, thereby, rich on words and expressions, can express almost all concepts with all their nuances or degrees of strength, and it thus reveals its early and long culture, but a culture without taste and sensitiveness.

Adelung's description of 'Upper German' has clear negative connotations, which are expressed through words such as *rough*, *hardness*, and *extensive pomp*. The last sentence then portrays 'Upper German', and by implication its speakers, as tasteless and insensitive. By contrast, Adelung's representation of Low German/Low Saxon sounds more positive, especially with regard to the pronunciation, which is depicted as soft and easy flowing:

> Die Niederdeutsche oder Niedersächsische Mundart ist von ihr gerade das Gegentheil; eine Feindinn aller vollen Hauch= Zisch= und Blaselaute, aller harten Doppellaute, des vollen Oberdeutschen Mundes und des leeren Wortgepränges, und dagegen eine erklärte Freundinn aller sanften und leicht fließenden Töne, der höhern Vocale und einer viel sagenden, aber auch oft unperiodischen Kürze. Sie ist reich an Kunstwörtern für das Seewesen, hingegen arm an Ausdrücken für unsinnliche Gegenstände, weil sie weit weniger ausgebildet worden, daher sie in solchen Fällen immer genöthigt ist, von ihrer reichern und üppigern Schwester zu borgen. (Adelung 1781: 17f., § 31)

---

37 For Adelung, Upper German seems to refer to what is called High German (*Hochdeutsch*) in modern linguistic terminology, i.e. the German-speaking part south of the Benrath Line that underwent the second Germanic consonant shift, in contrast to Low German. Adelung, therefore, appears to place what in today's terminology is called Upper German and East Central German in the same group, i.e. 'Upper German', while – as can be seen below – he conceives High German (*Hochdeutsch*) as a sub-category within Upper German. In order to indicate this distinction to modern terminology, the term 'Upper German' in Adelung's understanding of High German is marked with apostrophes.

The Low German or Low Saxon vernacular is just the opposite of it [of the Upper German variety]; an enemy of all full aspirated, hissing and blowing sounds, of all hard diphthongs, of the full Upper German mouth and the empty word-pomp, and instead a professed friend of all soft and easy flowing sounds, of the higher vowels and a meaningful but also often un-periodical brevity. It is rich on coinages for naval matters, however poor on expressions for intellectual subjects because they have been cultivated to a much lesser extent, therefore, it is always forced to borrow from its richer and more opulent sister in these cases.

It appears that the northern German pronunciation, especially, carried some kind of prestige for Adelung, while the lexis is presented as somewhat impoverished in comparison to 'Upper German'. Indeed, von Polenz (1994: 143) states that the appreciation for north German pronunciation emanated from Luther's praise of the Brandenburgian and Low Saxon pronunciation, where Luther's request for a clear *Leselautung*, i.e. pronunciation when reading a text out loud, was followed more rigorously than in Upper Saxony. This would suggest that Adelung is referring to northern German, rather than Low German pronunciation. In any case, the prestige of this northern variety was restricted to pronunciation, while the prestigious variety with regard to grammar and lexis was High German, which is described as a "daughter of Upper German, but more of the northern than of the southern provinces" by Adelung (1781: 18).[38] Thus it is made clear that 'good' German is not found in the southern parts of the German-speaking area, such as Bavaria and Austria.

Faulstich (2008) illustrates the wider context of the 'verticalisation' of German varieties and stresses that the Upper Saxon variety had already gained considerable prestige in the 17th century. Grammarians – or more generally 'Sprachkundler' (Faulstich 2008), i.e. individuals dealing with language such as lexicographers, publicists, and literary scholars – of the 18th century further legitimated the supremacy of the Upper Saxon variety by highlighting its well-developed state of standardisation and its supra-regional use (ibid.). The position of Saxony as a cultural and commercial centre also contributed to Upper Saxon becoming the most highly ranked variety in the German-speaking area and being used synonymously to High German by various grammarians (e.g. Gottsched and Adelung) (ibid.). Upper Saxon was clearly more prestigious than UG in the 18th century[39] but this does not necessarily explain why the Habsburg Monarchy – as one of the most powerful empires in

---

38 See section 3.6 for the full original quotation.

39 This should not imply that UG necessarily carried more prestige before the 18th century. Stigmatisations of Austrian varieties can already be found in the 16th century, as the following quotation testifies: "Bauarorum lingua Sueuicae similis est, sed etiam crassior, ut audio: crassissima in Austria, uel aliqua eius parte. frow pronuntiant fraw; heuw / hauw." (Gesner 1555: 39). ("The language of the Bavarians is similar to Swabian, but even grosser, as I hear it: the grossest in Austria, or in some part of it. They pronounce frow fraw; heuw / hauw.") I am very grateful to Dr Raf van Rooy, KU Leuven, for providing this quotation and translation.

Europe at the time – felt it necessary to introduce this 'foreign' variety. The ideologies behind this language reform are discussed in the following section.

2.2 Enlightenment and language reform

Wiesinger (2008: 255) points out that the Enlightenment and the language reform went hand in hand in Austria. During the Enlightenment, the intelligentsia believed that language, the ability to think, and academic disciplines were closely connected (ibid. 263). This led to the impression that what was perceived as poor linguistic conditions (especially the non-standardised spelling, archaic morphological forms and the complex, long-winded syntax of the written language) prevented Austria from advancing in scientific and intellectual fields (ibid.):

> Wo aber die Sprache schlecht und mangelhaft ist, dort könne auch nicht ordentlich gedacht und weder geistige Leistung hervorgebracht noch Wissenschaft und Fortschritt erzielt werden. (Wiesinger 2008: 263)

> Where, however, the language is bad and deficient, one also cannot think properly and one can neither generate accomplishments nor achieve scholarship and progress.

Wiesinger bases this observation on various comments by grammarians and literary scholars throughout the 18th century. Johann Balthasar von Antesperg (1682/83–1763), a grammarian from Bavaria who spent most of his life in Vienna, highlights the connection between language awareness and the intelligence of a people:

> Die Gewißheit der Sprache ist das Merkmahl eines klugen Volkes. [...] Ein rüchtiger [sic] Werkzeug, ja ein unerschöpflicher Nutzen in allen guten Geschäften, Künsten und Wissenschaften; und die Ungewißheit derselben ist das Widerspiel. (Antesperg 1747: Vorrede §. XI)[40]

> The certainty of language is the characteristic of a wise people. [...] A proper instrument, yes an inexhaustible benefit to all good businesses, arts and sciences; and the uncertainty of it is the opposite.

Antesperg, who contributed to the standardisation of 18th-century Austrian German with his *Kayserliche Deutsche Grammatick* (*Imperial German Grammar*), suggests that Austrians are not certain about their language yet:

> [...] So [durch Grammatiken] wird die reine deutsche Schreibart, Poesie und Beredsamkeit [...] in Oesterreich zu einem männlichen Alter gelangen. [...] So werden wir [...] in der eigenen Sprache wie andere gesittete Völker klug, hurtig, bescheiden, und Kenner und Liebhaber guter Künste und Wissenschaften werden [...]. (Antesperg 1747: Vorrede §. XXVIII)

---

40 A number of the quotations presented in this section can also be found in Wiesinger (2008).

Thus [through grammars] the pure German way of writing, poetry and eloquence will soon [...] reach a manly age in Austria. Thus we will [...] in our own language become wise, swift, modest, and adepts and enthusiasts for good arts and sciences like other civilised people [...].

By listing what will happen once the Austrians have grammars, Antesperg implies what has not happened yet, i.e. Austrians are perceived as unwise, slow, and as people who do not know anything about good arts and sciences; and these perceptions are linked to language. For Friedrich Wilhelm Gerlach (1728–1802), a history teacher from Thuringia, who participated in the 18th-century language norm discourse, language use seems to be the predominant factor for how people are perceived:

Je ordentlichere, und je mehr Worte also, eine Sprache hat, desto vollkommener und besser können die Menschen dänken, von denen sie geredet wird. Folglich soll eine jede Menge der Menschen die Fehler ihrer Sprache verbessern [...] und selbe in der Richtigkeit zu erhalten, sich befleißen. Es ist ein Zeichen, daß Unwissenheit, unrichtige Gedanken, und kleine Geister in einem Land seyn: wo der vorige Satz nicht beobachtet wird. (Gerlach 1758: 2f.)

The more proper, and so the more words a language has, the more complete and better the people by whom it is spoken can think. Consequently, a great many people should correct the mistakes of their language [...] and work hard on keeping it correct. It is a sign that nescience, incorrect thoughts and small minds are in a country, where the previous sentence is not obeyed.

In his *Kurzgefasste Deutsche Sprachlehre* (*Brief German Grammar*) (1758), Gerlach explicitly connects the ability to think with the number of ('proper') words a language has. He also urges people to use their language correctly if they do not wish to be perceived as ignorant and unintelligent. For Joseph von Sonnenfels (1732/33–1817), an Austrian literary scholar who advocated the foundation of a German society, language stands at the beginning of a chain of perceptions:

Denn, wirklich beruhet ein nicht geringer Theil der Hochachtung, welche Ausländer einem Lande entweder einräumen, oder versagen, schon auf der Sprache desselben. Je nachdem diese, geschmeidig, rein und bearbeitet ist, urtheilen sie, daß auch dessen Geschmack fein, und geläutert seyn müsse. Von dem Geschmacke schliessen sie auf die Wissenschaften; und von diesen ziehen sie weitere Folgen auf die Sitten. (Sonnenfels 1761: 23)

Because it is true that not a small part of the respect which foreigners either grant or deny a country is based on the language of this very country. Depending on whether it is smooth, pure and well-formed, they judge that the taste of this country must be refined. From the taste they draw conclusions regarding the academic studies; and from these they draw further conclusions on the mores.

In his speech entitled *Ankündigung einer deutschen Gesellschaft in Wien* (*Announcement of a German society in Vienna*), which he gave on 2 January 1761 on the occasion of its foundation[41], Sonnenfels develops a kind of hierarchical structure of perceptions: the language leads to judgments of the taste, which in turn influences the assessment of academic studies, which then affects the perception of the manners of a country, or rather of its inhabitants. Adelung, by contrast, suggests a more interactive relation between the condition of a people and its language:

> Jede Sprache stehet mit der Erkenntniß eines Volkes und dessen Art zu denken, in dem genauesten Verhältnisse. Bey einem armen, rohen und ungesitteten Volke ist sie arm, rauh und ganz auf sinnliche Gegenstände eingeschränkt; bey einem gesitteten, blühenden und ausgebildeten Volke wortreich, biegsam, aller Begriffe und ihrer Schattirungen fähig; bey einem durch den Luxus entnervten Volke aber, so weich, üppig und kraftlos, als das Volk selbst. (Adelung 1781: 4, §. 4).

> Every language reflects the knowledge of a people and its way of thinking. A poor, rough, and uncivilised people has a language that is poor, rough and completely limited to sensuous subjects; when it comes to a civilised, flourishing, and educated people the language is rich in words, flexible, able to express all terms in their nuances; but with respect to a people strained by luxury, it is as soft, luxuriant, and weak as the people itself.

While Sonnenfels indicates that he is referring to perceptions, Adelung presents the link between a people and its language as general facts. Similarly, Johann Heinrich Gottlob (von) Justi (1720–1771), who was appointed to a professorship for German eloquence at the *Theresian Academy* in 1750, declares the existence of a connection between the condition of academic studies and language with unquestionable certainty. In his inaugural lecture entitled *Abhandlung von dem Zusammenhang der Vollkommenheit der Sprache mit dem Blühenden Zustand der Wissenschaften* (*Essay on the connection between the perfection of language and the thriving state of academic studies*), Justi claims the following:

> Ein blühender Zustand der Wissenschaften stehet [...] mit der Vollkommenheit der Sprache in der genauesten Verbindung. (Justi 1750: 20)

> A thriving state of academic study is most closely connected to the perfection of the language.

Justi believes that language can and should be changed by expanding its vocabulary and by ensuring a pleasant pronunciation as well as consistent inflection (Wiesinger 2008: 321). Thus perfection of a language can be achieved, which will, in turn, lead to a growth in academic studies. Academic studies were of particular

---

[41] The *Wiener Deutsche Gesellschaft* only existed for two years and their activities were, according to Wiesinger (2008: 331), limited to a number of lectures.

importance to Justi since they would advance the *Glückseligkeit* of human society to make a state rich, powerful and happy:

> Da es eine unleugbare Wahrheit ist, daß die Wissenschaften dasjenige Mittel sind, wodurch ein Volk an seiner gemeinschaftlichen Glückseeligkeit arbeiten muß; und da ein Staat ohne Mitwirkung der Wissenschaften niemahls reich, mächtig und glücklich werden kan; so kan man von den jezigen weisen Grundsätzen und Einrichtungen mit vollkommener Zuversicht eine solche Erwartung haben. Ein blühender Zustande der Wissenschaften hat nämlich mit denjenigen Mitteln, welche einen Staat mächtig und glücklich machen, einen unzertrennlichen Zusammenhang. (Justi 1750: 32)

> Because it is an undeniable fact that academic studies are the means for a people to work on its collective *Glückseligkeit* and because a state can never become rich, powerful and happy without the involvement of academic studies, one can now with full confidence have such an expectation from the current wise principles and institutions. Thriving academic studies are inseparably linked to the means which make a state powerful and happy.

The term *Glückseligkeit* was a central concept in 18th-century Austria and referred to a state of individual 'happiness' for the common good as well as the benefit of the state (Klippel 1999: 77f.). The idea of promoting *Glückseligkeit* for the common good is also evident in the *Allgemeine Schulordnung* (1774).[42] This school policy states under the subheading *Beweggrund zur Festsetzung einer allgemeinen Landschulordnung* (*Motives for the regulations of a common school policy*) that it was realised "that the education of the youth, of both sexes, requires closer attention since it is the most important basis of the true *Glückseligkeit* of the nations"[43]. In other words, it was believed that education and academic studies, which – as outlined above – were connected to language, can generate *Glückseligkeit* as well as power.

2.3 Empress Maria Theresa and her educational reforms

Naturally, Empress Maria Theresa, the ruler of the Habsburg Empire from 1740 to 1780, not only absorbed the ideas outlined above but also followed them in order to ensure the powerful position of her empire. Maria Theresa was the only sovereign female ruler in the history of the Habsburg Monarchy and her 40-year-long reign is considered highly successful by Habsburg standards, not only on account of the territorial expansion the empire underwent during her reign (Yonan 2011: 2f.). She induced a number of political consolidations, introduced administrative reforms,

---

42 See the next section for further details on this school policy.
43 German original: "[...] so haben Wir wahrgenommen, daß die Erziehung der Jugend, beyderley Geschlechts, als die wichtigste Grundlage der wahren Glückseligkeit der Nationen ein genaueres Einsehen allerdings erfordere." (*Allgemeine Schulordnung* 1774).

and initiated cultural developments, thus helping the Habsburg Empire to gain political as well as cultural influence on an international scale (ibid. 3).

In the context of my research, Maria Theresa's views on the intellectual state of Austrian society are of great importance since they crucially influenced the path of the language reform in Austria. Maria Theresa herself was of the opinion that Austrians had a "very bad language".[44] This statement was made in a letter to Gottsched's wife Luise Adelgunde Victoria Gottschedin after a visit to Vienna in 1749, where both Gottsched and his wife were received by Maria Theresa at Schönbrunn Palace (Wiesinger 2008: 260). Soon after meeting Gottsched, Maria Theresa set up a professorship for German eloquence at the *Theresian Academy* in 1750, which was – as mentioned before – given to Johann Heinrich Gottlob (von) Justi (ibid. 272). Originally, Maria Theresa had wished to appoint Johann Christoph Gottsched for this position but since he declined the offer, an alternative way to disseminate Gottsched's language norms was employed: By imperial decree, the empress prescribed the use of Gottsched's *Grundlegung einer deutschen Sprachkunst* (first edition 1748), which was largely based on the ECG variety, at the *Theresian Academy* (ibid.). Of course, a general dissemination of the ECG norms within Austria could not be provided by this decree, given that the *Theresian Academy* was restricted to members of the aristocracy. However, the abolition of censorship in 1751 resulted in the distribution of scientific and literary texts from the Protestant central and northern German areas (ibid. 273). This does not necessarily mean that no ECG and north German literature was circulating in the Habsburg Monarchy before the middle of the 18th century. Indeed, von Polenz (1994: 176) regards the contact with ECG and north German literature since the 17th century as a reason for Austria's open-mindedness towards the ECG language norms, in contrast to the greater conservatism in Bavaria.

Another step in the language reform was Maria Theresa's appointment of Johann Siegmund Valentin Popowitsch (1705–1774) to the new professorship for German language and eloquence at the University of Vienna and at the *Savoyische Akademie* in 1753 (ibid.). Furthermore, Popowitsch, as the first domestic linguist, was asked to write a German grammar for schools, which he published in 1754 (ibid.). In his *Nothwendigste Anfangsgründe der Teutschen Sprachkunst zum Gebrauche der Österreichischen Schulen* (*Most necessary foundations of the German language for the use by Austrian Schools*), Popowitsch follows Gottsched's norms to a large extent, even though he became one of Gottsched's rivals.[45] In this way, Gottsched's norms were further disseminated, if indirectly.

---

44 German original, as cited in Wiesinger (2008: 260): "Wir Oesterreicher haben eine sehr schlechte Sprache."
45 See section 3.4 for further details.

The role of education in the implementation of a language norm should not be underestimated. Indeed, as Deumert & Vandenbussche (2003: 7) state

> novel forms of elementary national education which emerged from the late eighteenth and early nineteenth century in most European countries, and which provided prescriptive language education to large numbers of speakers, were a central force in the diffusion of standard languages and the formation of a standard/dialect diglossia.

In order to understand the influence of Popowitsch's schoolbook and education in general in the propagation of the ECG norm, 18th-century education in Austria is now outlined.

The education of the general public was closely connected to the ideas of the Enlightenment and was advocated by Maria Theresa as well as her son and co-ruler Joseph II (reigning from 1765 to 1790). In the 18th century, the Habsburg government began to intensify its influence on the Austrian school system, which, hitherto, had been in the hands of religious orders.[46] The state's increasing intervention in school affairs (especially the curricula and the textbooks) originated in the recognition that their subjects could be influenced by education (Engelbrecht 1984: 14, Jaklin 2003: 9). Education should be shaped according to ideas of the Enlightenment: all people, regardless of class, religion or race, should be able to participate in school education (Engelbrecht 1984: 68). It was, however, not only the ideas of the Enlightenment, but also the ruling style of Absolutism that led to the increasing intervention of the state into school affairs[47], thus limiting the influence religious orders had (ibid.). Nevertheless, religious and moral education was not dismissed (ibid.), since the aim of education remained to be the raising of devout Christians, who were faithful to their fatherland (Jaklin 2003: 67). Besides generating obedient subjects, loyal soldiers and dutiful civil servants to strengthen the power of the state, a standardised school system was to lead to the creation of a *Nationalgeist*, a state-wide patriotism, by unifying the cultural, historical and social characteristics of the Habsburg Monarchy's nations (ibid. 68). However, each citizen should only receive schooling adequate to their social class; thus the rigid class distinction in education was retained (ibid.). And as too much enlightenment was deemed to carry a risk, the basic education for every citizen was limited to religious education and the so-called *Trivium*, i.e. reading, writing and arithmetic (ibid.). These subjects were taught in

---

46 Engelbrecht (1984: 15–17) stresses that pedagogical advancements had been made since the 17th century in Western Europe and that these, slowly but surely, also began to spread in Austria.
47 The school reform was further incited by the defeats against Prussia (War of Austrian Succession 1741–1748, Silesian Wars 1740–1742, 1744–1745, 1756–1763): Improvements in the training and education of officers as well as soldiers should lead to victories in battles (Engelbrecht 1984: 72).

so-called '*Deutsche Schulen*', i.e. primary schools, which were further divided into '*Trivialschulen*', '*Hauptschulen*', and '*Normalschulen*'.[48]

Jaklin (2003: 72f.) describes the education situation of the majority of the population as being in disorder until the mid-18th century: The church and to a lesser extent the lords of the manor or representatives of the municipality in towns were responsible for primary education. The number of children attending school was very low, especially in the countryside, where teaching only took place in winter as children were needed to augment the workforce from spring to autumn (ibid.). Furthermore, parents were not keen to spend money on school fees (ibid.). A survey in 1770 revealed that in Vienna, some 42 % of children received no education at all, while in Lower Austria only 17 to 18 % received education (ibid.). Children of the aristocracy and wealthy citizens were given private tuition; consequently, private tuition encompassed as many children as the state schools (ibid.).[49] It can, therefore, be concluded that not many children came into contact with Popowitsch's *Nothwendigste Anfangsgründe der Teutschen Sprachkunst zum Gebrauche der Österreichischen Schulen* (1754) in or before 1770. In other words, the language norms prescribed in his textbook would have only reached a very limited number of children, which would have not led to any wide-spread dissemination of those norms.

In 1770, Maria Theresa ordered the introduction of a school committee (Engelbrecht 1984: 99). This newly formed *Niederösterreichische Schulkommission* (*Lower Austrian school committee*) was given supreme control over the entire German education system in the Archduchy of Austria (i.e. today's Vienna, Upper and Lower Austria) by Empress Maria Theresa in October 1770 and sought to improve the organisation and content of schools (ibid.). Hitherto, there had existed no state supervision of schools or guidelines for the training of teachers. In addition to the introduction of the school committee as well as teacher training, new schools, so-called *Normalschulen*, were founded, intended as ideal institutions that would set the norms for a homogeneous state education and would train future teachers (Jaklin

---

48 Secondary schools were referred to as '*Lateinische Schulen*', '*Gymnasien*' or '*niedere Schulen*'. Universities and other institutions of higher education could be attended after graduating from a secondary school (Engelbrecht 1984). This division into three main, successive types of educational institutions is simplified here since the variety of vocational schools, such as '*Arbeitsschulen*', '*Industrieschulen*', '*Real-Zeichnungs-Schulen*' and '*Real-Handlungs-Academien*' (Engelbrecht 1984: 171–179), that existed in 18th-century Austria is not listed here. As I am interested in the form of schooling accessible to all people, only information about '*Deutsche Schulen*' will be provided. See Engelbrecht (1984) for detailed descriptions of secondary and higher education in 18th- and 19th-century Austria, which offered only limited access to poorer students.

49 A number of religious orders, such as the Piarists and the Ursulines, offered free education (religion, reading, writing and arithmetic) but their schools were mostly located in towns and, therefore, not accessible for those living in the countryside (Jaklin 2003: 73).

2003: 75). The first *Normalschule* was opened in Vienna on 2 January 1771 (Engelbrecht 1984: 99).

After the foundation of the *Normalschule*, the *Niederösterreichische Schulkommission* lost its momentum due to financial restrictions as well as uncertainty in how to proceed in the school reform (ibid. 100f.). However, in 1773 the rescindment of the Jesuit order, which had remained influential in educational matters, forced Maria Theresa to act quickly but also led to an increase in funds, since the Jesuits' funds were confiscated (ibid. 101). Since Maria Theresa's advisors and the school commission could not agree on a definite procedure, Maria Theresa asked Johann Ignaz Felbiger (1724–1788), an educationist working for Frederick II[50] in Prussia, to consult on realising her school reform plans (ibid. 101f.). This step, i.e. to ask a northerner to reform school teaching, had fundamental consequences on the visibility of Austrian German (see section 4.3).

Felbiger's teaching materials and methods were highly regarded but interpreted in various ways in Austria and it was believed that only he himself could achieve the desired uniformity in schooling (ibid. 102). Felbiger's concepts, consequently, initiated new education models and led to the first nation-wide elementary education policy in 1774 (*Allgemeine Schulordnung für die deutschen Normal-, Haupt- und Trivialschulen in sämmtlichen Kayserl. Königl. Erbländern*). This school policy formed the basis for a uniform state primary education and instigated the formation of a school committee in every provincial government. Three types of elementary schools were envisaged (Jaklin 2003: 75–77):

1) *Trivialschulen*: These schools were situated in every place that had a church. Religion, reading, writing and arithmetic were taught in one or two classes.

2) *Hauptschulen*: These schools were based in bigger towns as well as in monasteries and were divided into three or four[51] classes. In addition to religion and reading, instructions in calligraphy, orthography, German grammar and essay writing were provided. Basic Latin skills were also taught to students who were going to continue their education in a *Gymnasium*.

3) *Normalschulen*: These schools were founded in every town with a school committee and, as previously mentioned, acted as models for the other types of schools. The subjects were identical to those taught in the *Hauptschulen* but

---

50 Frederick II agreed to Maria Theresa's request to send Felbiger to Austria (Engelbrecht 1984: 102). Originally, Felbiger estimated to be in Vienna for a few months only but his work took longer than expected (ibid. 111). When Frederick II issued an ultimatum to Felbiger, namely to either resign from his post in Prussia or to return immediately, Felbiger chose the first option, after being promoted by Maria Theresa in 1777 (ibid.).

51 According to Jaklin (2003: 15, 76), the *Hauptschule* was divided into three classes but the school policy by Felbiger provides a timetable for *Hauptschulen* divided into three as well as four classes (*Allgemeine Schulordnung* 1774: Lit. B).

further lessons (such as architecture, geography and natural history) were available in the four classes.

The *Allgemeine Schulordnung* not only dictated which subjects were to be taught in these three types of schools, but also the length and time of each lesson taking place.[52] Thus Felbiger's school policy, which remained in force until 1869, allowed the state to intervene in the organisation and content of schools. The influence of religious orders on primary education was thus reduced significantly (Jaklin 2003: 79).

Naturally, not all of Felbiger's demands were met immediately after their publication: Engelbrecht (1984: 113) states that barely one quarter of children attended schools in rural areas in the first few years after the introduction of compulsory schooling. Families working in agriculture, especially, wanted to save money by not paying for the school fees, textbooks and writing materials and by employing their children as workforce (ibid.). This resistance to schooling in rural areas had been anticipated: the *Allgemeine Schulordnung* (1774: point 10) states that children in rural areas between the ages of 9 and 13 years have to be taught from the beginning of December (in contrast to the beginning of November in towns) to the end of March in *Trivialschulen*. Furthermore, a 3-week-break during harvest time was scheduled in the summer term for children to help their parents (ibid.). Children between 6 and 8 years of age were taught in the warmer months of the year as walking to school was too troublesome for them in winter (ibid.). The difficulty in physically accessing schools was also one of the reasons why illegal *Winkelschulen* flourished, where teachers without formal training gave a basic education for a small school fee (Engelbrecht 1984: 114f.). The authorities did not take significant action against these *Winkelschulen* since there was a lack of state-trained teachers[53] and of teaching rooms in the state-run schools (ibid.). These inadequacies also kept wealthy citizens from sending their children to state schools, with many opting for their children to be privately educated (Jaklin 2003: 79).

After a survey conducted in 1781 showed that, on average, less than a third of the children complied with the compulsory 6-year-duration of school attendance, Joseph II introduced punitive measures[54] for parents who did not send their children

---

52 Translations of these timetables can be found in the appendix.
53 The teaching job was rather unappealing due to the low salary and the non-existence of a pension scheme as well as health insurance (Jaklin 2003: 79). In order to raise the status of this job, teachers were declared civil servants in 1788 and received a pension (ibid. 80). Furthermore, teachers were exempt from military service (ibid.).
54 If children were not sent to school, their parents had to pay twice the school fees or work for the public, such as carrying out building and renovation works on the school (Engelbrecht 1984: 119). Frühmann (2010: 23f.) states that the parents (usually the fathers) could opt to serve a sentence of five to eight hours on Sundays in a detention room instead of paying the fine of one guilder.

to school (Engelbrecht 1984: 119). Additionally, from 1785 onwards, only wealthy citizens would be required to pay for their children's education and more schools were opened in order to shorten the often excessive distance to the nearest state school (Jaklin 2003: 81). These measures increased the number of children attending state schools but still did not achieve full compliance (ibid.).

Nevertheless, the school reform introduced in 1774 increased literacy rates and led to more wide-spread schooling in 18th- and early 19th-century Austria (cf. Boyer 2002).[55] In order to guarantee uniformity of education, Felbiger's school policy (*Allgemeine Schulordnung* 1774: point 7) not only prescribed teaching methods but also textbooks.[56] Crucially, teaching materials which were not on this approved textbook list (see appendix) were proscribed for students in state schools:

> [...] Diese Bücher, so wie sie in dem unten angehängten Verzeichnisse E. enthalten sind, müssen von allen Schulleuten nach den Umständen jeder Schulen angeschaft, der Innhalt genau befolgt, und die Jugend aus keinen anderen, als aus den Vorgeschriebenen unterwiesen werden, doch können sich geschicktere Lehrer, wann sie wollen, auch andere Bücher, ähnlichen Innhalts, bedienen, um aus solchen ihre eigene Kenntnisse zu erweitern. (*Allgemeine Schulordnung* 1774: point 7)

> [...] These books, which are contained in the enclosed list E, have to be purchased by all school people according to the circumstances of every school, their content has to be strictly followed, and the young are not to be instructed by any other than the prescribed [books], but skilled teachers can, if they want to, use other books of similar content in order to further their own knowledge.

The task of ensuring that nothing other than the approved books were published and used in state schools was one of the remits of the school committee, which also had to verify that copies of the prescribed textbooks conformed precisely to the original books printed in Vienna (*Entwurf zur Instruction der Schul Commissionen* 1775: 18). As previously mentioned, not all the demands made in Felbiger's school policy were achieved instantly. A document entitled *Über den gegenwärtigen Zustand des deutschen Schulwesens in den deutschen Erblanden* (*On the current state of the German schools in the German Hereditary Lands*) (1777: 5f.) reveals that many of the listed textbooks (such as the *Anleitung zur deutschen Sprache*, which was awaiting corrections by the author, and the first two parts of the first volume of the

---

55 Boyer (2002: 270) points out that the effect of Felbiger's reading primers on the reduction of the illiteracy rate cannot be determined empirically due to the lack of statistical data. Nevertheless, Boyer (2002: 270f.) states that the impact of Felbiger's reading primers (which remained to be used in primary schools for about 20 years) on the reduction of the illiteracy rate must not be underestimated, even if the impact was usually limited to literacy skills in reading (rather than reading and writing).

56 In the preamble to the first edition of his *Saganer Fibel* (1763), Felbiger states that his teaching methods are not new inventions but adopted from the *Berliner Real-Schule* (Boyer 2002: 254).

Lesebuch) had yet to be printed in 1777. The same document (1777: 8) further speci-fies that only 37 of the 182 *Landschulen*, i.e. schools in the countryside, had received the approved textbooks by 31 December 1776. It is, therefore, not surprising that most of the books located in the schoolbook collection of the *Austrian Federal Minis-try of Education* (*BMB*) date from the years after 1777.

A letter by the Imperial Chancellery (*Böhmische und Österreichische Hofkanzlei*) to Maria Theresa on the condition of the *Normalschulen* (dated 15 April 1775) states that Felbiger not only wrote most of the textbooks himself but also drafted further books and edited others. Rössler (1995: 55f.) states that all together 47 pedagogical documents and textbooks were either written or edited for publication by Felbiger between 1763 and 1785. This reveals that Felbiger had considerable influence on the content as well as the language used in schoolbooks. An analysis of a selection of these textbooks as well as reading primers printed before 1774 will show to what extent the language used in teaching materials changed with Felbiger's influence on Austria's education system.[57]

Without a doubt, Felbiger and Justi (as outlined in the previous section) played significant roles in the acceptance of ECG norms in Austria, at least in written lan-guage use (von Polenz 1994: 176). However, their work has to be seen in the context of the socio-political circumstances at the time. The ideas of the Enlightenment and their propagation by the Habsburg Empire's leaders, Maria Theresa and Joseph II, certainly played a major role in the rapid dissemination of the ECG norms in Austria.

---

57 See section 4.3.

3 Grammarians' norm prescriptions

3.1 Grammarians' role in the development of German

The previous chapter discussed to what extent the ideologies of the Enlightenment provoked an urge to change the linguistic landscape in 18th-century Austria. Empress Maria Theresa followed these ideologies and turned to grammarians, most notably Johann Christoph Gottsched, to realise her plans of language reform. Gottsched has been described as the most – but certainly not the only – influential 18th-century grammarian (cf. Wiesinger 2008, Rössler 1997[58]). This chapter investigates the works of a number of 18th-century grammarians[59], deemed important for the development of the language reform.[60] The selection of the grammarians follows modern linguists' assessments (notably von Polenz 1994, Rössler 1997 and Wiesinger 2008) of the importance of these grammarians in 18th-century Austria. While all of the grammarians discussed here (i.e. Antesperg, Gottsched, Popowitsch, Felbiger and Adelung) fall into this category, their influence on actual language use has been questioned. Piirainen (1980: 599), who focuses on graphemics, claims that the theoretical works of grammarians did not have a significant effect on the standardisation of German. Indeed, Piirainen (ibid.) believes that the role of grammarians such as Gottsched and Adelung has been overemphasised in linguistic research on the development of German. Von Polenz (1994: 136) notes that, in general, grammarians and lexicographers merely codified the language use common in socially influential, educated circles and institutions *subsequently*. In other words, the language norms found in 18th-century grammars were based on certain linguistic varieties that had been established prior to their codification. Furthermore, the codices written by

---

58 Rössler (1997: 86f.) stresses that Adelung's grammar became "*the* standard grammar in the late 18th century", which was mainly due to Adelung's ability to summarise previous grammars, thus rendering them superfluous.

59 Naturally, these grammarians were influenced by their 17th-century predecessors, such as Justus Georg Schottelius and Gottfried Wilhelm Leibniz, and their views on language have to be seen as continuous trends rather than radical new ideas. In general, 17th-century linguists strove to enhance the status of German in comparison to Latin and French, which led to a kind of democratisation since the use of German in, for example, scientific and religious contexts allowed broader circles of the general public to understand and participate in these contexts (Gardt 1999: 134f.). On the other hand, only 'High German' was accepted as the 'correct' variety and its proficiency was a requirement for participating in the discourse on religion, science etc. (ibid. 135). Thus 'High German' became a means of social identification and exclusion (ibid.). Undoubtedly, these developments influenced the linguistic concepts of 18th-century grammarians, who continued to describe and define 'High German' more extensively. For more detailed information on the works of linguists in the 17th century, see, for example, von Polenz (1994), Gardt (1994, 1999), and Leweling (2005).

60 See Rössler (1997) for an in-depth analysis of further grammars.

DOI 10.1515/9783110547047-003

grammarians and lexicographers were influenced by four role models (Josten 1976, von Polenz 1994: 137):

- commendable language regions, especially *Meißen* (Upper Saxony) but also the most northern parts of the German-speaking area with regard to pronunciation,
- commendable scripts and authors, especially Martin Luther,
- commendable institutions, especially those of the empire (e.g. the Imperial Chancellery, i.e. the *Wiener Hofkanzlei*),
- commendable principles of model language use (*Sprachkulturprinzipien*), especially with the establishment of concrete spelling, grammar and style guides, as well as dictionaries in the 17th century.

Even though the grammarians' prescriptions were influenced by these models and based on certain existing varieties, the grammarians of the 16th to 18th century, without any doubt, intervened in the development of German in a regulating and standardising way, at least with regard to certain linguistic features (von Polenz 1978: 99).

The question of how effective the grammarians' prescriptions really were in changing language use has been discussed by several linguists (cf. Konopka 1996, Takada 1998, Langer 2001, McLelland 2011). Konopka (1996), for example, focuses on German syntax and investigates metalinguistic statements as well as language use from the 18th century to ascertain to what extent the language norms found in grammars and other prescriptive texts (e.g. translation instructions) influenced the use of syntactic variants. Langer (2001), too, studies the effect of language prescriptions, analysing the use of auxiliary *tun*, polynegation and the double perfect. Both scholars conclude that "metalinguistic statements did indeed have a measureable degree of influence at least on the choice of some linguistic properties of modern standard German" (Langer 2001: 108). Similarly, McLelland's (2011) work on Schottelius's grammar *Ausführliche Arbeit von der Teutschen HaubtSprache* (1663) showed that Schottelius' influence on the emerging standard German language was limited to particular features.

While some influence can be attributed to the work of 17th- and 18th-century grammarians, other factors, too, account for the implementation of certain linguistic variants. Konopka (1996: 43–45) lists four factors: the standing of a grammarian and the spread of his works, the influence of professional writers and the impact of schooling. This means that not every grammarian was influential in the development of standard German but mainly those who were well-known and whose works were widely disseminated and re-printed, such as Gottsched's *Grundlegung einer deutschen Sprachkunst* (1748, 5th ed. 1762). The influence of grammarians on professional writers becomes clear when investigating revised versions of texts and the corrections made (Konopka 1996: 44f.).[61] These revised texts, in turn, circulated the language norms of the influential grammarians. Another factor, which has not received much attention from linguistic scholars yet, is the role of schooling. It seems obvious that education would lead to the propagation of certain linguistic variants, i.e. those taught in school. This, however, poses two major questions: Who decides what is taught in schools and which language norms are used as a basis for teaching materials? We will return to these issues in chapter 4. First, however, it is necessary to study the language prescriptions of influential grammarians in order to establish which variants were considered 'correct' German. Particular attention is paid to the prescriptions concerning the linguistic variants described in section 1.1.6 and analysed in chapter 4.

3.2 Johann Balthasar von Antesperg

The first linguistic work by Johann Balthasar von Antesperg (1685–1765)[62], a Bavarian who spent most of his adult life as a civil servant in a higher position in Vienna, was published in various cities (Vienna, Nuremberg, Prague, Dresden, Leipzig, Regensburg, Augsburg and Frankfurt) in 1734 (Mraz 1980: 60f.). This *Kayserliche deutsche Sprachtabelle zur Verbesserung der deutschen Sprache* (*Imperial German language table for the improvement of the German language*) was based to a large extent on the UG language norm and sent to Gottsched for suggestions of improvement on 4 August 1734 (Rössler 1997: 35). Gottsched recommended linguistic adjustments to the variety used by the *Deutsche Gesellschaft*, i.e. ECG (ibid. 35f.):

> So nehmen wir uns mit Dero Erlaubniß die Freyheit, beykommende Umschrift von Dero Vorrede beyzulegen, so wie wir dieselbe nach unsrer Mundart gesetzet haben würden. Dieses ist nur ein bloßer Versuch, um zu sehen, wie Eurer Hochwohlgebohren diese Verbesserung anstehen wird: denn aus Furcht, daß Denenselben unsre Freyheit zu groß scheinen möchte, haben wir es nicht gewagt, weiter zu gehen, bis wir hören würden, wie Dieselben solches aufgenommen hätten. Gefällt es Denenselben, daß Dero Tabelle auch in hiesigen Gegenden und in ganz Niedersachsen Beyfall finden soll: So würde wohl die Schreibart auf diesen Schlag durchgehends geändert werden müssen. (*Mitteilungen der Deutschen Gesellschaft* 1902: 28ff., as cited in Rössler 1997: 35f.)

> Thus, with your permission, we take the liberty of attaching the enclosed transcript of your preamble, as we would have it set in our variety. This is but a mere attempt to see how your

---

61 See also Leweling's (2005: 210–218) observations on editorial corrections in the *Braunschweigischen Anzeigen*, a journal published twice a week from 1745 onwards. Leweling (2005: 216) suggests that the editor consulted a grammar when correcting contributions to this journal.
62 Wiesinger (2010) was able to determine Antesperg's date of birth, which was stated as 1682 or 1683 in previous research literature on Antesperg.

Hochwohlgebohren[63] will receive these improvements: For because of fear that you may regard our liberty as too great, we did not dare to go any further until we might hear how you have received our suggestions. If you would like that your table will meet approval in the whole of Lower Saxony, the writing style would have to be changed throughout forthwith.

Thus Gottsched indicates that Antesperg's *Sprachtabelle* would not be successful in Lower Saxony if it was written in Antesperg's UG variety. Furthermore, Gottsched warns Antesperg of a 'rushed' publication, which Antesperg meets with little enthusiasm (Rössler 1997: 36). Antesperg had wished for more concrete corrections by Gottsched and the *Deutsche Gesellschaft*, which would allow him to revise and publish his *Sprachtabelle* quickly (ibid.):

[Denn] (...) das Papier [ist] schon gekauft, das Werk schon wirklich gesetzet und bis gegenwärtige Stund noch unter der Preß lieget, auch monatlich 2 f.: extra bezahlen mus, so lang es also lieget, so bin ich gezwungen alhier fort zufahren, und eine hochansehnl...: e deutsche Gesellschaft abermahlen ganz freundlich zu ersuchen nicht allein ihr gut Achtung, sondern auch zugleich die wirkliche correction, und ausstellung der Sprach-Kunst-, oder Buchstaben fehler ohne einzige Barmherzigkeit auf das schärfeste mit zu theilen, damit das Werk seinen zuverläßlichen Stand. haben möge, so lang Deütschland stehet. (Letter by Antesperg to Gottsched, 3 September 1734, as cited in Rössler 1997: 36)

[Because] the paper [has] already [been] bought, the work readily typeset and because I am charged to pay 2 f [guilders] per month until it is placed under the printing press; as long as this is the case, I am forced to proceed here and politely ask a highly respectable *Deutsche Gesellschaft* once again to not only pay good attention to any grammatical or spelling mistakes but also to correct these and to communicate them to me without any mercy and most harshly, so that the work may retain its reliability as long as Germany remains.

According to Wiesinger, Antesperg revised his *Sprachtabelle* only minimally before it was published in 1734. Given the financial pressures depicted above it is not surprising that the work was not edited to the extent that Gottsched and the *Deutsche Gesellschaft* recommended. Furthermore, Antesperg's subsequent works, the *Josephinische Erzherzogliche A. B. C. Oder Namenbüchlein* (a reading primer published in 1744) and the *Kayserliche Deutsche Grammatick* (*Imperial German Grammar*) (1747, 2nd ed. 1749), include a number of UG features.[64] Indeed, Antesperg frequently presents both ECG and UG variants as being equally appropriate, giving freedom of choice to the reader, or rather writer.[65] Rössler (1997: 37) regards this absence of a uniform norm in Antesperg's grammars as well as the almost simultaneous publication of Gottsched's *Grundlegung einer deutschen Sprachkunst* in 1748 as the main

---

63 *Hochwohlgeboren* is a polite form of address.
64 See section 4.3 for an analysis of Antesperg's *Namenbüchlein* (1744).
65 See below for examples.

reasons for Antesperg's lack of success.[66] According to Rössler (1997: 42), Antesperg did not play any significant role in the reform of the written German language after 1750. Von Polenz (1994: 157), too, states that Antesperg's impact on the language reform was limited due to the great success of Gottsched's grammar in Vienna. However, Antesperg certainly initiated the debate about the ECG language norms propagated by Gottsched in 18th-century Austria (ibid.). His grammar, therefore, deserves closer attention.

The preface of Antesperg's *Kayserliche Deutsche Grammatick* (1747) reveals his view on language and his attitudes towards norms. In his address to the readers of his grammar, Antesperg (1747: Vorrede § II.) laments the current state of the German language in Austria and wishes people, especially learned people, would pay closer attention to the 'purity' and 'correctness' of German.

> Dann es ist §. II. [n]icht wenig zu betauren, daß unsere schöne und herrliche Sprache [...] nicht wie andere von uns Deutschen hochgeschätzet, verbessert und ausgeübet worden. §. III. Daß die meisten vom Adel, auch lateinisch gelehrte Männer in Deutschland auf fremde Sprachen so viel Zeit und Geld; hingegen aber auf die allerprächtigste hochdeutsche Grundsprache den allerwenigsten Fleiß anwenden. §. IV. Daß sie sich um derselben Reinigkeit und Richtigkeit nicht bekümmern, sondern in solcher öfters mit groben Schnitzern nur nach Gutdünken daher lallen, und ohne Wissenschaft dahin sudlen, und vermeynen, es sey schon genug, wann man sie zu unseren Zeiten mit harter Mühe verstehet. (Antesperg 1747: Vorrede § II–IV)[67]

> Because it is §. II. quite regrettable that our beautiful and glorious language [...] is not prized, improved and practised by us Germans as we do others. §. III. That the majority of the nobility, even men in Germany who are learned in Latin, spend so much time and money on foreign languages, whilst only applying the most meagre of diligence to the most magnificent High German base language §. IV. They do not care about its purity and correctness, but often just babble along stumbling over blunder after blunder, as they see fit, quite without any expertise haphazardly botching their mistakes, and then supposing that it suffices if understanding is successful on our part if we exert a great deal of effort.

Wiesinger (2008: 259) points out that when Antesperg complains about the lack of awareness of 'purity' and 'correctness' he refers to Austria's non-standardised written language use with accepted variables in orthography and morphology but also to spoken language. Antesperg aims to promote a better sense of language awareness, i.e. of what is 'correct' and what is 'wrong', since it signalises the intelligence of a people:

> Die Gewißheit der Sprache ist das Merkmahl eines klugen Volkes. Eine Zierde des Hofes. Ein rüchtiger [sic] Werkzeug, ja ein unerschöpflicher Nutzen in allen guten Geschäften, Künsten

---

66 Mraz (1980: 84), by contrast, regards Antesperg's age – he was in his 70s when the first steps of the educational reforms were taken in the 1750s – as the reason for Antesperg's lack of influence in linguistic matters, in comparison to Gottsched and Popowitsch.

67 A number of the quotations used in chapter 3 can also be found in Wiesinger (2008).

und Wissenschaften; und die Ungewißheit derselben ist das Widerspiel. (Antesperg 1747: Vorrede § XI.)

The certainty of language is the characteristic of a wise people. An ornament of the court. A proper instrument, yes an inexhaustible benefit to all good businesses, arts and sciences; and the uncertainty of it [language] is the opposite.

Antesperg thus stresses the link between the language and the perception of its speakers: If somebody is well-spoken, they are perceived as intelligent while people who do not talk 'properly' are perceived as the opposite. Since Antesperg found the written German language in Austria in disarray, he decided to write his grammar (Antesperg 1747: Vorrede § XVI.), which – together with other grammars – should improve Austria's language and the perception of its speakers:

Ich habe gethan, was ich als ein getreuer Patriot habe können, ein anderer thue noch mehr hinzu, so werden wir des reinen Ausdruckes in eigener Sprache bald mächtig werden. So wird die reine deutsche Schreibart, Poesie und Beredsamkeit ihre Kinderschuhe bald vertreten und in Oesterreich zu einem männlichen Alter gelangen. [...] So werden wir in dem eigenen Vernunftlicht (ich meyne in der eigenen Sprache) wie andere gesittete Völker klug, hurtig, bescheiden, und Kenner und Liebhaber guter Künste und Wissenschaften werden, auch uns von dem kostbaren Last des ausländischen Blendwerks nach und nach mit vielem Vortheile befreyen können. (Antesperg 1747: Vorrede § XXVIII.)

I have done what I could do as a faithful patriot, someone else should do some more, thus we will soon be able to express ourselves purely in our own language. Thus the pure German way of writing, poetry and eloquence will soon grow out of its children's shoes and reach a manly age in Austria. [...] Thus we will in our own light of reason (I mean in our own language) become wise, swift, modest, and adepts and enthusiasts for good arts and sciences like other civilized people, it will also be able to free us by and by from the heavy burden of the foreign illusion, with many advantages.

In his grammar, Antesperg (1747: Vorrede § XXI.) states that he did not derive his norms from any particular 'dialect' (*Mundart*) but rather from the 'base' of the German language and the usage of scholars:

Betreffend nun die Sprache selbst, so habe ich mich hierinne nach keiner Mundart, deren in Deutschland wenigstens 37. gezehlet werden, gerichtet, sondern nur auf den Grund und auf die von den Gelehrten angenommene deutsche Sprache gesehen: Dann man findet ganz gründlich, daß man weder in Griechenland, weder in Latio, weder in Italien, weder in Spanien, weder in Frankreich jemals also geredet habe, als die von den Gelehrten angenommene Sprache eingerichtet gewesen. (Antesperg 1747: Vorrede § XXI.)

With regard to the language itself, I did not go by any particular 'dialect', of which there are at least 37 in Germany, but rather only looked at the base and at the German language accepted by the scholars: Because one clearly finds that neither in Greece, nor in Latium, Italy, Spain and France one ever spoke in the language accepted by scholars in the way it was constructed.

Antesperg thus rejects prescription of a certain regional variety but rather extracts his language norms from the varieties used by educated people. At the same time, Antesperg recognizes that people do not speak the language accepted by scholars. In other words, the language norms prescribed by scholars are constructed and not based on actual language use. Even though he points out that his grammar is largely based on this constructed written language, he does, in some parts, refer to actual UG pronunciations. In the second part of his grammar, Antesperg (1747: 240) lists the following examples of 'wrong' pronunciation, which teachers should not allow.

Tab. 3: Examples of UG spoken language in comparison to written language (Antesperg 1747: 240)

'wrong' pronunciation	instead of	'correct' pronunciation
Eä laft a mid	anstatt	Er lauft auch mit.
Göbtsjems	anstatt	gebet es ihm.
Sö kemä scho	anstatt	sie kommen schon.
Jo frälä zu wö diets enk	anstatt	ja freylich, zu was dienet es euch.
Mir sän do	anstatt	wir sind da.
Gehet rein	anstatt	gehet herein.
Wirds jem eper nöt recht sä	anstatt	wird es ihm etwann nicht recht seyn.
Jetz kimt dä Heä Vodä und Fau Muedä	anstatt	jetzt kommt der Herr Vater und die Frau Mutter.
Oes geht in aim hin	anstatt	es gehet in einem hin.
I sag enks, gehts nöt aba	anstatt	ich sage es euch, gehet nicht hinab.
Mähn den Däbt ä, set da mät ä	anstatt	mähen dann die Aebte auch, sehet da mähet auch.

It is worth noting that Antesperg's list provides us with data of spoken language at a time when such forms had long since disappeared from general writing, similar to the reading primer printed around 1750 discussed in the previous chapter.[68] As such, it presents a form of language that is usually 'invisible' (cf. Langer & Havinga 2015) to modern-day researchers, who have to rely on texts which usually depict written, not spoken language.

---

[68] Indeed, the *Teutsches Namen- oder Lehrbüchl* (c. 1750) exhibits a number of similarities to Antesperg's (1744) reading primer and also includes the example of "Er laft a mid" presented in his grammar. There is no clear evidence that Antesperg was the author of the *Teutsches Namen- oder Lehrbüchl*, which generally focuses more strongly on religion than Antesperg does. However, it seems that the *Teutsches Namen- oder Lehrbüchl* is based on Antesperg's work to some extent. If it was the case that other schoolbooks were influenced by Antesperg's works, it could be argued that his language norms were disseminated through schooling in mid-18th-century Austria.

Antesperg's list above indicates that he considered the spoken UG language varieties 'wrong'. He (1747: 240) urges teachers to make their pupils aware of their mistakes and correct the UG pronunciation, which goes against German etymology and syntax:

> so müssen die Schul- und Lehrmeister auch auf die deutsche Pronuntiation ein obachtsames Aug tragen, und der Iugend nicht gestatten, dass sie die Wörter falsch ausspreche; [...] sondern dieselbe fleissig corrigiren und auf den rechten Weg führen, das ist, ihr die wider die deutsche Etymologie und den Syntax beganene Fehler daselbst zeigen. (Antesperg 1747: 240)

> so the schoolmasters must also pay attention to the German pronunciation and must not allow the students to pronounce the words incorrectly; [...] but correct them diligently and lead them onto the right path, i.e. to show them those mistakes they make, which go against German etymology and syntax.

While Antesperg generally rejects the UG pronunciation as 'wrong', he does prescribe some UG features in his grammar, as the following sections show.

3.2.1 Antesperg on *e*-apocope in nouns

In his *Kayserliche Deutsche Grammatick* (1747), Antesperg frequently lists both variants, i.e. nouns with *e*-apocope and with final -*e*. For many words both variants are presented as equally acceptable:

Tab. 4: Nouns presented with UG and ECG variant (Antesperg 1747: 51–59)

masculine nouns	Erb(e), Knab(e)[69], Nam(e)[70], Lay(e)
feminine nouns	die Farb(e), Gab(e), Garb(e), Lieb(e), Grub(e), Haub(e), Stub(e), Sylb(e), Begierd(e), Heerd(e), Sünd(e), Eul(e), Harpf(e), Hülf(e), Tauf(e), Leich(e), Kirsch(e), Ell(e), Ahl(e), Stimm(e), Wärm(e), Bühn(e), Pfann(e), Sonn(e), Kapp(e), Lipp(e), Supp(e), Hur(e), Lehr(e), Ameis(e), Buß(e), Achs(e), Gant(e), Senft(e), Au(e), Klau(e), Reu(e), Hitz(e)
neuter nouns	Vieh(e), Glück(e)

In other cases, however, only the UG or the ECG forms are listed:

---

69 This word is listed only in the UG form, i.e. *Knab*, on page 63 (Antesperg 1747).
70 The UG form, i.e. *Nam*, is listed on page 44 (Antesperg 1747).

Tab. 5: Nouns presented with either the UG or the ECG variant (Antesperg 1747: 51–59)

	UG *e*-apocope	ECG ending *-e*
masculine nouns	Bub, Rab, Fried[71], Scherb, Aff, Bürg, Funk, Rapp, Has, Ochs, Wais	Laye, Saame or Saamen, Wille
feminine nouns	Salb, Schwalb, Herd, Erbsünd, Todsünd, Straf, Pfeif, Herberg, Arch, Zech, Eul, Meil, Mühl, Woll, Bien[72], Lamp, Schupp, Todtenbahr, Beer, Pfarr, Thür, Waar, Münz, Katz	Brücke, Buche, Ehe, Ehre, Erde, Gnade, Güte, Grösse, Klippe, Klinge, Eile, Schaubühne, Kolbe, Kutsche, Zwetschke, Leiste, Pflege, Heerde, Pfründe, Reue, Reihe, Ruhe, Seife, Sohle, Stunde, Taube, Treppe, Wette, Weyde, Weide, Weyhe oder Weihe
neuter nouns	Erb, Aug[73]	Ende[74]

Antesperg (1747) appears to be inconsistent in some of his prescriptions. The German word for *peace* is, for example, listed without *-e* (i.e. *Fried*) on pages 51 and 247 but with the ending *-e* on pages 27 and 272 (*Friede*). Similarly, both, the UG and ECG variant for *bee*, i.e. *Bien* (page 56) and *Biene* (page 272), are presented. On the other hand, these inconsistencies could be regarded as descriptions, rather than prescriptions, of language use. Indeed, Antesperg (1747: 267) does comment on differences between the spelling and pronunciation of words, thus providing an insight into actual language use:[75]

> §. I. Der Vocal *e* wird am Ende des Wortes, wie das französische, gar oft nicht gehöret, aber gleichwohl geschrieben; Z. E. *die Seele, Gnade, Sache, Bitte, Ehre, Erde, Hülfe, Tiefe, Dicke, Poesie, Historie, Glorie, Mode, der Poete, Knabe, die Artillerie*, u. (Antesperg 1747: 267)

> §. I. At the end of the word, the vowel *e* is, as in French, often not heard at all, but still written; e.g. *die Seele, Gnade, Sache, Bitte, Ehre, Erde, Hülfe, Tiefe, Dicke, Poesie, Historie, Glorie, Mode, der Poete, Knabe, die Artillerie* etc.

---

71 In a comment on noun declination, Antesperg (1747: 27, 272) lists this noun with the ending *-e*, i.e. *Friede*.

72 This noun is presented with the ending *-e* on page 272.

73 In his chapter on the declension of nouns, Antesperg (1747: 32) includes the variant with *-e*, i.e. *Auge*.

74 In his section on plural forms, Antesperg (1747: 69) includes the UG form without *-e*, i.e. *End*.

75 Rössler (1997: 131) stresses that Antesperg incorporates everyday UG language use, evoking a sense of discrepancy between the prescribed ECG norm and the actual language use in the UG language area.

It is striking that Antesperg does not judge the *e*-apocope negatively; on the contrary, he compares the UG pronunciation to a very prestigious language, i.e. French[76], which implies that he does not consider the UG pronunciation to be inferior.

Similarly, Antesperg (1747: 25, 42f., 45) accepts the *e*-apocope in strong masculine nouns in the dative singular form when he lists both variants in his declension paradigms: *dem Kopf(e), dem Geist(e), dem Sporn(e), dem Sinn(e), dem Tag(e)*. The examples following his statement that these nouns "can end in -*e* in the dative and ablative case", e.g. "*am Kayserlichen Hofe seyn*" and "*in dem Hause wohnen*" (ibid. 26), reveal that the *e*-apocope is also acceptable in neuter nouns in the dative singular form. For Antesperg, the ending -*e* is, therefore, not obligatory in the dative case.

With regard to plural forms, Antesperg appears more prescriptive by stating rigorous rules for the use of the ending -*e*:

> Die erste Regel.
> Die männliche Nennwörter (*Nomina masculina*) welche sich auf einen Consonanten endigen, nehmen im Plurali gemeiniglich den Vocalen *e* an sich. Z.E. *Der Bart, Die Bärte; Der Berg, Die Berge; Der Baum, Die Bäume* [...] (Antesperg 1747: 61)

> The first rule.
> The masculine nouns (*Nomina masculina*) which end in a consonant generally take on the vowel *e* in plural. E.g. *Der Bart, Die Bärte; Der Berg, Die Berge; Der Baum, Die Bäume* [...]

Comments on individual words follow these lists of examples, such as: "*Der Theil, Die Theile*. 3. Dass man also nicht schreiben soll *bayde Thail sollen erscheinen*, &c. anstatt *bayde Theile*" ("One should not write *bayde Thail sollen erscheinen*, instead of *bayde Theile*") (Antesperg 1747: 62). This addition clearly stigmatises the UG variant as wrong, while presenting the ECG form as correct. As for feminine and neuter nouns, Antesperg (1747: 64–69) prescribes the following.

> Die zweyte Regel.
> Die weibliche Nomina oder die *Fœminina* nehmen in dem Plurali gemeiniglich die Sylbe *en* an sich. [...] Von dieser Regel werden erstlich ausgenommen nachfolgende *Fœminina*, welche im *Nominativo* des Pluralis nur ein *e* haben. Z.E. *Die Gans, Die Gänse; Die Hand, Die Hände, Die Kuh, Die Kühe* [...] (Antesperg 1747: 64–66)

> The second rule.
> The feminine nouns or *feminina* usually take on the syllable *en* in their plural form [...] Firstly, the following *feminina*, which only have an *e* in the nominative of the plural, are excluded from this rule. E.g. *Die Gans, Die Gänse; Die Hand, Die Hände, Die Kuh, Die Kühe* [...]

---

76 While many 18th-century grammarians criticised the use of French loan words, French remains the prestige variety among the nobility (Faulstich 2008: 7).

Die dritte Regel.
Die *Nomina neutra* gehen in dem Nennefall der Vielheit (im *Nominativo plurali*) gemeiniglich aus auf die Sylbe *er*. [...] Von dieser Regel werden ausgenommen die nachfolgende *Neutra*, welche in dem *Nominativo plurali* in dem Vokal *e* ausgehen. Z. E. *Das Creuz, Die Creuze, Das Netz, Die Netze, Das Pferd, Die Pferde* [...] (Antesperg 1747: 67, 69)

The third rule.
The neuter nouns in their nominative plural form (in the *Nominativo plurali*) generally end in the syllable *er*. [...] The following neuter nouns, which end in the vowel *e* in the nominative plural, are excluded from this rule. E.g. *Das Creuz, Die Creuze, Das Netz, Die Netze, Das Pferd, Die Pferde* [...]

This shows that Antesperg does not accept the *e*-apocope in plural forms, while he tolerates and in some cases even favours it in singular nouns.

3.2.2 Antesperg on past participles

With regard to the conjugation of verbs, and in particular the formation of regular past participles, Antesperg (1747: 93) states the following rule:

7. Daß die Deutschen nur eine einzige *Conjugationem regularem*, nemlich das *Verbum lieben* haben, über welche sie in *active & passiva voce* viele 1000. *Verba regularia* conjugiren, und diese sind alle die jenige, welche in *præsenti tempore indicativi* in (*e, est, et,*) und in dem *Imperfecto* in (*ete, etest, ete,*) und im *Suppino* oder besser zu sagen **in dem *Participio præteria temporis* in *et*, wie die dritte Person des *Indicativi singularis* (mit Beysetzung der Sylbe *ge*) ausgehen** [...] (Antesperg 1747: 93, my emphasis)

7. The Germans [i.e. German-speaking people] have only one singular regular conjugation, namely the verb *lieben* [love], by which they conjugate many 1000 regular verbs in the active and passive voice, and these are all those, which **end** in (*e, est, et,*) in the present indicative tense, in (*ete, etest, ete,*) in the imperfect, and **in *et*** in the *Supine* or rather **in the past participle, like the third person of the indicative singular (with the addition of the syllable *ge*)** [...]

Antesperg (1747: 93) thus prescribes the use of the prefix *ge-* and of the suffix *-et* in past participles. Whereas he himself appears to adhere to the prefix rule, he does not always observe his rule for the use of the ending *-et* and frequently uses *-t* instead. In the introduction to conjugations, *geliebet* is used first, followed by *geliebt* further down the same page (Antesperg 1747: 92). On pages 95 to 104, Antesperg (1747) then conjugates the verb *lieben* in the active voice and in all tenses. While he now first gives *geliebt* as the past participle of *lieben* (1747: 95), he presents both forms ("*geliebet*, oder *geliebt*") as equally appropriate in the conjugation of the verb in the perfect (p. 98) and pluperfect tenses (p. 99). While Antesperg's rule on page

93 only prescribes the *-et* ending, his actual use of language indicates that variation between both forms was the norm.[77]

As with *e*-apocope in nouns, Antesperg (1747: 167) addresses actual (spoken) language use by mentioning that *e*-syncope often occurs in conjugations:

> §. II. Das *e* wird im Decliniren und Conjugiren und andern Fällen *per syncopen* gar oft ausgelassen; Z.E. *dieß, Geists, liebte, er redt, unsern, unsren, habt, eur, schönster, u.* Anstatt *dieses, Geistes, liebete, er redet, unseren, habet, euer, schönester, u.* (Antesperg 1747: 167)

> §. II. By way of *syncope*, the *e* is often left out in the declination and conjugation and in other cases; E.g. *dieß, Geists, liebte, er redt, unsern, unsren, habt, eur, schönster,* etc. Instead of *dieses, Geistes, liebete, er redet, unseren, habet, euer, schönester,* etc.

While Antesperg (1747: 167) compared the *e*-apocope in nouns with the pronunciation in French, i.e. a prestigious language, he uses more negative terms to describe *e*-syncope: 'left out' implies that the *-e-* should be there and 'instead of' suggests that the succeeding forms with *-e-* are the 'correct' variants. However, not a single past participle is given as an example for *e*-syncope in the quotation above, which might indicate that, in these cases, Antesperg did not judge it negatively, which would be in line with his use of both variants, i.e. the suffixes *-t* and *-et*. In sum, it can, therefore, be argued that Antesperg saw both suffixes as equally appropriate, while prescribing the use of the prefix *ge-* in regular past participle more rigorously.

With regard to irregular verbs, Antesperg also generally uses the prefix *ge-* in his list of examples (1747: 130–156).[78] There are, however, two interesting exceptions: for the verb *to eat*, Antesperg lists three possible past participles: "*ich habe gessen, geessen, nec sperne gegessen*" (p. 135). Antesperg's addition of 'nec sperne', meaning 'do not condemn', implies that the previous two forms without the prefix *ge-* were more commonly used in the Upper German language area. The second exception is the verb *to give* with two possible past participles, one with and another one without the prefix *ge-*: "*gegeben & geben*" (p. 136). Other past participles, which can drop the prefix *ge-* in Upper German varieties (such as *geblieben, gebraten, gebracht, gegangen, gekommen*) are, however, only listed with the prefix. The UG variants without *ge-* are thus invisibilised.

---

77 See also the conjugation of the verb *lieben* in the passive, with both variants of the past participle ending appearing in the conjugation lists, resulting in the co-occurance of *geliebt* and *geliebet* (Antesperg 1747: 104f.).

78 This list includes modal verbs, which will not be discussed here since it is unclear whether Antesperg allows the use of forms without *ge-* in connection with accusative objects, e.g. *Nils hat es nicht wollen*. Similarly, the auxiliary verb *werden* is included in the list but the form *worden* might only be mentioned in its function as an auxiliary verb for passive constructions (e.g. *Markus ist zum Professor befördert worden*), rather than as a copula verb (e.g. *Markus ist Professor worden*).

3.2.3 Antesperg on alternative forms of *wir/sie sind*

Antesperg (1747: 116f.) conjugates the verb *to be* in the present indicative in the following way:

Ich bin	Wir sind oder seynd
du bist	ihr seyd
er ist nicht ißt	sie sind oder seynd

Antesperg thus allows two variants in the 1ˢᵗ and 3ʳᵈ person plural present indicative, namely the ECG form *sind* and the UG variant *seynd*. Antesperg seems to prefer the use of the ECG variant[79] in his grammar but *seynd*[80] is also employed occasionally.

Rössler (1997: 302) states that Antesperg and Friedrich Wilhelm Gerlach (1728–1802) are the only two influential 18ᵗʰ-century grammarians who allowed alternative forms to *wir/sie sind*.[81] The following section will investigate Gottsched's language norms.

3.3 Johann Christoph Gottsched

After publishing his *Grundlegung einer deutschen Sprachkunst* (1748, 5ᵗʰ ed. 1762)[82], Johann Christoph Gottsched (1700–1766), born in East Prussia (Juditten) and later working in Saxony (Leipzig), became *the* German language authority, not just in Saxony and Prussia but also in Austria (cf. Rössler 1997, Wiesinger 2008). His condensed version entitled *Kern der deutschen Sprachkunst* (1753) was similary successful. Furthermore, Gottsched was a well-known literary scholar, which – together with his engagement in journalistic and institutional activities, e.g. his leading role in the *Deutsche Gesellschaft* in Leipzig[83] – accelerated his influence as a language

---

79 For example, in the preface and first chapter (p. 1–14) of his grammar, *wir/sie seynd* is never used, while *wir/sie sind* occurs 13 times.

80 See, for example, pp. 24, 74, 93 and 198. In his reading primer, too, which is discussed in section 4.3, Antesperg uses *seynd* occasionally.

81 Gerlach (1758) opts for the alternative variants *wir/sie seyen* rather than *wir/sie seynd* in present indicative, thus eliminating the morphologic and phonetic difference from the conjunctive form of the verb *to be* (Rössler 1997: 302).

82 While the first three editions are entitled *Grundlegung einer deutschen Sprachkunst*, the title of the fourth and fifth edition is *Vollständigere und Neuerläuterte Deutsche Sprachkunst*. I am mainly using the 3ʳᵈ edition (published in 1752) since it is more readily available. A comparison between the 3ʳᵈ and the 5ᵗʰ edition, which was also consulted, revealed only insignificant differences between these two editions.

83 This 'German society' intended to exert normative influence over the development of German language and literature (Döring 2002: 303). Leweling (2005: 220) stresses the importance of 'German societies' in general: with their discussion and exercises on language use, the 'German societies'

authority (von Polenz 1994: 158). Rössler (1997: 29f.) describes Gottsched as being the one grammarian "hauptverantwortlich für die Durchsetzung einer ostmitteldeutsch geprägten Reform der Schriftsprache in Österreich seit der Mitte des 18. Jahrhunderts" ("primarily responsible for the implementation of Austria's written language reform, which was strongly influenced by ECG, since the mid-18th century"). Konopka (1996: 52), too, stresses Gottsched's importance in the language reform and deems Gottsched to be the best-known grammarian of the time. Gottsched's linguistic works were the most influential of the 18th century and forced other grammarians to either adopt Gottsched's norms or to critically engage with them (ibid. 55).

Gottsched bases his language norms on the written language of educated people since

> [e]ine jede Mundart hat in dem Munde der Ungelehrten, ihre gewisse Mängel: ja aus Nachläßigkeit und Uebereilung im Reden ist sie mit sich selbst nicht allemal einstimmig. Daher muß man auch den Gebrauch der besten Scribenten zu Hülfe nehmen, um die Regeln einer Sprache fest zu setzen: denn man pflegt sich im Schreiben viel mehr in acht zu nehmen, als im Reden. (Gottsched 1752: 3)

> [e]very variety[84] has its shortcomings when spoken by the uneducated: indeed, due to negligence and hasty speech it is not uniform in itself. Therefore, one has to consult the usage of the best writers in order to determine the rules of a language: because one tends to be a lot more careful when writing than when speaking.

Consequently, Gottsched derives his language norms from – what he considers – the language of the best writers:

> Die guten Schriftsteller setzen die Sprache des Volkes fest, ungeachtet sich in dem Munde des Volkes die Sprachen von Zeit zu Zeit ändern. (Gottsched 1752: 18)

> Good writers determine the language of the people, irrespective of the changes that occur in the spoken language of the people from time to time.

Rössler (1997: 29) points out that all the writers that Gottsched lists in his grammar are from the East Central German and North German (NG) language area. In other words, Gottsched's grammar is not based on UG but on ECG, and to some extent, NG. Indeed, Gottsched regards the UG variety (as well as Low German) as deviations from the 'best dialect' and UG variants as 'mistakes':

---

assisted in the linguistic education and the education of the speakers. This is particularly relevant since 'German societies', especially the one in Leipzig, implemented Gottsched's language norms in linguistic exercises and thus contributed to their dissemination (ibid. 221).

84 Gottsched uses the term 'Mundart' to refer to dialects as well as sociolects (Faulstich 2008: 108). I, therefore, decided to translate 'Mundart' into the more neutral term 'variety'.

Dieser Theil [der Syntax-Teil in Gottscheds Grammatik] ist desto nöthiger, da in einem so großen Lande, als Deutschland ist, vielerley Mundarten im Schwange gehen, die öfters auch in der Verbindungsart der Wörter von einander abgehen. Manche Landschaften nämlich **weichen** sehr von den andern, und **fast alle einigermaßen von der besten Mundart**, die man das wahre Hochdeutsche nennet, auch in den Wortfügungen **ab**: nicht, als ob sie ihre eigene Art zu reden für besser, oder nur für eben so gut hielten; sondern **weil sie die bessere nur nicht wissen, oder aus Nachläßigkeit nicht zu beobachten pflegen**. So **fehlen z.E. Ober- und Niederdeutsche**, in den Fällen der Fürwörter, bey den Zeitwörtern, **sehr häufig**; wenn jene z.E. sprechen: *ich bin bey Sie gewesen, ich bitte Ihnen*, u. d. m. (Gottsched 1752: 22, my emphasis)

This chapter [the chapter on syntax in Gottsched's grammar] is even more necessary since in a country as large as Germany, there are so many dialects which quite frequently deviate from each other, also with regard to the connection between words. Some regions deviate a lot from the others, and **almost all of them deviate to some extent from the best dialect**, known as the true High German, even when it comes to word formation: the **reason for this deviation** is not that they consider their own way of speaking better or just as good but that **they just do not know the better way of speaking or** that they do not observe the better way of speaking due to **carelessness**. Thus for example **Upper** [= Southern] **and Lower** [= Northern] **Germans very frequently fail** when using pronouns and verbs; when, for example, they say: *ich bin bey Sie gewesen, ich bitte Ihnen* etc.

In the quotation above, Gottsched does not specify what he regards as the 'best dialect' – it remains unclear what precisely the best variety is but Upper and Low German varieties are certainly excluded from Gottsched's ideal language. The fact that Gottsched equates this 'best dialect' with the language used in Upper Saxony becomes clear in the following quotation.

Nach wem wird man sich also richten sollen? Aber es bedarf dieser Frage gar nicht. Ganz Deutschland ist schon längst stillschweigend darüber eins geworden. Ganz Ober= und Niederdeutschland hat bereits den Ausspruch gethan: **daß das mittelländische, oder obersächsische Deutsch, die beste hochdeutsche Mundart sey:** indem es dasselbe überall, von Bern in der Schweiz, bis nach Reval in Liefland, und von Schleswig bis nach Trident in Tyrol, ja von Brüssel bis Ungarn und Siebenbürgen, auch im Schreiben nachzuahmen und zu erreichen suchet. (Gottsched 1762: 69, my emphasis)

So who should one conform to? But this question is not needed. All of Germany has long implicitly agreed on it. All of Upper and Lower Germany has already expressed: **that the Middle, or Upper Saxon German, is the best High German variety:** as attempts are made everywhere to imitate and to successfully mimic it, including in written form, from Bern in Switzerland, to Reval in Liefland, and from Schleswig to Trident in Tyrol, from Brussels to Hungary and Transylvania.

In contrast to Antesperg, Gottsched thus derives his norms from a certain regional variety. For Gottsched there is not any doubt that Upper Saxon is the 'best High German dialect' and the variety that all German-speaking people strive for. Gottsched's assessment that all of the Upper and Low German areas agree with his judgment is, however, premature. Carl Friedrich Aichinger (1717–1782), a head master, preacher, church and school inspector from Vohenstrauß, Upper Palatinate, criticised Gottsched for excluding Upper German from his concept of High German (von Polenz 1994: 161). In his *Versuch einer teutschen Sprachlehre* (*Attempt of a German Grammar*) (1753), Aichinger advocates a supra-regional standard language, which should be agreed upon by all German-speaking areas (ibid. 162), i.e. a "mundartübergreifende Ausgleichssprache" (Rössler 1997: 55). Johann Siegmund Valentin Popowitsch, whose views will be discussed below, shared Aichinger's notions. Two Swiss linguists, Johann Jakob Bodmer and Johann Jakob Breitinger (1746), as well as Friedrich Carl Fulda (1774) and Johannes Nast (1777) also criticised the supremacy lent to the Upper Saxon language area and, instead, tried to raise the prestige of Upper German varieties (Faulstich 2008: 97–105, 166–173). Besides these Upper German linguists, a number of grammarians from more northern German areas, such as Johann Friedrich Heynatz (1771) and Johann Friedrich Zöllner (1796), raised concerns about equating High German with Upper Saxon (Faulstich 2008: 173–176). Gottsched's concept of High German as the Upper Saxon variety was clearly critized and his assessment cited above is, therefore, questionable. At the same time, Gottsched himself admits that not everybody knows how to speak the Upper Saxon variety.

> Dieß Verzeichniß [die Abwandlung der regelmäßigen Verben] wird aber auch den Nutzen haben, daß man in den verschiedenen Provinzen von Deutschland, wo man in Ansehung der Abwandelungen oft sehr von einander abgeht, oder ungewiß ist, ob sie richtig oder unrichtig zu bilden sind, **den guten Gebrauch von Obersachsen, oder des wahren Hochdeutschen** ersehen könne. **Viele wüßten es gern, wie man hier spricht, um sich darnach zu richten.** (Gottsched 1762: 320, my emphasis)

> This list [of the conjugation of regular verbs], however, will also be of use, in that one can see **the proper use of Upper Saxon, or of the real High German**, in different provinces in Germany, where people often deviate considerably with regard to conjugation, or where people are unsure whether the verbs are regular or irregular. **Many would like to know how one speaks here** [in Upper Saxony] **in order to adjust to it.**

In this case, i.e. if one does not know how the variety is spoken, it is surely difficult to imitate the Upper Saxon variety accurately. Gottsched's assessment of the Upper Saxon variety as the 'best dialect' and people's striving towards it does not necessarily mean that the variety was actually used by people outside Upper Saxony. In fact, it does not even mean that what Gottsched calls "[Sprach]Gebrauch von Obersachsen" ("[language] use of Upper Saxony") in the quotation above refers to the language used by all people in Upper Saxony. Gottsched further distinguishes between the language used by higher social classes, educated people, and literary scholars and that of 'ordinary people' (the *Pöbel*), which he stigmatises. Gottsched argues that the latter, i.e. the variety/variants used in everyday life by 'ordinary people', should not form part of a literary language (Rössler 1997: 30f.).[85] Gottsched's account of the dissemination of Upper Saxon variants, therefore, seems exaggerated or naïve. More generally, von Polenz (1994: 161) describes Gottsched's concepts of language as naïve since Gottsched regarded German as it was at his time as perfect and, therefore, wished for an end to German language change.

Despite his 'naïve' concepts of language, Gottsched was a major catalyst for the dissemination of Upper Saxon variants. In contrast to other grammarians, such as Antesperg (see above), Gottsched clearly propagated the language variety used by higher social classes in Upper Saxony, i.e. an ECG variety. UG variants were usually (but not always!) stigmatised as 'wrong' in Gottsched's grammar, as the next section will show.

3.3.1 Gottsched on *e*-apocope in nouns

Gottsched (1752: 212f.) prescribes the ending -*e* for feminine words and the *e*-apocope for weak masculine as well as neuter nouns beginning in *Ge*- explicitly:

> 18 §. Wie also diejenigen unrecht thun, die den weiblichen Wörtern das Endungs *e* rauben, wenn sie z.E. sprechen und schreiben, *die Kron', die Lieb', die Gnad'* u.s.w. als welches die Sprache ohne Noth hart und rauh machet: also fehlen andre dadurch eben so sehr, daß sie ohne Ursache den männlichen Wörtern am Ende ein *e* anflicken; indem sie sprechen, *der Franke, der Franzose, der Pohle, der Sachse, Schwabe, Türke* u. ja wohl gar *der Fürste, der Grafe, der Herre, der Pfarre, der Poete, der Prophete* und *der Narre*. Noch andere hängen solches auch ohne Noth den Wörtern des ungewissen Geschlechts, die sich mit *Ge* anfangen, an: als das *Gesichte, Gedichte, Gerüchte, Gespräche, Geheule*, u. d. gl. die doch solches weder fodern [sic] können, noch irgend nöthig haben. (Gottsched 1752: 212f.)

> 18 §. Just as some wrongly remove the ending *e* in feminine words, when saying and writing, *die Kron', die Lieb', die Gnad'* etc., making the language unnecessarily hard and rough, others fail just as much by patching an *e* at the end of masculine words without cause by saying, *der Franke, der Franzose, der Pohle, der Sachse, Schwabe, Türke* and even *der Fürste, der Grafe, der Herre, der Pfarre, der Poete, der Prophete* and *der Narre*. Others unnecessarily attach such an *e* to neuter words beginning in *Ge*: such as *das Gesichte, Gedichte, Gerüchte, Gespräche, Geheule*, etc. which neither require nor necessitate it.

In other words, Gottsched prescribes the ECG variant (the ending -*e*) for feminine but the UG variant (*e*-apocope) for weak masculine nouns, which would ease the

---

[85] For ease of reading, the variety propagated by Gottsched will be referred to as 'Upper Saxon' or ECG variety. It should, however, be kept in mind that this regionally determined variety has to be regarded as a specific 'sociolect' since – in the discourse presented here – it only refers to the variety used by the higher social classes.

distinction between feminine (with *e*) and weak masculine nouns (without *e*) (Rössler 1997: 133).

Gottsched (1752: 221–223) further lists nouns according to their gender, stating that the ending *-e* is used for all feminine nouns ending in *b, f, p* (e.g. *Nabe, Hufe, Puppe*) and for most feminine nouns ending in *z* (e.g. *Hitze*). The following quotation presents further examples for the use of the ending *-e* in feminine nouns and reveals Gottsched's uncertainty when applying his own rule of *e*-apocope in weak masculine nouns.

> 17 §. Alle Wörter, die sich auf ein kurzes *e* enden, sind weibl. Geschlechts: als z.E. *Ähre, Ebbe, Ehre, Gabe, Glocke, Gnade, Grube, Habe, Haube, Hütte, Krone, Laube, Stube, Tiefe,* u. s. w. Nur einige wenige sind ausgenommen; als der *Glaube, Name, Saame, Knabe, Rabe, Bube,* u. d. gl. wiewohl es noch zweifelhaftig ist, ob nicht *der Glaub* ohne *e,* wie *der Raub,* oder mit einem *n, der Glauben,* wie die zween folgenden, *Namen, Samen,* von *Nomen, Semen;* und die drey letzten, als männliche Benennungen, lieber *der Bub, der Knab,* und *der Rab,* heißen sollen? Wenigstens schrieben die Alten, *der Knapp, der Rapp,* für *Rab* und *Knab;* [...] (Gottsched 1752: 212)

> 17 §. All words, which end in a short *e,* are of feminine gender; such as *Ähre, Ebbe, Ehre, Gabe, Glocke, Gnade, Grube, Habe, Haube, Hütte, Krone, Laube, Stube, Tiefe* etc. There are only a few exceptions; such as der *Glaube, Name, Saame, Knabe, Rabe, Bube,* etc. albeit whether or not *der Glaub* should rather be without *e,* like *der Raub,* or with a final *n, der Glauben* is still questionable, like the following two, *Namen, Samen,* from *Nomen, Semen;* and the latter three, as masculine denotations, rather *der Bub, der Knab,* and *der Rab?* At least the old [i.e. previous grammarians, authors] write, *der Knapp, der Rapp,* for *Rab* and *Knab;* [...]

Rössler (1997: 141f.) points out that Gottsched's propagation of *e*-apocope in weak masculine as well as mixed-declension neuter nouns (e.g. *das Aug*) is not based on a geographical preference but rather due to systematic considerations since the *e*-apocope in weak masculine and mixed-declension neuter nouns results in a clear morphological distinction between them and feminine nouns.[86]

By contrast, Gottsched (1752: 231, 240) prescribes the use of the ending *-e* in the dative singular form of strong masculine and neuter nouns (e.g. *dem Stande, dem Amte*). The only exception that Gottsched (1752: 493) notes is that the dative *-e* is not used when two or more nouns immediately follow a preposition:

---

86 With regard to Rössler's (1997: 140) reference to Jellinek (1913: 243) who states that Gottsched rejected the ending *-e* in weak masculine and mixed-declension neuter nouns in the nominative singular consistently ("rundweg"), it should be pointed out that Gottsched himself was not as consistent and systematic as described by Rössler and Jellinek (see quote above and Gottsched's (1752) use of *Auge* (pp. 85, 108, 189, 395, 400, 659) instead of *Aug* (pp. 237, 562) in the nominative and accusative case).

Man saget sonst recht, *in der Noth und im* (d. i. *in dem*) *Tode*. Allein wenn man sie beyde vereiniget, so heißt es: *in Noth und Tod*. Eben so saget man: *Mit Gut und Blut, in Freud und Leid, mit Rath und That*; (Gottsched 1752: 493)

One rightly says *in der Noth und im* (d. i. *in dem*) *Tode*. Only when the two are combined, it is: *in Noth und Tod*. One equally says: *Mit Gut und Blut, in Freud und Leid, mit Rath und That*;

Gottsched (1752: 226, 240) further states that only nouns ending in *-el, -en* and *-er* can[87] have zero plural endings. Words of German origin ending in different letters or letter combinations take an *-e, -n, -en* or *-er* in their plural form (Gottsched 1752: 227–240). In summary, Gottsched prescribes the ending *-e* for feminine nouns, strong masculine and neuter nouns in the dative singular form and plural forms of nouns.

3.3.2 Gottsched on past participles

Similarly to Antesperg, Gottsched provides a certain model for the conjugation of regular verbs:

Durch richtige Zeitwörter versteht man solche, die in der jüngstvergangenen Zeit ein *te*, und in der völlig vergangenen ein *et* annehmen. Als *ich labe, ich labete, gelabet; ich lebe, ich lebete, gelebet; ich liebe, ich liebete, geliebet; ich lobe, ich lobete, gelobet; ich ruhe, ich ruhete, geruhet*, u.d.gl. Diese machen nun im Deutschen die größte Anzahl aus, und man bemerket, daß sie durch alle Gattungen, Arten und Zeiten, ja in allen Personen, durchgehends den Selbstlaut des Stammwortes beybehalten: [...]. Dieses erleichtert nun die Abwandlung dieser Zeitwörter ungemein, und weil sie alle auf einen Schlag gehen, so brauchen wir auch nur ein einziges Muster davon. (Gottsched 1752: 305)

Regular verbs are those which take on the ending *te* in the preterite and *et* in the perfect tense. Such as *ich labe, ich labete, gelabet; ich lebe, ich lebete, gelebet; ich liebe, ich liebete, geliebet; ich lobe, ich lobete, gelobet; ich ruhe, ich ruhete, geruhet* etc. These [kinds of verbs] constitute the majority in German, and one notices that they keep the vowel of the stem in all categories, types and tenses, even in all persons: [...]. Now this eases the conjugation of these verbs immensely, and because they are all conjugated in the same way, we only need a single model.

In the examples Gottsched lists in his first section about regular verbs, he forms every past participle with the prefix *ge-* and the suffix *-et* (*gelabet, gelebet, geliebet, gelobet, geruhet*). He then presents a more detailed description of his conjugation model for regular verbs:

4 §. Es bilden sich aber in der richtigen Abwandlung die verschiedenen Zeiten folgender Gestalt. Von der gebiethenden Art *lob*, oder wie man itzo gelinder spricht, *lobe*, entsteht die

---

87 The plural forms of nouns ending in *-el* or *-er* can, of course, also end in *-n*.

erste Person der gegenwärtigen Zeit, durch Anhängung des *e*, und Vorsetzung des *ich*; *ich lobe*. Zu diesem *e* setzet man noch den Buchstab *n*, so hat man die unbestimmte Art, *loben*. Will man die jüngst vergangene Zeit haben, so setzet man anstatt des *n*, das *te* hinten zu: *ich lobete*. Läßt man das letzte *e* hier weg, und setzet die Syllbe *ge* voran, so hat man die völlig vergangene Zeit: *gelobet*, die auch in der längst vergangenen bleibt. [...] (Gottsched 1752: 306)

4 §. Regular verbs are formed in the following way in the different tenses. The 1ˢᵗ person in the present tense is formed by adding the ending *e* and putting *ich* in front of the imperative *lob*, or as one nowadays says more mildly, *lobe*; *ich lobe*. To this *e* one adds the letter *n* to get the infinitive form, *loben*. If one wants the preterite form, one adds *te* instead of *n* at the end: *ich lobete*. If one leaves out the last *e* here, and one adds the syllable *ge* in front [of the stem], one gets the present perfect form: *gelobet*, which also stays that way in the pluperfect tense. [...]

In this more detailed description, Gottsched prescribes the prefix *ge-* and the suffix *-et*, i.e. the ECG variants. He sticks to his prescription in the conjugation examples he lists for every person on page 309, 311 and 312. Furthermore, Gottsched mentions and explains some exceptions to his model, but these refer to the present tense only:

Selbst in den Zeitwörtern, die sich auf *eln* und *ern* zu enden, und also eine Ausnahme zu erfordern scheinen, als *mangeln, klingeln, segeln, hindern, rudern, wettern*, u. d. gl. scheint das *e* nur darum weggefallen zu seyn, weil es zwischen zween flüßige Mitlauter, oder halbe Selbstlaute zu stehen gekommen. Man findet auch in alten Schriften wirklich *seglen, hindren, klinglen*, u. (Gottsched 1752: 307)

Even in verbs ending in *eln* and *ern*, and thus seemingly presenting an exception, such as *mangeln, klingeln, segeln, hindern, rudern, wettern* etc., the *e* seems only to have dropped because it was between two sonorants or semivowels. In old documents, one really finds *seglen, hindren, klinglen* etc.

While Antesperg allowed the use of both variants, the suffix *-t* and *-et*, in regular past participles, Gottsched clearly propagated the latter form. With regard to the prefix *ge-*, however, both grammarians agreed on the compulsory use of the ECG variant, i.e. regular past participles with *ge-*. In his lists of irregular verbs, Gottsched (1752: 330–338) consistently records past participles with the prefix *ge-* (such as *gekommen, gethan, getroffen, getrunken, geblieben, gegangen, gebissen, gepfiffen, gegossen, gekrochen, gebacken, gegraben, getragen*) without mentioning that these past participles can be formed without the prefix in the Upper German language area. Whereas Antesperg acknowledges the variants *gessen/geessen* and *geben*, Gottsched invisibilises all Upper German forms without *ge-* by not mentioning them at all.

3.3.3 Gottsched on alternative forms of *wir/sie sind*

As previously shown, Antesperg allowed the use of the UG variants *wir/sie seynd* as well as the ECG form *wir/sie sind*. Gottsched, by contrast, stigmatises the UG variant in the 3rd person plural in his conjugation of the verb *to be*:

Ich bin,	Wir sind,
Du bist,	Ihr seyd,
Er ist.	Sie sind, (nicht seyn.) (Gottsched 1752: 297)

In the 3rd person plural, Gottsched adds 'not *seyn*' in brackets after the 'correct' ECG variant '*Sie sind*'. While the UG form is thus stigmatised explicitly in the 3rd person plural, it is stigmatised indirectly in the 1st person plural as it is not mentioned at all. Again, Gottsched prescribes the ECG variants, while dismissing their UG equivalents. The following sections will show to what extent other grammarians followed Gottsched's language norms.

3.4 Johann Siegmund Valentin Popowitsch

Johann Siegmund Valentin Popowitsch (1705–1774) was born in Lower Styria, today Slovenia, and moved to Graz in 1714 or 1715, where he had several jobs and studied (Faninger 1996: 17, 19). Faninger (1996: 18) states that Popowitsch's mother tongue was Slovenian; Popowitsch described himself as "kein gebohrner Teutscher" ("not German by birth") in his scientific monograph *Untersuchungen vom Meere* (1750: Vorbericht [p. 9]).[88] Popowitsch's adversaries construed his statement to mean that he had learnt German as a foreign language and was, therefore, unqualified to write a German grammar (Faninger 1996: 18). Popowitsch (1754b: Vorrede, 30) responded to his adversaries, insisting that he had learnt German from his parents. Faninger (1996: 18) assumes that Popowitsch was raised in a bilingual environment, speaking Slovenian and German in the form of a Styrian dialect, while learning 'High German' in Graz. Popowitsch's desire for improving his 'High German' was the starting point for his work on German grammar (ibid.).

Before working in Vienna (1741–1744) and Kremsmünster (1744–1746), he had established contact with Gottsched about his linguistic research, who advised him against publishing a grammar.[89] Popowitsch followed this advice and refrained from

---

88 Popowitsch's *Untersuchungen vom Meere* (1750) was published anonymously and covered a wide range of scientific topics, including geography, archeology, natural sciences, and linguistics (Faninger 1996: 31).

89 Faninger (1996: 22) and Rössler (1997: 44) point out that, similarly to Antesperg's work, Popowitsch's grammar would have meant competition for Gottsched.

publishing his work (Rössler 1997: 44). Rössler (1997: 44f.) states that this fact and the subsequent success of Gottsched's grammar were reasons for Popowitsch's change from a follower to an opponent of Gottsched in the 1740s. Furthermore, the concept of standardisation differed between the two grammarians: While Gottsched based his norm on the Upper Saxon literary language, Popowitsch believed that a supra-regional agreed language (*Ausgleichssprache*) should constitute the standard language (Rössler 1997: 45). Popowitsch's adverse position against Gottsched comes to the fore when he mentions Gottsched's advice in his *Untersuchungen vom Meere* (1750):

> Hr. Gottsched, welcher [...] glaubte, ich würde eine Teutsche Sprachlehre schreiben, ließ mich in seinem Beantwortungsschreiben ernstlich warnen, ich sollte ja keine vergebliche Arbeit anfangen. Was ich vorhätte, wäre längst mit allem Fleiße bereits vollbracht worden. Ich könnte mich noch darzu vor der gelehrten Welt lächerlich machen, wie Hr. A=sperger in Wien [...], [dem seine] angebohrne Mundart nicht erlaubet hätte, etwas geschicktes in der Hochteutschen Sprache auszurichten. Wenn die Gelehrten meine hier beigebrachten Gedanken, von der Beschaffenheit der oberländischen Mundarten, und andere dergleichen Nachrichten, gerne eher erfahren hätten [...] so wissen sie, wer diese Bekanntmachung hintertrieben habe. (Popowitsch 1750: 312)

> Mr Gottsched, who [...] believed that I would write a German grammar, delivered a stern warning in his response letter, saying I should not start any work in vain. What I intended had [according to Gottsched] long been achieved with the greatest diligence. Also, I could make a fool of myself in the learned world, such as Mr A=sperger in Vienna [...], [whose] native dialect had [according to Gottsched] not allowed him to accomplish anything sophisticated in the High German language. Had scholars already wanted to learn about my thoughts on the nature of Upper German dialects, and other such information, they [now] know who has thwarted this publication.[90]

The rivalry between Popowitsch and Gottsched increased further after Popowitsch's appointment as a professor for German language and eloquence at the University of Vienna and at the *Savoyische Akademie* in 1753 (Rössler 1997: 46). The open conflict peaked when Popowitsch published his own grammar entitled *Die nothwendigsten Anfangsgründe der Teutschen Sprachkunst, zum Gebrauche der Österreichischen Schulen herausgegeben* (*The most necessary elements of German grammar, published for use in Austrian schools*) in 1754, in which the name *Gottsched* was used to exemplify the declension of masculine proper nouns. Gottsched and his Viennese followers took this as a vilification of the name *Gottsched* and wanted it to be removed from the grammar, a revision not realised (Rössler 1997: 47). However, Gottsched's followers, particulary Franz Christoph von Scheyb (a poet and writer who grew up in Vienna from the age of ten) managed to reduce Popowitsch's influence by en-

---

90 It should be noted that Popowitsch (1750: 312f.) added a second reason for not publishing his linguistic research: a lack of financial support.

couraging and writing pasquils about him (Faninger 1996: 42, 52–60). Furthermore, Popowitsch had to endure opposition from the Jesuits and the chancelleries, who disapproved of his language reforms (ibid. 60). Faninger (1996: 71) believes that – besides the grammatical and orthographic changes advocated – Popowitsch also attracted rivals because of his wilful and short-tempered nature. Popowitsch's rivalries resulted in his exclusion from the foundation of the *Viennese German Society* in 1761 (ibid. 70f.) and the rejection of his grammar in Austria's schools and academies (Rössler 1997: 50). After Popowitsch's retirement from his post at the University of Vienna in 1766, his grammar also disappeared from the spheres of higher education (Faninger 1996: 79). His successor, Josef Heinrich von Engelschall, replaced it with Gottsched's *Kern der deutschen Sprachkunst* (1753) and Justi's *Anweisung zu einer guten deutschen Schreibart* (1755) (ibid.). These facts lead Faninger (1996: 232) to the conclusion that Popowitsch's influence on the language use of his contemporaries as well as on other grammarians was marginal.

Furthermore, Popowitsch's interest in 'dialects' and the linguistic varieties used by 'simple' and 'uneducated' people was incomprehensible to many of his contemporaries, even though the German philosopher and mathematician Gottfried Wilhelm von Leibniz had already advocated the study of "the words of the common man" ("Landworten des gemeinen Mannes") in 1697 in his *Unvorgreifliche Gedanken, betreffend die Ausübung und Verbesserung der Deutschen Sprache* (*Nonprejudicial thoughts on the use and improvement of the German language*) (Faninger 1996: 34, 98). Popowitsch (1750: appendix [p. 22])[91] refers to Leibniz and, according to Faninger (1996: 99), highlights the value of 'dialects' as a pool of lexical variants for the enrichment of the High German vocabulary as well as their usefulness in establishing the etymology and orthography of words. Popowitsch's advocacy for the inclusion of Austrian German (and other regional varieties) in the formation of a standard German is also evident in the preamble by the publisher of his *Versuch einer Vereinigung der Mundarten von Teutschland als eine Einleitung zu einem vollständigen Teutschen Wörterbuche* (*Attempt at uniting the German dialects as an introduction to a complete German dictionary*) (1780).

[W]ie sehr könnte die Hochteutsche Sprache bereichert werden, wenn man aus jenen die deutlichsten und geschicktesten Benennungen in das Hochteutsche aufnähme? wie viele Wörter sind durch das schädliche Vorurtheil der Anhänger Gottscheds, daß die Sächsische Mundart für die Hochteutsche Sprache müsse angesehen werden, in das Hochteutsche eingeschlichen, welche dunkel, unbestimmt, mehrdeutig, oder aus einer fremden Sprache

---

91 This section of Popowitsch's *Untersuchungen vom Meere* is entitled "Schreiben / des Verfassers / vorhergehender Abhandlung / an / Einige vornehme Gelehrte / in / Leipzig" ("Letters to a few noble scholars concerning the author's work"). It follows Popowitsch's third part "Nachlese von etlichen Zusätzen" (pp. 275–432) and is not numbered consecutively.

entlehnet sind, und die durch die geschicktesten Benennungen aus andern ländlichen Mundarten könnten ersezet werden? (Popowitsch 1780: Vorbericht des Herausgebers J. L.)

[T]o what great extent could the High German language be enriched if one was to incorporate the most precise and most sophisticated terms into High German? how many words that are dark, vague, ambiguous or borrowed from a foreign language, and which could be replaced by the most sophisticated terms from other regional varieties, have crept into High German due to the harmful preconception of Gottsched's followers that the Saxon dialect must be regarded as the High German language?

Faulstich (2008: 127) stresses that Popowitsch's questioning of Upper Saxon as the 'leading variety' (*Leitvarietät*) does not go hand in hand with an increase in status of the Upper German varieties. Instead, Popowitsch seeks to improve the state of Upper German (ibid.). Indeed, despite propagating the inclusion of Austrian German in the language norm discourse, Popowitsch describes certain regional features as 'mistakes' in his preamble to *Anfangsgründe der Teutschen Sprachkunst* (1754a).

Die meisten Fehler, welche man in den Schriften der Österreicher antrifft, werden wider die Biegungen der Nennwörter, wider die Abwandlung der unrichtigen Zeitwörter, und wider den bewährten Gebrauch der Haftwörter begangen. Alle diese Unrichtigkeiten können durch fleißige Lesung des hier mitgetheilten Auszuges vermieden werden. (Popowitsch 1754a: Vorrede)

Most mistakes, which one finds in texts written by Austrians, are made in the following areas: the inflection of nouns, the conjugation of irregular verbs, and the use of prepositions. All these mistakes can be avoided by reading the relevant sections in this grammar diligently.

Popowitsch's grammar aims to eliminate these 'mistakes', especially by applying principles of analogy to establish what is correct (Faninger 1996: 105). For Popowitsch, it was analogy rather than language use that determined whether a variant was 'wrong' or 'correct' (ibid.). The elimination of Austrians' 'mistakes' would result in an enhancement of the status of Austrian German, even outside Austria's borders:

Das müssen die [...] Lehrer sich zuvörderst angelegen seyn lassen, und nicht zu frühzeitig sorgen, ob noch etwas von der Teutschen Sprachlehre nachkommen wird, oder nicht. Wenn auch nichts mehr nachfolgete, so wird damit schon ein Vieles, ja beinahe das Meiste ausgerichtet seyn, und die auswärtigen Verächter der Österreichischen Schreibart sollen auch bald schwelgen, wenn man nur das Jztgedachte auf unsern Schulen erst die Jugend lernen läßt. (Popowitsch 1754a: Vorrede)

The teachers must firstly concentrate on this [excerpt], and they should not worry prematurely about any succession of the German grammar. Even if nothing else follows, much or almost the most will have already been done by this excerpt, and the foreign dispraisers of the Austrian way of writing would also soon be silenced, if only the youth are allowed to learn this grammar in our schools.

Despite Popowitsch's efforts to advertise his grammar and propagate a 'correct' form of the Austrian German variety, his grammar was not used outside higher education and was soon replaced by Gottsched's *Grundlegung einer deutschen Sprachkunst*. An analysis of the prescription of certain features in Popowitsch's grammar will reveal to what extent these two grammars differed.

3.4.1 Popowitsch on *e*-apocope in nouns

Popowitsch (1754a: 8–29) lists paradigms for the inflection of feminine, masculine and neuter nouns. The paradigm for feminine nouns ending in -*e* is shown by declining the word *Ehre*, which ends in -*e* in all its forms (ibid. 11). Further examples of feminine nouns with the ending -*e* are listed on page 12 (*die Aalraupe, Achse, Ahle, Ameise, Amme, Aspe, Ähre, Änte, Bahre*)[92], while *e*-apocope never occurs and is never mentioned by Popowitsch. This is also the case for the examples of the plural forms of feminine nouns: *Äxte, Bänke, Bräute, Brüste, Einkünfte, Fäuste, Früchte, Hände, Häute, Kühe, Künste, Läuse, Mächte, Mägde, Mäuse, Mäute, Nächte, Nüsse, Säue, Städte, Wände, Werkstätte, Würste, Zünfte* (ibid. 13). In the extended version of his grammar, Popowitsch (1754b: Vorrede, 11f.) stigmatises the *e*-apocope in feminine nouns explicitly, when explaining that

> [d]as Verzeichniß der weiblichen, die sich in *e* endigen, ist [...] auch deswegen etwas weitläuftiger [sic] geworden, weil unsere Mundart sie anders bildet. Denn einigen wird ihr *e* entzogen, da man, *die Achs, Ahl, Ameis, Bahr, Beut, Birn, Blum, Buß* u. spricht. Andre werden hingegen, durch die Anflickung des veralteten *n*, von unsern Landesleuten verlängert, welche noch *die Binden, die Birken, Breiten, Brillen, Butten, Büchsen, Dicken, Dinten, Docken* u. sprechen, und gleichwol nur *eine Binde, Birke* u. verstehen. (Popowitsch 1754b: Vorrede, 11f.)

> [t]he list of the feminine nouns which end in *e* is somewhat more extensive, because our 'dialect' [i.e. UG] forms them differently. Because some nouns are deprived of the *e*, as one says *die Achs, Ahl, Ameis, Bahr, Beut, Birn, Blum, Buß* etc. Others, by contrast, are extended by patching on the obsolete *n* by our countrymen, who still say *die Binden, die Birken, Breiten, Brillen, Butten, Büchsen, Dicken, Dinten, Docken* etc., even though they only mean *one Binde, Birke* etc.

The ending -*e* is also prescribed in the dative singular form of strong masculine nouns (e.g. *dem Fuße, dem Bache, dem Baume* etc.) as well as neuter nouns (e.g. *dem Gebote, dem Jahre* etc.)[93] (1754a: 23–25). These nouns also end in -*e* in the nominative, genitive and accusative plural case (ibid.).

---

92 Rössler (1997: 133) states that in Popowitsch's extended grammar (1754b: 37–39) even more examples of feminine nouns ending in -*e* are given.

93 See also the paradigm for strong neuter nouns on p. 27 (*dem Volke*), with examples following on the subsequent page (e.g. *Dorf, Holz, Kind*), which end in -*e* in the dative singular case.

With regard to weak masculine nouns, on the other hand, Popowitsch (1754a: 20f.) prescribes the *e*-apocope in the nominative form: e.g. *der Bub, Aff, Bot, Buchstab, Bürg, Drach, Erb, Falk, Genoß, Gesell, Has, Hirt, Holunk, Knab, Knapp (Bergknapp), Kund, Löw, Ochs, Path, Pfaff, Rab, Scherg (der Büttel), Schurk, Schüz, Zeug.*[94] This rule also applies to names of peoples, which do not end in *-er*, such as *der Böhm, Britt, Dän, Finn, Franzos, Griech, Portugies, Preuß, Türk* etc. (ibid. 21). Thus Popowitsch creates a clear distinction between feminine and weak masculine nouns.

In summary, Popowitsch prescribes the ending *-e* for feminine nouns, strong masculine and neuter nouns in the dative singular form as well as for plural forms. In this way, he closely follows Gottsched's prescription and distances himself from the Upper German variety, which was accepted in Antesperg's grammar. Similar to Gottsched but less forceful, Popowitsch stigmatises the *e*-apocope in feminine nouns directly by describing it as "deprivation" ("Entzug") in the extended version of his grammar (see quotation above). In the shorter version, by contrast, Popowitsch invisibilises the *e*-apocope in feminine nouns by not mentioning it at all. In weak masculine nouns, Popowitsch prefers the *e*-apocope since this allows for a clear distinction from other types of nouns.

3.4.2 Popowitsch on regular past participles

Popowitsch (1754a: 84–97), like Gottsched, uses the verb *loben* to exemplify the conjugation of regular verbs. He (1754a: 84f.) lists the following forms for the present and preterite tense:

ich lobe	ich lobete
du lobest	du lobetest
er lobet	er lobete
wir loben	wir lobeten
ihr lobet	ihr lobetet
sie loben	sie lobeten.

In a note (1754a: 85), he adds: "Man kann auch schreiben, *ich lobte, du lobtest* u." ("One can also write, *ich lobte, du lobtest* etc."). Similarly, he allows both endings (*-et* as well as *-t*) for the past participle, which he lists as "*gelobet*, oder *gelobt*" (ibid.). While Popowitsch (1754a: 86–94) opts for the use of the former in the active voice as well as in the passive voice formed with *werden* (e.g. *ich werde gelobet*), he (1754a: 94–97) prefers the latter in the passive voice formed with *sein* (e.g. *ich bin gelobt*).

---

94 *Der Gefährte* seems to be an exception in this list of examples (Popowitsch 1754a: 20).

Popowitsch uses both past participle endings (the suffix -*et* as well as -*t*) in his conjugation of the verb *loben*, thus distancing himself from Gottsched's prescription of the ending -*et*. Nevertheless, he seems to have a slight preference for the suffix -*et*. With regard to the prefix *ge-*, Popowitsch follows previous grammarians (Antesperg and Gottsched) in deeming this prefix compulsory in the formation of regular past participles. Similar to his contemporaries, Popowitsch (1754a: 103–134) provides a catalogue of irregular verbs, with all irregular verbs that can take the prefix *ge-* listed as such (e.g. *gebacken, gebissen, geblasen, geblieben, gebrochen, gebracht, gedacht, gegessen, gegeben, gegangen, gegriffen, geklungen, gekommen, getragen, getrieben, getrunken*). Variants without *ge-* are neither mentioned nor used.

3.4.3 Popowitsch on alternative forms of *wir/sie sind*

Popowitsch (1754a: 79f.) conjugates the verb *sein* in the following way:

Ich bin,	Wir sind,
du bist,	ihr seyd,
er ist.	sie sind.

This conjugation is in line with Gottsched's norm prescriptions. While Gottsched explicitly stigmatises UG variants as 'wrong', Popowitsch does not mention any specific Upper German forms in his paradigm. Thus he stigmatises the Upper German variants (*wir/sie seynd/t*) indirectly by not mentioning them and only using their Central German counterparts. In other words, Popowitsch renders the Upper German variants invisible to modern-day researchers. However, in the extended version of his grammar, Popowitsch (1754b: 231) writes "*wir sind*, nicht *seynd* [...] *sie sind*, nicht *seynd*, vielweniger *seyn*", thus explicitly stigmatising the Upper German variant as 'wrong'.

3.5 Johann Ignaz von Felbiger

Johann Ignaz von Felbiger (1724–1788) was born in Glogow (Silesia), to an Austrian postmaster and a Bavarian mother, and was a loyal Prussian subject after Glogow became part of Prussia in 1742 (Engelbrecht 1984: 102). As mentioned in chapter 2, Felbiger was commissioned by Maria Theresa in 1774 to advise on her school reform. Felbiger's school policy introduced compulsory elementary education and his textbooks on German language, most of which were published anonymously, were used in schools until 1848, with a few revisions in line with Adelung's norms (von Polenz 1994: 175). One of these textbooks is entitled *Anleitung zur deutschen Sprachlehre* (*Instruction on German Grammar*) (1775) and will be discussed in more detail below.

Rössler (1997: 71f.) states that Felbiger's grammar is based on Gottsched's *Kern der deutschen Sprachkunst* (1753) but it distinguishes itself from other grammars by addressing a broader audience, i.e. students of all social classes. Felbiger himself aimed to sell his *Sprachlehre* as cheaply as possible, which he achieved by limiting the content to what was absolutely necessary (Rössler 1995: 60f.).[95] This meant that Felbiger only mentioned additional information on specific features or structures if he felt that these may pose difficulties to students (Rössler 1997: 75). Consequently, Felbiger goes into less detail about UG variants than, for example, Gottsched (ibid.). Furthermore, the publishing house of the so-called *Deutsche Schulen* (*Verlag der deutschen Schulanstalten bei St. Anna in der Johannesgasse*), which was awarded the exclusive right to print textbooks and teaching materials by Maria Theresa in 1772, enabled cheap production (ibid. 72). Poor children received Felbiger's textbooks for free (ibid.). It can, therefore, be argued that Felbiger's grammar was probably the most widely disseminated in Austria in the second half of the 18th century, especially among 'ordinary people'. While Felbiger's *Anleitungen* were not particularly innovative with regard to language use since they followed Gottsched's norms, their wide dissemination formed a strong basis for the implementation of the language reform in 18th-century Austria (Rössler 1995: 72).

Despite its condensed form, Felbiger's *Spachlehre* (1775) covers all central grammatical topics, from nouns and their declination to syntax. Instructions on spelling are dealt with separately in his *Anleitung zur deutschen Rechtschreibung* (*Instruction on German Spelling*) (1774) and guidance on pronunciation is given in Felbiger's reading primer (Felbiger 1775: 3).[96] The introduction to his *Sprachlehre* (1775) is, however, very short: Before going into detail about grammatical rules and structures, Felbiger (1775: 3) only states that "[d]ie deutsche Sprachlehre enthält die Regeln die deutsche Sprache richtig zu reden und zu schreiben" ("[t]he German *Sprachlehre* contains the rules for speaking and writing correctly in German"). On the basis of this statement it can be argued that Felbiger believes that there is *a* correct German, rather than different varieties of German. At the same time, this implies that there is also a 'wrong' German. While Felbiger does not stigmatise a particular regional variety explicitly, in contrast to Gottsched (see above), he describes particular features, such as the use of auxiliary *tun* and *drüber/drunter* instead of *darüber/darunter*, as mistakes in a number of footnotes:

---

95 His *Anleitung zur deutschen Sprachlehre* (1775) is only 124 pages long, which is significantly shorter than, for example, Gottsched's (1752) 678-page-long grammar (excluding the preface and the index).

96 See section 4.3 for analyses of a number of reading primers designed to be used in state schools (1777, 1778, 1779, 1782, 1783, 1804, 1833), which were written by Felbiger but published anonymously.

> Den Fehler höret man oft in gemeinen Reden, daß man das Zeitwort *thun* anstattt [sic] eines Hilfswortes brauchet; als: *wir thun arbeiten, ihr thut spielen, wenn ich wissen thäte.* (Felbiger 1775: 96)

> Often in common discourse, one can hear the mistake of using the verb *thun* instead of an auxiliary verb; such as: *wir thun arbeiten, ihr thut spielen, wenn ich wissen thäte.*

The use of auxiliary *tun* had been evaluated negatively since the 16th century in poetry and was considered sub-standard in all formal writing by 1740 (Langer 2001: 221). Felbiger follows this stigmatisation of auxiliary *tun* and mentions other variants that he considers "incorrect" ("unrichtig"), such as the omission of /a/ in *darüber* and *darunter*:

> *Darüber* und *darunter* werden oft unrichtig zusammengezogen, wenn von keinem Orte die Rede ist; als: *ich werde drüber* (anstatt *darüber*) denken; *drunter* anstatt *darunter* verstehen. (Felbiger 1775: 102)

> *Darüber* and *darunter* are often shortened incorrectly if they do not refer to places; such as: *ich werde drüber* (instead of *darüber*) denken; *drunter* instead of *darunter* verstehen.

These are two examples of Felbiger's clear distinction between 'correct' and 'incorrect' language use. The following sections will discuss Felbiger's prescriptions with regard to noun endings, past participles and forms of the verb *to be*.

3.5.1 Felbiger on *e*-apocope in nouns

Felbiger (1775) categorizes German noun declensions into five groups. The first declension concerns weak masculine nouns and includes the following words: *Der Aff, Both, Buchstab, Bub, Bürg, Drach, Erb, Falk, Gefährt, Genoß, Gesell, Has, Hirt, Insaß, Knab, Kund, Lay, Löw, Neff, Ochs, Path, Pfaff, Rab, Schütz, Sklav, Vorfahr, Wais, Zeug (der Zeugnis giebt)* (ibid. 8f.). This list of examples indicates that Felbiger prescribes the *e*-apocope for weak masculine nouns. It is striking that Felbiger's examples resemble those of Popowitsch (1754a: 20f.).[97] The only differences are that Felbiger writes *Gefährt* without the *-e*, in line with the other nouns, and lists *Insaß* (after which he adds "ein Provinzialwort", i.e. a regional word) instead of *Holunk* as well as *Sklav* instead of *Scherg*. Furthermore, he does not include *Knapp* and *Schurk* but adds *Lay, Neff, Vorfahr* and *Wais*. This resemblance to Popowitsch's examples suggests that Felbiger based his textbook on the textbook previously used in Austrian

---

97 Ten of these examples (*Aff, Bub, Falk, Knab, Leu, Ochs, Path, Pfaff, Rab, Sklav*) can also be found in Gottsched (1752: 236f.) but Gottsched's list is considerably more extensive. Popowitsch might have picked some of the examples from Gottsched with Felbiger, in turn, copying them from Popowitsch.

schools, i.e. Popowitsch's *Nothwendigsten Anfangsgründe* (1754a). As in Popowitsch (1754a), the prescription of *e*-apocope in weak masculine nouns also applies to names of peoples not ending in *-er*, e.g. *Böhm, Franzos, Jud, Israelit* and *Kroat* (Felbiger 1775: 9).

Felbiger's description of the second declension briefly covers feminine words, giving *die Frau, der Frau, der Frau, die Frau,* pl. *die Frauen* as a declination paradigm (ibid. 10). In a footnote he adds that it is wrong to say *mit der Frauen, auf Erden, bey der Kirchen.* Instead one ought to say: *mit der Frau, auf der Erde, bey der Kirche* (ibid.). While Felbiger does not give any other feminine nouns ending in *-e* as examples in his chapter on noun declension, feminine nouns with *e*-apocope never appear in his grammar, apart from *Hilf,* which he consistently spells without final *-e.* Similar to Popowitsch, Felbiger thus implicitly prescribes the ending *-e* for feminine nouns while invisibilising the *e*-apocope by not mentioning it. For the plural forms of feminine nouns, he explicitly dictates the ending *-e*:

> Die Hauptwörter auf *iß*, welche in der mehrern Zahl auf *e* ausgehen, als die *Finsternisse, Hindernisse* [sowie] folgende Wörter, die sich in der mehrern Zahl auch auf *e* endigen, und den Selbstlauter zugleich ändern; als: *die Axt, Bank, Braut, Brust, Faust, Frucht, Hand, Haut, Kluft, Kruft, Kuh, Laus, Luft, Lust, Macht, Maus, Mauth, Noth, Nuß, Sau, Schnur, Stadt, Wand, Wurst, Zunft.* (Felbiger 1775: 9f.)

> The nouns ending in *iß*, which end in *e* in their plural form, such as *Finsternisse, Hindernisse* [as well as] the following words, which also end in *e* in the plural, and change the vowel at the same time; such as: *die Axt, Bank, Braut, Brust, Faust, Frucht, Hand, Haut, Kluft, Kruft, Kuh, Laus, Luft, Lust, Macht, Maus, Mauth, Noth, Nuß, Sau, Schnur, Stadt, Wand, Wurst, Zunft.*

Felbiger's examples are again largely copied from Popowitsch (1754a: 13), who lists the same nouns alphabetically, except for *Kluft, Kruft, Luft, Lust, Noth* and *Schnur.* Instead, Popowitsch (ibid.) also provides the following examples: *Einkunft, Kunst, Magd, Nacht* and *Werkstatt.* Therefore, it can be argued that Felbiger's *Sprachlehre* is – to a large extent – based on Popowitsch (1754a) with regard to the declension of nouns.

The third declension in Felbiger (1775) concerns masculine and neuter nouns ending in *-el, -en, -er* as well as loanwords ending in *-ier* and *-ör*, and is, therefore, irrelevant here. Felbiger's fourth declension, on the other hand, discusses dative and plural forms of strong masculine and neuter nouns. Felbiger (1775: 11) states that these nouns end in *-e* in the dative case. In their plural forms, the vowel either stays unchanged and the ending *-en* is added or its vowel is changed and the noun ends in *-er* (ibid. 12). Most of the nouns, however, end in *-e* in their plural forms, with the addition of *-n* in the dative plural case (ibid.). The ending *-n* in the dative plural case is also compulsory for nouns ending in *-er.* Felbiger (ibid.) declines one noun in all cases to provide an example: singular: *das Ey, des Eyes, dem Eye, das Ey*; plural: *die Eyer, der Eyer, den Eyern, die Eyer.* For the dative singular form (i.e. *dem*

Eye) he adds a footnote, in which he denotes the *e*-apocope in the dative case a mistake:

> Kein Fehler kömmt so oft vor, als dieser, daß das *e* in der einzelnen und mehrern Zahl ausgelassen wird. Man redet und schreibt nur *dem Fuß, dem Stock, dem Zahn, dem Gesicht, dem Aug*, da es doch heißen sollte: *dem Fusse, dem Stocke, dem Zahne, dem Gesichte, dem Auge*. (Felbiger 1775: 12)

> No mistake occurs more often than the one in which the *e* is left out in the singular and plural. One says and writes only *dem Fuß, dem Stock, dem Zahn, dem Gesicht, dem Aug*, when it should actually be: *dem Fusse, dem Stocke, dem Zahne, dem Gesichte, dem Auge*.

Thus Felbiger clearly prescibes the ending *-e* for strong masculine and neuter nouns in the dative case as well as for certain nouns in the plural, while stigmatising the *e*-apocope explicitly. As mentioned above, a number of nouns in Felbiger's fourth declination category end in *-er* or *-en*. Felbiger's (1775: 12) list of examples for these nouns includes the neuter nouns *das Aug* and *das End*, which indicates that he proposes the use of *e*-apocope for mixed-declension neuter nouns.

After presenting the fifth declension (proper nouns and loan words), Felbiger (1775: 20) further comments on common mistakes with regard to plural forms:

> Man vermeide folgende Fehler, die in der gemeinen Aussprache so oft gehöret werden:

> [...] 2.) Das *e* soll niemals in der mehrern Zahl ausgelassen werden. Man merke sich deßwegen die allgemeine Regel, daß die allgemeinen Nennwörter die nicht auf *el, en, er, lein* in der vielfachen Zahl ausgehen, das *e* annehmen, als: *die Haare, die Hüte, die Schuhe, die Strümpfe, die Tische, die Schafe*.

> 3.) Unrichtig sagt der Pöbel: *die Schattener, Staner, Bämer, Bäner, Gebäuer* [sic], *die Mauthen, Zünften, Kräften, die Mantel, Handel, mit den Handen*, anstatt *die Schotten, die Steine, Bäume, Beine, Gebäude, Mäuthe, Zünfte, Kräfte, Mäntel, Händel, mit den Händen*. (Felbiger 1775: 20)

> One should avoid the following mistakes, which are often heard in common speech:

> [...] 2.) The *e* should never be omitted in the plural. One should, therefore, remember the general rule that general nouns not ending in *-el*, *-en*, *-er*, and *-lein*, in the plural take an *e*, such as: *die Haare, die Hüte, die Schuhe, die Strümpfe, die Tische, die Schafe*.

> 3.) 'Ordinary people' incorrectly say: *die Schattener, Staner, Bämer, Bäner, Gebäuer* [sic], *die Mauthen, Zünften, Kräften, die Mantel, Handel, mit den Handen*, instead of *die Schotten, die Steine, Bäume, Beine, Gebäude, Mäuthe, Zünfte, Kräfte, Mäntel, Händel, mit den Händen*.

Thus Felbiger stresses the importance of the compulsory ending *-e* in plural forms. It must not be ommitted or changed to *-er/-en* in the examples given above. Felbiger's third point in the quotation above reveals that he distinguishes between the varieties used by the upper and by the lower classes and links this distinction to 'correctness': the way lower class people speak is 'wrong', which implies that the language use of other, i.e. higher social classes is 'correct' or 'better'.

In summary, Felbiger prescribes the ending -*e* for feminine nouns, for strong masculine and neuter nouns in the dative case and for plural forms but the *e*-apocope for weak masculine and mixed-declension neuter nouns, establishing a clear difference between these latter and feminine nouns. In these prescriptions, Felbiger follows Popowitsch (1754a) to a large extent and even uses very similar lists of examples. As mentioned before, Popowitsch's *Anfangsgründe* (1754a) are, on the other hand, based on Gottsched's grammar (1748). While Rössler's (1997: 76) statement that Felbiger's *Anleitungen* "adopt Gottsched's instructions to a large extent" ("übernehmen weitgehend die Angaben des Leipziger Sprachreformers Gottsched") is, therefore, still legitimate, Popowitsch's influence on Felbiger should not be underestimated.

3.5.2 Felbiger on past participles

Felbiger (1775: 46) provides a general rule for the formation of regular past participles: he states that regular past participles begin with *ge-* and end in -*et*.

> Das Mittelwort selbst, welches sich auf *t* oderauf [sic] *n* endiget, kann man von der unbestimmten Art und zwar in den einfachen Zeitwörtern der 1ten Abwandlung so bilden, daß man im Ausgange des Wortes anstatt des *n* ein *t* ** von Anfang aber noch die Sylbe *ge* *** setzet, als: *loben, lobet, gelobet*, das *ge* bleibt in den fremden Wörtern aus, die auf *iren* ausgehen; als *kommandiren, konsekriren, dividiren*. (Felbiger 1775: 46)

> The past participle, which ends in *t* or in *n*, can be formed on the basis of the indefinite form [= infinitive], for regular verbs of the first verb class [i.e. regular verbs], by adding a *t* instead of an *n* at the end of the word ** but also by putting the syllable *ge* at the beginning ***, such as *loben, lobet, gelobet*; the *ge* is absent in loan words which end in *iren*, such as *kommandiren, konsekriren, dividiren*.

Felbiger bases the formation of regular past participles on the first person present tense (e.g. *ich lobe*), which is turned into a past participle by adding the prefix *ge-* and the ending -*t*, resulting in, for example, *gelobet*. Felbiger thus prescribes the prefix *ge-* and the ending -*et* explicitly. Furthermore, he mentions common mistakes in footnotes (indicated with asterixes in the quotation above). In the first footnote (**), Felbiger (1775: 46) stresses that it is wrong to say *geredt* and *gearbeit* instead of *geredet* and *gearbeitet*, i.e. it is a mistake to omit the -*e*- if the verb ends in a dental suffix. The omission of -*e*- in other past participles, e.g. *gekauft* instead of *gekaufet*, is, however, not mentioned. Either Felbiger did not consider the ending -*t* instead of -*et* to be a mistake in this case or he thought that using the ending -*et* would not pose any problems to students. Given that Felbiger (1775: Mustertabelle)[98] consistently uses the ending *-et* in his conjugation of the verb *lieben* (with the sole exception of *ich werde geliebt werden*)[99], the latter suggestion seems more plausible. In other words, Felbiger explicitly prescribes the ending *-et* for regular past participles while implicitly stigmatising the ending *-t* by generally not using it.[100]

By contrast, Felbiger stigmatises the omission of the prefix *ge-* in past participles explicitly in his second footnote (***):

> Das *ge* wird sehr oft unrichtig ausgelassen in folgenden und ander [sic] Sätzen; *er ist kommen, vorbeygangen, aufstan= ich habe gessen, trunken, brochen.* (Felbiger 1775: 46)

> The *ge* is often omitted incorrectly in the following and other sentences; *er ist kommen, vorbeygangen, aufstan= ich habe gessen, trunken, brochen.*

Felbiger's explicit stigmatisation of the omission of the prefix *ge-* as well as his consistent use of *ge-* in past participles make it clear that he, as his predecessors discussed above, prescribes the prefix. With regard to the ending of past participles, too, Felbiger follows Gottsched and prescribes the suffix *-et*.

3.5.3 Felbiger on alternative forms of *wir/sie sind*

In his conjugation table, Felbiger (1775: Mustertabelle)[101] conjugates the verb *to be* in the following way:

Ich bin   wir sind *
du bist   ihr seyd
er ist   sie sind

This conjugation is in line with Gottsched (1752) and Popowitsch (1754a). In the first person plural, Felbiger adds a footnote stating that the UG variants are incorrect:

> Man saget insgemein, aber fehlerhaft *sie seyn* oder *seynd*, so auch irrig in der verbindenden Art *sie seyen.* (Felbiger 1775: Mustertabelle)

---

98 This table of examples, in which the verbs *sein, werden, haben, lieben* as well as a number of irregular verbs are conjugated in every person, number and tense, is inserted between page 58 and 59 in Felbiger's *Spachlehre* (1775).
99 The use of the ending *-t* in this one particular construction could be considered as merely a mistake on the part of the author or the typesetter since all the other 46 forms are listed with *-et*.
100 All examples of regular past participles that Felbiger (1775: 40–55) provides in his section on verbs end in *-et* (e.g. *gelobet, gestrafet, belohnet, ausgeruhet, gefraget, angelanget, erlaubet, gelebet, gereiset, gelachet* etc.)
101 This table is inserted between page 58 and 59.

One says in private, but incorrectly *sie seyn* or *seynd*, and it is also wrong to say *sie seyen* in the subjunctive form.

Thus Felbiger, similar to Gottsched (1752) and Popowitsch (1754b), prescribes the ECG variants *wir/sie sind*, while dismissing the UG variants *wir/sie seyn/seynd* as incorrect.

3.6 Johann Christoph Adelung

Johann Christoph Adelung (1732–1806) was born in Pomerania, at the time part of Prussia, and spent his life in Prussia until 1758. He then moved from Halle, where he studied theology, to Erfurt, where he worked as a teacher until 1762 (Rössler 1997: 78). From 1765 to 1787, Adelung worked in Leipzig, Saxony, during which time he published his monumental dictionary, the *Versuch eines vollständigen grammatisch-kritischen Wörterbuches der Hochdeutschen Mundart mit beständiger Vergleichung der übrigen Mundarten, besonders aber der oberdeutschen*[102] (5 volumes, published 1774–1786) as well as his grammar, the *Deutsche Sprachlehre: Zum Gebrauche der Schulen in den Königl. Preuß. Landen*[103] (1781) with additional comments in his *Umständliches Lehrgebäude der Deutschen Sprache, zur Erläuterung der Deutschen Sprachlehre für Schulen*[104] (1782). Rössler (1997: 86f.) refers to Adelung's *Deutsche Sprachlehre* (1781), together with his *Umständliches Lehrgebäude der Deutschen Sprache* (1782), as *the* standard grammar in the late 18th century. After the publication of Adelung's grammars, Gottsched's *Grundlegung* was no longer reprinted. Since Adelung summarised all previous linguistic insights and suggestions for language norms, his predecessors became obsolete (Rössler 1997: 87). As a result, Rössler (ibid.) argues that Adelung's grammars mark the end of the period of linguistic reform, in which Austria's written language was adjusted to the ECG ideal.[105]

However, Adelung (1781) himself believed that his grammar was unique as he tried to find the essence of the German language within itself, rather than just copying Latin grammars and make them fit to the German language – a technique employed by Antesperg, Gottsched and Popowitsch.[106]

---

102 English translation: *Attempt at a complete grammar-critical dictionary of the High German variety with consistent comparisons with the other varieties, in particular the Upper German varieties.*
103 English translation: *German grammar: for school use in the Kingdom of Prussia.*
104 English translation: *Detailed teaching guide of the German language, commenting on the German grammar for schools.*
105 The last grammar written in this period was, however, Felbiger's *Deutsche Sprachlehre*, which was published anonymously in 1794 (Rössler 1997: 88).
106 See, for example, their adoption of the Latin 6-case-system for the four cases in German.

Ich habe mich bemühet, das Wesen der Deutschen Sprache in ihr selbst aufzusuchen, und daraus ist denn auch die Einrichtung der gegenwärtigen Sprachlehre entstanden, dagegen andere immer noch Copien der Lateinischen sind. (Adelung 1781: Vorrede)

I have tried to find the essence of the German language within itself, and from it the arrangement of this grammar was developed, while others are still copies of the Latin grammar.

The aim of Adelung's grammar was to raise language awareness and to act as a kind of guide for young language enthusiasts to provide them with more clarity about the foundation of German.

Wird indessen gegenwärtiger Versuch nur dazu dienen, den jungen Liebhaber der Sprache auf ihre bisher so sehr verkannten Gründe aufmerksam zu machen, ihm ein wohlthätiges Licht über Gegenstände, welche bisher mit einer undurchdringlichen Finsterniß umgeben waren, wo nicht anzuzünden, doch wenigstens vorzubereiten, und ihm den Pfad auch nur von weitem zu zeigen, welcher ihn mit gewissen und sichern Schritten durch das so sehr verwilderte Sprachgebieth leiten kann [...]. (Adelung 1781: Widmung: 4f.)

This attempt will, by contrast, only serve to point the young language enthusiast to the hitherto so misjudged bases of language, to at least prepare, if not shed, a beneficial light on the matters which were surrounded by an impervious darkness until now, and to show him, if only from a distance, the path which can lead him with certain and confident steps through this ever so feral language area [...].

The importance of language awareness is a recurring theme in the language discourse of the 18th century. As mentioned above, Antesperg lamented the lack of language awareness and linked it to the level of intelligence of a people. In other words, language is linked to thoughts – an idea that is also apparent in Adelung's *Mithridates* (published in four volumes from 1806–1817), in which he compares the Lord's Prayer in hundreds of language varieties. As Gardt (1999: 187) points out, Adelung believed that only 'developed languages' enabled the expression of complex thoughts. Adelung regarded High German a 'developed language', which he intended to describe, rather than prescribe in his grammar, in contrast to Gottsched. Adelung (1781) stresses that language rules should not be set arbitrarily. They have to be proven by examples and are always subject to change in a living language.

Es folget [...]: 1. daß die Sprachregeln [...] nicht willkührlich gemacht werden müssen. 2. Das sie bloß wahrscheinlich sind, und [...] durch Beyspiele erwiesen werden müssen; und 3. daß sie in einer lebendigen Sprache nicht unveränderlich sind, sondern ihr in allen ihren Veränderungen folgen müssen. (Adelung 1781: 22, § 42)

It follows [...]: 1. that the language rules [...] must not be set arbitrarily. 2. That they are merely presumed and [...] have to be proven through examples; and 3. that they are not unchangeable in a living language but have to follow the language in all its changes.

In that way, the task of a grammarian is not to set laws and norms but to help the language users to abide by their own language rules, according to Adelung:

> Hieraus fließen zugleich die Pflichten und Befugnisse des Sprachlehrers. Er ist nicht der Gesetzgeber der Nation, sondern nur ihr Sprecher und Dolmetscher. Er dringet ihr keine Vorschriften auf, sondern sammelt nur die von ihr von Zeit zu Zeit gemachten und in dem Herkommen aufbehaltenen Gesetze, spüret ihren Gründen und Gränzen nach, bemerkt die Fälle, wo sie sich widersprechen oder zu widersprechen scheinen, zeigt der Nation, wo sie aus Übereilung, aus Mangel der Aufmerksamkeit oder aus Unkunde wider Willen ihre eignen Gesetze übertreten, und überläßt endlich alles der Entscheidung der meisten und weisesten Stimmen. (Adelung 1781: 22f., § 43)

> From this [§ 42 above], the responsibilities and authorisations of a grammarian emerge. He is not setting laws for the nation, but is merely its speaker and interpreter. He does not impose any prescriptions on the nation, but simply collects the laws that are periodically passed or changed by the nation and the ones that have remained the same, he traces their rationale and limits, notices the cases in which they contradict or seem to contradict one another, shows the nation where it violates its own laws against its will due to lack of attention or awareness, and he finally leaves everything to the decision of the most and wisest voices.

While the quotations above depict Adelung as a descriptive, non-judgmental grammarian, he does favour a particular variety, the written language called High German. Adelung describes High German as one of the daughters of Upper German, softened by the Upper Saxon dialect, and having incorporated just as many Low German elements as was necessary to plane the UG roughness.

> Die unter dem Nahmen des Hochdeutschen bekannte jüngere Schriftsprache ist eine Tochter des Oberdeutschen, doch mehr der nördlichen als der südlichen Provinzen. Es ist die durch den Obersächsischen Dialect gemilderte und durch Geschmack, Künste und Wissenschaften ausgebildete und verfeinerte Oberdeutsche Mundart. Sie hat nebst ihren ältern Schwestern, den Fränkischen, Thüringischen und Obersächsischen Dialecten von der weichen, schlüpfrigen und kurzen Sprache des Niederdeutschen nur gerade so viel angenommen, als zur Milderung der rauhen und schwülstigen Oberdeutschen nöthig war, und ist seit der Reformation nicht allein die Büchersprache aller Schriftsteller von Geschmack, sondern auch die Hofsprache des gesittetern und verfeinerten Umganges geworden. (Adelung 1781: 18, § 32)

> The younger literary language known as High German is a daughter of Upper German, but more of the northern than the southern provinces. It is the Upper German variety, softened by the Upper Saxon dialect, cultivated and refined by taste, the arts and sciences. It has, besides its older sisters the Franconian, Thuringian and Upper Saxon dialects, adopted only as much from the soft, slithery, and short language of Low German as was necessary to soften the rough and pompous Upper German, and is not only the language of books of every author with good taste since the reformation but also the language of the court of the well-mannered and refined interaction.

This quotation illustrates Adelung's language perceptions: While High German is the best variety, Low and Upper German are inferior in some, rather ambiguous ways (*soft, rough* etc.). He continues to describe this High German variety as *pure, good and beautiful German*, in contrast to 'dialects'.

> Sie wird daher auch gemeiniglich vorzugsweise gemeinet, wenn man von der Deutschen Sprache überhaupt, von dem was rein Deutsch, gut Deutsch, schön Deutsch u. s. f. ist, spricht, in welchem Falle sie als die herrschende allgemeine Sprache den Mundarten der Provinzen entgegen gesetzt wird. (Adelung 1781: 18f., § 33)

> It is, therefore, this High German language which is commonly and primarily meant, if one talks about the German language per se, of that which is pure German, good German, beautiful German etc., in which case it, as the ruling common language, is contrasted to the dialects of the provinces.

Adelung, in contrast to Gottsched, does not explicitly equate High German with the Upper Saxon variety. Indeed, Adelung (1782: 84f.) stresses that 'Upper Saxon' cannot be used as a synonym for 'High German'. Instead, High German is depicted as a superordinate ideal language, which is not identical to any regional variety (Adelung 1782: 72ff.). However, since this ideal language cannot be constructed from all existing varieties, it is dependent on historical-pragmatic circumstances, such as economic prosperity, thriving arts and sciences, as well as fine tastes and manners (Gardt 1999: 188f.). Consequently, High German is implicitly linked to geographical areas where these circumstances are given (ibid.), i.e. Upper Saxony. Indeed, Adelung (1782: 82) highlights the prestige of the Upper Saxon variety, which arose from thriving arts and sophisticated tastes. Faulstich (2008: 155), too, points out that Adelung relates High German to the Upper Saxon variety.

In order to establish the norms of this High German language, Adelung devised a hierarchical line, which will lead to the 'correct' linguistic forms:

> Die gesetzgebenden Theile einer Sprache stehen demnach in folgender Ordnung unter einander: 1. der Sprachgebrauch, als die höchste und unumschränkteste Macht. Was diese nicht bestimmt, entscheidet 2. die Sprachähnlichkeit oder Analogie. Wenn auch diese schweigt, so nimmt 3. die Abstammung oder Etymologie das Wort, und wenn in einem Falle alle diese nichts entscheiden, so gebühret 4. dem Wohlklange eine Stimme. (Adelung 1781: 22, § 41)

> The law-giving parts of a language are placed in the following order below each other: 1. the language use, as the highest and almightiest power. Whatever language use does not determine is decided by 2. the language similarity or analogy. If this also remains silent, 3. the derivation or etymology has its say, and should none of these be sufficient in determining a rule 4. the agreeable sound has its say.

The fact that Adelung does not refer to the language use of the general public but primarily to the language use of the best authors becomes clear in the following quotation.

> In einer durch Schrift und Geschmack ausgebildeten Sprache, dergleichen die Hochdeutsche ist, bestehet dieser Gebrauch in der herrschenden und übereinstimmigen Gewohnheit des besten und weisesten Theiles der Nation, besonders der besten und weisesten Schriftsteller. (Adelung 1781: 21, § 40)

> In a language developed through writing and taste, such as High German, this use consists of the prevailing and congruent habits of the best and wisest parts of the nation, especially of the best and wisest authors.

Similarly to Gottsched, Adelung bases his language norms, which have largely been carried over from previous grammars, on written language and in particular, the language of professional writers. The following, closer analysis will show to what extent Adelung's prescriptions differ from previous grammars.

3.6.1 Adelung on *e*-apocope in nouns

In his chapter on word formation, Adelung (1781: 100–115) lists a number of words in alphabetical order of their endings. The ending -*d* and/or -*de* is, as Adelung (1781: 103) explains, primarily used to form abstract nouns but it can also be used for concrete nouns, such as *Herde*, *Behörde* and *Gemählde*. Words ending in -*e* are, according to Adelung (1781: 103), concrete things in the feminine grammatical gender, e.g. *Leuchte, Schere, Ähre, Änte, Bahre, Beere, Base, Asche, Äsche, Biene, Platte, Eiche, Eule*. There are, however, also many abstract nouns ending in -*de* and -*e*, such as *Freude, Zierde, Sünde, Gnade, Bürde, Würde, Begierde, Güte, Liebe* etc. (Adelung 1781: 110). A further group of nouns that is specifically listed by Adelung (1781: 108) is collective nouns formed with the prefix *ge*-, such as *Getreide, Gebirge, Gesinde* and *Gehäuse*.[107] These lists give a first insight into Adelung's preference for the ECG variants with the ending -*e*, instead of the UG forms without final -*e*. Adelung (1781: 138–160) further divides German nouns into eight classes of declension and provides endings for all cases in the singular and plural:

Tab. 6: Adelung's eight classes of declension for German nouns (1781: 138–160)

	1st decl.	2nd decl.	3rd decl.	4th decl.	5th decl.	6th decl.	7th decl.	8th decl.
sg.								
nom.	-	-	-	-	-	-	-	-
gen.	es, s	es, s	s	en, n	ens	es, s	-	-

---

107 Adding an -*e* to *Gehölz, Geblüt, Gewölk* and *Geripp* is, however, described as *fehlerhaft*, i.e. a mistake (Adelung 1781: 108).

	1st decl.	2nd decl.	3rd decl.	4th decl.	5th decl.	6th decl.	7th decl.	8th decl.
dat.	e	e	-	en, n	en	e/-	-	-
acc.	-	-	-	en, n	en	-	-	-
pl.								
nom.	e	er	-	en, n	en	en, n	en, n	e
gen.	e	er	-	en, n	en	en, n	en, n	e
dat.	en	ern	n	en, n	en	en, n	en, n	en
acc.	e	er	-	en, n	en	en, n	en, n	e
e.g.								
	Tag	Wort	Vater	Zeuge	Schmerz	Bett/ Auge	Pfarre	Hand

The table above illustrates that Adelung prescribes the ending *-e* for strong masculine and neuter nouns in the dative singular form (see 1st, 2nd and 6th declension).
While admitting that there are only a few general rules with regard to the declension
of German nouns, Adelung lists four universal rules that apply to all (or most[108])
nouns, among which is rule number 3:

> Alle Wörter, welche im Genitiv *es* haben, müssen im Dativ *e* bekommen; welche aber nur *s*
> allein haben, lassen den Dativ unbezeichnet. (Adelung 1781: 138)

> All words which have the ending *es* in the genitive case, must be given the ending *e* in the da-
> tive; the words which only end in *s*, stay unmarked in the dative.

More generally it can be said that nouns ending in *-e* in the nominative case are not
given another *-e* in the dative case (see, for example, *Auge* in the 6th declension).
With regard to the 1st declension, Adelung (1781: 138f., § 178f.) further specifies the
following:

> Das *e* ist in dieser Declination ein charakteristischer Biegungslaut, daher es auch in eigentlich
> Deutschen Wörtern im Genitiv und Dativ nie verbissen werden sollte, ob es gleich im
> gesellschaftlichen Umgange häufig geschiehet, *Baums, Arms* [...] für die richtigern *Baumes,
> Armes* [...].

> Wo das *e* im Genitiv nicht verbissen werden darf, da darf es im Dativ noch weniger wegfallen,
> *Baume, Arme, zu seinem Wohle, an diesem Abende*. Die es aber im Genitiv nicht leiden, dulden
> es auch im Dativ nicht, *dem Gehorsam, Athem, Brodem, Bräutigam*. (Adelung 1781: 138f., §
> 178f.)

---

108 Adelung's (1781: 138) second rule states that all feminine nouns stay unchanged in their singular forms but that there are a few exceptions, which will be discussed later in his grammar.

The *e* is a characteristic inflection ending in this declination, therefore it should never be suppressed in actual German words in the genitive and dative, even if this frequently happens in social interaction, *Baums, Arms* [...] for the more correct *Baumes, Armes* [...].

In those instances where the *e* must not be suppressed in the genitive, its omission is even less acceptable in the dative, *Baume, Arme, zu seinem Wohle, an diesem Abende*. Where the *e* is rejected in the genitive, however, it is similarly discarded in the dative, *dem Gehorsam, Athem, Brodem, Bräutigam*.

Thus Adelung stigmatises common language use and explicitly prescribes the dative *-e*. Furthermore, the examples given in the table above for weak masculine nouns and feminine nouns (*Zeuge, Pfarre*) end in *-e*. With regard to the former example and the 4th declension more generally, Adelung (1781: 151, § 197) states the following:

Nach dieser Form gehen: 1. Männliche Wörter mit dem Hochdeutschen mildernden *e* am Ende, welche daher in der ganzen Declination nur ein *n* annehmen dürfen: *Affe*, [...] *Bube*, [...] *Bürge*, [...] *Erbe* [...] *Hase, Hirte* **(oder nur *Hirt*)**, *Knabe*, [...] *Zeuge* [...]. Ausgenommen ist hiervon nur *Bursche*, welches im Plural gemeiniglich *Bursche* für *Burschen* hat.

Dahin auch viele Volkesnahmen, welche sich nicht auf *er* endigen, und im Hochdeutschen das mildernde *e* erfordern: *Böhme, Britte, Däne, Finne, Franke, Franzose, Grieche, Hesse, Jude, Irre, Lette, Pohle, Portugiese, Preusse, Russe, Sachse, Schotte, Schwabe, Schwede, Slave, Türke, Wende.* (Adelung 1781: 151, § 197, my emphasis)

This pattern is followed by: 1. Masculine words with a High German softening *e* at the end, which, therefore, can only take an *n* in the whole declination: *Affe* [...] *Bube*, [...] *Bürge*, [...] *Erbe* [...] *Hase, Hirte* **(or just *Hirt*)**, *Knabe*, [...] *Zeuge* [...]. The only exception is *Bursche*, which commonly has *Bursche* for *Burschen* as the plural form.

Also many names of peoples, which do not end in *er*, require the softening *e* in High German: *Böhme, Britte, Däne, Finne, Franke, Franzose, Grieche, Hesse, Jude, Irre, Lette, Pohle, Portugiese, Preusse, Russe, Sachse, Schotte, Schwabe, Schwede, Slave, Türke, Wende.*

In contrast to Gottsched, Adelung thus prescribes the use of the ending *-e* for weak masculine nouns, with one exception: The ending *-e* is not compulsory for the German word for shepherd (*Hirte* or just *Hirt*). The ending *-e* is also prescribed for the names of various peoples, with the following exceptions:

[...] Volkesnahmen, deren letzte Sylbe betont ist, und welche das mildernde *e* noch nicht angenommen haben, *Bosniak, Heidamak, Polak*, (besser *Pohle*,) *Kalmuck, Israelit, Kroat*, [...]. (Adelung 1781: 152)

[...] names of peoples with a stressed last syllable, which have not taken on the softening *e* yet, [such as] *Bosniak, Heidamak, Polak*, (better *Pohle*,) *Kalmuck, Israelit, Kroat*, [...].

Adelung's phrasing reveals that the compulsory *-e* is a new rule which is spreading but it has not yet made it into all weak masculine nouns. Indeed, Gottsched stressed that the ending *-e* was unnecessary in these cases (see section 3.3.1).

According to Adelung (1781: 153), the fifth declension arose from the third and fourth declension. It can be seen as a modified version of the fourth declension since it is weak masculine nouns that are inflected according to this pattern, such as *Friede, Glaube, Hirte, Knabe* etc., all of which can also be counted in the third (with an added *-n*: *Frieden, Glauben*) or fourth declension (*Hirte, Knabe*) (ibid.). Furthermore, Adelung (1781: 154) mentions that the noun *Buchstab*, which is considered a compound form (*Buch* plus *Stab*) without the ending *-e*, fits into the fifth as well as the third declension.

The examples for the sixth and seventh declension further reveal that Adelung (1781: 155, 157f.) prescribed the ending *-e* for mixed-declension neuter nouns as well as for feminine nouns in their nominative forms: *das Auge, das Ende, die Ameise, Pfarre, Sache, Schule* etc. Furthermore, the ending *-e* is also compulsory in the plural forms of nouns that belong to the first and eighth declension, e.g. *Tage, Hände*, while zero plural endings can only occur in the plural forms of strong masculine nouns (see table above). On the other hand, the omission of *-e*, especially in feminine nouns and nouns in plural, leads to a variety sounding 'hard', according to Adelung (1782: 74).

In summary, Adelung prescribes the ending *-e* for feminine nouns as well as for weak masculine and mixed-declension neuter nouns in the nominative case. Furthermore, the ending *-e* is compulsory to mark the dative singular and plural forms.

3.6.2 Adelung on past participles

Similar to Popowitsch, Adelung uses the ECG ending *-et* as well as the UG ending *-t* in his examples of regular verbs in the perfect tense. After explaining the formation of the perfect tense with the verbs *haben* and *sein*, Adelung (1781: 272) gives the following examples: *ich habe gelobt, ich bin gereiset*, i.e. one example with the ending *-t* and another with the ending *-et*. Adelung's conjugation of the verb *loben* reveals that he prefers the ending *-t* for regular past participles in active indicative forms while prescribing the ending *-et* for active subjunctive as well as all passive and infinitive forms:

	I. Das Activum. [active]	
	1. Indicativ.	2. Conjunct. [subjunctive]
Perfect.	Ich habe gelobt.	Ich habe gelobet.
Plusq.	Ich hatte gelobt.	Ich hätte gelobet.
Fut. exact.	Ich werde gelobet haben.	Ich werde gelobet haben.

II. Das Passivum. [passive]

	1. Indicat.	2. Conjunct. [subjunctive]
Präs. [pres.]	Ich werde gelobet.	Ich werde gelobet.
Imperf.	Ich ward, (wurde) gelobet.	Ich würde gelobet.
Perf.	Ich bin gelobet worden.	Ich sey gelobet worden.
Plusq.	Ich war gelobet worden.	Ich wäre gelobet worden.
Fut. absol.	Ich werde gelobet werden.	Ich werde gelobet werden.
exac.	Ich werde gelobet worden seyn.	Ich werde gelobet worden seyn.

3. Infinitiv.

Präs. [pres.]	Gelobet werden.
Perf.	Gelobet worden seyn.
Fut.	Werden gelobet werden. (Adelung 1781: 280f.)

Below this paradigm, Adelung states the following:

> Der Wohlklang muß entscheiden, wo die Zusammenziehung in den Endsylben statt findet oder nicht; die Sprache des gesellschaftlichen Umganges ziehet gern zusammen, wenn es ohne Härte geschehen kann, die feyerliche Sprache nicht so gern. Im Conjunctiv vermeidet man um der Deutlichkeit willen lieber die Zusammenziehung. Die Verba auf *eln* und *ern*, werfen, wenn es seyn kann, lieber das letzte *e* weg als das erste: *ich sammele, du sammlest*, nicht *sammlest, er sammlt, ich sammlete, gesammlet*; *dauern, dauere, du dauerst, er dauert, dauerte, gedauert.* (Adelung 1781: 281f., § 418)

> Whether or not the sound is agreeable determines if the contraction of the final syllables takes place or not; the language of social interaction likes to contract them, if it can happen without harshness, the ceremonial language does not like to contract as much. In the subjunctive one prefers to avoid the contraction due to clarity. Verbs ending in *eln* and *ern* prefer to throw away the last rather than the first *e*, if possible: *ich sammele, du sammelst*, not *sammlest, er sammelt, ich sammelte, gesammelt*; *dauern, dauere, du dauerst, er dauert, dauerte, gedauert.*

Adelung does not give a strict rule for the use of both variants. However, as discussed above, he does prefer the use of *-et* in the subjunctive. Furthermore, the context dictates which ending is used: while *-et* is the preferred variant in higher register, the ending *-t* is used in everyday speech.

Adelung does not mention the formation of past participles without the prefix *ge-*. It seems that the ECG form with *ge-* had suppressed its UG equivalent to such an extent that it did not strike Adelung as worth mentioning. A similar observation can be made when looking at the forms of *to be* below.

3.6.3 Adelung on alternative forms of *wir/sie sind*

Adelung (1781: 277) only lists the ECG forms of the verb 'to be' in the first and third person singular present indicative:

Ich bin.	Wir sind.
Du bist.	Ihr seyd.
Er ist.	Sie sind.

Thus Adelung follows the ECG norm prescribed by Gottsched and other grammarians before him. In contrast to Gottsched, Popowitsch, and Felbiger, Adelung does not denote the UG variants as explicitly wrong but, instead, does not mention them at all, thus rendering them invisible in his grammar. Rössler (1997: 303) believes that, by the time Adelung wrote his grammar, the UG variants *wir/sie seynd* had been suppressed from standard language usage to such an extent that this violation of the ECG rules did not even seem worth mentioning.

3.7 Further prescriptive texts

The grammars discussed above are only a selection of prescriptive texts. Others were, of course, published, such as the grammars by Carl Friedrich Aichinger (1717–1782), Friedrich Wilhelm Gerlach (1728–1802), and Franz Joseph Bob (1733–1802). Many of them, however, followed the norms established in previous grammars and their influence on the formation of standard German in Austria was, therefore, limited.[109] Generally, it can be assumed that the norm prescriptions which were intended for use in primary and secondary schools were more influential since they addressed a wider readership. Before discussing two prescriptive works intended for schools in sections 3.7.2 and 3.7.3, an essay on what were considered mistakes in the Upper German dialect is summarised below.

3.7.1 *Abhandlung* (1772)

The *Abhandlung von den Hauptfehlern der österreichischen Mundart* (*Essay on the main mistakes of the Austrian 'dialect'*) (1772) by Paul Graf Amor von Soria was published by his teachers Joseph Burkard and Michael Denis in a collection of student essays entitled *Jugendfrüchte des k. k. Theresianums* (Wiesinger 2008: 282f.). It lists, as its title suggests, Austrian German variants that were considered mistakes, some of which were later also mentioned by Joseph von Sonnenfels in his writing guide *Über den Geschäftsstil* (1784) (ibid.). Soria (1772) considers the following constructions and features 'mistakes':

---

109 Cf. Rössler's introductory chapters on Aichinger (1997: 51–61), Gerlach (1997: 61–65) and Bob (1997: 65–69).

1. auxiliary *tun*, e.g. *Wann thut die Frau in die Kirche gehen?*
2. using *derer* and *denen* instead of *der* and *den*, e.g. *Verzeichnis derer Jahrmärkte; Abhandlung von denen Tugenden und Lastern.*
3. using *vor* for *für* and vice versa, e.g. *Bitte vor uns; Fürhang.*
4. using *wann* for *wenn* and vice versa
5. conjugating irregular verbs according to the paradigm for regular verbs in the preterite, e.g. *Wenn Sie auf die Nacht nicht so viel esseten, so schlafeten Sie besser.*
6. using strong inflected adjectives after definite articles in plural noun phrases, e.g. *die dicke Folianten; die gelehrte Winde.*
7. using *-ist* or *-ister* instead of *-ste, -ster* or *-ester* in superlative forms, e.g. *der Herr Obrist, verbundnister Diener.*
8. ellipsis of first person pronouns, e.g. *Bitte mich entschuldiget zu halten, kann morgen nicht kommen.*
9. using *Ihnen* instead of *Sie* in the accusative case, e.g. *Ich kenne Ihnen schon. Darf ich Ihnen morgen heimsuchen?*
10. extensive use of the perfect tense, e.g. *Er hat es aus der Tasche genommen, hat es allen gezeiget, und alle haben es bewundert.* instead of *Er nahm es aus der Tasche, zeigte es allen, und alle bewunderten es.*
11. 'incorrect' pronunciation, esp. pronouncing the *a* in too low a tone (*in einem zu tiefen Tone*), not distinguishing *ö* from *e* and *ü* from *i*, e.g. *heren* instead of *hören*, *Ibel* for *Übel*; suppressing the *e* in final syllables, e.g. *laufn* for *laufen*, *Himml* for *Himmel*; using the diphthong *ue* instead of *u*, e.g. *Muetter* for *Mutter*, *Huet* for *Hut*.

Most of these 'mistakes' were and are, however, not restricted to Austria or even the Upper German language area. Auxiliary *tun* had been stigmatised since the 16th century, in the northern as well as the southern German areas (cf. Langer 2001), which implies that it was also commonly used there. Similarly, *vor* and *für* as well as *wann* and *wenn* were used interchangeably in large parts of the German-speaking area in the 18th century. Soria himself admits that other provinces make mistakes but that this should not be an excuse to use language incorrectly.

> Alle diese von mir angeführten inländischen Fehler müßen Niemanden verleiten zu glauben, als ob ich der Meynung wäre, daß andere Provinzen nicht eben so wohl wider die Grammatik, Wortsetzung, und Aussprache verstießen. Aber seine eigenen Fehler durch fremde schützen wollen, habe ich noch immer für die schwächste Art sich zu vertheidigen gehalten. (Soria 1772: 235f.)

> All the regional mistakes I have listed here should not lead to the assumption that I was of the opinion that other provinces would not violate the rules of grammar, word order, and pronunciation. But I believe that protecting one's own mistakes through foreign ones is still the weakest sort of defence.

In Soria's view, the only way to combat these mistakes is the introduction of a language policy 'from above' coupled with the establishment of a language academy:

> Ueberhaupts scheint mir kein Mittel hinlänglich diesem Uebel [Aenderungen und Abweichungen im Sprachgebrauch] zu steuern, als ein fürstlicher Befehl, und die Errichtung einer Sprachakademie. (Soria 1772: 228)

> Generally, no means seem to suffice in order to control this evil [changes and deviations in language use] except for a governmental order and the establishment of a language academy.

While a language academy was never founded, Maria Theresa herself advocated the use of 'proper' German. Her school reform may have played a significant role in disseminating what were considered 'proper' German norms. The following sections discuss two prescriptive works intended for school use.

3.7.2 *Anweisung* (1794)

As stated in its preface, the anonymous *Anweisung die deutsche Sprache richtig zu sprechen, zu lesen und zu schreiben* (*Instruction on speaking, reading and writing the German language correctly*) (1794) replaced Felbiger's *Anleitung zur deutschen Rechtschreibung* in elementary schools (so-called '*Trivialschulen*'[110]) and was intended as a teachers' rather than a students' book. With regard to spelling, it closely follows, as is stated in the preface, Adelung's norm prescriptions: "Im 4. Hauptstücke wird die Rechtschreibung nach Adelungischen Grundsätzen gelehrt." ("In the 4th part, the spelling is taught according to Adelung's conventions") (*Anweisung* 1794: preface [p. 3]). Indeed, it is difficult to find any deviations from Adelung's *Deutsche Sprachlehre* for Prussian schools in the whole book. With regard to the UG features discussed here, it is, therefore, not surprising that the ECG ending -*e* is prescribed for strong masculine and neuter nouns in the dative singular (e.g. *dem Baume, dem Sohne, dem Hunde, dem Tage, dem Thiere, dem Manne*) and for plural forms (e.g. *Thiere, Künste*) (ibid. 34–39). The declination of the noun *Auge* further reveals that the ending -*e* is compulsory for this weak neuter noun. With regard to feminine nouns, however, the noun *Thür* is inflected, which is, to this day, codified in both variants, i.e. *Türe* and *Tür*. Nevertheless, it cannot be argued that the *Anweisung* prescribes the *e*-apocope for feminine nouns since the few examples given below the paradigm of the seventh declination end in -*e*: *Achse, Ameise, Aehre* (ibid. 39).[111]

Similarly, the verb *to be* is conjugated in exactly the same way as in Adelung's grammar, thus prescribing the ECG forms *wir/sie sind*. With regard to regular past participles, the *Anweisung* (1794: 69f.) lists examples with both endings next to each other for the perfect (*ich habe gelobet, gelobt*) and the pluperfect (*ich hatte gelobet, gelobt*) in the active as well as for present tense in the passive (*ich werde gelobet,*

---

110 See chapter 2 for more details on this type of schools.

111 In fact, the variant *Thüre* was the plural form of *Thür* but was used as a singular form in MHG (Grimm & Grimm 1854–1961: Vol. 21, col. 458). It seems that this singular versus plural distinction was taken into account in the *Anweisung*, with *Thür* being provided as an example for a feminine noun in the singular. For other feminine nouns, the ending -*e* is prescribed.

gelobt). While stressing that the *-e* in the final syllable is compulsory in the subjunctive forms, as prescribed by Adelung, both variants are listed as examples for the present singular subjunctive (ibid. 70f.). While variation seems to be the norm as regards past participle endings, the prefix *ge-* is always given, in regular as well as irregular past participles, and, therefore, implicitly prescribed.

3.7.3 *Deutsche Sprachlehre* (1798)

The anonymous *Deutsche Sprachlehre* is a more extensive version of the *Anweisung* (1794) and was intended for *Normal-* and *Hauptschulen* (*zum Gebrauche der deutschen Normal- und Hauptschulen in den k. k. Staaten*). Its title suggests a close connection to Adelung's grammar and its differences to the *Anweisung* (1794) are limited to examples and more detailed explanations, with many identical sections. The prescriptions discussed above also apply to the *Deutsche Sprachlehre* (1798). The introduction to this textbook is of interest, owing to the number of language ideologies it reveals. While different varieties are acknowledged, there is a variety that is 'better' than the others, namely High German:

> Die deutsche Sprache ist nicht in allen Provinzen des deutschen Reiches ganz dieselbe. Jede Provinz hat ihre besondere Mundart. Vorzüglich unterscheidet sich die oberdeutsche und niederdeutsche Mundart. Das oberdeutsche gemeine Volk spricht *Mueter, Voder, bischt*, anstatt *Mutter, Vater, bist*; und der Niederdeutsche spricht *Biwel, Kleeder*, anstatt *Bibel, Kleider*.

> So verschieden auch die deutschen Mundarten sind, so gibt es doch in Deutschland eine gewisse Art zu reden, die überall verständlich, und unter gelehrten und andern Leuten von guter Erziehung üblich ist. Mann nennet diese auserlesene Mundart Hochdeutsch, Schriftdeutsch, Büchersprache. (*Sprachlehre* 1798: 7f., § 3f.)

> The German language is not completely the same in all provinces of the German Empire. Each province has a special dialect. Primarily, the Upper German can be distinguished from the Low German dialect. The Upper German common folk say *Mueter, Voder, bischt*, instead of *Mutter, Vater, bist*; and the Low German says *Biwel, Kleeder*, instead of *Bibel, Kleider*.

> As different as the German dialects may be, there is a certain way of talking in Germany, which is mutually intelligible everywhere and which is common among learned and other people with good education. This selected variety is called High German, written German, the literary language.

High German is connected to good education and comprehensibility. Furthermore, as discussed in chapter 2, the correct use of one's mother tongue shows one's ability to think clearly.

> Ein geborner Deutscher muß sich befleißigen, seine Muttersprache richtig zu reden und zu schreiben. Denn es ist meisten Theils ein sicheres Zeichen, daß derjenige nicht klar und

deutlich denket, welcher sich nicht klar und deutlich in seiner Muttersprache auszudrucken weiß. (*Sprachlehre* 1798: 8, § 5)

A German must strive to speak and write his mother tongue correctly. Because it is usually a reliable sign that one who does not think clearly and coherently, cannot express himself clearly and coherently in his mother tongue.

The language ideology of one 'correct' way of speaking, with anything deviating from it being considered a mistake, prevails in 18th-century grammars intended for school use. The following chapter investigates if these ideologies, the norm prescriptions by 18th-century grammarians, and the introduction of the school policy in 1774 had an observable effect on the language use in Austrian writing.

4 The implementation of the language reform

The previous chapter illustrated how 18th-century grammarians implicitly or explicitly prescribed certain variants (see table below for a summary of these prescriptions). A central question in the field of historical sociolinguistics is to what extent such prescriptions, and more generally, language policies 'from above' can influence linguistic behaviour. In order to assess the impact of linguistic prescriptions on 18th- and early 19th-century language use in Austria, the variables discussed above and summarised in the table below will be analysed in the following three corpora: reading primers, newspaper issues, and petitionary letters. A comparison between these corpora will show if the language use differed between these types of texts. Before discussing the results of these analyses, the corpora will be described in the following section.

Tab. 7: Summary of prescribed variants by 18th-century grammarians

	Antesperg (1747) (2nd ed. 1749)	Gottsched (1748) (5th ed. 1762)	Popowitsch (1754)	Felbiger (1775) (2nd ed. 1779)	Adelung (1781)
e-apocope:					
fem. sg.	acceptable	not acceptable	not acceptable	not acceptable	not acceptable
masc./neutr. dat.	acceptable	not acceptable	not acceptable	not acceptable	not acceptable
pl.	not acceptable	not acceptable	not acceptable	not acceptable	not acceptable
past participles:					
prefix *ge-*	compulsory (though exceptions)	compulsory	compulsory	compulsory	compulsory
ending *-t/-et*	both acceptable	ending *-et*	both acceptable (ending *-t* for passive formed with *sein*)	ending *-et*	ending *-t* in active ind., ending *-et* in active subj., inf., and passive & for higher register
verb *to be*:					
wir/sie seyn(d/t)	acceptable	not acceptable	not acceptable	not acceptable	not mentioned
wir/sie sind	acceptable	compulsory	compulsory	compulsory	compulsory

DOI 10.1515/9783110547047-004

4.1 The selection and characteristics of the corpus texts

To address variation according to text type, it is important that the analysis is based on a broad range of texts. For this reason, three corpora of language use, all spanning a time period of about 90 years (from 1744 to 1834) were compiled; namely, reading primers, newspaper issues, and petitionary letters. These three corpora represent different usages of language and views on language.

4.1.1 Reading primers

The first corpus contains reading primers[112], i.e. books designed to teach reading. Mauthe (2008: 178) states that the oldest German reading primer is the *Modus legendi*, handwritten by Christoph Hueber, a schoolmaster from Landshut (Bavaria), in 1477 (Mauthe 2008: 178, Voeste 2008: 55). According to Brüggemann (1975: 1), the first German reading primers instructing people how to read and containing religious indoctrination appeared in the first half of the 16th century. Furthermore, reading primers in Latin were used in German-speaking areas, such as the reading primer written for Maximilian I from around 1466, which is Austria's oldest preserved reading primer.[113] In the first half of the 18th century, when the early and systematic teaching of children became more important, pedagogy and theology were still closely connected (Wild 1990: 51f.). This connection remained intact in the second half of the 18th century[114] but the focus shifted to the promotion of independent thinking and reasoning (ibid. 66). Indeed, many of the reading primers compiled for this corpus contain moral slogans and stories that are designed to teach children how to reason. The following example is taken from a reading primer printed in 1778, which was designed to be used in elementary schools in the Austrian Empire.

> Ein Knab, der auf einem Steckenpferde ritt, peischte [sic] immer auf dasselbige los, damit es fortgehen sollte: aber es gieng nicht, weil der Knab selbst nicht gieng. Ein anderer klügerer Knab sagete: er wolle ihm bald forthelfen, nahm eine Ruthe und schlug jenen unter die Füsse. Da er fort lief, lief sein Pferd auch mit fort.

---

112 All reading primers apart from Antesperg's *Josephinische Erzherzogliche A B C Oder Namenbüchlein* (1744) were available at the largest known schoolbook collection in Austria at the *Austrian Federal Ministry of Education* (*BMB*; previously called the *Austrian Ministry for Education, the Arts and Culture, BMUKK*) in Vienna. This collection has now been moved to the library of the University of Vienna. The first corpus is compiled of *all* monolingual German reading primers available in this schoolbook collection for the period specified, apart from multiple primers that were published in the same year.

113 Cf. Boyer's (2004) pedagogical analysis of this reading primer, containing a full version of the original book.

114 Many of the 18th-century reading primers I analysed contain prayers and religious texts.

Du suchst oft, mein Kind, den schlechten Fortgang, den du in deinem Lernen machst, auf etwas ausser dir zu schieben: aber du bist selber Schuld. Mache nur selbst in deinem Fleisse Schritte, so wird dein Verstand auch weiter kommen. (*ABC oder Namenbüchlein zum Gebrauche der Schulen in den kaiserlich-königlichen Staaten* 1778: 45)

A boy, who was riding a hobbyhorse, whipped it continuously, so that it would move: but it didn't because the boy himself did not move. Another boy, who was cleverer, said: he would soon help him, took the whip, and beat the boy under his feet. Since the boy ran, his horse also ran.

You, my child, often try to blame something external for the lack of progress in your learning: but you yourself are to blame. You yourself have to work hard to progress, in this way your intellect will also advance.

While the general pedagogical aims are certainly highlighted in these moral stories, reading primers also aimed at teaching a particular variety of German. In other words, these primers represent the target language in education. As mentioned in chapter 2, education is a central force in the dissemination of language norms (Deumert & Vandenbussche 2003: 7) and reading primers can certainly aid in the transmission of certain varieties and variants. While it is uncertain whether teachers used the variants prescribed in schoolbooks, the pupils reading the books would have been exposed to what was considered the 'norm' in writing.

As mentioned in chapter 2, Felbiger introduced compulsory elementary schooling with uniform curricula and textbooks in December 1774. Most of the reading primers (11 out of 15) in this corpus were printed in the Austrian Empire after the introduction of this school policy (see table below).[115]

Tab. 8: List of reading primers

Title of book (abbreviated)	Place of publication	Year of publication	To be used in state schools
Das Josephinische Erzherzogliche A.B.C. Oder Namenbüchlein (Antesperg)	Vienna	1744	no
Teutsches Namen- oder Lehrbüchl	Vienna	c. 1750	no
Ein sehr nutzliches Stimmen-Büchlein	Graz	c. 1770	no
Catholisches Namen-Büchl	Linz	1774	no
ABC und Buchstabirbüchlein zum Gebrauche der Landschulen	Prague	1777	yes

---

115 The titles of the reading primers are abbreviated in this table. The full titles can be found in the bibliography.

Title of book (abbreviated)	Place of publication	Year of publication	To be used in state schools
ABC oder Namenbüchlein zum Gebrauche der Schulen in den kaiserlich-königlichen Staaten	Ljubljana[116]	1778	yes
ABC oder Namenbüchlein zum Gebrauche der Schulen in den kaiserlich-königlichen Staaten	Prague	1779	yes
ABC oder Namenbüchlein zum Gebrauche der Oesterreichischen Normalschule	Vienna	1782	yes
ABC oder Namenbüchlein zum Gebrauche der Landschulen	Vienna	1783	yes
Neuestes ABC-Buch oder Uebungen im Syllabieren oder Buchstabiren und im Lesen	Vienna	1802	no
Nahmenbüchlein zum Gebrauche der Stadtschulen in den kaiserl. königl. Staaten	Graz	1804	yes
ABC und Buchstabierbüchlein nebst Leseübungen für Anfänger	Bolzano[117]	1809	no
Der kleine Abc-Schüler	Salzburg	1818	no
Syllabier-Büchlein zum Privatgebrauche (Kirchmayr)	Vienna	1828	no
Nahmenbüchlein für Stadtschulen in den kaiserl. königl. Staaten	Linz	1833	yes

Apart from two reading primers, the *Josephinische Erzherzogliche A.B.C. Oder Namenbüchlein* (1744) written by the grammarian Johann Balthasar von Antesperg and the *Syllabier-Büchlein zum Privatgebrauche* (1828) written by Laur[entius] Kirchmayr (a school teacher), all books in the corpus were published anonymously. However, it is known that Felbiger himself wrote and/or edited several of the textbooks designed to be used in schools after 1774 (see chapter 2). In fact, the reading primers printed in 1777, 1778, 1779, 1782 and 1783 may have been written by Felbiger himself.[118] After about 1790, the reading primers designed to be used in state schools were revised, which means that the *Nahmenbüchlein zum Gebrauche der Stadtschulen* (1804, 1833) represent completely new textbooks, not based on Felbiger's original reading primers (Boyer 2002: 267f.).

These two textbooks from the 19th century reveal the cost of schoolbooks at the time. The *Nahmenbüchlein zum Gebrauche der Stadtschulen* (1804) cost 9 kreutzer unbound in hardcover, while the *Nahmenbüchlein für Stadtschulen* (1833) cost 7

---

116 German: *Laibach*.
117 German: *Bozen*.
118 Cf. Boyer (2002: 260), who refers to an earlier version of the *ABC oder Namenbüchlein, zum Gebrauche der Schulen in den kaiserlich-königlichen Staaten* (1776) as "Felbiger Fibel".

kreutzer unbound and 10 kreutzer bound in a leather cover (see cover page).[119] Engelbrecht (1984: 88) notes that the cost of schoolbooks was kept to a minimum by restricting the content to what was absolutely necessary and by not using any illustrations. Since pupils owned their own copies of textbooks after the school reform in 1774 (*Allgemeine Schulordnung*: point 7), they were designed to be affordable for their parents. The cost of reading primers designed to be used at home only (i.e. the reading primers printed in 1802, 1809, 1818 and 1828) and schoolbooks printed before the introduction of Felbiger's school policy, which were illustrated, was probably higher.[120]

Reading primers were certainly one of the most basic textbooks available to pupils since they were designed to teach students how to read. It can, therefore, be assumed, that the children attending school in the 18th century had access to reading primers.[121] Indeed, for children attending school for a very limited amount of time, they might have been the only books that they read themselves.[122]

The format and structure of the reading primers compiled for the first corpus is very similar. Beginning with individual letters, the reading primers become gradually more difficult: syllables, monosyllabic words, polysyllabic words, whole sentences and then texts (either prayers or stories conveying moral values). The shorter reading primers, particularly the ones printed in 1744, c. 1770, and 1774, and the *Kleine ABC-Schüler* (1818), which was published to be used at home, started off with more difficult constructions or did not dwell on individual syllables. For example, the first sentence in Antesperg's reading primer (1744) is "Wann der Knabe singet, so schreyet er a, a, a." ("When the boy sings, he shouts a, a, a."). In other words, the letters of the alphabet were introduced in whole sentences, which even include

---

119 In comparison, a teacher's basic salary was 130 guilders per year in 1786 (Weißenböck 2010: 36), which could be raised to 300 or 400 guilders per year with the help of other jobs, money collections, and bonuses but was – according to Engelbrecht (1984: 114) – still considered a rather low salary. 1 guilder equated to 60 kreutzer. The textbooks for state schools can, therefore, be described as affordable.

120 Boyer (2002: 255) notes that schoolbooks were relatively expensive before the introduction of Felbiger's school reform in 1774. Before then, the pupils would usually bring any book to school in order to learn to read.

121 Engelbrecht (1984: 87f.) states that reading primers, arithmetic books, and catechisms were the most common schoolbooks before the introduction of the school reform in 1774, when books dealing with, for example, grammar, history and agriculture were added to the list of textbooks (cf. *Allgemeine Schulordnung*: Lit. E).

122 The appendix of Felbiger's school policy (1774: Lit. B) reveals that the curriculum for first year students in *Hauptschulen* was limited to spelling and religious education. Students would learn how to read and write from the second year onwards (see appendix for the complete curricula and taught subjects). Even if pupils dropped out of school after their first two years, they would have come across reading primers.

subordinate clauses, in Antesperg's primer, while other primers started with a simple list of the letters of the alphabet.

In contrast to the basic structure of reading primers, their volume varied considerably, with the shortest reading primer consisting of 37 pages and the longest of 150 pages. In order to achieve greater comparability, only the first 37 to 48 pages of each primer were analysed, with results being provided in absolute numbers as well as percentages in section 4.3.[123] Furthermore, passages composed in verse were left out since these represent a more artificial use of language.[124]

4.1.2 Newspaper issues

The second corpus consists of nineteen issues of the *Wienerisches Diarium* (*Wiener Zeitung* from 1780 onwards), published between 1744 and 1834. In a modern context, Ammon (2003: 2) refers to texts written by professional writers (e.g. journalists) as 'model texts', meaning that readers of the newspaper perceive these texts to be exemplary for their 'correct' language use. The regular use of certain linguistic constructions in newspapers by journalists can render these variants "standard by usage" or "standard by mere usage" (Ammon 2003: 2) if the features are not standard for any other reason, e.g. because they are codified in grammars or dictionaries (ibid.). While I only consider variants that were codified in contemporary grammars and do not investigate any possible "standard by mere usage" features, it is important to consider the model role newspapers may have played for their 18th-century readership. In other words, newspapers may not have created standard forms but they would have disseminated the language that was used in them. However, it has to be noted that readership was very limited in the 18th and early 19th century. Hosokawa (2014: 24) states that newspapers only became reading material for the masses from the 1830s onwards when relatively cheap tabloids began to appear. Before then, the vast majority of newspaper readers belonged to the nobility and the bourgeoisie (ibid. 39). It was only in the first half of the 19th century that newspapers also began to spread among the peasant population in the countryside (ibid. 40). It is, therefore, very unlikely that newspapers would have influenced the language use of 'ordinary people' before the 1830s.

---

123 The oldest reading primer analysed, i.e. Antesperg's *Josephinische Erzherzogliche A.B.C. Oder Namenbüchlein* (1744), is 48 pages long. An analysis of further pages in longer reading primers has shown that the language use does not change radically after the first 48 pages. Including further pages in the analysis is not likely to have changed the overall results gained by analysing the first 48 pages.

124 Poems often contained a disproportionately high number of nouns with *e*-apocope due to the metre and rhyme of the poem. Counting these instances would have distorted the overall results.

However, newspapers are a valuable source to establish whether the prescriptions by 18th-century grammarians changed the language use of professional writers and their 'model texts'. The *Wienerisches Diarium/Wiener Zeitung* was selected for the analysis due to its continuous publication since its very first issue on 8 August 1703[125], which means that individual newspaper issues with a set period of time between them (in this case, five years) can be chosen for analysis.[126] The initial title of the first issue printed by Johann Baptist Schönwetter essentially summarises what would be the content of the newspapers for many years (Zenker 1903: 4):

> Wiennerisches *Diarium* / Enthaltend Alles Denkwürdige / so von Tag zu Tag so wohl in dieser Käyserlichen Residentz=Stadt Wienn selbsten sich zugetragen / als auch von andern Orthen auß der gantzen Welt allda nachrichtlich eingeloffen / Mit diesem besondern Anhang / Daß auch alle die jenige Persohnen / welche wochentlich allhier gestorben / hingegen was von Vornehmen gebohren / dann *copuliret* worden / ferner anhero und von dannen verreiset / darinnen befindlich. (*Wiennerisches Diarium* 1703: title)

> Viennese *Diarium* / Containing everything noteworthy / which has happened in the imperial residence of Vienna as well as what has been reported from other places in the whole world / With a special appendix / containing a list of all people who have died here [in Vienna] during the week / those of nobility who have been born / who got married / also those who have travelled to and away from here [Vienna].

Indeed, this title accurately describes the structure of the newspaper, which first not only reported on local as well as global news and included an appendix containing death notices, and information on notable figures, but also provided advertisements for books and notices of auctions. A short weather report was published from 10 January 1784 onwards. Zenker (1903: 4) describes the *Wienerisches Diarium* as relatively up-to-date by contemporary standards: hardly any piece of news was older than eight days. From 1788, the *Wiener Zeitung* was published three times a week (previously it was printed twice a week – on Wednesdays and Saturdays), but there were hardly any changes regarding the general layout of the newspaper (ibid. 18). Also, its relation to the government remained the same during the whole 18th century: the *Wienerisches Diarium/Wiener Zeitung* was a private company with certain privileges from the emperor, not an official institution of the empire (*Hofzeitung*), and its content was subject to censorship (ibid.).

Journalism, similar to teaching, was usually a sideline in the 18th century, resulting in officers, diplomats, lawyers, doctors, librarians etc., who had received an

---

125 Since the *Wiener Zeitung* is still published today, it is the oldest operating daily newspaper in the world (Czeike 1992–1997: 648).

126 By contrast, the corpus of reading primers and the corpus of petitionary letters were compiled by collecting all the materials available at the time. Furthermore, the *Wienerisches Diarium/Wiener Zeitung* can be easily accessed via the online newspaper archive of the Austrian National Library (*ANNO – AustriaN Newspapers Online*), URL: http://anno.onb.ac.at/ [accessed 26.04.2017].

academic education and could read and translate foreign newspapers, writing newspapers articles (Hosokawa 2014: 56). Indeed, teachers, too, worked as part-time journalists. According to Hosokawa (ibid.), journalism gradually developed into an independent profession in the 19th century, with most journalists belonging to the bourgeoisie.[127] However, the death notice of Hieronymus Gmainer, who worked as a journalist and editor for the *Wienerisches Diarium* from at least 1721 to his death on 27 April 1729, provides the title "Zeitung=Schreiber" ("newspaper writer") next to his name (Zenker 1903: 7).[128] It seems that – at least for a few people – journalism had reached a stage of professionalism before the 19th century. For these few people, journalistic and editorial tasks were closely connected: Schönwetter, the founder of the *Wienerisches Diarium*, for example, not only wrote articles, but also edited and printed them (ibid. 5). It can, therefore, be argued that these individuals determined the language used in articles at the early stages of the newspaper. As the *Wienerisches Diarium/Wiener Zeitung* grew, more people were involved in its production, and from 1805, sections (local versus international) were assigned to different editors. This editorial division was the result of an imperial resolution from 2 January 1805, which ordered the subordination of the editorial office to the imperial authorities (ibid. 21). Consequently, the *Wiener Zeitung* suddenly became an official institution (ibid. 22). Henceforth, an employee of the imperial authorities, Joh. Michael Armbruster, was the editor of the local news, while the articles on international news remained in the editorial hands of employees of van Ghelen's company, which owned the leasehold on the *Wienerisches Diarium/Wiener Zeitung* from 1721 to 1 January 1858 (ibid. 22, 39).

Of particular relevance is the fact that the sections on global news in the *Wienerisches Diarium/Wiener Zeitung* were mostly copied from foreign newspapers (Zenker 1903: 4)[129], which means that the authors of these news articles were not necessarily

---

127 Zenker (2003: 32) argues that it was in the year 1848 (i.e. the year of the March Revolution) that journalism became a profession – before then articles were written by political or literary amateurs.

128 See the list of death notices in the *Wienerisches Diarium* published on 30 April 1729: http://anno.onb.ac.at/cgi-content/anno?aid=wrz&datum=17290430&seite=8&zoom=33 [accessed 26.04. 2017].

129 Sometimes quotation marks indicated that these were copied articles whilst at other times they were introduced by stating that the news was presented as received. In the issue of the *Wienerisches Diarium* published on 1 July 1769, for example, it is stated that the news given in Russian newspapers was so contradictory that the editors of the *Wienerisches Diarium* could not resolve the ambiguities and, therefore, reprinted them as presented in the *Petersburger Zeitungen*: "Von den Wirkungen der Rußisch=Kaiserlich und Ottomanischen Waffen, laufen so widersprechende Nachrichten ein, daß man der Ungewißheit worein man dadurch versetzet wird, nicht anderst abzuhelfen weiß, als daß man diese Nachrichten, so wie sie angekommen, dem Publikum mittheilet." ("The news of the impact of the Imperial Russian and Ottoman weapons are so contradictory that one cannot resolve the ambiguity in any other way than reporting the news to the readers in [exactly] the way they were received.") (*Wienerisches Diarium*, 1 July 1769, first paragraph).

from the UG language area. Indeed, von Polenz (1994: 18) states that the content and form of newspapers were relatively uniform due to their supra-regional nature:

> Der Nachrichtenfluß wurde überregional organisiert: Da das Sammeln dieser Fern-Nachrichten zunehmend von professionellen Agenten (*Zeitungsschreyber*) besorgt wurde, die für mehrere Zeitungen arbeiteten und deshalb dem Verleger ein Alibi gegenüber der lokalen Zensur boten, waren Inhalt und Form der Zeitungen weiträumig relativ einheitlich. Zeitungen wurden so – nach der Luther-Bibel – auch zum wirksamsten Mittel der Popularisierung und Verbreitung einheitlicher Sprachvarianten auf dem Wege zur nationalen Schriftsprache. (von Polenz 1994: 18)

> The flow of information was organized supra-regionally: Since the collection of global news increasingly became a task of professional agents (*newspaper writers*) who worked for several newspapers, and thus provided the publisher with an alibi for the local censorship, the content and form of newspapers was relatively uniform across a large area. Thus newspapers – after the Luther Bible – also became one of the most effective means of popularizing and disseminating uniform linguistic variants during the creation of a national written language.

Von Polenz thus highlights the crucial role that newspapers played in the standardisation process of German. Durrell's (forthcoming) analysis of the *GerManC* corpus, on the other hand, shows that the language in newspapers did not differ from the language in other 18th-century texts written by educated social classes, such as scientific texts. In other words, newspapers were not the only text types that were supra-regional in the 18th century. It can, therefore, be concluded that the educated classes in general – not merely newspapers – contributed to the standardisation of the German language (Durrell ibid.). Durrell thus does not ascribe any significant role in the standardisation process of German in the 17th and 18th century to newspapers. Instead, he argues that newspapers follow the norms that were selected by the educated classes and codified by grammarians, such as Adelung. In contrast to grammarians, newspaper correspondents did not prescribe certain norms explicitly, i.e. certain variants were not described as 'bad' or 'wrong'. Instead, a more tolerant "selection and dissemination of variants" ("Variantenaussonderung und -verbreitung") (von Polenz 1994: 374) took place in newspapers, with the editors largely accepting the variants used by the different correspondents (ibid.). Since the original reports written by the correspondents are not preserved, it is difficult to establish to what extent the editors changed these original texts or where the correspondents were from (Durrell et al. 2008: 265). The analysis of newspaper issues from the *Wienerisches Diarium/Wiener Zeitung* in section 4.4 will reveal whether the linguistic features in the newspaper articles can provide insights into the origin of individual correspondents. More importantly, the results of the analysis will shed light on the use of regional features in newspaper issues published between 1744 and 1834 and assess to what extent correspondents followed the prescriptions by Adelung and other 18th-century grammarians.

For the analysis, nineteen issues – each printed in the first week of July in 5-year-intervals (starting with 1744 and finishing with 1834) – were selected and up to the first nine pages were analysed, depending on the frequency of the linguistic features that were selected for the analysis. Since the layout between newspapers changed over the years, with generally more text on individual pages in the 19th century, and since the frequency of the linguistic features varied between the different issues of newspapers, the number of pages or rather columns was adjusted to the occurrences of the features.[130] The number of columns of each newspaper issue as well as the minimum and average number of instances for each feature can be found in the following tables:

Tab. 9: Number of columns analysed in each newspaper issue

Publishing date	Number of columns analysed in each issue
1 July 1744	1–14
2 July 1749	1–12
3 July 1754	1–18
4 July 1759	1–15
4 July 1764	1–14
1 July 1769	1–14
2 July 1774	1–14
3 July 1779	1–12
3 July 1784	1–14
1 July 1789	1–12
2 July 1794	1–14
3 July 1799	1–14[131]
4 July 1804	1–14
1 July 1809	1–8[132]
1 July 1814	1–8
1 July 1819	1–4
1 July 1824	1–8

---

130 The content of the newspaper, too, changed slightly within the 91 years under investigation. Since the sections on the local as well as international news remained a constant and since they were always printed at the beginning of the *Wienerisches Diarium/Wiener Zeitung*, the first few pages of each newspaper issue were analysed. In this way, the comparability of individual issues was given.

131 The list of officers on the third page was not included in the analysis.

132 The scans of columns 5 to 8 of the newspaper issue published on 1 July 1809 were misplaced on the ANNO website and can be found in the issue published on 3 July 1809.

Publishing date	Number of columns analysed in each issue
1 July 1829	1–4 & 7
1 July 1834	1–7

Tab. 10: Minimum and average number of occurrences of variables per newspaper issue

Variable	Minimum and average number of occurrences per issue	
e-apocope/ending -e	minimum	average[133]
fem. sg.	23	43
masc./neutr. sg. dat.	27	55
pl.	18	36
past participles		
prefix ge-	11	27
ending -t vs -et	38	61
verb to be		
wir/sie seynd vs sind	5	10

4.1.3 Petitionary letters

The growing interest in petitionary letters as sources for historical research in the last 20 years is linked to the relatively new 'history from below' approach, which emerged in the 1970s and aimed to research how 'ordinary people' experienced and/or influenced historical developments.[134] Within the discipline of historical sociolinguistics, Klenk (1997) analysed 95 petitionary letters by miners (1816–1918), which proved to be conceptually oral. Similarly, Fairman's (1999, 2003, 2007) research illustrates that the language used in so-called 'pauper letters'[135] is conceptu-

---

133 The average number of occurrences illustrates the relative frequency of the different features in the newspaper corpus. As in the reading primers, the frequency of the verb to be in the 1st or 3rd pers. pl. pres. ind. act. is rather low.

134 Cf. van Voss's (2002) edited volume on petitions in social history, Ulbricht's (1996) analysis of 17th-century petitionary letters from the Duchies of Schleswig and Holstein, and Ulbrich (1996) for historical research on 18th-century petitionary letters written by women. Rudolph (2005) and Würgler (2005), too, deal with German petitionary letters, while Sokoll (1996, 2001), for example, focuses on English 'pauper letters', Grateau (2001) on French letters of complaints, and Nubola (2005) on the role of petitions in Italian states from the 15th to the 18th century.

135 The term 'pauper letters', which is translated as 'Armenbriefe' into German by Sokoll (1996), seems too narrow for the letters I analysed since the corpus of petitionary letters also contains, for

ally oral and, therefore, provides an insight into actual language use in the past.[136] In comparison to the letters analysed by Fairman, the petitionary letters that I compiled for my third corpus appear to be more formal, i.e. they are, in general, conceptually closer to written language than Fairman's texts.

In order to assess to what extent the language use in these handwritten petitions differed from printed texts (reading primers and newspaper issues), a corpus of 60 petitionary letters from outside Vienna, 31 of which were found in the Styrian Provincial Archives (Graz) and 29 in the Archives of Upper Austria (Linz), is analysed.[137] It can be assumed that the writers of these petitions aimed at writing what they considered to be 'standard German' since these petitionary letters were addressed to local sovereigns (*Landesfürsten*), lords of the manor (*Grundherren*), city councils (*Stadtrat*) or other legal entities (e.g. the *Salzoberamt*[138] in Gmunden, Upper Austria). Schennach (2004: 572f.) stresses that the fundamental characteristics of petitions remain the same, despite different addressees. While the salutation in the letter would obviously change, the overall content of petitions would not: an obedient appeal for grace (ibid.). According to Schennach (2004: 575) and Würgler (2005: 17), anyone – regardless of their age, social standing or sex – had the right to submit a petition and a large proportion of the population made use of this right (Schennach 2004: 575).[139] Indeed, the submission of petitions was encouraged since it functioned as a means of communication between the sovereigns and their subjects as well as an outlet for complaints at times of social tension (ibid. 573).[140] Furthermore, it served as an instrument for monitoring the implementation of orders (ibid.). While petitioners did not have a subjective right to the grant of grace, they had a de facto right to the administration of their petitions (ibid.). Indeed, the vast majority of the petitionary letters that I analysed contain a short summary of the addressee's reply, indicating that the petition was processed and whether the petitioner was success-

---

example, requests for permissions to build sheds or houses. Therefore, I use the terms 'petitionary letters' and 'petitions'.

136 Cf. the summary of Fairman's (1999, 2003, 2007) research in section 1.1.5.

137 The majority of petitionary letters were found in archives of sovereigns and important families. These *Herrschafts-* or *Familienarchive* often contained a section entitled *Untertanenarchive* (*subjects' archive*), which held petitionary letters, wills, various official documents, and – in very few cases – personal letters. The archival reference for each petition can be found in the bibliography (see *Petitionary letter*).

138 The *Salzoberamt* was an imperial authority, which controlled the extraction and trade of salt (Jakob 2003).

139 Würgler (2005: 35) notes that – according to the state of research in 2005 – more men than women (with women's petitions being often submitted by widows) and more adults than adolescents made use of this right.

140 Cf. Rudolph (2005), who illustrates how the petitionary system stabilized the power relation between the authorities and their subjects.

ful.[141] These replies as well as dates of the submission of letters (abbreviated as 'praes.' for *praesentatum* in the petitions) provided by the addressee proved particularly valuable for determining when a petition was written if no date was given in the letter itself. From letters with dates and replies, it can be inferred that the turn-around was fairly quick. For example, Ingnaz Grishoffer's petition[142] was written on 9 October 1801, 'presented' on 10 October 1801, and the summary of the reply is dated 31 October 1801. In some cases, the letter was even received on the day it was written.[143] It can, therefore, be assumed that the petitionary letters without dates were written in the same year as the replies were issued if they were dated between February and December. If the reply was from January, it was assumed that the letter was written in the previous year. The reference of each petitionary letter was marked with 'r' (reply – year inferred by reply), 'p' (presented – year inferred from note of receipt) or 'w' (written – year provided in the petition itself) after the year to indicate how the year of writing was determined.

Ascertaining the writer of the letter is more difficult since it was usually not the petitioners themselves writing the letters. Indeed, Schennach (2004: 579) points out that, in the 16th century, the authorities pronounced the use of scribes authorised to compose petitions, while so-called *Winkelschreiber*[144] – i.e. semi-educated people from the lower-middle class or farmers, who could read and write, writing petitions professionally or only occasionally (Valentinitsch 1983: 195) – should be avoided.[145] In other words, the petitioners were usually not the authors of the petitionary letters. In a few cases, however, a 'manu propria' sign, indicating that the actual petitioners signed the letters, follows the signatures. If the signature matches the handwriting in the text, it can be assumed that the petition was not only signed, but also written by the petitioners themselves. When this is the case, the petition is marked with an 'M' at the end of its reference. Despite the fact that petitionary letters were usually recorded by a scribe and not the petitioners themselves, petitionary letters can be considered 'ego-documents', i.e. "[t]exts in which an author writes about his or her own acts, thoughts and feelings" (Dekker 2002: 7) since they are usually written in the first person singular and convey the aspects of the life and living conditions of an individual (Ulbricht 1996: 150).

The extent to which an (un)authorised writer influenced the content and language of petitionary letters depended on their stage of professionalism – with dif-

---

141 Schennach (2004: 579) states that no general estimation about the success rate of petitions can be given since it depended too much on the subject.

142 STLA_1801w_Pflindsberg

143 Cf. STLA_1788w_b_Lamberg – the petitionary letter was dated 26 March 1788 and an added note at the top of the letter states "Empfangen den 26ten Merzen 788" ("Received 26 March 1788").

144 Cf. the term *Winkelschulen* mentioned in chapter 2.

145 Valentinitsch (1983: 195f.) reports that these *Winkelschreiber* encouraged people to hand in petitions for their own financial profit since they charged people for writing petitionary letters.

ferences in the intervention between, for example, an adept solicitor and an ordinary court secretary – as well as on the rate of payment (Schennach 2004: 580). These factors determined whether the linguistic varieties and variants of the petitioners were largely adopted – merely adapting them to the formal requirements of the text genre – or whether the requests of the petitioners were brought to paper in some 'polished' form (ibid.). The basic structure of petitions is, however, consistent throughout the corpus. Schennach (ibid. 574) lists the following components of petitions: 1. salutation (*titulatio*), 2. reasons for the application (*exordium*), 3. detailed depiction of the circumstances, coupled with a plea for help (*narratio* and *petitio*), and 4. an affirmation of loyalty and submission or an expression of hope for resolving the depicted grievances (*conclusio*).[146] This fixed structure results in frequent formulaic constructions as well as repetitions, as shown in grey in the following petitionary letter (presented on 1 July 1757):

Tab. 11: Formulaic constructions (in grey) in STLA_1757p_Saurau[147]

Line	Transcription: STLA_1757p_Saurau	Notes
	<pb n="1">	
1	<p><lb/>Ihro Hochgräffliche Excellenz</p>	Formulaic salutation.
2	<p><lb/>Hoch und Wohl gebohrner ReichGraff	Formulaic salutation.
3	<lb/>auch gnädig und Hochgebiettender Herr Herr p.p: </p>	
4	<p><lb/>Da mir die Milde und *Hoche gnade*	Reasons for the application
5	<lb/>*Euer Hochgräfflichen Excellenz* <unclear>mehr den bevindt</unclear>	(usually introduced with *because* and containing
6	<lb/>unterfinnge mich beÿ *Eure Excellenz* mit meiner	expressions of submission).
7	<lb/>unterthanigst gehorsambster bitt anzuhalten.	
8	<lb/><unclear>Wes mass</unclear> ich Vormahls die hoche gnad gehabt auf	Depiction of circumstances and plea for help (usually
9	<lb/>dem Gschlossberg meine *S: h:* Gaÿß zu Weÿden, soliches	containing expressions of
10	<lb/>mir aber anjezo Von Herren Verwalter schörffist	submission)
11	<lb/>abgebotten, so bitte Vnterthänigst und fußfallend	More detailed reasons for
12	<lb/>Ihro Hochgräfflichen Excellenz Wollen gnädigst	the petition (usually containing personal infor-
13	<lb/>zu erlauben belieben mir gemelte Gaÿss an	mation on the petitioner,
14	<lb/>einen Strikh gebunden an gemelten Gschlossberg	esp. marital status and
15	<lb/>zu Weÿden, in erwegung wie d ich ein arme	number of children).
16	<lb/>Wittib, so annoch 3 Vnmündige /: so zu sag. / Kinder	

---

146 Karweick (1989: 32) illustrates that the second part, which he terms *captatio benevolentiae* instead of *exordium*, as well as the *conclusio* closely resemble religious pleas.
147 See Table 12 for annotation conventions. Annotations are printed in grey in order to ease readability.

Line	Transcription: STLA_1757p_Saurau	Notes
17	‹lb/›nur mit der Allmosen, und Gaÿss=Milich zu	
18	‹lb/›Erhalten mich befleiss. muß, und da eine am Strikh	
19	‹lb/›gebundene Gaÿss Keinen schaden zu Verursachen	
20	‹lb/›in Stand sich befindet‹/p›	
	‹pb n="2"›	
21	‹p›‹lb/›Ihro Hochgrafflichen Excellenz‹/p›	Formulaic salutation.
22	‹p›‹lb/›Bitte also Knÿefällig meiner unterthänigsten	Plea for help, affirmation of
23	‹lb/›bitt zu gewähren und ein gnädiges fiat zu	loyalty and submission
24	‹lb/›ertheillen, vor Weliche hoche gnad ich stets	(often containing a promise
25	‹lb/›befliss. seÿn werde, ‹unclear›umb‹/unclear› ein zeitlich langes und	to pray for the addressee and wishes for the ad-
26	‹lb/›Ewiges leben Euer Hochgräfflich. Excellenz	dressee's well-being
27	‹lb/›beÿ Gott Täglich ᵐᵉⁱⁿ Gebett auszugiess. in Hoffnung	and/or long reign).
28	‹lb/›Gott d Allmächtige wird solche Gnad hundertfältig	Formulaic closing phrase
29	‹lb/›ersezen. Dahin mich allerunterthänigst	(usually followed by the
30	‹lb/›Empfehle‹/p›	petitioner's name).
	‹pb n="3"›	Note by authorities on the
	‹p›‹lb/›[pras. den 1ᵉⁿ July 1757]‹/p›	'presentation' date.
31	‹p›‹lb/›An	Addressee's Address.
32	‹lb/›Ihro Hochgräfflichen	(including formulaic saluta-
33	‹lb/›Excellenz dem Hoch und	tions)
34	‹lb/›Wohl gebohrnen Herrn Herrn	
35	‹lb/›Reichs Graffen Corbinian	
36	‹lb/›*Saverau* Ihro Kaÿßerl. Königl.	
37	‹lb/›Majest: geheimen Rath, und	
38	‹lb/›Stadthaltern in Steÿer ‹gap quantitiy="1" unit="words"/›	
39	‹lb/›der Herrschaft Schwannberg p. p.	
40	‹lb/›Ihro Hochgrafflichen *Excellenz* meinen	
41	‹lb/›Gnädigsten herrn Herrn p: p: ‹/p›	
42	‹p›‹lb/›Vnterth‹unclear›ä‹/unclear›nigstes bitten‹/p›	Purpose of the letter.
43	‹p›‹lb/›Elisabeth Fridrichin	Name of petitioner (usually
44	‹lb/›Wittib.‹/p›	followed by their marital status, profession and/or place of residence).

The petitionary letter above starts with a highly formulaic salutation, setting the submissive tone continued throughout the letter. After stating general reasons for writing this petition, the petitioner describes her circumstances in more detail. In the past, she was allowed to graze her goat on the land of the lord of the manor. At the time of the letter, this became forbidden, which resulted in the loss of the essential grazing land for the petitioner's goat. Since the petitioner is a widow with three underage children, she depends on the goat's milk and alms for her and her family to survive. Therefore, she begs the addressee, lord of the manor Count Palatine Saurau, to allow her goat to graze on his land again, assuring him that the goat will not cause any damage since it will be tied to a rope. The petitionary letter closes with a formulaic and highly submissive plea for help and with a common closing phrase.

Karweick (1989: 32) points out that the *narratio*, i.e. the depiction of the petitioner's circumstances, was the element of a petition that was least confined to set linguistic constructions, which meant that the petitioner could write more freely (see lines 8–20 in the transcription above). On the other hand, this part could present linguistic problems for the writer, given that formulaic structures could simply be copied (Karweick 1989: 32).

Guide books on letter writing, so-called *Briefsteller*, certainly provided many of these formulaic constructions and a basic structure for petitions. From a variety of these *Briefsteller*, two are mentioned here to illustrate how they may have influenced the language, structure, and style of the petitions that I compiled. In the 17th century, Brauser's *Hurtige[r] Briefsteller* (1687: 518–609) contained a list of formulaic constructions for, as well as examples of, various petitionary letters. The final two paragraphs of a request for an increase in salary, for example, include phrases that are very similar but not identical to those found in the petitionary letter transcribed above and to Austrian petitions from the 18th and early 19th century in general:

> Gelanget dannenhero an Eure Gnaden mein höchst sehn= und flehentliches Bitten / Sie geruhen / Ihro angebornen hohen Güte und Milde nach / Dero dürfftig=nothleidenden Diener mit gnädigen Augen anzusehen / und mein [sic] ohne dem geringe Besoldung jährlich in etwas zu verbessern.

> Wie Ihre Gnaden hieran ein höchstlöbliches Werk verrichten / als werde ich / so lange ich lebe / nicht nachlassen solche Eurer Gnaden vortreffliche Milde mit schuldigster Dankbarkeit zu rühmen / und dabey den grossen GOtt kindlichst anzuflehen / daß er Eure Gnaden mit lang= beharrlicher Lebens=Fristung und höchstglücklichem WolErgehen überschütten wolle / wie ich dann E. Gnaden der allgewaltige Beschirmung Gottes getreulichst mich aber dero hohen Gnade demühtigst empfehle und verbleibe

> Eurer Gnaden unterthänigst=gehorsamster Diener (Brauser 1687: 549–551)

> My most ardent and pleading request reaches Your Grace [in the hope that] you – according to your innate kindness and mildness – deign to view your poor destitute servant with merciful eyes and to improve my low salary a little bit each year.

As Your Grace does the most commendable work, I will – as long as I live – not cease to praise Your Grace's admirable mildness with all due gratitude and to beg the great God in the most pure way[148] that he may whelm Your Grace with long-lasting life and the most prosperous well-being / thus I then faithfully commend Your Grace to the almighty protection of God and bid Your Grace farewell most humbly, remaining

Your Grace's most submissive and obedient servant

Similar to the petitonary letter transcribed above, this extract conveys a strong sense of submission and obedience. A number of the formulaic expressions used in this extract can also be found in the petitionary letters that I analysed. Wolfgang Stainparzer's (1749) petition, for example, closes in the following way:

<lb/>Alß gelanget an *Euer Hochgräfl: Excell^{ia}_{pp}* mein ganz
<lb/>vnterthänigst gehorsambstes Bitten, zu geruehen mir die
<lb/>bißhero auß dero müld= vnd Güette hergeflossene nach=
<lb/>sehung, verers anwiderumben auf 3. Jahr, nemblichen *pro*
<lb/><unclear>A</unclear>*: 1749: 750: A* 1751: iedes Jahr mit 3. K. in hochen Gnaden
<lb/>angedeÿen Zulassen, worgegen wie vorhin, nicht ermangle.
<lb/>mein vnablässiges gebett, vmb *Euer Hochgräfl: Excellenz pp*
<lb/>vnd des ganzen *Hochgräfl: Excellenz pp* Hauses, Seel= vnd Leibes
<lb/>vergniegliche Regierung imerhin Zu Gott Zu Bitten. Zur gnädigen
<lb/>fiats Gewehrung. mich vnterthänigst gehorsambst Empfilhe.
(OOLA_1749r_Neuhaus)

So my most submissive and obedient request reaches
Your High Excellency You may again grant me the charitableness,
which originates from your mildness and kindness,
of 3 kreutzer for another 3 years, namely for
the years 1749, 1750, and 1751, in great graciousness,
for which [I] will not cease to
always pray to God for the healthy and pleasurable reign of
Your High Excellency and the whole *House of Your High Excellency*.
I bid farewell most submissively and obediently
for the granting of fiat.

Guide books published in the early 19th century also contained sections on German orthography and grammar. The 10th edition of Karl Philipp Moritz's[149] *Allgemeiner deutscher Briefsteller* (*General German letter writing guide*) (1793, 10th ed. 1832), for example, dealt with orthographic rules, prepositions, irregular verbs and the

---

148 According to the German dictionary by Jacob and Wilhelm Grimm (1854–1961: Vol. 11, col. 769f.), the term *kindlich* was also used to express the desirable characteristics of children, such as purity and innocence. The translation of *kindlich* to *pure* seems appropriate in this quotation.
149 Karl Philipp Moritz was a literary scholar from the northern German language area (born in Hamelin, later living in Hanover, Brunswick, and Berlin, among other places) (Schrimpf 1980: 10–20).

distinction between accusative and dative case, before providing stylistic rules and examples of letters. Moritz's examples, too, contain formulaic phrases, such as:

> Die Milde und Güte, mit der Sie, gnädige Frau, stets fremdes Fehlen beurtheilen und fremdes Unglück zu mildern suchen, geben mir heute den Muth, mich mit einer Bitte an Sie zu wenden [...] (Moritz 1832: 130)

> The mildness and kindness, with which you, madam, seek to assess the deficiencies and mitigate the misfortunes of others, encourage me to approach you with my request [...]

Such guide books on letter writing as well as the (un)authorised writers would have certainly influenced the language used in petitionary letters, which may have differed considerably from the varieties used by the petitioners themselves. It should also be noted that the majority of the petitions follow the stylistic norms expected in petitionary letters. Indeed, it seems that almost all petitions compiled for the third corpus were written by professional writers. However, the stage of professionalism seems to vary between the writers, and despite the usually rather carefully drafted letters, the handwriting of these writers was not always easy to decipher. The first page of Elisabeth Fridrichin's petition (see table above for the transcription) should illustrate this point.

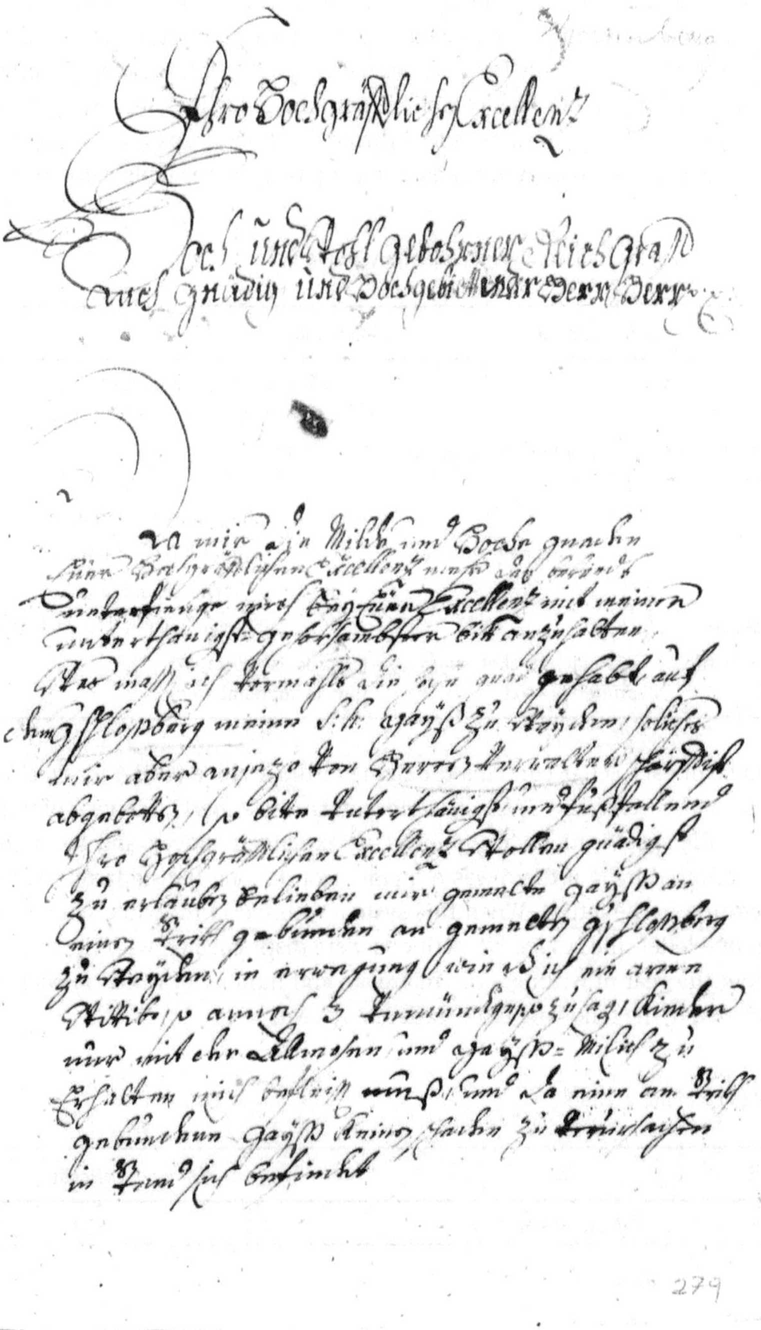

Fig. 4: First page of Elisabeth Fridrichin's petition (STLA_1757p_Saurau)

At the same time, this petitionary letter should serve as an example which explains the most common conventions employed in the transcription of the 60 petitionary letters. Apart from replacing the long *s* (ſ) with *s*, the transcriptions keep the original spellings and layout. Annotations compliant with the guidelines set out by the Text Encoding Initiative (TEI)[150] were used to indicate deletions, gaps due to illegibility, line breaks, page breaks, paragraphs and unclear passages (see table below).

Tab. 12: Annotations in the transcription of petitionary letters[151]

Case	Annotation	Example
Deletions	<del/>	in: OOLA_1784w_Weinberg: Jeder<del>zeit</del>
Indecipherable words or characters	<gap/> (plus indication of extent)	<gap quantitiy="1" unit="words"/> (line 38)
Line breaks	<lb/>	<lb/> (at the beginning of each line)
Page breaks	<pb/> (plus page number)	<pb n="1"/> (lines are not numbered)
Paragraphs	<p/>	<p>[text]</p> (for each paragraph)
Unclear passages	<unclear/>	<unclear>mehr den bevindt</unclear> (line 5)
Added notes by the authorities	in square brackets and printed in Arial	[pras. den 1en July 1757] (line is not numbered)

The reference of each letter contains the name of the archive (*OOLA* for *Oberösterreichisches Landesarchiv* and *STLA* for *Landesarchiv Steiermark*), the year of writing (followed by the specifications 'r', 'p' or 'w' as explained above), and the archival reference (followed by M if there was a 'manu propria' and the signature matched the handwriting in the letter). When this system resulted in the same reference for more than one letter, the respective petitions were distinguished with the letters 'a' and 'b' (after the year of writing). The reference and number of words of each petition is provided in the following table, ordered by year.

Tab. 13: List of petitionary letters

Reference[152]	Words
STLA_1744w_Lamberg, Fam. K. 319 H. 1390	339

---

150 Cf. http://www.tei-c.org/Guidelines/P5/ [accessed 26.04.2017].
151 Annotations are printed in grey here in order to ease readability.
152 These references are abbreviated in sections 4.5 and 4.6.

Reference[152]	Words
STLA_1746w_Lamberg, Fam. K. 320, H. 1393	266
STLA_1747r_Lamberg, Fam. K. 320, H. 1393	335
OOLA_1749r_Neuhaus, Herrsch. Nr. 149, VI, 18	290
OOLA_1751r_a_Weinberg, Herrsch. Sch. 1061, B70	332
OOLA_1751r_b_Weinberg, Herrsch. Sch. 1061, B70	354
OOLA_1752r_Weinberg, Herrsch. Sch. 1061, B70	289
STLA_1752p_Lamberg, Fam. K. 329, H. 1428	349
STLA_1754p_Saurau, Fam. K. 154, H. 1479	244
STLA_1754r_Donnersbach, Herrsch. K. 41, H. 154	384
STLA_1755w_Saurau, Fam. K. 56, H. 928	211
STLA_1757p_Saurau, Fam. K. 154, H. 1479	235
STLA_1758p_Saurau, Fam. K. 188, H. 1860	236
STLA_1760r_Rothenfels, Herrsch. K. 211 H. 730	362
OOLA_1763w_Schwertberg, Herrsch. Sch. 134_M	230
OOLA_1764w_Schwertberg, Herrsch. Sch. 134	127
STLA_1766p_Rothenfels, Herrsch. K. 211, H. 730	215
OOLA_1768p_Waldenfels, Herrsch. Sch. 330, 4	362
OOLA_1769r_Weinberg, Herrsch. Sch. 1061, B70	338
OOLA_1771w_Weinberg, Herrsch. Sch. 1061, B70	531
OOLA_1772r_Weinberg, Herrsch. Sch. 1061, B70	349
OOLA_1773r_a_Weinberg, Herrsch. Sch. 1061, B70	285
OOLA_1773r_b_Weinberg, Herrsch. Sch. 1061, B70	367
OOLA_1773w_Weinberg, Herrsch. Sch. 1061, B70	285
OOLA_1775r_Weinberg, Herrsch. Sch. 1061, B70	286
OOLA_1776r_Weinberg, Herrsch. Sch. 1061, B70	263
OOLA_1777r_Zunftarchivalien, Sch. 68	381
OOLA_1778r_Weinberg, Herrsch. Sch. 1061, B70	546
OOLA_1781r_a_Weinberg, Herrsch. Sch. 1061, B70	386
OOLA_1781r_b_Weinberg, Herrsch. Sch. 1061, B70	320
STLA_1782r_Lamberg, Fam. K. 177, H. 764	439
STLA_1783w_St. Lambrecht, Stiftsarchiv, K. 149 H. 70	211
OOLA_1784w_Weinberg, Herrsch. Sch. 1061, B70	298
OOLA_1786w_Weinberg, Herrsch. Sch. 1061, B70	138
STLA_1786w_Lamberg, Fam. K. 177, H. 764_M	224
STLA_1787w_Rothenfels, Herrsch. K. 211, H. 730	189
STLA_1788w_a_Lamberg, Fam. K. 177, H. 764	108
STLA_1788w_b_Lamberg, Fam. K. 177 H. 764	208
OOLA_1792w_Obernberg, Herrsch. Nr. 878, XX, 55	230

Reference[152]	Words
STLA_1792w_Rothenfels, Herrsch. K. 211, H. 730	255
STLA_1796w_Lamberg, Fam. K. 192, H. 823	389
STLA_1797w_Saurau, Fam. K. 154, H. 1479	147
STLA_1801w_Oberradkersburg, Herrsch. K. 150, H. 564	286
STLA_1801w_Pflindsberg, Herrsch. K. 25, H. 167	228
STLA_1802w_Pflindsberg, Herrsch. K. 25, H. 161	272
STLA_1803w_Pflindsberg, Herrsch. K. 25, H. 159	115
STLA_1804w_Oberradkersburg, Herrsch. K. 150, H. 564	149
STLA_1806w_Pflindsberg, Herrsch. K. 25, H. 173	164
STLA_1810w_Oberradkersburg, Herrsch. K. 150, H. 564_M	280
STLA_1811w_Oberradkersburg, Herrsch. K. 150, H. 564_M	536
OOLA_1812w_Vöcklabruck, Stadtarchiv Sch. 29, Nr. 15_M	412
STLA_1820w_Rothenfels, Herrsch. K. 211, H. 730	353
OOLA_1822w_a_Neuhaus, Herrsch. Nr. 149, VI	216
OOLA_1822w_b_Neuhaus, Herrsch. Nr. 149, VI	564
OOLA_1824w_Vöcklabruck, Stadtarchiv Sch. 29, Nr. 29_M	489
OOLA_1824w_Vöcklabruck, Stadtarchiv Sch. 29, Nr. 29	671
OOLA_1825w_Neuhaus, Herrsch. Nr. 149, VI, 19_M	628
STLA_1828w_Pflindsberg, Herrsch. K. 24, H. 155	156
STLA_1829w_Pflindsberg, Herrsch. K. 24, H. 141_M	358
OOLA_1830p_Ort, Herrsch. Sch. 85 VI	168

Overall, the petition corpus comprises 18,378 words and covers a period of almost 90 years (1744 to 1830). Apart from a period of eight years between the petitions written in 1812 and 1820, the maximum time span between petitions is four years.

4.2 Presentation of results

The following sections deal with the analyses of the texts from these three corpora. A comparison between these corpora will reveal whether the language use differed between reading primers, newspaper issues and petitionary letters. The results for each variable are presented in three separate sections:

- *e*-apocope in nouns, i.e. the absence of *e* in final word position, e.g. *Schul* versus *Schule, in dem Wald* versus *in dem Walde, drei Jahr* versus *drei Jahre.*
- past participles: the absence of the prefix *ge-* in past participles (e.g. *kocht* versus *gekocht*) and variants of regular past participle endings (e.g. *gelernt* versus *gelernet*)

– variants of the verb *to be* in the 1st and 3rd pers. pl. ind. pres., i.e. *wir/sie seyn/d/t* versus *wir/sie sind*.

For each feature, the quantitative results are given in tables presenting the absolute number of tokens. In sections 4.3 and 4.4, which present the findings from the analyses of the reading primers and newpaper issues, figures (in percentages) illustrate the quantitative results if the number of occurrences of the variables was reasonably high. Due to the low number of variables in single petitionary letters, the figures in section 4.5 present absolute numbers (not percentages). The quantitative results are discussed in detail and qualitative analyses were employed in order to uncover possible explanations for the quantitative results.

While quantitative analyses might appear relatively straightforward, there are a number of cases that have to be considered in more detail. With regard to *e*-apocope in nouns, only feminine nouns, strong masculine and neuter nouns in the dative singular form, and plural nouns were included in the results since the number of weak and mixed-declension masculine nouns and strong declension neuter nouns was very low in the three corpora.[153] On the other hand, compound nouns were included in the results, e.g. *Reisleibwagen* with *Reis* being counted as *e*-apocope in feminine nouns, or *Reisegefolge* with *Reise* being counted as a feminine noun with the ending *-e*. Loan words ending in final *-e* (e.g. *die Affaire*) were not counted since the 18th- and early 19th-century pronunciation of these words cannot be determined.

Particularly problematic cases were encountered when analysing the texts for dative *-e*. In a number of instances, writers used accusative case endings for articles, pronouns or adjectives when grammatical rules prescribed the use of dative, e.g. "Der Herzog von Huescar gewester spanischer Bottschafter **an den** Französischen Hof, [...]" (*Wienerisches Diarium* 1749: col. 1, my emphasis). In these cases, which were very rare overall and mostly occurred in the petitionary letters, it was unclear whether these writers used the accusative case deliberately or 'mistakenly', and the noun was not counted as an instance of *e*-apocope or dative *-e*. In a few texts, instances of dative *-e* in accusative objects could be found, e.g. "Obgleich die Kalmucken den Feind von allen Seiten umringt hatten, auch einige Mursen ihre unterhabende Truppen vom Pferde absteigen, und ein heftiges Feuer **auf den Feinde** machen ließen, [...]." (*Wienerisches Diarium* 1769: col. 4, my emphasis). Since the article appears in the accusative case here – conforming to the rules of standard German – this example and similar cases were not counted as instances of dative *-e*.

With regard to past participles, it should be noted that past participles which were used as adjectives were included in the results of the past participles prefix

---

153 Strong declension neuter nouns occurred more frequently than weak and mixed-declension masculine nouns. However, they often appeared in the dative case, which made it impossible to determine whether the final *-e* was a dative *-e* or the final *-e* of the noun stem, e.g. *am Ende*.

variable, e.g. *angekommenen, gedruckten*. For the ending *-t* versus *-et*, they were noted but listed separately. The same method was applied for past participles used as nouns, e.g. *das Erlernte*. The list of past participles with the suffix *-t/-et* only contained regular verbs, irregular verbs with weak verb endings, e.g. *gebracht, gedacht*, were not included. However, verbs that nowadays occur with *Rückumlaut* in standard German, e.g. *erkannt*, were included if they were formed regularly, e.g. *erkenn(e)t*.

The following sections present the results obtained from the reading primers first, followed by the newspaper issues and petitionary letters. A summary of the results for each corpus can be found at the end of each section and a comparison between the three corpora is provided in section 4.6. It has to be kept in mind that these three corpora are not representative for the language use of the population in 18th- and early 19th-century Austria.[154] Instead, they exemplify how language was used in particular text types at that time.

4.3 Language use in reading primers

4.3.1 *e*-apocope in nouns

As mentioned above, all of the 18th-century grammarians discussed, apart from Antesperg, prescribed the ending *-e* for feminine nouns, strong masculine and neuter nouns in the dative singular form as well as nouns in plural.[155] Antesperg accepted the absence of final *-e* in feminine nouns and in the dative singular form of strong masculine and neuter nouns as 'correct' language use. Nouns in plural, by contrast, had to end in *-e*. It is, therefore, not surprising to find instances of *e*-apocope in Antesperg's reading primer (1744). The following table provides the absolute numbers of tokens for both variants in feminine, strong masculine and neuter nouns in dative singular, and plural nouns for all reading primers.

---

154 Cf. Wegera (2013: 64), who points out that "linguistic corpora can never be representative in a strictly statistical sense for a language or a historical stage of a language, because there is a lack of precise knowledge of the so-called overall population".

155 As mentioned before, the *e*-apocope can additionally occur in weak and mixed-declension masculine nouns (e.g. *der Bursch*) as well as strong neuter nouns (e.g. *das End*). Since these types of nouns appear very infrequently in the three corpora and since their inclusion would not significantly change the overall results, they were not counted.

Tab. 14: *e*-apocope versus using the ending *-e* in reading primers: overall (absolute numbers)

Title of book	Place and year of publication	*e*-apocope	ending *-e*
Das Josephinische Erzherzogliche A.B.C. Oder Namenbüchlein (Antesperg)	Vienna, 1744	19	154
Teutsches Namen- oder Lehrbüchl	Vienna, c. 1750	59	68
Ein sehr nutzliches Stimmen-Büchlein	Graz, c. 1770	35	11
Catholisches Namen-Büchl	Linz, 1774	34	6
ABC und Buchstabirbüchlein zum Gebrauche der Landschulen	Prague, 1777	13	163
ABC oder Namenbüchlein zum Gebrauche der Schulen in den kaiserlich-königlichen Staaten	Ljubljana, 1778	3	236
ABC oder Namenbüchlein zum Gebrauche der Schulen in den kaiserlich-königlichen Staaten	Prague, 1779	3	240
ABC oder Namenbüchlein zum Gebrauche der Oesterreichischen Normalschule	Vienna, 1782	2	237
ABC oder Namenbüchlein zum Gebrauche der Landschulen	Vienna, 1783	15	231
Neuestes ABC-Buch oder Uebungen im Syllabieren oder Buchstabiren und im Lesen	Vienna, 1802	8	174
Nahmenbüchlein zum Gebrauche der Stadtschulen in den kaiserl. königl. Staaten	Graz, 1804	3	361
ABC und Buchstabierbüchlein nebst Leseübungen für Anfänger	Bolzano, 1809	46	189
Der kleine Abc-Schüler	Salzburg, 1818	3	122
Syllabier-Büchlein zum Privatgebrauche (Kirchmayr)	Vienna, 1828	1	242
Nahmenbüchlein für Stadtschulen in den kaiserl. königl. Staaten	Linz, 1833	5	360

As the following figure illustrates, the percentage of nouns displaying *e*-apocope in Antesperg's *Erzherzogliche A.B.C.* (11 %) is rather low in comparison to the reading primers printed in c. 1750, c. 1770, and 1774. In the *Teutsche Namen- oder Lehrbüchl* (c. 1750), the occurrences of *e*-apocope and ending *-e* are relatively balanced, with 46 % versus 54 % respectively, while the *e*-apocope is clearly dominant in the *[S]ehr nutzliches Stimmen-Büchlein* (76 %) and in the *Catholisches Namen-Büchl* (85 %). In some sense, Antesperger's primer seems relatively 'modern', i.e. closer to today's standard, compared to other *Namenbüchlein* printed within 20 years of its publication. All of the primers printed between 1744 and 1774 contain prayers, but only the latter two specifically state that they are Catholic reading primers or that they contain Catholic prayers: *Catholisches Namen-Büchl* (1774) and *Ein sehr nutzliches*

Stimmen-Büchlein [...] *auch mit Schönen Catholischen Gebethlein / Morgens und Abends / vor= und nach dem Essen in allen verbessert* (c. 1770). This might confirm Rössler's argument (2005: 247) of the intentional use of *e*-apocope in Catholic texts in order to indicate distance to ECG Protestant texts.[156]

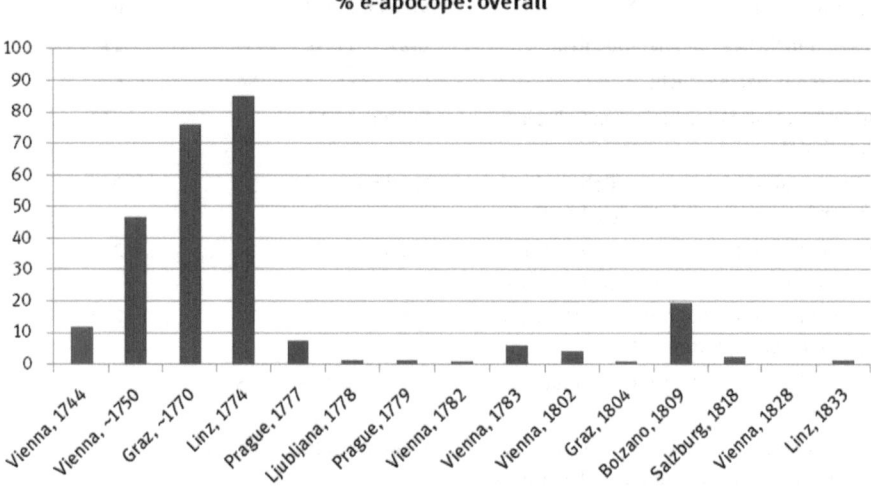

Fig. 5: *e*-apocope in reading primers: overall (in percentages)

After 1774, a sharp drop in the occurrences of *e*-apocope (to 7 %)[157] can be observed in the *ABC und Buchstabirbüchlein zum Gebrauche der Landschulen* (1777) – the first reading primer analysed from Felbiger's list of approved textbooks. This percentage decreases further to just 1 % in the subsequent three reading primers, with only eight nouns displaying *e*-apocope: *Gnad, Plag* (both printed in 1778, 1779 and 1782), *beim Doppelpunkt* (1778) and *im Verlag* (1779). With regard to the feminine nouns, it should be noted that these occur in a list of monosyllabic words in these reading primers. This formal constraint has probably resulted in the inclusion of nouns that would otherwise have been spelt with final -*e*.

This constraint is also noticeable in both editions of the *Namenbüchlein zum Gebrauche der Landschulen* (1777 and 1783), which contain almost the same percentage

---

156 Antesperg's reading primer and the reading primer printed around 1750 may also have been Catholic books but they do not state so explicitly. In other words, while the primers printed around 1770 and in 1774 are clearly identified as Catholic, the other two books are not, and a religious affiliation may have been of less importance to the authors of these primers.
157 This equates to 13 nouns with *e*-apocope, which will be mentioned below.

of *e*-apocope (7 % and 6 %). Ten out of the 13 (1777) / 15 (1783) nouns with *e*-apocope appear in the monosyllabic word lists on pages 10 and 12 of those primers (see figure below).

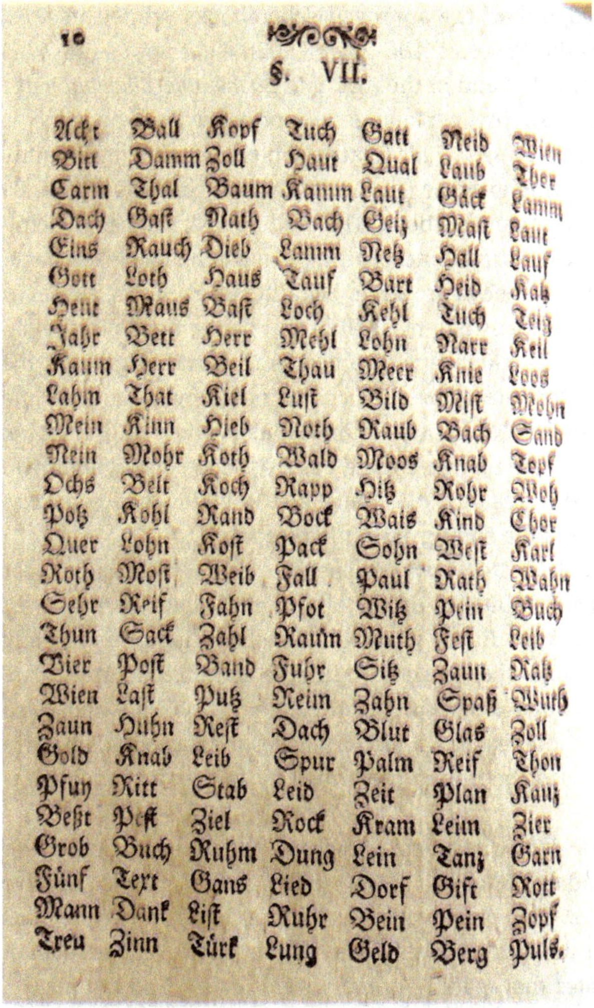

10

§. VII.

Ackt	Ball	Kopf	Tuch	Gatt	Neid	Wien
Birt	Damm	Zoll	Haut	Qual	Laub	Ther
Carm	Thal	Baum	Kamm	Laut	Gäck	Lamm
Dach	Gaſt	Nath	Bach	Geiz	Maſt	Laut
Eins	Rauch	Dieb	Lamm	Netz	Hall	Lauf
Gott	Loth	Haus	Tauf	Bart	Heid	Katz
Heut	Maus	Baſt	Loch	Kehl	Tuch	Teig
Jahr	Bett	Herr	Mehl	Lohn	Narr	Keil
Kaum	Herr	Beil	Thau	Meer	Knie	Loos
Lahm	That	Kiel	Luſt	Bild	Miſt	Mohn
Mein	Kinn	Hieb	Noth	Raub	Bach	Sand
Nein	Mohr	Koth	Wald	Moos	Knab	Topf
Ochs	Beit	Koch	Rapp	Hitz	Rohr	Woh
Poß	Kohl	Rand	Bock	Wais	Kind	Chor
Quer	Lohn	Koſt	Pack	Sohn	Weſt	Karl
Roth	Moſt	Weib	Fall	Paul	Rath	Wahn
Sehr	Reif	Fahn	Pfot	Witz	Pein	Buch
Thun	Sack	Zahl	Raum	Muth	Feſt	Leib
Bier	Poſt	Band	Fuhr	Sitz	Zaun	Ratz
Wien	Laſt	Putz	Reim	Zahn	Spaß	Wuth
Zaun	Huhn	Reſt	Dach	Blut	Glas	Zoll
Gold	Knab	Leib	Spur	Palm	Reif	Thon
Pfuy	Ritt	Stab	Leid	Zeit	Plan	Kauz
Beßt	Peſt	Ziel	Rock	Kram	Leim	Zier
Grob	Buch	Ruhm	Dung	Lein	Tanz	Garn
Fünf	Text	Gans	Lied	Dorf	Gift	Rott
Mann	Dank	Liſt	Ruhr	Bein	Pein	Zopf
Treu	Zinn	Türk	Lung	Geld	Berg	Puls.

Fig. 6: List of monosyllabic words in the *Namenbüchlein zum Gebrauche der Landschulen* (1777: 10)

The content between the two editions of the *Namenbüchlein zum Gebrauche der Landschulen* is, however, very different. The introductory parts on letters remain the same – with increasing difficulty from monosyllabic words to polysyllabic words – but the 1777 edition continues with reading exercises (i.e. children's stories with moral messages) while the *Namenbüchlein* printed in 1783 proceeds with prayers and *Der kleine Katechismus* (i.e. a list of questions and answers on Catholic doctrines). The majority of the texts analysed in these primers were, therefore, not the same.

It is also striking that two of the reading primers designed for home use display higher percentages of *e*-apocope than the approved schoolbooks printed in 1778, 1779, 1782, 1804, and 1833. In the *Neuestes ABC-Buch* (1802), eight nouns (i.e. 4 %) are spelled without the prescribed -*e* and in the *ABC und Buchstabierbüchlein nebst Leseübungen für Anfänger* (1809), the percentages of nouns with *e*-apocope is significantly higher (20 %, i.e. 46 nouns). This relatively high percentage is mainly due to an eleven-page-long reading exercise (pp. 13–23), which contains 38 (i.e. 83 %) of the 46 instances of *e*-apocope in this book. The reading task teaches the children about God in monosyllabic words. Since writing a meaningful eleven-page-long text in monosyllabic words will have proven to be rather difficult, the author of the book never used the suffix -*e* for strong masculine and neuter nouns in the dative singular form in this text. The *e*-apocope also occurs in plural forms (e.g. *die Leut, die Stein)*. Furthermore, the author uses 28 abbreviated nouns (such as *die Sonn', das Aug', im Staub', die Stern'*) to fulfil the monosyllabic-word requirement of the task.[158] These abbreviations were neither counted as *e*-apocope nor as ending -*e* since they indicate that *e*-apocope was possible, whilst also implying that *e*-apocope was not perceived as 'correct' and the ending -*e* should be used.[159]

Kirchmayr's *Syllabier-Büchlein* (1828), which specifies that it is designed for home use in its title (*zum Privatgebrauche*), on the other hand, contains the lowest percentage of nouns with *e*-apocope in the whole corpus of reading primers. Only one out of 243 nouns (i.e. 0.4 %) is spelled without final -*e* and this occurrence appears in a binomial pair: *Speis und Trank* (p. 19). The title page of this book also states that Kirchmayr was a school teacher, which indicates that at least some 19th-century teachers had internalised the norms prescribed by 18th-century grammarians.

In the last reading primer included in this corpus – the *Nahmenbüchlein für Stadtschulen in den kaiserl. königl. Staaten* (1833) – only 1.4 % of nouns (i.e. five nouns) appear without final -*e*. This percentage was slightly lower in the previous edition printed in 1804 (0.8 %, i.e. three nouns). This slight change in the number of nouns without final -*e* indicates that reading primers were revised and not just reprinted. Both editions include the feminine noun *Kloak* in a list of two- and three-syllable words but the binomial pair *nach Maß und Gewichte* (1804) was changed to

---

158 It would be interesting to see whether reading primers from Northern and Central German areas contained similar passages and how the monosyllabic-word requirement was dealt with in these primers.

159 A significantly smaller number of similar abbreviated nouns were found in the other primers and the same procedure (i.e. neither counting them as *e*-apocope nor final -*e*) was applied.

nach Maß und Gewicht in the 1833 edition. Furthermore, the absent dative *-e* in *zum Verkauf* (1804) was added in the later edition. In turn, however, the neuter singular dative construction *aus dem Mehl* appears without *-e* in the 1833 edition. In this edition, also the noun *Wäsche* is spelled without final *-e* in the phrase *rein sey Wäsch und Kleid* (changed from *rein sey Wäsche und Kleid*).

These changes are very minor in comparison to the more radical development between c. 1750 and 1777. With regard to noun endings, Felbiger's school reform appears to have had a strong impact on the language used in reading primers designed to be used in school and at home. The analysis of textbooks further revealed that Antesperg's primer published in 1744 was 'modern' in comparison to the three subsequent primers. Even though Antesperg accepted the *e*-apocope in feminine nouns as well as strong masculine and neuter nouns in the dative case as 'correct' language use in his grammar, he clearly preferred using the ending *-e* in his reading primer, especially in feminine nouns, as the following table illustrates.

Tab. 15: *e*-apocope versus using the ending *-e* in reading primers: feminine nouns (absolute numbers)

Title of book	Place and year of publication	*e*-apocope	ending *-e*
Das Josephinische Erzherzogliche A.B.C. Oder Namenbüchlein (Antesperg)	Vienna, 1744	5	96
Teutsches Namen- oder Lehrbüchl	Vienna, c. 1750	32	33
Ein sehr nutzliches Stimmen-Büchlein	Graz, c. 1770	19	7
Catholisches Namen-Büchl	Linz, 1774	20	4
ABC und Buchstabirbüchlein zum Gebrauche der Landschulen	Prague, 1777	10	87
ABC oder Namenbüchlein zum Gebrauche der Schulen in den kaiserlich-königlichen Staaten	Ljubljana, 1778	2	120
ABC oder Namenbüchlein zum Gebrauche der Schulen in den kaiserlich-königlichen Staaten	Prague, 1779	2	120
ABC oder Namenbüchlein zum Gebrauche der Oesterreichischen Normalschule	Vienna, 1782	2	120
ABC oder Namenbüchlein zum Gebrauche der Landschulen	Vienna, 1783	11	131
Neuestes ABC-Buch oder Uebungen im Syllabieren oder Buchstabiren und im Lesen	Vienna, 1802	1	98
Nahmenbüchlein zum Gebrauche der Stadtschulen in den kaiserl. königl. Staaten	Graz, 1804	1	165
ABC und Buchstabierbüchlein nebst Leseübungen für Anfänger	Bolzano, 1809	6	108

Title of book	Place and year of publication	e-apocope	ending -e
Der kleine Abc-Schüler	Salzburg, 1818	1	61
Syllabier-Büchlein zum Privatgebrauche (Kirchmayr)	Vienna, 1828	1	150
Nahmenbüchlein für Stadtschulen in den kaiserl. königl. Staaten	Linz, 1833	2	165

Only five feminine nouns are spelled without final -*e* in Antesperg's *Erzherzogliche A.B.C.* (1744): *Gems, Katz, Waar, Wag, Stund*, with the first three appearing in a list of four-letter-words (p. 20) and *Wag* occurring in a list of monosyllabic words (p. 21). The noun *Stunde*, by contrast, is spelled without -*e* in the Hail Mary (p. 28). This Catholic prayer is also included in the subsequent three reading primers (printed c. 1750, c. 1770, and 1774), where *Stunde* is also spelled without final -*e*.

Apart from Antesperg's reading primer and the *ABC und Buchstabierbüchlein nebst Leseübungen für Anfänger* (1809), which also displays significantly fewer feminine nouns with *e*-apocope than the overall results would suggest, the following figure of percentages for *e*-apocope in feminine nouns closely resembles that of the overall findings.

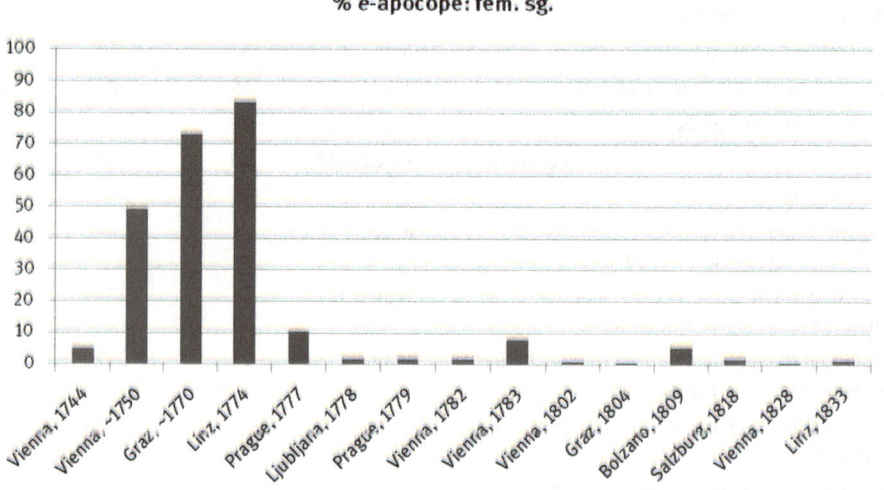

Fig. 7: *e*-apocope in reading primers: feminine nouns (in percentages)

In order to find out if the instances of *e*-apocope are limited to certain feminine nouns, the following table lists all feminine words that display *e*-apocope alphabetically, with numbers in square brackets indicating how often these words occur in the same reading primer, if exceeding 1. Feminine nouns without final -*e* that appear in more than one reading primer (excluding different editions of the same textbook) are marked in grey.

Tab. 16: Feminine nouns without final -*e* in reading primers

Title of book	Place and year of publication	nouns with *e*-apocope
Das Josephinische Erzherzogliche A.B.C. Oder Namenbüchlein (Antesperg)	Vienna, 1744	Gems, Katz, Stund, Waar, Wag
Teutsches Namen- oder Lehrbüchl	Vienna, c. 1750	Bien, Blum, Ehr [2], Erd, Feil, Fers, Gnad [3], Hülf, Kält, Kirch, Lehr, Lieb [2], Morgenstund, Münz, Reu, Sach, Schlang, Schul, Seel [3], Sonn, Sprach [2], Stund [3], Ungnad
Ein sehr nutzliches Stimmen-Büchlein	Graz, c. 1770	Blum, Ehr [2], Freud, Glock, Gnad [2], Herberg, Lichtmeß, Lieb, Müh, Schneck, Seel [2], Sorg, Speis, Stund [2], Sünd
Catholisches Namen-Büchl	Linz, 1774	Blum, Ehr [3], Freud [2], Glock, Gnad [3], Katz, Lieb, Milchsupp, Pfeif, Seel [2], Speis, Spritz, Stund, Turteltaub
ABC und Buchstabirbüchlein zum Gebrauche der Landschulen	Prague, 1777	Bitt, Fahn, Fuhr, Hitz, Katz, Lung, Pfot, Quitt, Rott, Tauf
ABC oder Namenbüchlein zum Gebrauche der Schulen in den kaiserlich-königlichen Staaten	Ljubljana, 1778	Gnad, Plag
ABC oder Namenbüchlein zum Gebrauche der Schulen in den kaiserlich-königlichen Staaten	Prague, 1779	Gnad, Plag
ABC oder Namenbüchlein zum Gebrauche der Oesterreichischen Normalschule	Vienna, 1782	Gnad, Plag
ABC oder Namenbüchlein zum Gebrauche der Landschulen	Vienna, 1783	Bitt, Fahn, Fuhr, Hitz, Katz, Lung, Pfot, Quitt, Rott, Stund, Tauf
Neuestes ABC-Buch oder Uebungen im Syllabieren oder Buchstabiren und im Lesen	Vienna, 1802	Birn
Nahmenbüchlein zum Gebrauche der Stadtschulen in den kaiserl. königl. Staaten	Graz, 1804	Kloak

Title of book	Place and year of publication	nouns with *e*-apocope
ABC und Buchstabierbüchlein nebst Leseübungen für Anfänger	Bolzano, 1809	Birn, Katz, Quitt, Schand, Speis, Sünd
Der kleine Abc-Schüler	Salzburg, 1818	Sonn
Syllabier-Büchlein zum Privatgebrauche (Kirchmayr)	Vienna, 1828	Speis
Nahmenbüchlein für Stadtschulen in den kaiserl. königl. Staaten	Linz, 1833	Kloak, Wäsch

The noun *Stund(e)* is spelled without -*e* in five different reading primers, most notably also in one reading primer printed after 1774. However, in this second edition of the *ABC oder Namenbüchlein zum Gebrauche der Landschulen* (1783), the noun *Stund* only occurs in the Hail Mary (p. 25), i.e. in a very formulaic text. Another re-occurring feminine noun is *Gnad*, which appears in the reading primers printed in c. 1750, c. 1770, 1774, 1778, 1779, and 1782. It should, however be noted that *Gnad* is included in a list of monosyllabic words in the latter three textbooks and spelled with final -*e* in other parts of the books. Similarly, the noun *Birn* is included as part of a monosyllabic-word list in the *Neuestes ABC-Buch* (1802: 12) and appears in the text exclusively containing monosyllabic words in the primer printed in 1809 (p. 22). The noun *Speis* appears in conjunction with *Trank* in all reading primers, i.e. in the binomial pair *Speis und Trank*. It is rather unexpected that the noun *Speis* was spelled with -*e* in the same binomial pair in the second edition of the *Namenbüchlein zum Gebrauche der Landschulen* (1783: 18), given the highly formulaic nature of this construction.

The only feminine noun with *e*-apocope in *Der kleine Abc-Schüler* (1818) is *Sonn* (p. 38). The ECG variant *Sonne*, however, also appears in this reading primer (p. 37). In the *Teutsches Namen- oder Lehrbüchl* (c. 1750), only the UG variant without -*e* occurs. This reading primer contains a few nouns with variation between *e*-apocope and final -*e*. For example, both variants *Erd* and *Erde* are written on page 42, with the first referring to the earth as a globe and being preceded by the definite article *die*, and the second variant referring to earth as one of the four elements (*earth*, *air*, *fire*, and *water*) without any article (as *Erde* here refers to a mass noun). In other words, there may be a semantic distinction between the noun spelled with and without final -*e*. The definite article preceding a noun does not appear to influence the use of final -*e* since other nouns preceded by a definite article are spelled with -*e* (e.g. *die Zunge* on p. 22) and nouns without definite article also display *e*-apocope (e.g. *Stund*, *Sach* on p. 16). It can, therefore, not be argued that there is a systematic morpho-syntactic rule behind the use of one of the variants.

In summary, the *e*-apocope in feminine nouns was widely used in the *Teutsches Namen- oder Lehrbüchl* (c. 1750), and is even dominant in the reading primers printed in c. 1770 and in 1774. In Antesperg's *Erzherzogliche A.B.C.* (1744), on the other hand, only 5 % of feminine nouns are spelled without final -*e*, which indicates Antesperg's preference for the ECG norm with -*e*. Similar to the overall results, all reading primers printed after 1774 display a low percentage (not more than 10 %) of feminine nouns with *e*-apocope. Even in the *ABC und Buchstabierbüchlein nebst Leseübungen für Anfänger* (1809), which showed a relatively high percentage of *e*-apocope in the overall findings, only 5 % of feminine nouns were spelled without final -*e*. This indicates that either strong masculine and neuter nouns in the dative singular form or nouns in plural were frequently spelled without final -*e* in this particular reading primer. The following table reveals that the number of *e*-apocope in strong masculine and neuter nouns in the dative singular form almost equals the number of nouns with dative -*e* in the *ABC und Buchstabierbüchlein nebst Leseübungen für Anfänger* (1809).

Tab. 17: *e*-apocope versus using the ending -*e* in reading primers: strong masculine and neuter nouns in the dative singular form (absolute numbers)

Title of book	Place and year of publication	*e*-apocope	ending -*e*
Das Josephinische Erzherzogliche A.B.C. Oder Namenbüchlein (Antesperg)	Vienna, 1744	16	18
Teutsches Namen- oder Lehrbüchl	Vienna, c. 1750	21	0
Ein sehr nutzliches Stimmen-Büchlein	Graz, c. 1770	9	0
Catholisches Namen-Büchl	Linz, 1774	13	0
ABC und Buchstabirbüchlein zum Gebrauche der Landschulen	Prague, 1777	3	41
ABC oder Namenbüchlein zum Gebrauche der Schulen in den kaiserlich-königlichen Staaten	Ljubljana, 1778	1	67
ABC oder Namenbüchlein zum Gebrauche der Schulen in den kaiserlich-königlichen Staaten	Prague, 1779	1	69
ABC oder Namenbüchlein zum Gebrauche der Oesterreichischen Normalschule	Vienna, 1782	0	69
ABC oder Namenbüchlein zum Gebrauche der Landschulen	Vienna, 1783	4	46
Neuestes ABC-Buch oder Uebungen im Syllabieren oder Buchstabiren und im Lesen	Vienna, 1802	7	25
Nahmenbüchlein zum Gebrauche der Stadtschulen in den kaiserl. königl. Staaten	Graz, 1804	2	57
ABC und Buchstabierbüchlein nebst Leseübungen für Anfänger	Bolzano, 1809	35	41
Der kleine Abc-Schüler	Salzburg, 1818	2	8

Title of book	Place and year of publication	*e*-apocope	ending -*e*
Syllabier-Büchlein zum Privatgebrauche (Kirchmayr)	Vienna, 1828	0	30
Nahmenbüchlein für Stadtschulen in den kaiserl. königl. Staaten	Linz, 1833	3	54

As mentioned before, the majority of nouns without dative -*e* (30 out of 35) in the *ABC und Buchstabierbüchlein nebst Leseübungen für Anfänger* (1809) occur in the 11-page-long text composed of monosyllabic words. After this text, the dative -*e* occurs frequently, with just a few exceptions: *am Weinstock, mit Sauerteig, zum Fluch und Schwur, am späten Abend.* In other words, the *e*-apocope in strong masculine and neuter nouns in the dative singular form was mainly dictated by the formal constraints of one text in this reading primer.

In Antesperg's *Erzherzogliche[s] A.B.C.* (1744), by contrast, variation seems to be the norm (see table below, with prepositional phrases being ordered alphabetically).[160] In the case of *nach Haus* versus *nach Hause* as well as *im 2. Theil* versus *im zweiten Theile* the same prepositional phrases are spelled once with and once without dative -*e*. Generally, the prepositions do not seem to dictate the use of dative -*e* in Antesperg's primer. The prepositions *an, in, mit,* and *nach* are followed by nouns with and without dative -*e*. There are, however, a few similarities to other reading primers: There is no dative -*e* after the preposition *mit* if it is immediately followed by a noun (*mit Fleiß*). This principle also applies to the reading primers printed in 1777 (*mit Sauerteig*), 1802 (*mit Zuckerwerk*), and 1809 (*mit Sauerteig*). Furthermore, the noun *Gott* appears without dative -*e* (cf. the primers printed in 1809 and 1818).

Tab. 18: *e*-apocope versus dative -*e* in Antesperg's *Erzherzogliche[s] A.B.C.* (1744)

e-apocope	dative -*e*
ab dem großen Gott	
am Fuß, am Verstand	am dritten Tage, am Leibe [2]
bey dem Tisch	
im Feld, im Heil. Röm. Reich, im 2. Theil, in dem Wort	im Jahre, im zweiten Theile [4], in dem Werke, in einem Worte

---

160 Nouns without any preceding preposition are not provided in the table. In Antesperg's primer, the only strong masculine or neuter noun in dative singular case without any preceding preposition is *dem Schulkinde* (p. 11).

e-apocope	dative -e
mit dem Heiligen Creuz, mit Fleiß [2]	mit einem Hunde, mit einem jeden Worte [2], mit einem mündlichen Fleiße, mit seinem kostbarlichen Blute
nach dem Vorbild, nach Haus	nach Hause
	unter Königlichem Schutze
vor deinem Angesicht, vor dem Tisch	
zu Haus	

In Antesperg's reading primer (1744: 32), final -e is added once to a mixed-declension neuter noun in the accusative case [my emphasis]: "Hierbey soll man die Schul-Kinder mündlich unterweisen, [...] wie es [das Schulkind] sodann sich manierlich abkleiden, und **ins Bette** legen soll." ("Hereby one should instruct the pupils how they should properly undress, and go to bed"). This shows that Antesperg also used the dative -e in an accusative construction, but he did not use it consistently. Instead, it seems that variation was acceptable and normal to him.

While the use between e-apocope and dative -e is fairly balanced in Antesperg's primer, dative -e never occurs in the reading primers printed in c. 1750, c. 1770 and 1774. In the reading primers printed in 1782 and 1828, on the other hand, strong masculine and neuter nouns in the dative singular form are always spelled with final -e.[161] Also in all further textbooks that were to be used in schools and printed after 1774, the percentage of e-apocope in strong masculine and neuter nouns in the dative singular form was very low, as the following figure illustrates.

---

161 Since there is no variation with regard to dative -e in these five primers, they will not be discussed in detail.

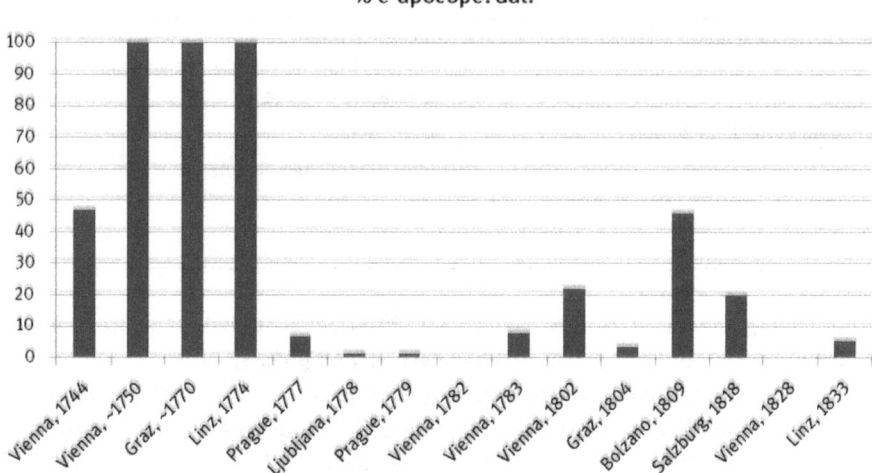

Fig. 8: *e*-apocope in reading primers: strong masculine and neuter nouns in the dative singular form (in percentages)

This figure presents a rather different picture from the overall results and highlights the importance of distinguishing between different nouns with regard to *e*-apocope. The *e*-apocope in strong masculine and neuter nouns in the dative singular form seemed to be more accepted than the *e*-apocope in feminine nouns in the reading primers printed before 1777 and in most of the reading primers designed for home use. However, it has to be pointed out that the number of strong masculine and neuter nouns appearing in the dative case is very low in a number of reading primers, most notably in the *[N]utzliches Stimmen-Büchlein* (c. 1770, 9 nouns) and *Der kleine Abc-Schüler* (1818, 10 nouns). In the latter primer, 20 % of *e*-apocope equate to just two instances: *mit dem lieben Gott* and *dem lieben Gott*. The figure of percentages is, therefore, somewhat misleading.

The data is more reliable for the *Neuestes ABC-Buch* (1802), in which seven nouns (22 %) occur without and 25 nouns (78 %) with dative *-e*. The following nouns appear without dative *-e*: *von* [...] *dem Gebrauch, mit Zuckerwerk, von Lorenzens Fleiß überzeugt, dem lieben Gott, zum kleinsten Wurm, zum Unglück, zum Abend*. It is striking that three out of these seven instances are preceded by the preposition *zu* in connection with the definite article *dem*. There is only one counter example in this reading primer: *zum Frühstücke*. If the preposition *zu* is followed by a spelled-out article, a pronoun or just the noun, the dative *-e* is added: *zu diesem Geschäfte, zu diesem Zwecke, zu einem größern Verdienste, zu Hause, zu Mittage*. Furthermore, the preposition *von* is followed by *e*-apocope and no counter examples are given in the reading primer. The same is true for the preposition *mit* if it is not followed by any article or pronoun (*mit Zuckerwerk*).[162] The final *-e*, however, occurs if there is an article or pronoun between *mit* and the noun: *mit seinem Sohne, mit einem Stocke, mit dem* [...] *Fleische, mit seinem Weibe*. Also after the prepositions *in, aus, auf*, and *bei*, nouns always take dative *-e* in the *Neuestes ABC-Buch: in jedem Falle, im vollen Maaße, in einem Gerichte, in keinem Falle, im Felde, aus diesem Beyspiele, aus dem Wege, auf dem Lande, bey seinem großen Geschäfte*. Furthermore, the noun *Gott* does not take dative *-e* (as in the reading primers printed in 1744 and 1818). The occurrence of dative *-e* versus *e*-apocope, therefore, does not seem completely arbitrary, even if the patterns behind the use of dative *-e* are difficult to establish.

In other cases, the *e*-apocope in strong masculine and neuter nouns in the dative singular form may have been 'mistakes' made by the author or typesetter. In the textbook printed in 1778, the only noun without dative *-e* is *beim Doppelpunkt* (p. 29), while *beim Beistriche, beim Strichpunkte*, and *beim Schlusspunkte* – written immediately before or after *beim Doppelpunkt* – appear with dative *-e*. Even *bei dem Doppelpunkte* is spelled with dative *-e* further down the same page. Similarly, the dative *-e* was added to *zum Verkauf* (p. 28) in the second edition of the *Nahmenbüchlein für Stadtschulen* (1833), while being spelled without final *-e* in first edition (1804). Additionally, *aus dem Mehl* (p. 28), which had dative *-e* in the first edition, could be seen as a spelling mistake in the textbook printed in 1833, given that 54 nouns appear with dative *-e* in the same primer. Just two other neuter nouns, which formed part of a binomial pair, were spelled without final *-e*: *nach Maß und Gewicht* (p. 25). Another instance of *e*-apocope in strong masculine and neuter nouns in the dative singular form that could be considered a spelling mistake is the noun *Samstag* in the *Namenbüchlein zum Gebrauche der Landschulen* (1783). It occurs without final *-e* in the construction *am Feyertage und Samstag* (p. 27). The same construction was used in the textbooks printed in 1778, 1779, and 1782, where *Samstag* was spelled with dative *-e*. However, given that spelling mistakes overall are very rare in these textbooks, the absence of dative *-e* is not necessarily a 'spelling mistake' but a deliberate use of *e*-apocope.

Even if the cases discussed above were 'spelling mistakes', they do not change the overall trend towards the dative *-e* in all reading primers printed after 1774. The reading primers from Felbiger's approved list of textbooks showed a very low percentage of *e*-apocope in strong masculine and neuter nouns in the dative singular form. The reading primers designed for home use generally followed this trend. The relatively high percentage of *e*-apocope in the *ABC und Buchstabierbüchlein* (1809) is due to the formal constraints of one particular text and the low number of total occurrences (10 nouns) has to be taken into account when looking at the percentages given for *Der kleine Abc-Schüler* (1818).

---

162 Cf. the reading primers printed in 1744, 1777, and 1809.

Insufficient data in two reading primers also presents a problem when analysing plural forms. Only eleven nouns occur in plural in the *[N]utzliches Stimmen-Büchlein* (c. 1770) and this number is even lower in the *Catholisches Namen-Büchl* (1774), with just three nouns in plural (see table below). Even the inclusion of the one case of *e*-apocope in plural forms in the latter reading primer is questionable since the noun ending is *-en* (not just *-e*) in *alle meine Sünd* (p. 37) or similar constructions in other reading primers. *Alle meine Sünden* appears, for example, in the *Teutsches Namen- oder Lehrbüchl* (c. 1750: 39) and *alle Sünden* in the reading primer printed in 1778 (p. 20).[163] The cases with plural *-e* are, however, clear: *Hände* and *Gebothe*. Interestingly, the same nouns occur in the reading primer printed in c. 1770, which includes the Ten Commandments and the same evening prayer as the primer printed in 1774. In the *[N]utzliches Stimmen-Büchlein* (c. 1770), *alle meine Sünd* as well as *deine Händ* appear without final *-en/-e*. The plural is also unmarked in *zehn Gebott, viel schöne Ding, drey Halbdoppellaut* and *alle Tag*. While *deine Händ* appears without plural *-e* twice, it is once marked – as are three other nouns: *acht Zwillinge, elf Hauptdoppellaute*, and *die Steine*. Since both *Händ(e)* and *Halb-/ Hauptdoppellaut(e)* appear in both variants, it can be argued that the author of this reading primer found variation in plural markings acceptable.

Tab. 19: *e*-apocope versus using the ending *-e* in reading primers: plural (in total numbers)

Title of book	Place and year of publication	*e*-apocope	ending *-e*
Das Josephinische Erzherzogliche A.B.C. Oder Namenbüchlein (Antesperg)	Vienna, 1744	0	41
Teutsches Namen- oder Lehrbüchl	Vienna, c. 1750	6	34
Ein sehr nutzliches Stimmen-Büchlein	Graz, c. 1770	7	4
Catholisches Namen-Büchl	Linz, 1774	1	2
ABC und Buchstabirbüchlein zum Gebrauche der Landschulen	Prague, 1777	0	35
ABC oder Namenbüchlein zum Gebrauche der Schulen in den kaiserlich-königlichen Staaten	Ljubljana, 1778	0	49
ABC oder Namenbüchlein zum Gebrauche der Schulen in den kaiserlich königlichen Staaten	Prague, 1779	0	51
ABC oder Namenbüchlein zum Gebrauche der Oesterreichischen Normalschule	Vienna, 1782	0	48

---

163 Since not marking feminine nouns in plural with *-(e)n* is rather unusual in the 18th century (cf. Solms & Wegera 1993: 179) and due to the low number of nouns in plural, these instances were included in the results of the analysis.

Title of book	Place and year of publication	*e*-apocope	ending -*e*
ABC oder Namenbüchlein zum Gebrauche der Landschulen	Vienna, 1783	0	54
Neuestes ABC-Buch oder Uebungen im Syllabieren oder Buchstabiren und im Lesen	Vienna, 1802	0	50
Nahmenbüchlein zum Gebrauche der Stadtschulen in den kaiserl. königl. Staaten	Graz, 1804	0	139
ABC und Buchstabierbüchlein nebst Leseübungen für Anfänger	Bolzano, 1809	5	40
Der kleine Abc-Schüler	Salzburg, 1818	0	53
Syllabier-Büchlein zum Privatgebrauche (Kirchmayr)	Vienna, 1828	0	62
Nahmenbüchlein für Stadtschulen in den kaiserl. königl. Staaten	Linz, 1833	0	141

Apart from the reading primers printed in c. 1770 and in 1774, only two other reading primers included plural nouns that were not marked with final -*e*. The *Teutsches Namen- oder Lehrbüchl* (c. 1750) included the following nouns in plural (ordered alphabetically).

Tab. 20: *e*-apocope versus plural -*e* in the *Teutsches Namen- oder Lehrbüchl* (c. 1750)

e-apocope	plural -*e*
(zehn) Gebot, (24) Stund, (sieben) Täg, (vier) Theil, Zähn [2]	Aufsätze, Bäume [2], Birnbäume, Dinge, Dünste, Fische, Gänse, Gebeine, Hände [2], Höfe, Hüte [2], Klötze, Köpfe, Körbe, Künste, Metalle, Nüsse, Osternächte, Reime, Röcke, Sprüche, Ströme, Täge [2], Tausenddienste, Winde, Worte, Zähne [3], Zäune

The majority of nouns in plural (85 %) were marked with -*e* in this reading primer but some variation can be detected: *Täg(e)* is spelled without final -*e* once, and with plural -*e* twice. Similarly, *Zähn(e)* occurs without plural -*e* twice but with -*e* three times. As in the reading primer printed in c. 1770, the *Zehn Gebot* are not marked with plural -*e*. In general, however, the plural -*e* is clearly dominant. This is also the case for the *ABC und Buchstabierbüchlein* (1809), which contains four unmarked plural nouns in its monosyllabic text (*Erd=Beer, Leut* [2], *Stein*) plus one plural noun without final -*e* on page 26: *(zwölf) Jahr*. Since the *e*-apocope in the first four cases can be attributed to the formal constraints of the monosyllabic text[164], it is the last occurrence that is particularly interesting as the plural of temporal nouns (*Stund, Täg*) is also unmarked in the *Teutsches Namen- oder Lehrbüchl* (c. 1750). By contrast, plural forms are always marked with final -*e* in Antesperg's *Erzherzogliche[s] A.B.C.* (1744) – in line with the prescriptions in his grammar.

Overall, the results of the analysis of *e*-apocope in plural nouns suggest that the *e*-apocope was less accepted in these cases than in feminine singular nouns and in strong masculine and neuter nouns in the dative singular form. The plural is usually marked with -*e(n)*, while the *e*-apocope only appears in four reading primers and is only dominant in one of them. In the other 11 reading primers, the *e*-apocope is completely invisible in plural nouns.

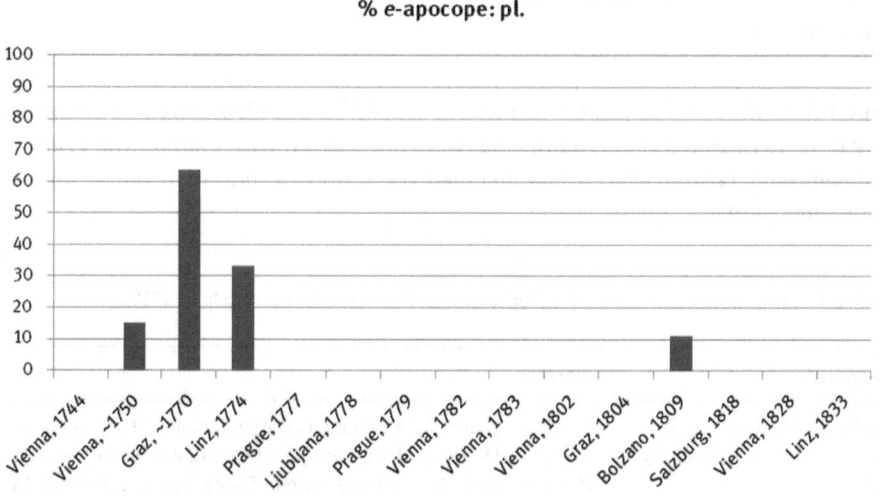

Fig. 9: *e*-apocope in reading primers: plural (in percentages)

A comparison between the figures above reveals that the use of final -*e* developed differently in feminine nouns, strong masculine and neuter nouns in the dative singular form, and plural nouns. This highlights the importance of distinguishing between these nouns. In general, it can, however, be argued that the introduction of the school reform in 1774 had a significant effect on the language use in reading primers with regard to the number of instances of *e*-apocope in nouns. The follow-

---

164 Indeed, *Leute* occurs with plural -*e* six times in the rest of the primer, and *Edelsteine* can be found on page 48 with plural -*e*.

ing section will show if a similar development can be observed in the use of past participle prefixes and endings.

4.3.2 Past participles

With regard to the prefix *ge-* in past participles, quite remarkably, not a single instance of the UG variant without *ge-* can be found in any of the reading primers. The number of past participles that can be formed without *ge-* is, however, rather low in several reading primers in comparison to the overall numbers of *e*-apocope, especially in the *[N]utzliches Stimmen-Büchlein* (c. 1770), the *Catholisches Namen-Büchl* (1774), and *Der kleine Abc-Schüler* (1818), as the following table illustrates.[165]

Tab. 21: Past participle prefixes in reading primers (absolute numbers)

Title of book	Place and year of publication	without *ge-*	with *ge-*
Das Josephinische Erzherzogliche A.B.C. Oder Namenbüchlein (Antesperg)	Vienna, 1744	0	17
Teutsches Namen- oder Lehrbüchl	Vienna, c. 1750	0	30
Ein sehr nutzliches Stimmen-Büchlein	Graz, c. 1770	0	9
Catholisches Namen-Büchl	Linz, 1774	0	10
ABC und Buchstabirbüchlein zum Gebrauche der Landschulen	Prague, 1777	0	31
ABC oder Namenbüchlein zum Gebrauche der Schulen in den kaiserlich-königlichen Staaten	Ljubljana, 1778	0	32
ABC oder Namenbüchlein zum Gebrauche der Schulen in den kaiserlich-königlichen Staaten	Prague, 1779	0	31
ABC oder Namenbüchlein zum Gebrauche der Oesterreichischen Normalschule	Vienna, 1782	0	31
ABC oder Namenbüchlein zum Gebrauche der Landschulen	Vienna, 1783	0	36
Neuestes ABC-Buch oder Uebungen im Syllabieren oder Buchstabiren und im Lesen	Vienna, 1802	0	17
Nahmenbüchlein zum Gebrauche der Stadtschulen in den kaiserl. königl. Staaten	Graz, 1804	0	18

---

165 The low frequency of past participles that can be formed without *ge-* in reading primers is mainly due to the fact that the main parts of these books are comprised of lists of nouns and simple structures, e.g. active rather than passive structures and sentences in present tense rather than perfect tense.

Title of book	Place and year of publication	without *ge-*	with *ge-*
ABC und Buchstabierbüchlein nebst Leseübungen für Anfänger	Bolzano, 1809	0	30
Der kleine Abc-Schüler	Salzburg, 1818	0	10
Syllabier-Büchlein zum Privatgebrauche (Kirchmayr)	Vienna, 1828	0	14
Nahmenbüchlein für Stadtschulen in den kaiserl. königl. Staaten	Linz, 1833	0	19

Despite the low number of occurrences in a number of textbooks, it can be argued that the UG variant without *ge-* had been stigmatised to such an extent by the mid-18th century that it was not used in schoolbooks anymore.

One reading primer, which deserves closer attention with regard to the prefix *ge-* in past participles, is the *Catholisches Namen-Büchl* (1774). This reading primer (1774: 28) lists 49 past participles without the *-e-* (such as *bhalten, bstochen, gfallen, gstickt*) or *-er-* (*zhauen, zrissen, ztrennt*) in the prefix (see figure below).[166]

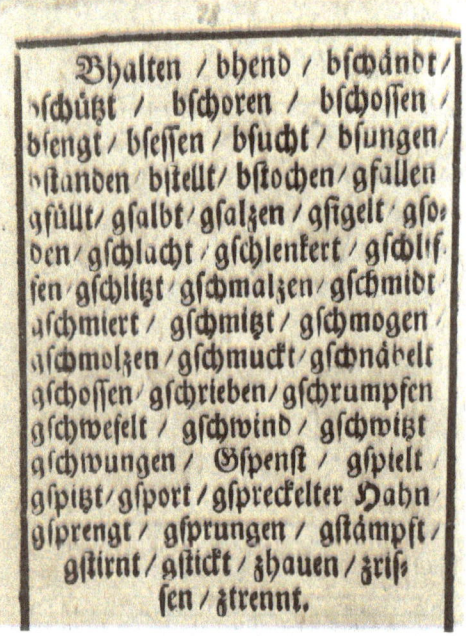

Fig. 10: *e-/er-*syncope in the *Catholisches Namen-Büchl* (1774: 28)

---

166 The *ge-* prefix could not be dropped completely in any of the listed past participles.

This *e-/er*-syncope in the prefix of the past participle is another linguistic feature typical for the UG language area[167] and certainly provokes a sense of orality to the modern ear. It does not appear on any other page of the reading primer, though. The structure of this reading primer might provide an explanation for the absence of *-e-/ -er-* in past participle prefixes on this one page: Similar to the other textbooks, this primer first lists the alphabet, followed by individual words, some of which are illustrated by pictures. On page 25, the pronunciation of certain word-initial letters (such as *V, J, C*) is explained briefly, followed by a set of short words beginning with two consonants (*Frosch, Stein, Klee* etc.) on pages 26 and 27. Given that these three pages deal with the pronunciation of certain letters, the author might have intended to introduce the learners to variants which sound familiar to them before presenting them with the linguistically complex prayers on the subsequent pages.

With regard to the endings of regular past participles, the results appear to be more complex than for any other feature. Whereas the ending *-t* is dominant in the primers printed in 1774[168], 1802, 1809, 1818 and 1828, the ending *-et* is more frequent in the primers published in 1744, c. 1750, c. 1770[169], 1777, 1778, 1779, 1782, 1783, 1804 and 1833 (see table and figure below). When examining these findings in more detail, a number of patterns can be found. Firstly, the majority of reading primers of the later group, i.e. the primers published in 1777 and thereafter, are textbooks from the approved list of Felbiger's school policy (cf. *Allgemeine Schulordnung* 1774: Lit. E), i.e. they were – as their titles suggest – intended to be used in state schools. By contrast, the primers in which the ending *-t* was more common were mostly designed for private tuition. In other words, the language use in Felbiger's approved schoolbooks differs from that of the more general reading primers with regard to regular past participle endings.

Tab. 22: Regular past participles ending in *-t* versus *-et* in reading primers (absolute numbers)

Title of book	Place and year of publication	ending *-t*	ending *-et*
Das Josephinische Erzherzogliche A.B.C. Oder Namenbüchlein (Antesperg)	Vienna, 1744	16	51

---

167 Solms & Wegera (1993: 239) attribute the syncope of *-e-* in the prefix *ge-* mainly to the West Upper German area.

168 It should be noted that the past participle ending *-t* only appears in the list of past participles with *-e-/-er*-syncope mentioned above. In the rest of the *Catholisches Namen-Büchl* (1774), the ending *-et* is used.

169 The number of regular past participles in this primer was rather low with 10 past participles ending in *-t* and 12 ending in *-et*. It is, therefore, more appropriate to regard the frequency of the two past participle endings as balanced.

Title of book	Place and year of publication	ending -*t*	ending -*et*
Teutsches Namen- oder Lehrbüchl	Vienna, c. 1750	20	26
Ein sehr nutzliches Stimmen-Büchlein	Graz, c. 1770	10	12
Catholisches Namen-Büchl	Linz, 1774	27	15
ABC und Buchstabirbüchlein zum Gebrauche der Landschulen	Prague, 1777	6	37
ABC oder Namenbüchlein zum Gebrauche der Schulen in den kaiserlich-königlichen Staaten	Ljubljana, 1778	11	46
ABC oder Namenbüchlein zum Gebrauche der Schulen in den kaiserlich-königlichen Staaten	Prague, 1779	14	42
ABC oder Namenbüchlein zum Gebrauche der Oesterreichischen Normalschule	Vienna, 1782	12	44
ABC oder Namenbüchlein zum Gebrauche der Landschulen	Vienna, 1783	4	49
Neuestes ABC-Buch oder Uebungen im Syllabieren oder Buchstabiren und im Lesen	Vienna, 1802	23	12
Nahmenbüchlein zum Gebrauche der Stadtschulen in den kaiserl. königl. Staaten	Graz, 1804	17	40
ABC und Buchstabierbüchlein nebst Leseübungen für Anfänger	Bolzano, 1809	22	17
Der kleine Abc-Schüler	Salzburg, 1818	17	4
Syllabier-Büchlein zum Privatgebrauche (Kirchmayr)	Vienna, 1828	18	15
Nahmenbüchlein für Stadtschulen in den kaiserl. königl. Staaten	Linz, 1833	19	40

The ending -*t* is, however, not completely replaced by -*et* in any of the reading primers designed for state schools or home use. Indeed, there is some variation of the endings of the same verb within a number of textbooks. For example, in the *ABC oder Buchstabirbüchlein zum Gebrauche der Landschulen* printed in 1777, both variants are presented for the past participle of *machen*, i.e. *gemacht* as well as *gemachet*, and in the textbooks printed in 1778, 1779 and 1782 *gesagt* as well as *gesaget* occur. Since this variation only appears in a few words, it cannot be argued that variation was the norm. It seems, however, that no general rule was consistently applied in the use of past participle endings.

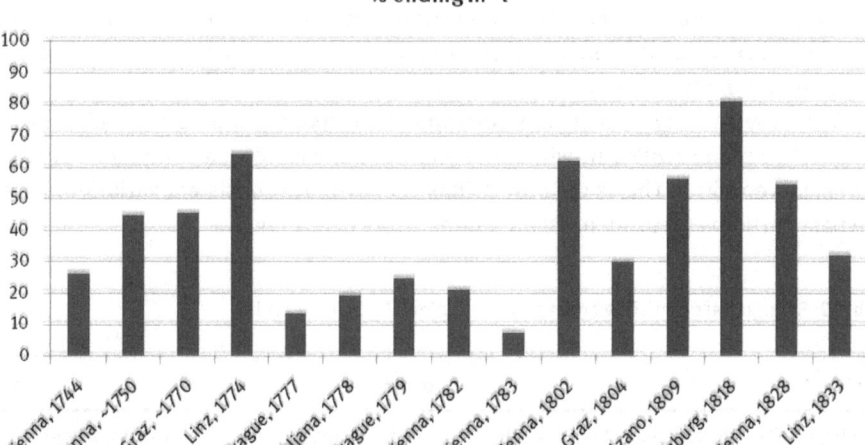

% ending in -*t*

Fig. 11: Regular past participles ending in -*t* in reading primers (in percentages)

Indeed, most grammarians radically simplified the rules for past participle endings by simply prescribing the ending -*et* (see chapter 3).[170] In fact, there are several cases, in which the use of the regular past participle endings is phonetically determined. The past participle of verbs with their stem ending in -*el* or -*er* is formed with -*t* (e.g. *befördert* and *geadelt*, not *beförderet/geadelet*). This general rule was usually applied in the reading primers.

The past participle of verbs with stems ending in either -*d/-t* or a fricative/plosive plus nasal sound, on the other hand, is formed with the ending -*et* (e.g. *vollendet, behütet, gewidmet*).[171] Due to these general rules, it is not surprising that both variants (-*t* and -*et*) occur in every reading primer. In the vast majority of cases, these morpho-phonological rules were applied. The only exceptions are *befreundt* in Antesperg's *Erzherzogliche[s] A.B.C.* (1744), and *bschändt, gschmidt*, both of which

---

170 In fact, only Adelung mentions that the past participles of verbs with stems ending in -*eln* and -*ern* take the ending -*t*, instead of -*et* (see section 3.6.2).

171 This rule also applies to past participles which are used as adjectives (e.g. *abgehärteten, gezeichnete, verordneten*). In all other cases, past participles used as adjectives are consistently spelled with -*t*-, apart from *gesäeten* in the *ABC oder Buchstabirbüchlein zum Gebrauch der Landschulen* (1777). Solms & Wegera (1993: 237) point out that the ending -*et* is only occasionally used in past participles of verbs ending in a vowel. A further curiosity can be detected in the textbooks printed in 1778 and 1779, in which the past participle of *erlernen* is used as a noun, creating the form *das Erlernete*. Later editions of these textbooks (1782 and 1783) changed this variant to *das Erlernte*. Past participles used as nouns or adjectives were not included in the table and figure above.

are given in the list of past participles without *-e/-er-* in the prefix (see Figure 10) in the *Catholisches Namen-Büchl* (1774). According to Solms & Wegera (1993: 237), the complete absence of the ending *-(e)t* was still common for verb stems ending in a dental sound in the 17th century.

The only reading primer that corresponds to today's standard German is *Der kleine Abc-Schüler* (1818), in which the ending *-t* is used consistently, except when verb stems end in *-t*. This is the only primer that displays consistent variation, i.e. all the past participles ending in *-et* are phonetically determined.

Tab. 23: Regular past participle endings in *Der kleine Abc-Schüler* (1818)

ending *-t*	ending *-et*
gehört, gelernt, gesagt, gemacht, angefüllt, angespritzt, geträumt, gelebt, gelebt, gemacht, gemacht, gemacht, geschenkt, erlaubt, gefragt, gesagt, gesagt	gekostet, ausgerichtet, geantwortet, eingerichtet

It should be noted that *Der kleine Abc-Schüler* (1818) was printed in Salzburg, which did not continuously belong to the Habsburg Monarchy until 1816, previously belonging to Bavaria and being an independent principality.[172] It could, therefore, be argued that the standardisation of regular past participle endings was implemented to a greater extent in Salzburg/Bavaria than in the (rest of the) Habsburg Monarchy.

While further patterns can be detected for the variation in other reading primers there are no consistent rules for the use of one variant or another. Antesperg, for example, prefers to use the ending *-et* (rather than *-t*) when the past participle is part of an active perfect construction.[173] Out of 29 perfect constructions, 25 past participles end in *-et*, while only the verbs *gemacht* [3] and *zugesagt* are formed with the ending *-t* in perfect constructions. This indicates that there is not only a phonetic and morphological, but also a lexical pattern behind the variation between the endings *-t* and *-et*. Indeed, the past participle of *machen* is formed with the ending *-t* 27 times in the corpus of reading primers (in eight primers). The variant *gemachet* only occurs twice in the *ABC und Buchstabirbüchlein zum Gebrauche der Landschulen*

---

172 However, Engelbrecht (1984: 139) states that Felbiger's school reform was also implemented in Salzburg, slightly after its introduction in the Habsburg Monarchy. Indeed, Boyer (2002: 263) mentions that a reading primer published in the Archbishopric of Salzburg in 1777, entitled *A, B, C, Buchstabir- und Lesebüchlein für die deutschen Trivialschulen in den hochfürstlich-salzburgischen Landen,* is almost identical to Felbiger's reading primer printed in 1776.

173 The preference for the past participle ending *-et* in active perfect constructions is also apparent in most of the other reading primers, with the exception of the primers printed in 1802, 1809, and 1818.

(1777), which – as mentioned above – also includes the variant with the ending -t. Another pattern that emerges when investigating Antesperg's *Erzherzogliche[s] A.B.C.* (1744) more closely is that the *sein*-passive is usually formed with past participles ending in -et.[174] This is the case for 12 out of 13 *sein*-passive constructions in Antesperg's primer, the sole exception being *gelobt seyst du* (p. 31). More generally, the percentage of the ending -t (26 %) is fairly low in Antesperg's *Erzherzogliche[s] A.B.C.* (1744). Despite accepting both endings in his grammar, he uses the ending -et considerably more often in his reading primer.

In summary, the use of -t or -et depends on phonetic, morphological, and lexical factors. The authors of the reading primers did not consistently follow the prescriptions of 18th-century grammarians, which appear to be vague (for example, describing the *Wohlklang*, i.e. an agreeable sound, as decisive) or too detailed (distinctions between active and passive). A clear shift away from the ending -t can be detected in the textbooks from Felbiger's prescribed list of schoolbooks, which generally show a lower percentage of the ending -t than the primers designed for home use. This shift seems to be reversed at the beginning of the 19th century when the ending -t became more widely used again, especially in the reading primers designed for home use.

4.3.3 Alternative forms of *wir/sie sind*

The UG form *wir/sie seynd* only appears in two reading primers. In Antesperg's *Erzherzogliche[s] A.B.C.* (1744), it occurs 16 times (i.e. 18 %), while the ECG variant *wir/sie sind* is used 75 times (82 %). In other words, the ECG variant is clearly dominant in Antesperg's primer. In the *Teutsches Namen- oder Lehrbüchl* (c. 1750), by contrast, the UG form is used exclusively. However, the verb *to be* was not used frequently in the 3rd person plural present indicative active and never occurred in the 1st person plural: *sie seind* was used four times and *sie seynd* appeared three times. The infrequent use of the verb *to be* in the 1st and 3rd person plural was also problematic in other reading primers, especially in the primers printed in c. 1770 and 1774, in which not a single instance occurred. This lack of data means that the development of this variable in reading primers published after c. 1750 and before 1777 cannot be determined. From 1777 onwards, the ECG variant was used exclusively, as the following table shows.

---

174 As mentioned in section 3.4.2, Popowitsch preferred the ending -t in the passive voice formed with *sein* while using the ending -et for the passive formed with *werden*, contrary to Antesperg's use of past participle endings. Popowitsch's principle is not applied consistently in any of the reading primers, indicating that his prescriptions with regard to regular past participle endings were not influential.

Tab. 24: Variants of the verb *to be* in the 1st and 3rd pers. pl. pres. ind. act. in reading primers (absolute numbers)

Title of book	Place and year of publication	*wir/sie seind/seynd*	*wir/sie sind*
Das Josephinische Erzherzogliche A.B.C. Oder Namenbüchlein (Antesperg)	Vienna, 1744	16	75
Teutsches Namen- oder Lehrbüchl	Vienna, c. 1750	7	0
Ein sehr nutzliches Stimmen-Büchlein	Graz, c. 1770	0	0
Catholisches Namen-Büchl	Linz, 1774	0	0
ABC und Buchstabirbüchlein zum Gebrauche der Landschulen	Prague, 1777	0	10
ABC oder Namenbüchlein zum Gebrauche der Schulen in den kaiserlich-königlichen Staaten	Ljubljana, 1778	0	14
ABC oder Namenbüchlein zum Gebrauche der Schulen in den kaiserlich-königlichen Staaten	Prague, 1779	0	14
ABC oder Namenbüchlein zum Gebrauche der Oesterreichischen Normalschule	Vienna, 1782	0	14
ABC oder Namenbüchlein zum Gebrauche der Landschulen	Vienna, 1783	0	60
Neuestes ABC-Buch oder Uebungen im Syllabieren oder Buchstabiren und im Lesen	Vienna, 1802	0	4
Nahmenbüchlein zum Gebrauche der Stadtschulen in den kaiserl. königl. Staaten	Graz, 1804	0	12
ABC und Buchstabierbüchlein nebst Leseübungen für Anfänger	Bolzano, 1809	0	11
Der kleine Abc-Schüler	Salzburg, 1818	0	13
Syllabier-Büchlein zum Privatgebrauche (Kirchmayr)	Vienna, 1828	0	23
Nahmenbüchlein für Stadtschulen in den kaiserl. königl. Staaten	Linz, 1833	0	12

Antesperg's *Erzherzogliche[s] A.B.C.* (1744) is the only reading primer that includes both the UG and the ECG variant. The UG variant is, however, limited to three pages, two of which provide tables for multiplication and addition, giving 15 instances of *seynd* and 48 of *sind* (see figure below).

Das Einmaleins.

9. Cap. Von der Lesung der Ziffer und Zahlen. 35

1mal	1.	ist	1.	4mal	10.	sind 40.
2mal	2.	sind	4.	5mal	5.	sind 25.
2mal	3.	sind	6.	5mal	6.	sind 30.
1mal	4.	sind	8.	5mal	7.	sind 35.
2mal	5.	sind	10.	5mal	8.	sind 40.
2mal	6.	sind	12.	5mal	9.	sind 45.
2mal	7.	sind	14.	5mal	10.	sind 50.
2mal	8.	sind	16.			
2mal	9.	sind	18.	6mal	6.	seynd 36.
2mal	10.	sind	20.	6mal	7.	seynd 42.
				6mal	8.	seynd 48.
3mal	3.	sind	9.	6mal	9.	seynd 54.
3mal	4.	sind	12.	6mal	10.	seynd 60.
3mal	5.	sind	15.	7mal	7.	sind 49.
3mal	6.	sind	18.	7mal	8.	56.
3mal	7.	sind	21.	7mal	9.	63.
3mal	8.	sind	24.	7mal	10.	70.
3mal	9.	sind	27.	8mal	8.	sind 64.
3mal	10.	sind	30.	8mal	9.	72.
				8mal	10.	80.
4mal	4.	sind	16.	9mal	9.	sind 81.
4mal	5.	sind	20.	9mal	10.	90.
4mal	6.	sind	24.	10mal	10.	sind 100.
4mal	7.	sind	28.	10mal	100.	sind 1000.
4mal	8.	sind	32.			*Nota 7.*
4mal	9.	sind	36.			

36 9. Cap. Von der Lesung der Ziffer und Zahlen.

Nota 7. Die Kinder sollen bald anfänglich nicht allein das Einmaleins, sondern auch das Einsundeins lesen und aussprechen können, also folget auch solches.

Das Einsundeins.

1. und 1.	sind	2.		4. und 9.	sind	13.
2. und 2.	seynd	4.		5. und 5.	sind	10.
2. und 3.	seynd	5.		5.	6.	11.
2. und 4.	seynd	6.		5.	7.	12.
2. und 5.	seynd	7.		5.	8.	13.
2. und 6.	seynd	8.		5.	9.	14.
2. und 7.	seynd	9.		6. und 6.	sind	12.
2. und 8.	seynd	10.		6.	7.	13.
2.	9.	seynd 11.		6.	8.	14.
3. und 3.	sind	6.		6.	9.	15.
3. und 4.	sind	7.		7. und 7.	sind	14.
3. und 5.	sind	8.		7.	8.	15.
3.	6.	sind 9.		7.	9.	16.
3.	7.	sind 10.		8. und 8.	sind	16.
3.	8.	seynd 11.		8.	9.	17.
3.	9.	seynd 12.				
4. und 4.	sind	8.		9. und 9.	sind	18.
4. und 5.		9.		9.	10.	19.
4.	6.	10.		9.	11.	20.
4.	7.	11.		9.	12.	21.
4.	8.	12.				

Nota 8. Allhier soll man der Jugend verschiedene leichte Exempel und Fragen aufgeben, und dieselbe aus dem Einmaleins oder Einsundeins entscheiden lassen: Z.E. Eine Elle Tuch kostet 2. fl. wie viel

Fig. 12: The use of *seynd* and *sind* in Antesperg's *Erzherzogliche[s] A.B.C.* (1744: 35f.)

The use of one or the other variant seems to be random but the ECG variant is clearly the dominant one in Antesperg's reading primer. Apart from the instances depicted in the figure above, the UG variant only occurs once again in Antesperg's reading primer (1744: 48): "die Nisse **seynd** in Haaren und heissen *lendes*" [my emphasis] ("The nits are in the hair and are called *lendes*").

With the introduction of the school reform in December 1774, the UG variant disappears completely from reading primers. Since the UG variants are still common in everyday language use in today's Austria[175], it is more appropriate to speak of a process of invisibilisation rather than morphological language change. The UG variants are completely invisible in reading primers printed after the introduction of the school reform (1774), but they did not disappear from actual language use.

---

[175] Cf. the map of everyday language use in the German-speaking areas today (Elspaß & Möller 2003): http://www.atlas-alltagssprache.de/runde-2/f23a-c/ [accessed 26.04.2017]. This map illustrates that the variants *san*, *sand*, *sen*, *sein*, *sin*, and *sind* are used on an everyday basis by Austrians today. Below the map it is noted that no adjustment to the standard form (i.e. *wir/sie sind*) can be observed in Austria and Bavaria.

4.3.4 Conclusion: Analysis of reading primers

The findings described above indicate that Felbiger's school policy from 1774 had a significant effect on the language used in reading primers. The UG *e*-apocope is almost invisible in the textbooks intended for state schools printed after the introduction of the school policy, with the use of *e*-apocope in feminine nouns usually being restricted to lists of monosyllabic words and the *e*-apocope never occurring in plural nouns. In the three reading primers printed between c. 1750 and 1774, on the other hand, the *e*-apocope appears frequently in feminine singular nouns and also occurs in plural forms. In strong masculine and neuter nouns in the dative singular form, the UG variant without final -*e* is used exclusively in these three primers. Antesperg (1744), too, often spells strong masculine and neuter nouns in the dative singular form without final -*e* but adds the -*e* in feminine singular nouns in 95 % of cases and always in plural forms, which corresponds to the norms prescribed in his grammar. In the reading primers printed in 1802, 1809, and 1818, the dative -*e* is also not used as often as in the primers that appear on Felibger's list of approved textbooks for school use, while Kirchmayr's *Syllabier-Büchlein* (1828) designed for home use employs the dative -*e* consistently.

In summary, a clear trend away from the UG *e*-apocope towards the ECG norm can be detected after the introduction of Felbiger's school reform. Before this reform, there was a considerable degree of variation with regard to *e*-apocope in reading primers, with the *e*-apocope being most common in strong masculine and neuter nouns in the dative singular form. Antesperg's *Erzherzogliche[s] A.B.C.* (1744) generally appears more 'modern', i.e. closer to the language used in later primers, than the three books printed between c. 1750 and 1774. After 1774, many of the instances of *e*-apocope, particularly in the *ABC und Buchstabierbüchlein nebst Leseübungen für Anfänger* (1809), are due to formal constraints (monosyllabic-word lists or texts), which result in a more artificial use of language.

In comparison to Rössler's (2005: 245) findings, which show that the occurrence of *e*-apocope had dropped to 37 % by about 1765, it is striking how often the *e*-apocope occurs in the reading primers printed between c. 1750 and 1774. With regard to feminine and plural nouns, Durrell's (2016) results, too, suggest a very low frequency of *e*-apocope in the East Upper German area from 1751 onwards. Furthermore, the exclusive use of *e*-apocope in strong masculine and neuter nouns in the dative singular form in the reading primers published between c. 1750 and 1774 is not in line with Rössler's (2005: 261) and Durrell's findings. After 1774, i.e. with the introduction of Felbiger's textbooks, the frequency of *e*-apocope is drastically reduced in reading primers and the results match those of Rössler and Durrell more closely.

The analysis of the prefix in past participles, too, led to different results than those presented by Rössler. While Rössler (2005: 306) encounters variation in the printed UG texts during the entire time period under investigation (1530–1765), past participles always occur with the prefix *ge-* in every reading primer. By 1744, the UG variant without prefix must have been stigmatised to such an extent that it was not used in reading primers anymore.

With regard to the ending of regular past participle (*-t* versus *-et*), a wavelike development can be observed in the reading primers under consideration. The ending *-et* was dominant in Antesperg's *Erzherzogliche[s] A.B.C.* (1744), while the use of the two variants was fairly balanced in the subsequent three reading primers. Between 1777 and 1783, the ending *-et* was clearly preferred. At the turn of the century, though, the ending *-t* became more popular again, particularly in reading primers that were designed for home use. Since the use of the ending is partly determined by the stem of the verb (ending in *-el* or *-er* versus in either *-d/-t* or a fricative/plosive plus nasal sound), it is not surprising that variation occurs in every reading primer. Furthermore, certain morphological and lexical principles influenced the use of the variants, with the ending *-et* being preferred in active perfect constructions in several reading primers and the verb *machen* usually taking the ending *-t*.

As mentioned in section 3.6.2, Adelung (1781) prescribed the ending *-t* for the active indicative but the ending *-et* for the active subjunctive, the infinitive, and passive as well as for higher register. These specific rules were not applied in any of the reading primers, but the ending *-t* did become more widely used at the beginning of the 19th century. In general, however, the rather vague or too detailed prescriptions of 18th-century grammarians seemed to have little effect on the use of one variant or another with regard to regular past participle endings.

The analysis of *wir/sie seynd* versus *wir/sie sind* leads to clearer findings, with the former variant, i.e. the UG form, only occurring in the *Erzherzogliche A.B.C.* (1744) and the *Teutsches Namen- oder Lehrbüchl* (c. 1750), and the latter being used exclusively from 1777 onwards. In other words, the UG variant seems to disappear from textbooks with the introduction of Felbiger's school reform. However, the ECG form *wir/sie sind* had been introduced to UG texts before 1774. In Antesperg's primer, the ECG form is used significantly more frequently than the UG variant. The lack of data in the reading primers printed in c. 1770 and 1774 results in uncertainties as to what happened in the time between c. 1750 and 1777.[176]

Rössler's (2005: 220) findings suggest that the change from UG *seynd* to ECG *sind* occurs before c. 1770, with the ECG variant clearly dominating but not completely replacing the UG form. As mentioned above, *sind* is used considerably more often (82 %) than *seynd* (18 %) in Antesperg's reading primer (1744), indicating that the replacement of the UG variant had started before Gottsched's grammar was published in 1748.[177] Felbiger followed Gottsched's prescription and it is, therefore, not

---

176 This gap will be bridged by the analysis of newspapers in the following section.
177 Gottsched may have influenced Antesperg in his use of the ECG variant. As discussed in section 3.2, Antesperg sent his *Kayserliche deutsche Sprachtabelle* (1734) to Gottsched for suggestions of

surprising that *wir/sie seynd* never occurs in any of the schoolbooks from Felbiger's approved list of textbooks. The 19th-century primers designed for home use, too, adhered to Gottsched's and Felbiger's prescriptions, only using the ECG variant.

Overall, the influence of 18th-century grammarians, particularly Felbiger, is apparent in the language used in reading primers. The following section will reveal if similar changes in the writing practices of newspaper correspondents can be observed.

4.4 Language use in newspaper texts

4.4.1 *e*-apocope in nouns

Instances of *e*-apocope in nouns can be found in every newspaper issue of the newspaper corpus, with the highest number (78) occurring in 1754 and the lowest number in 1784 (see table below). In the latter issue, just three nouns in the dative case appear without final *-e* (*zum Druck, zum Gebrauch, am Schluß*), while feminine nouns and nouns in plural always end in *-e*. As the discussion below will show, variation within individual newspaper issues mainly occurs in strong masculine and neuter nouns in the dative case.

Tab. 25: *e*-apocope versus using the ending *-e* in newspaper issues: overall (absolute numbers)

Year of publication	*e*-apocope	ending *-e*
1744	51	63
1749	45	83
1754	78	51
1759	49	52
1764	57	61
1769	35	90
1774	20	126
1779	22	102
1784	3	139
1789	9	112
1794	9	141
1799	10	100

improvements. It is certainly plausible to suggest that Antesperg followed these suggestions in his later works, i.e. his reading primer (1744) and his grammar (1747).

Year of publication	e-apocope	ending -e
1804	15	135
1809	8	88
1814	17	148
1819	8	96
1824	22	177
1829	19	112
1834	13	191

Nevertheless, the overall results are revealing as they indicate that the ending -e was the preferred variant in all newspaper issues, with the exceptions of the 1754 issue, in which the e-apocope appeared in 60 % of the cases (see figure below), as well as the issues published in 1759 and 1764, in which no particular variant seemed to be preferred. It is striking that the percentage of e-apocope is slightly higher in the issues printed between 1754 and 1764 (with 60 % in 1754, 49 % in 1759, and 48 % in 1764) than in the issues published in 1744 (45 %) and 1749 (35 %). Since the basic structure of the newspaper remains the same between 1744 and 1764 (international news preceding local news), it cannot be argued that the high percentage of e-apocope is due to the type of news (local versus supra-regional). The percentage of e-apocope drops from 48 % in 1764 to 28 % in 1769 and continues to decrease, reaching the lowest point of 2 % in 1784. After that, the ending -e is used in at least 85 % of the cases.

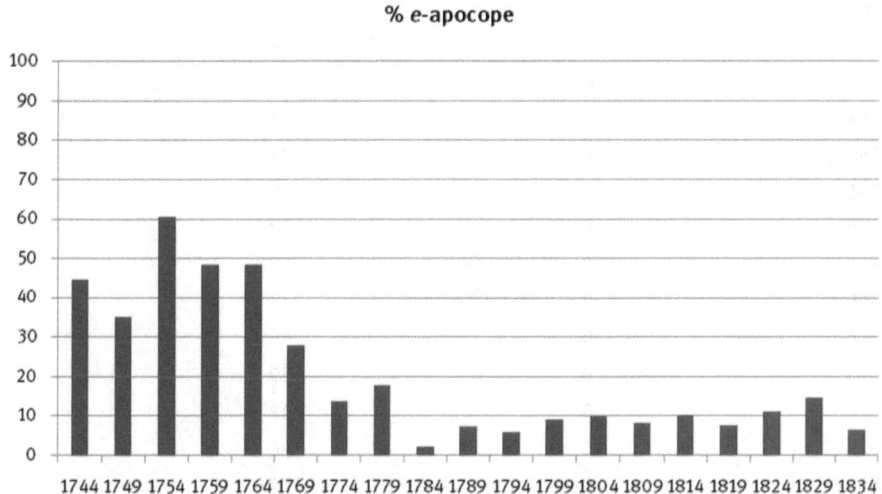

Fig. 13: e-apocope in newspaper issues: overall (in percentages)

The following analyses will show that variation between *e*-apocope and final *-e* mainly occurs in strong masculine and neuter nouns in the dative singular form. In these cases, preferences of individual correspondents can be observed. In newspaper issues with particularly high variation between *e*-apocope and final *-e* (about 50:50), the occurrences are, therefore, listed for each individual article. When no striking differences between individual articles were observed, which was the case for *e*-apocope in feminine and plural nouns, the lists are not sub-divided into articles but the particular columns, in which instances of *e*-apocope occurred, are provided.

With regard to feminine nouns, instances of *e*-apocope can only be observed in the newspaper issues printed between 1744 and 1769. The highest number of occurrences of *e*-apocope (11) can be found in 1754, but feminine nouns with the ending *-e* are clearly dominant in this and all the other newspaper issues, as the following table illustrates.

Tab. 26: *e*-apocope versus using the ending *-e* in newspaper issues: feminine nouns (absolute numbers)

Year of publication	*e*-apocope	ending *-e*
1744	2	37
1749	3	37
1754	11	22
1759	5	25
1764	6	30
1769	1	34
1774	0	54
1779	0	56
1784	0	44
1789	0	23
1794	0	49
1799	0	42
1804	0	59
1809	0	23
1814	0	55
1819	0	29
1824	0	49
1829	0	44
1834	0	77

It can generally be said that the *e*-apocope in feminine nouns was avoided by 1744 and became invisible after 1769 in the *Wienerisches Diarium*. The instances of *e*-apocope that do appear in the newspaper issues are listed in the table below (in alphabetical order, with the number of occurrences given in square brackets if exceeding 1, and the column in round brackets for instances of *e*-apocope).

Tab. 27: Variation in feminine noun endings in newspaper issues (1744–1769)

Newspaper issue	*e*-apocope	ending -*e*
1 July 1744	Schantz (col. 14), Scheld (river, col. 9)	Brücke, Flagge, Flotte [2], Freude, Fruhe [= Frühe] [3], Kapelle, Kirche, Lage, Menge [2], Reise, Rhede, Rukreise, Sache, Schantze, Schärffe, Schelde [4], Schifbrüke, Schleusse, Seele, Seite [4], Senfte, Spitze, Stelle, Stunde [2], Tauffe, Weile
2 July 1749	Aufnahm (col. 6), Ursach [2] (col. 3, 6)	Anfrage, Begierde [2], Elle [2], Flotte [2], Gemeinde, Gnade, Hitze [2], Höhe, Kirche [2], Leiche [2], Liebe, Meer=Enge, Meile [2], Menge, Milde, Prise, Sache [2], Seite [3], Stelle, Stunde [3], Tiefe, Treue, Weise, Wolke, Würde
3 July 1754	Freud (col. 3), Prob (col. 12), Reis [4] (col. 2, 4), Ruh[stätte] (col. 17), Sprach (col. 15), Straf (col. 5), Weis (col. 15), Wolzeil (street, col. 11), Zuruckreis (col. 4)	Anhöhe, Aufnahme, Beute, Einöde, Farbe [2], Flotte, Fruhe [= Frühe] [2], Grube, Hebamme, Herbst=freude, Kirche [2], Natur=lehre, [Ruh]stätte, Schaubühne, Seite, Sprachlehre, Taufe, Todten=farbe, Woche
4 July 1759	Freud (col. 5), Hülf (col. 4), Neiß [3] (river, col. 12)	Anklage, Anrede, Freude, Fruhe [= Frühe], Güte [2], Hauptstrasse, Hauptwache, Hülfe, Kirche, Küste, Länge, Milde [2], Münze, Pyramide, Reise [2], Reserve, Rose, Sorge, Stelle, Tauffe, Weise, Woche
4 July 1764	Auflag (col. 11), Sonn (col. 11), Stund (col. 12), Thür (col. 8), Waldzeil (street, col. 11), Windmühl (col. 10)	Anrede, Anzeige, Danksagungs=rede, Erde [2], Flasche, Gränze [3], Haupt=wache, Hitze, Lebens=strafe, Menge, Pforte, Rede, Reise [3], Sache [2], Schlagbrücke, Schweizer=wache, Seite, Stelle, Stille, Strasse, Stufe, Woche, Zugehörde [2]
1 July 1769	Reis[leibwagen] (col. 14)	Anhöhe, Aussage, Ferne, Flanke, Folge [2], Freude, Frühe, Gnade, Granatapfelblühe, Gränze [3], Hofdame, Hülfe, Lage, Menge [4], Niederlage, Pforte, Reise, Reise[gefolge], Sache, Schlappe, Seite [2], Spitze [2], Stärke, Stelle, Weise, Woche

In the 1744 newspaper issue, both variants for the feminine nouns *Schantz(e)* and *Scheld(e)* (a river in France/Belgium/the Netherlands) occur but in different articles. This indicates that the choice of one variant depended on individual correspondents. The same is true for the variants of the feminine noun *Hülf(e)* in the issue published in 1759. However, variation within the same article can also be observed, as is the case for *Freud(e)*, which occurs in both variants in an article on the birth of a prince (1759: col. 5). In this case, both, the UG and ECG variant seemed to be acceptable for the newspaper correspondent. The only feminine nouns displaying *e*-apocope that appear in more than one newspaper issue are *Reis* (1754 and 1769 – as part of a compound noun in the latter issue) and *-zeil* (as part of street names, in 1754 and 1764).

The noun *Thür(e)*, which is included in the 1764 newspaper issue, presents an interesting case since both variants became part of modern standard German, with the form without final *-e* being presented as the default form in the *Duden* (2006: 1029).[178] Indeed, *Türe* is not listed as a separate entry[179] and labelled as "regional, besides *Tür*" ("landsch. neben *Tür*") in the *Duden* (ibid.). This regional distribution of the variants *Tür* – *Türe* is confirmed by the *Atlas zur deutschen Alltagssprache* (Elspaß & Möller 2003). This modern atlas on everyday language use in the German-speaking areas shows that *Türe* is most commonly used in Saxony but also occurs in Switzerland and the south west of modern-day Germany in spoken language. This distribution is significantly different in written discourse (e.g. on signs): in this case, *Türe* is the more common form everywhere south of the river Main and in the area around Cologne.[180] The editors of the atlas explain that the variant with final *-e* may have been regarded as more 'correct' in the south of the German-speaking area, where the *e*-apocope is common in regional varieties. This explanation seems convincing, given that the *e*-apocope in feminine nouns had largely disappeared from newspapers by 1769, as illustrated in the following figure.

---

178 As mentioned in section 3.7.2, *Thüre* was actually the plural form of *Thür* but used as an equivalent to *Thür* since MHG (Grimm & Grimm 1854–1961: Vol 21, col. 458). This fact may explain why both variants are codified in modern standard German, with the singular form being presented as the default in the *Duden* (2006: 1029).

179 *Türchen*, *Türdrücker*, and *Türe* are listed in the same line in the *Duden* (2006: 1029).

180 Cf. Elspaß & Möller (2003), http://www.atlas-alltagssprache.de/runde-5/f16a-b/ [accessed 26.04.2017].

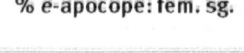

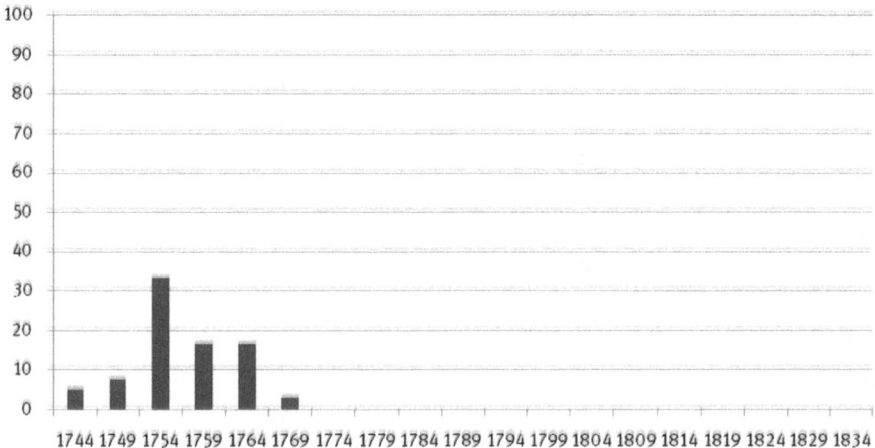

Fig. 14: *e*-apocope in newspaper issues: feminine nouns (in percentages)

The vast majority of feminine nouns in newspapers are formed with final -*e* by the mid-18th century. This means that the ECG norm was introduced to Austrian newspapers before it was prescribed by Gottsched and subsequent grammarians in their normative works. The ending -*e* in feminine nouns was also clearly dominant before the introduction of the school reform in December 1774. With regard to the dative -*e*, the findings present a very different picture.

The *e*-apocope is clearly more frequent in strong masculine and neuter nouns in the dative case than in feminine nouns (see table below). The newspaper issue printed in 1744 displays the lowest number of dative -*e*, which occurs in just two dative constructions: *auf einem Stücke* and *am Kopfe*. Both of these constructions appear in the same article on the town Maassluis in South Holland, dated 14 June 1744. As Durrell et al. (2008: 265) point out, the origin of the correspondents cannot be determined with any certainty. All we can say is that this correspondent was aware of the dative -*e* and used it in half of the cases in her/his article (*im Gefecht* and *mit Maltz* are spelled without -*e* in the same article).

Tab. 28: *e*-apocope versus using the ending -*e* in newspaper issues: strong masculine and neuter nouns in the dative singular form (absolute numbers)

Year of publication	*e*-apocope	ending -*e*
1744	49	2
1749	41	15

Year of publication	e-apocope	ending -e
1754	60	7
1759	43	9
1764	50	14
1769	33	32
1774	20	42
1779	22	21
1784	3	54
1789	9	37
1794	8	40
1799	8	29
1804	15	31
1809	8	19
1814	17	51
1819	8	34
1824	22	71
1829	19	40
1834	13	58

The newspaper issue printed in 1749 contains a considerably higher number of instances of dative -e. The 15 instances of dative -e occur in just six out of 24 articles: in two articles from Stockholm and one each from Copenhagen, Wilda, Posen, and Breslau, i.e. places north of Vienna. While the two Stockholm articles and the article from Breslau are consistent in their use of dative -e, variation can be found in the other three articles (see table below).

Tab. 29: e-apocope versus dative -e in the newspaper issue printed in 1749

Newspaper article	e-apocope	dative -e
Copenhagen, 7 June 1749	an selbigem Tag, am Donnerstag, zu Dero Conferenz-Raht	nach des Hrn. Grafen [...] Land=Gute, von des Hrn. Grafen [...] Eisenwerke
Wilda, 7 June 1749	zum Vorscheln	von dem grossen Mißwachse
Posen, 18 June 1749	am verwichenen Donnerstag	am verwichenen Dienstage

While it could be argued that the use of dative -e is dependent on the preposition in the first two articles (an and zu do not take dative -e while nach and von do take dative -e), the article from Posen with an almost identical construction, once spelled with and once without dative -e (am verwichenen Donnerstag versus am verwichenen

Dienstage), indicates that variation may have been the norm. In general, however, the *e*-apocope was the preferred variant in dative constructions in issues of the *Wienerisches Diarium* printed before 1765.

As the following figure illustrates, the *e*-apocope in dative constructions further decreased after 1764, with 52 % of strong masculine and neuter nouns being spelled without final -*e* in the dative case in 1769 and 1779. This percentage is significantly lower in the newspaper issue printed in 1774 (32 % of *e*-apocope) and in all issues printed after 1779 (with a maximum of 33 % of *e*-apocope). The lowest percentage of *e*-apocope can be found in the issue published in 1784, with just two dative constructions without final -*e* (see above).

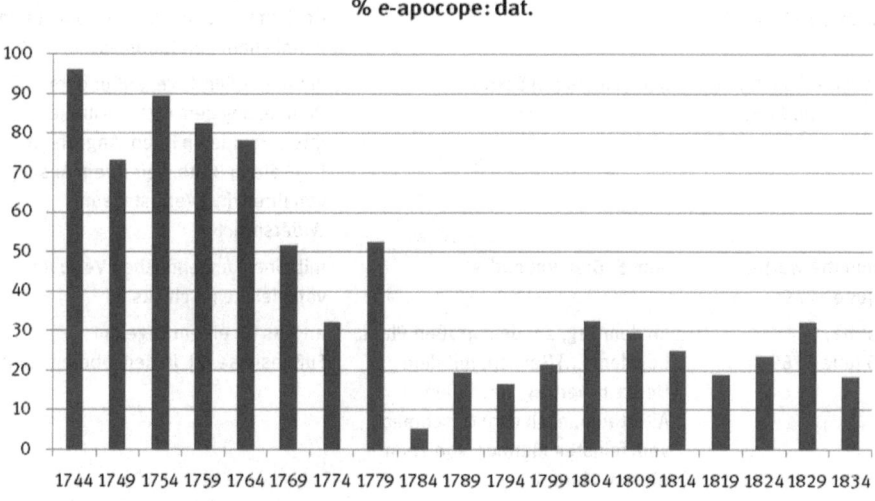

% e-apocope: dat.

Fig. 15: *e*-apocope in newspaper issues: strong masculine and neuter nouns in the dative singular form (in percentages)

Since the issues published in 1769 and 1779 display the greatest variation, they deserve closer attention. The following tables list all instances of strong masculine and neuter nouns in the dative case, categorized into the articles they appear in. The occurences are ordered alphabetically and the number of instances is provided in square brackets if exceeding 1.

Tab. 30: *e*-apocope versus dative *-e* in the newspaper issue printed in 1769

Newspaper article	*e*-apocope	dative *-e*
Introduction	dem Publikum, in dem Anhang	
St. Petersburg, 29 May 1769	am Fuß, bey dem dritten Kanonenschuß, bey dem Fluß [4], dem Obristlieutenant, in seinem Bericht, mit Anbruch, mit dem größten Muth, mit dem Rest, mit einem Theil, nach dem Ausbruch, nebst dem Obristlieutenant, zum Glück	auf dem Fuße, dem Feinde, im Anzuge, im türkischen Gebiete, in diesem Thale, keinem Feinde, vom Feinde, vom Pferde [3], vom schwarzen Meere
From the Turkish border, 26 May 1769		in dem Augenblicke, in dem Gesichte, in eben dem Zeitpuncte, in heimlichem Verständnisse
From the Polish border, 4 June 1769	nach einem [...] Bericht	am folgenden Tage, außer dem Puncte, bey dem ersten Anfalle, ihrem Feinde, in ihrem Angriffe, mit [...] kaltem Blute, seit ihrem Auszuge, von ihrem [...] Verluste, zum Widerspruche
From the Warta, 5 June 1769	vom 5. Brachmonath	mit einem ansehnlichen Verluste, von gleichem Schicksale
Parma, 13 June 1769	an dem Tag, auf dem großen Platz, bey dem [...] Besuch, mit dem Heurathsvertrag, nach dem Alterthum, nach dem Geschmack, vom feinsten Marmor, von eben diesem Marmor	an was für einem Tage, im Fußgesimse [2], in dem oberen Theile
Livorno, 16 June 1769	auf einem englischen Schif, bey dem General Paoli, von dem General [...], von dem Volk	
Vienna, 1 July 1769	auf dem Burgplatz, dem Erzherzog Ferdinand, zu Pferd	vom Hofe, zu Pferde

The table above indicates that the use of dative *-e* depended on the correspondent – three of them were consistent in their choice of either *e*-apocope (Introduction and Livorno) or dative *-e* (Turkish border). Furthermore, the variation between *e*-apocope and dative *-e* is not completely random. The writer of the St. Petersburg article, for example, never used the dative *-e* in constructions with the prepositions *bey* and *mit*. By contrast, the dative *-e* always occurs in nouns following the preposition *von* in this particular article. Furthermore, the preposition *nach* is followed by strong masculine nouns without dative *-e* in three different articles. However, with such a low number of instances, whether or not the writers deliberately used *e*-

apocope or dative *-e* with certain prepositions cannot be ascertained. The article on Vienna suggests that these choices were not always made deliberately or consistently, with *zu Pferd* and *zu Pferde* appearing in close proximity. A closer look at these two constructions reveals, however, that the former is preceded by a singular noun (*ein Postofficier zu Pferd*), while the latter follows a plural noun (*von der kön. hungarischen adel. Leibgarde zu Pferde*). Even in this case, there seems to be a morphological pattern behind the variation of *e*-apocope versus dative *-e*.

Similar findings can be revealed with a qualitative analysis of the newspaper issue published on 3 July 1779 (e.g. constructions following the preposition *mit* are spelled without dative *-e*) but again, these are from individual correspondents preferring a particular variant (see table below, in which the occurences are ordered alphabetically and the number of instances is provided in square brackets if exceeding 1).

Tab. 31: *e*-apocope versus dative *-e* in the newspaper issue printed in 1779

Newspaper article	*e*-apocope	dative *-e*
Versailles, 16 June 1779	an diesem Hof, dem König, in ihrem Grund	
Paris, 18 June 1779	aus einem Schif, bey dem Vorgebürg, bey ihrem Anfang, einem jeden Bootsmann, in dem günstigsten Augenblick, vom Regiment, von dem [...] Feldzug, zu einem [...] Gefängniß, zu Grund	dem Könige, im völligen Stande, in einem Schiffe, zu Pferde
Brest, 9 June 1779	zum Theil	
Rome, 9 June 1779	nach Maaß	in dem Vaticanischen Pallaste
Venice, 17 June 1779	auf dem St. Markus Platz	
Addition concerning the plan of a college	ihrem Institut	aus jedem Zöglinge, dem Staate, in welchem Stande, nach dem Plane
Haag, 19 June 1779	im Jahr	
London, 18 June 1779	mit dem letzten Entschluß, mit ihrem Gut und Blut, zum Schutz	am folgenden Tage [2], bey dem gesammten brittischen Reichsrathe, dem Hause, dem Oberhause [2], dem Parlamente, im grossen Ausschusse, in dem Oberhause, von seinem Hofe, zu Lande
Rotterdam, 19 June 1779	nebst dem Herzog [...]	

The differences between articles, i.e. between the language use of individual correspondents, highlights the importance of considering a newspaper issue as a compilation of different texts rather than one homogeneous text. As explained in section 4.1.2, the articles and reports of correspondents were usually printed without any major editorial changes, which resulted in variation in the language use between different correspondents. This variation did not seem to be of any concern to the editors. Indeed, a number of correspondents used both variants, *e*-apocope and dative *-e*, within the same article, which indicates that variation was accepted with regard to this particular feature in the second half of the 18th century. In fact, *e*-apocope in dative constructions can be found in all newspaper issues of my corpus. Nevertheless, a clear trend away from the *e*-apocope can be observed in the period under investigation, particularly after 1764.

The *e*-apocope in plural nouns, by contrast, hardly ever appears in the newspaper issues, with the highest number of instances (7) occurring in 1754 (see table below).

Tab. 32: *e*-apocope versus using the ending *-e* in newspaper issues: plural (absolute numbers)

Year of publication	e-apocope	ending -e
1744	0	24
1749	1	31
1754	7	22
1759	1	18
1764	1	17
1769	0	24
1774	0	30
1779	0	26
1784	0	41
1789	0	52
1794	1	52
1799	2	29
1804	0	45
1809	0	46
1814	0	42
1819	0	33
1824	0	57
1829	0	28
1834	0	56

The *e*-apocope in plural nouns was clearly avoided by 1744 and is restricted to particular lexical items in the newspapers issues. The following table shows all instances of *e*-apocope in plural forms and lists all plural nouns with the suffix -*e* in the same newspaper issues (in alphabetical order, with the number of occurrences provided in square brackets, if more than one, and the column, in which the instances of *e*-apocope occurs, in round brackets). For the instances of *e*-apocope, the preceding words or numbers are also supplied in square brackets.

Tab. 33: *e*-apocope versus suffix -*e* in plural nouns in newspaper issues

Newspaper issue	*e*-apocope	suffix -*e*
2 July 1749	[in ihre] Quartier (col. 1)	Bäume, Berge, Diebstähle, Dienste, Fahrzeuge, Gemählde, Geräte, Gründe, Jahre, Kräfte, Leute [3], Räthe [2], Schiffe [8], Steine, Tage, Täge, Umstände, Wasserfälle, Wege, Wolkenbrüche, Zölle
3 July 1754	[keine] Brief (col. 5), [6] Monat (col. 4), [alle] Sonntäg (col. 15), [zwey/alle/14] Tag [3] (col. 1/15/17), [8] Täg (col. 14)	Amt=leute [2], Briefe [2], Fahrzeuge [3], Geschenke, Grund=sätze, Rähte, Schiffe [2], Schlüsse [2], Spiele, Stucke, Tage, Theile [4], Trauer=spiele
4 July 1759	[80] Jahr (col. 10)	Artilleriestücke, Beglaubigungs=briefe, Früchte, Gefangene, Geschänknüsse, Kriegsschiffe, Lande, Nächstverwandte, Privatbriefe, Rechte, Rückstände, Schiffe, Steine, Stücke, Täge, Thiere, Umstände, Wälle
4 July 1764	[ihre] Sprüch (col. 12)	Aerzte, Bette, Fahrzeuge, Fußfälle, Hausgefässe, Herzoge, Preise, Quartiere, Schiffe [2], Sprüche, Städte, Stücke, Tage [2], Täge, Theile
2 July 1794	[3] Offizier (col. 7)	Arme, Bäume, Berge, Berichte, Briefe, Dinge, Distrikte, Fähnriche [2], Fahrzeuge, Feinde [2], Feste, Fortschritte, Früchte, Gebäude, Gebüsche, Hauptleute, Heere, Jahre, Leute [2], Kriegsschiffe, Linienschiffe [3], Mächte [2], Monathe, Oberlieutenante [2], Rechte, Säbelhiebe, Schiffe [4], Schritte, Ställe, Tage [2], Todte, Transportschiffe, Triumphe, Unterlieutenante, Verse, Verwundete, Vorräthe, Vorschläge [3], Zäune
3 July 1799	Oberlieutenant [Konyug und Terbojevich] (col. 4), [die] Offizier (col. 4)	Angriffe, Berichte, Bestimmungsgründe, Billete, Einkünfte, Fähnriche [4], Feldärzte, Fortschritte, Freunde, Hände, Hauptleute, Hauptpunkte, Hindernisse, Journale, Landmächte, Lehrsätze, Oberlieutenante [2], Preise, Punkte, Ritze, Schiffe, Tage, Umstände [2], Verhältnisse

The lexical items without plural marking can be categorized into two main groups, a) words referring to periods of time (*Sonntäg, Tag/Täg, Monat, Jahr*) and b) French loan words (*Oberlieutenant, Offizier, Quartier*). Furthermore, the noun *Brief* appears in both variants, with and without plural -*e*, within the same article (London, 7 June 1754). This word is unmarked in the accusative case while it is marked in the nominative case:

> Die Commissarien des Zolls haben [...] verboten, inskünftige keine Brief von dort herüber zu bringen. (*Wienerisches Diarium*, 03.07.1754: col. 5)

> The customs superintendents [...] forbid to henceforth bring letter(s)$_{acc}$ here from there.

> Verschiedene Briefe aus America melden, daß [...] (*Wienerisches Diarium*, 03.07.1754: col. 5)

> Various letters$_{nom}$ from America report that [...]

Since no similar instances of variation in different cases within one newspaper article[181] can be found in the rest of the newspaper corpus, it cannot be concluded that the marking of plural forms depended on the case system.

Apart from these few instances, the *e*-apocope in plural nouns is almost invisible in the whole period under investigation. By the beginning of the 19th century, the *e*-apocope had disappeared completely from the newspaper corpus (see figure below).

---

181 The plural form of *Spruch* occurs in both variants within the same newspaper issue (1764) but in two different articles.

Fig. 16: *e*-apocope in newspaper issues: plural (in percentages)

In summary, the number of instances of *e*-apocope in feminine and plural nouns is considerably lower than in strong masculine and neuter nouns in the dative case. With regard to feminine and plural nouns, the language use in newspapers had been largely adjusted to the ECG norms by 1744. The dative -*e*, by contrast, was used very rarely at that time and only became dominant in newspaper issues in 1774. Although a trend away from the *e*-apocope in dative constructions can be observed, the use of dative -*e* mainly depended on individual correspondents. This indicates that newspaper issues have to be considered as compilations of different texts rather than one homogenous text with consistent language use.

4.4.2 Past participles

Past participles without the prefix *ge*-, e.g. *geben* rather than *gegeben*, appear very rarely in the newspaper corpus, as the table below illustrates.

Tab. 34: Past participle prefixes in newspaper issues (absolute numbers)

Year of publication	without *ge*-	with *ge*-
1744	1	50
1749	0	36

Year of publication	without *ge-*	with *ge-*
1754	0	34
1759	1	28
1764	0	24
1769	0	33
1774	0	33
1779	1	22
1784	1	25
1789	0	21
1794	0	26
1799	0	27
1804	0	28
1809	0	11
1814	0	31
1819	0	17
1824	0	31
1829	0	17
1834	0	24

Only the newspaper issues printed in 1744, 1759, 1779, and 1784 contain one past participle without the prefix *ge-* each. These four instances are the following:

> Der geweste Com̃andant in Menin, Herr von Echten, ist nicht wie man **vorgeben**, daselbst gestorben; (*Wienerisches Diarium*, 01.07.1744: col. 10, my emphasis)

> Wann das nahe daran stehende Torf=magazin, und der nicht weit davon entfernte kleine Pulfer=thurn, worinnen 12. Tonnen Pulfer waren, auch vom Feuer wären ergriffen worden, würde das Elend allgemein **worden** seyn. (*Wienerisches Diarium*, 04.07.1759: col. 8, my emphasis)

> Gestern erhielte der Lord Weymuth von unserm Bothschafter zu Madrid, Lord Grantham Briefe, von deren Innhalt aber in dem Publico noch nichts bekannt **worden**. (*Wienerisches Diarium*, 03.07.1779: col. 12, my emphasis)

> Seit 25 Monaten, heißt es, hat dieses Thier weder **geessen** noch getrunken, und war dabey in einem engen Kasten eingeschlossen, ohne zu sterben. (*Wiener Zeitung*, 03.07.1784: col. 6, my emphasis)

It is striking that at least two of these cases (*vorgeben* and *geessen*) are in line with Antesperg's (1747: 135f.) prescriptions, with *gegeben* and *geben* listed in his grammar as equally appropriate and *gessen* as well as *geessen* as the more common variant (see section 3.2.2). Solms & Wegera (1993: 239, Anm. 6) state that *gessen* was still frequently used in the first half of the 17th century. In the East Upper German area, it seems to be used even longer, as Antesperg's prescriptions and the occurrence in the *Wienerisches Diarium/Wiener Zeitung* attest.

With regard to the past participle of the verb *werden*, it is uncertain whether Antesperg (1747: 155) includes the past participle without the prefix *ge-* as a variant of *geworden* or as an auxiliary verb for passive constructions (e.g. *Er ist getauft worden*) (cf. section 3.2.2). Solms & Wegera (1993: 238) explain that the past participle of *werden* was usually formed without the prefix *ge-* until the end of the 16th century, and this variant was still used in the 17th century. It was only during the 18th century that the variant with the prefix *ge-* prevailed (ibid.). The variant *worden* also occurs in texts printed around 1765 in Rössler's (2005: 307) corpus. This means that the variant without the prefix *ge-* had not disappeared completely from printed texts by the second half of the 18th century. From 1789 onwards, however, the UG variant is completely invisible in newspaper issues.

The number of occurrences of regular past participles ending in -*t* , e.g. *gesucht* as opposed to *gesuchet*, is considerably higher, which allows for a more detailed statistical analysis. As the following table shows, past participles ending in -*t* (as opposed to -*et*) are least common in the newspaper issue printed in 1749 (11 instances) and occur most frequently in 1834 (61 instances).

Tab. 35: Regular past participles ending in -*t* versus -*et* in newspaper issues (absolute numbers)

Year of publication	ending -*t*	ending -*et*
1744	17	84
1749	11	65
1754	15	56
1759	32	32
1764	12	53
1769	27	34
1774	31	33
1779	39	12
1784	21	38
1789	24	22
1794	25	22
1799	36	17
1804	45	7
1809	39	15
1814	43	27
1819	31	7

Year of publication	ending -*t*	ending -*et*
1824	40	11
1829	36	10
1834	61	19

Between 1744 and 1834, a relatively steady increase of the ending -*t* can be observed, as the figure below illustrates. While the ending -*t* is only used in about 20 % of cases in the newspaper issues published in 1744, 1749, 1754, and 1764, it occurs in about half of the cases in the issues printed in 1759, 1769, and 1774. The high percentage of the ending -*t* in the 1759 newspaper issue (50 %) is striking since it is considerably lower in the newspaper issues published five years before and after 1759, with 21 % in 1754 and 18 % in 1764. A similar increase in the use of the ending -*t* can be observed from 1774 (48 %) to 1779 (76 %), while the percentage of the ending -*t* is, again, considerably lower in the subsequent newspaper issue (36 % in 1784). It seems that the newspaper issues published in 1759 and 1774 are ahead of the trend towards the ending -*t*.

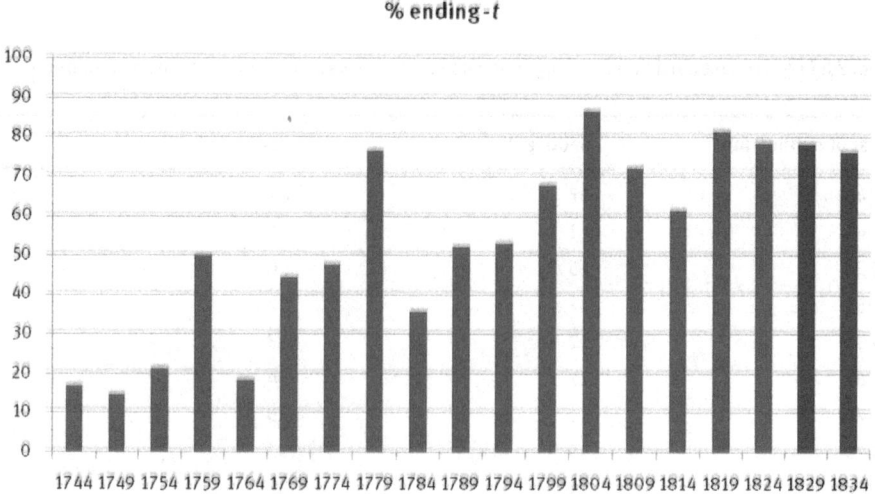

Fig. 17: Regular past participles ending in -*t* in newspaper issues (in percentages)

From 1789 onwards, the ending -*t* is used in more than half of the cases and becomes more dominant in 1799 (68 %). The highest percentage of the ending -*t* in regular past participles can be found in the newspaper issue published on 4 July 1804 (87 %), which is significantly higher than in the subsequent issues (72 % in

1809 and 61 % in 1814). From 1819 onwards, the percentage of the ending -*t* remains relatively stable, with about 80 % of regular past participles ending in -*t*.

Variation occurs in every newspaper issue, partly due to the morpho-phonological reasons mentioned in section 4.3.2: if the verb stem ends in -*el* or -*er*, the past participle ends in -*t*; if the verb stem ends in -*d/-t* or a fricative/plosive plus a nasal sound, the past participle ends in -*et*. These morpho-phonological principles are generally observed and only a few exceptions occur in the newspaper issues, such as the variants *geäusseret* (col. 11) and *fürgeforderet* (col. 13), which occur in the newspaper issue published in 1754. Similar examples can be detected in the newspaper issues published in 1764 (*gefeyeret*, col. 1) and 1769 (*gedauret*, col. 5). One case of *e*-syncope in a regular past participle with a verb stem ending in -*t* can be encountered in the newspaper issue printed in 1774:

> Zu Egelspach hat der Sturm viele Häuser abgedeckt, und bis auf Philippseich die Wälder dergestalt **verwüst**, daß man noch nicht im Stande ist, die grosse Anzahl der ausgerissenen Bäume zu bestimmen. (*Wienerisches Diarium* 1774: col. 12, my emphasis)

Similar cases can be observed in past participles that are used as adjectives, especially in the verbs *melden* and *achten* (see table below).

Tab. 36: *e*-synocope in regular past participles used as adjectives in newspaper issues

Newspaper issue	*e*-syncope in regular past participles used as adjectives
1744	erstgemeldten, unverrichter
1754	gemeldter, erst=gemeldten, ungeacht, obbemeldt, angemeldt= und elaßificirte
1764	hochgemeldten, erstgemeldten, bemeldte, gleichbemeldten, obbemelt
1769	uneracht
1804	hochgeachte

Apart from these instances, regular past participles ending in -*d/-t* or a fricative/ plosive plus a nasal sound are formed with the ending -*et* when used as adjectives as well as verbs. In all other cases, the ending -*t* is consistently found in past participles used as adjectives. Variation between the endings -*t* and -*et* that is not phonetically determined mainly occurs in past participles used as verbs. In order to establish whether this variation is dependent on individual correspondents or linguistic-internal factors, five newspaper issues were analysed in detail. All past participles from the newspaper sections stated in square brackets are listed in the table below, divided into the articles in which they occur (in the order they appear within the aricles) and with the auxiliary verbs provided in square brackets.[182] Phonetically determined variants are marked in grey.

Tab. 37: Regular past participle endings in the 1749 newspaper issue

Articles: 1749 [col. 1–12]	ending -t	ending -et
From Africa, 4 May		gesuchet [hat], [wurde] erkläret, [wurde] zuerkennet, [hat] erreget
From Spain, 3 June		angelanget [ist/war], [worden] aufgerichtet
Palermo, 28 May	[haben] ausgeplündert	[worden] verwundet [ist], retiriret [hatte], [haben] ruiniret, [ist...worden] massacriret
Turin, 11 June	gemacht [hatte]	[ist] abgereiset
Livorno, 13 June	[ist] abgesegelt, [seynd] angelangt, erobert [haben]	[haben solle] abgestattet, [ist...worden] eingeführet, [haben] errettet, [haben] eingebüsset, [seye] beschäftiget, [wird] berichtet
Genua, 14 June	[werden] ausgebessert	[0] vermischet, [seyen] bestimmet, [werden] ausgerüstet, [habe] abgeschicket, [haben] berichtet, [haben] geredet, [sollen...werden] ausgerüstet
Florence, 14 June		[hat] abgestattet
Rome, 14 June	[hat] gejagt, [hielten] bloquirt	[wurde] gewippet, begehret [hat], [hat] gestellet, [hat] vorgepasset, [hat] ertödtet, [worden] abgedecket [sind], [worden] verwundet [sind]
Castell Gandolfo, 14 June		gewürdiget [hat]
Haag, 16 June		niedergeleget [hat], [wurde] angezündet, angeordnet [hat], eingerichtet [hat], [waren] beleuchtet, [wurden] angezündet
Mastricht, 22 June		[waren] beschäftiget, [wurden] verwundet
Stockholm, 10 June	[wurde] gehenkt	[hatte] zugeschnürret
Copenhagen, 7 June		[haben] geruhet, [haben] paradiret, [seynd] durchpassiret, [werden können] geleget, [gewesen] gezieret [ist], [ward] creiret, [ward] beygesetzet
Gdansk, 9 June		[hätte] vertheidiget

---

182 In this table, the auxiliary verb is provided before the past participle if it is given in the sentence and after the past participle if it was omitted. Past participles without auxiliary verb (e.g. *mit Schlossen vermischt*) are marked with a zero in square brackets before the noun.

Articles: 1749 [col. 1–12]	ending -*t*	ending -*et*
Wilda, 7 June	[hat] befördert	[wird] gemeldet, ausgesenget [hat]
Posen, 18 June	[0] vermischt	[worden] geführet [sind], [sollen…werden] geführet, [worden] ausgebrüttet [sind]
Düsseldorf, 10 June		[soll…werden] abgeführet, [haben] erreget
Dresden, 11 June		[0] verlautet, [seynd] angelanget
Breslau, 13 June		[worden seynd] gesetzet, [waren] versammlet, [wurden] genöthiget, gefüget [hatten/haben], [wäre] eingestürzet, [hätte] getheilet

In the newspaper issue published in 1749, the ending -*et* is clearly dominant overall. However, the ending -*t* does occur occasionally and its use is not restricted to certain articles. The past participle of *machen* is formed with the ending -*t* in the article on Turin and occurs at least once in every newspaper issue of the corpus, in which it always (altogether 44 times) ends in -*t*, i.e. the variant *gemachet* is never used in the newspaper corpus. The past participle of *anlangen*, on the other hand, is more frequently formed with -*et* in the 1749 newspaper issue as well as in the whole newspaper corpus, with five cases of *angelangt* and 14 of *angelanget*.[183] Forming the past participle of *machen* with the ending -*t*, therefore, seems to have been an exceptional but established rule in the *Wienerisches Diarium/Wiener Zeitung*. Besides these lexical patterns and the morpho-phonological principles described above, it is difficult to determine any general morphological patterns being applied in the 1749 newspaper issue.

Tab. 38: Regular past participle endings in the 1769 newspaper issue

Articles: 1769 [col. 1–14]	ending -*t*	ending -*et*
Introduction	[0] verlegt	[wird] versetzet
St. Petersburg, 29 May	[waren] abgefertigt, gefaßt [hat], [hatten] umringt, [hatte] besetzt, [hatte] gepflanzt, [habe] erblickt, [sind…worden] niedergemacht	[worden] zugeordnet [war], [worden] getheilet [war], [wurde] berichtet, [hatte] zurückgeleget, [war] genöthiget, [hatte sich] retiriret, [hat] gedauret, [ist…worden] verfolget, [kann… haben] geglücket, [sind…worden] erbeutet, [haben sich]

---

183 It has to be pointed out that ten of these 14 instances occur in the 1744 newspaper issue.

Articles: 1769 [col. 1–14]	ending -*t*	ending -*et*
		vertheidiget, [war] entfernet, [ist...worden] verwundet
From the Turkish border, 26 May	[hat] vertheidigt, [sind] zurückgesetzt, [hatten] bemeistert, [hätte] vertheidigt, geplündert [hatten]	[hätte] unterstützet
From the Polish border, 4 June	[betrachtete als] besetzt, [betrachtete als] versorgt, [hätten] vereitelt, [hätte] gefaßt, [hätte] gesetzt, [hatten] gesteckt, [ward] befehligt, [haben] übersetzt	zugerichtet [haben], [wären... worden] veriret, [hätte] veranstaltet, [hätte] angestellet
From the Warta, 5 June	[haben soll] gewagt, [ward] beschuldigt	[hatte] unterstützet
Parma, 13 June	[wurde] aufgedeckt, [wurde] aufgedeckt	[ist] beschäftiget, [werden] errichtet, [ist...worden] gekrönet, [ist] verkleidet, [sind] gezieret, [wird...werden] aufgeführt, [wurde] reduciret, [ist...worden] beschenket
Livorno, 16 June		[ist] angelanget, [seynd] gelanget, [sind] abgereißet
Vienna, 1 July	[haben] abgelegt, [0] geführt	[ist...worden] ernennet, [hatten] beurlaubet, [0] geführet

The findings from the 1769 newspaper issue give a first indication that individual correspondents prefer a certain variant, with the writers of the Parma and Livorno articles using the ending -*et* clearly more frequently than the ending -*t*. The correspondents reporting on the Turkish and Polish borders, on the other hand, choose the ending -*t* more often. The hypothesis that writers used one or the other variant deliberately on the basis of morphological rules cannot be verified since both variants appear in similar constructions (active as well as passive). However, the writer of the article on Parma only uses the ending -*t* for the past participle of the verb *aufdecken*, which indicates that the selection of this variant may depend on the lexical item itself. This is certainly not the case for the verb *führen* since the past participle is formed with -*t* as well as -*et* within the same article in very similar constructions:

> [...] und nachdem sich höchstgedacht Ihre königl. Hoheit bey Dero durchlauchtigsten Familie auf das zärtlichste beurlaubet hatten, tratten Höchstdieselben, [...] von Sr. königl. Hoheit dem Erzherzog Ferdinand an der Hand bis zum Reisewagen **geführt**, ihre Reise an. (*Wienerisches Diarium* 1769: col. 14, my emphasis)

Der Reisleibwagen, von 2. k. k. Leibpostilions **geführet**, in welchem Ihre k. H. alleine oben an, und gegenüber die Frau Gräfin von Paar, als Obristhofmeisterin, sich befanden [...] (*Wienerisches Diarium* 1769: col. 14, my emphasis)

In this case it seems that variation was the norm. More generally, it can be noted that the degree of variation was significantly higher in the 1769 newspaper issue (ending -*t*: 44 %, ending -*et*: 56 %) than in that of 1749 (ending -*t*: 14 %, ending -*et*: 86 %). The use of the ending -*t* in regular past participles clearly increased between 1749 and 1769.

Tab. 39: Regular past participle endings in the 1789 newspaper issue

Articles: 1789 [col. 1–12]	ending -*t*	ending -*et*
Vienna	[werden soll] gemacht, [ist] festgesetzt	[ist...worden] bewilliget, [werden soll] erhöhet, [werden können] gebürdet, [werden] abgerechnet, [wird] verlanget, [haben] geruhet, [hat] eingestellet
Hungary	[sind] angelangt, [wurde] verfinstert, [wurden] durchlöchert, [sind] zerlöchert	[werden] erwartet, [hat] zernichtet
Transylvania	[ist] zugetheilt	[hat] ereignet, [hatte] verheeret
Austrian Netherlands	[haben] versammelt, [wurden] vorgelegt, [wird] unterdrückt, [wurden] getrennt, [war] versammelt, [wurde] angelegt	[worden sind] verleitet, [hatten] gegründet, [sah sich] genöthiget
Note by editors	[wird] gemacht	[werden] mitgetheilet, [findet sich] eingeschaltet, [wird] hergestellet, [werden sollen] bezahlet, [ist] erdichtet
France	[sind...worden] verhandelt, [hatten] verlangt, [wurde] gemacht, [wird] gezeigt, [hätte] versucht, [haben] vereitelt, [wäre] berechtigt	[wäre] berichtiget, [waren] beschäftiget, [habe] versäumet
Great Britain	[hat] aufgehört, [hatte] erklärt, [sind...worden] gemacht	

Similar to the newspaper issue printed in 1769, the analysis of the issue published in 1789 reveals that individual correspondents had preferences for one variant or another. It is particularly striking that the articles on supra-regional news contain fewer cases of the ending -*et* than local news (see Vienna) and the note by the editors. In their note, the editors use the regular past participle ending -*t* only once, namely in the verb *machen*, which seems to be – as mentioned before – lexically determined. On the other hand, in articles on supra-regional news, particularly those on the Austrian Netherlands, France, and Great Britain, the ending -*t* occurs significantly more often than the ending -*et*. This suggests that the editors did not adjust the language of individual correspondents to their own language use. Morphological patterns can be detected in the articles on Hungary, Transylvania, and the Austrian Netherlands, in which the correspondents use the ending -*t* consistently in passive structures (unless the verb stem ends in -*t*).

Tab. 40: Regular past participle endings in the 1809 newspaper issue

Articles: 1809 [col. 1–8]	ending -*t*	ending -*et*
Headline	[0] verlegt	
Proclamation	[hat] geführt, [hat] geäussert, [wurden] befreyt, [wurden] verurtheilt, [müssen…werden] angezeigt, [sind] bewilligt, [werden…werden] bestraft, [ist] geneigt	[ist] ermüdet, [haben] geleistet, [werden] verhaftet
Spain	[haben] verfügt, [waren…worden] entstellt, [wurde] geschickt, [hatte] aufgestellt, [standen] versammelt, [hatte] aufgeführt, [stand] angespannt, [wurden] abgeschickt, [wurde] bewirkt, [0] vermischt, [ist] geglückt, [haben] gemacht, [hatte] gesetzt, [hatten] gesucht, [schienen] geneigt	[wurden] getödtet, [hatte] gelandet, [hatten] genöthiget, [sah sich] genöthiget
France	[wird] eingeführt, [wird] gehandelt, [hat] gewählt, [sind] hergestellt, [dürfen…werden] eingeführt, [dürfen…werden] transportirt, [hat] geändert	
Great Britain	[war] versammelt	[ward] befreyet
Kingdom of Württemberg	[ist…worden] formirt, [werden] organisirt, [werden] gemacht	[ist…worden] bewaffnet
Miscellanea	[haben] erzählt	[wird] erwartet, [hat] beygewohnet
Reminder by the editors	[werden] ersucht, [werden] ersucht, [werden soll] ausgelöscht	[sieht sich] bemüssiget, [wird] eröffnet, [werden] ersuchet, [werden könne] bestimmet

By 1809, the ending *-t* is dominant in the majority of articles. A notable exception is the text by the editors of the *Wiener Zeitung*, who remind their readers to prepay their newspaper subscriptions. In this text, the ending *-et* is used more frequently than *-t* in regular past participles. This indicates that the language use of the editors differed from the language used by the correspondents in this newspaper issue. Given that the editors use both variants in their text – without any morphological distinctions being made (see *[werden] ersucht* versus *[werden] ersuchet*) – and that variation also occurs in other articles, it can be argued that the variation between the endings *-t* and *-et* was still accepted in newspaper texts at the beginning of the 19th century. A lexical pattern can be observed with regard to the past participle *genöthiget*. This form occurs twice in the article on Spain in the 1809 newspaper issue and once in four other newspaper issues (1749, 1769, 1774, and 1789), i.e. six times in the whole newspaper corpus. The variant *genöthigt*, on the other hand, appears only once in the newspaper corpus (in 1779). Whereas morpho-phonological principles are clearly applied in the 1809 newspaper issues, it is difficult to establish any morphological patterns for the use of the endings *-t* versus *-et*.

Tab. 41: Regular past participle endings in the 1829 newspaper issue

Articles: 1829 [col. 1–4 & 7]	ending *-t*	ending *-et*
Vienna		[haben] geruhet
Great Britain	[worden seyen] eingereicht, [habe] verlangt, [habe] verlangt, [würden] eingereicht, [sey...worden] festgesetzt, [wird] erlaubt	[habe] angeordnet, [werden möge] gestattet
France	[ist...worden] gemacht, [hat] erklärt, [seyen] controllirt	
Reports from the war zone	[ist] gelangt, [worden waren] ausgeschickt, [war] entfernt, [seyn würde] zurückgekehrt, [wurde] poussirt, [wurde] erlaubt, [0] vorausgesetzt, [wurde] aufgestellt, [war] maskirt, [hatten] versperrt, [hatten] erklärt, [hatte] gemacht, [war] vorgerückt, [0] zerstreut, [wurde] poussirt, [hielten] besetzt, [0] angefeuert, [war] besetzt, [0] verzögert, [sollten...werden] besetzt	[hatte] vermuthet, [0] gewendet, [0] benachrichtiget, [war] entmuthiget, [hatte] eröffnet, [hatte] gekostet
Footnote	[0] verlegt	
Note on prices	[bleibt] gestellt, [0] wiederholt, [wird] untersagt, [werden... werden]	[sind] verpflichtet

Articles: 1829 [col. 1–4 & 7]	ending -*t*	ending -*et*
	angezeigt, [findet sich] gekränkt, [wird] aufgefordert	

In the newspaper issue printed in 1829, regular past participles are usually formed with the ending -*t*, with morpho-phonological principles being applied consistently. Apart from past participles with verb stems ending in -*d*/-*t* or a fricative/plosive plus a nasal sound, only three regular past participles end in -*et*: *geruhet*, *benachrichtiget*, and *entmuthiget*. The ending -*et* is always used in past participles of the verb *geruhen* – not just in the 1829 newspaper issue, but also in the whole newspaper corpus, in which the form *geruhet* appears ten times while *geruht* never occurs. It seems that – as is the case for the verb *machen* – the lexical item determines which past participle ending is used. A convincing principle that was employed in the other two cases (*benachrichtiget* and *entmuthiget*) cannot be established.

In summary, the quantitative and qualitative analyses of regular past participle endings in newspaper issues reveal a clear trend from the ending -*et* to -*t* in the period under investigation. In newspaper issues with a high percentage of variation, such as 1769 and 1789, the choice of the variant depended on morpho-phonological principles, on the language use of writers of individual articles, and lexical patterns. The use of a certain variant on the basis of morphological principles (e.g. the use of the ending -*t* in passive structures) can only be observed in a few individual newspaper articles.

4.4.3 Alternative forms of *wir/sie sind*

The only alternative form to *wir/sie sind* that appears in the newspaper issues is *wir/sie seynd*. The latter variant can be found in six newspaper issues (1744–1769) and is used exclusively in two of them (in 1749 and 1754). From 1764 onwards, the ECG variant *wir/sie sind* is clearly dominant and the UG form is completely invisible from 1774 onwards in the *Wienerisches Diarium/Wiener Zeitung* (see table and figure below).

Tab. 42: Variants of the verb *to be* in the 1st and 3rd pers. pl. pres. ind. act. in newspaper issues (absolute numbers)

Year of publication	*wir/sie seynd*	*wir/sie sind*
1744	5	6
1749	11	0

Year of publication	*wir/sie seynd*	*wir/sie sind*
1754	9	0
1759	4	3
1764	1	12
1769	1	8
1774	0	13
1779	0	15
1784	0	10
1789	0	11
1794	0	15
1799	0	5
1804	0	7
1809	0	6
1814	0	8
1819	0	12
1824	0	7
1829	0	7
1834	0	16

The shift from UG *seynd* to ECG *sind* can already be observed in 1744, with the ECG variant being used in more than half of the cases. It is particularly striking that the ECG variant never occurs in the two subsequent newspaper issues (1749 and 1754). After that, the use of the UG variant decreases relatively quickly, as the following figure illustrates.

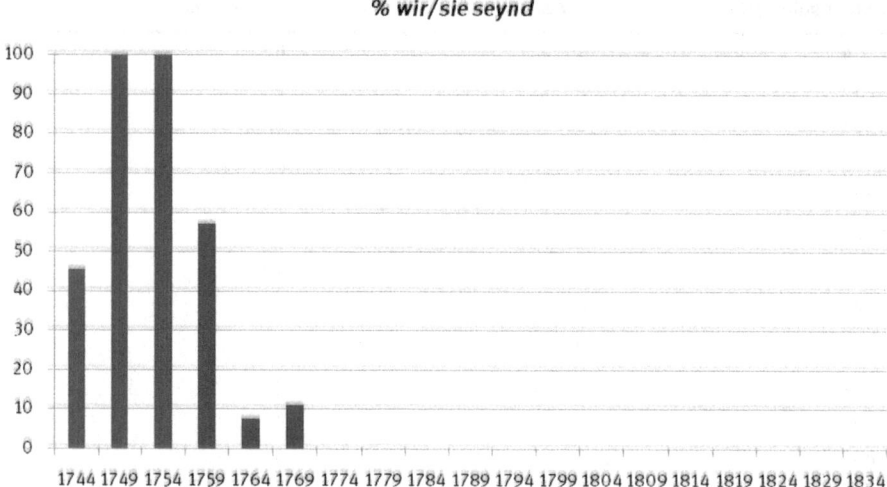

% wir/sie seynd

Fig. 18: *wir/sie seynd* in newspaper issues (in percentages)

When analysing the occurrences of *seynd* and *sind* in the newspaper issues printed between 1744 and 1769 in detail, a few patterns emerge. In the newspaper issue published in 1744, there is a clear regional distribution, with all instances of *seynd* appearing in articles from Italy (Rome, Nemi) and France (Marseille), while all instances of *sind* occur in articles from "Teutschland" (Aurich, Ketsch, and the Upper Rhine). A similar regional distribution can be observed in the newspaper issue printed in 1759, in which the three instances of *sie sind* appear in the articles on Cologne and Copenhagen. The majority of instances of *sie seynd* (three out of four), by contrast, occur in the article on Vienna.[184] However, *sie seynd* also occurs in an article on Cassel (i.e. Kassel in Hesse) once, which is situated in the same dialect area as Cologne (West Central German). Of course, it cannot be assumed that the writer of the article on Cassel is from that region, but his/her use of the ending *-ch* instead of *-g* in "rohem **Teich**" and "Das Brod und den **Teich**" (1759: col. 1, my emphasis) suggests that this writer is not from the very southern part of the German-speaking area. In their grammar of ENHG, Reichmann & Wegera (1993: 122) state that words being spelled with *ch* rather than *g* (e.g. *berch, tach*) are mainly found in texts from the Central German area and the adjacent northern part of the Upper

---

184 The only instance of *sie seynd* in the 1764 newspaper issue, too, occurs in a note from Vienna (1764: col. 14).

German area.[185] Based on this regional distribution, one may conclude that the newspaper correspondent came from this northern part of the Upper German language area – using both UG features (*sie seynd*) and features that are associated with areas north of Austria (*Teich*).

The instances of *sie seynd* in the 1749 newspaper issue, on the other hand, do not comply with the regional distribution described above. In this particular newspaper issue, in which *sie seynd* is used exclusively, the UG variant also appears in the articles on "Teutschland" (Düsseldorf, Dresden, Berlin, Breslau). This may suggest that the writers of these articles were from the Upper German language area. Another possible explanation for the exclusive use of the UG variant in this and the 1754 newspaper issue may be that the editors or printers of the newspaper standardised the forms for the 3rd pers. pl. ind. pres. act. of the verb *to be* before publishing the news. This, however, does not explain the variation between *sind* and *seynd* in other newspaper issues.

It seems that variation between *sie seynd* and *sie sind* was not uncommon in media texts printed before the 1760s. After that, the use of the UG variant decreased rapidly, with the UG variant being invisible in the *Wienerisches Diarium/Wiener Zeitung* from 1774 onwards. The article on Livorno in the 1769 newspaper issue contains the last visible instance of *sie seynd* in the newspaper corpus, while also containing the ECG variant:

> Die Herren Wood, ein engländischer Cavalier, Conte Carletti von Monte Pulciano, und der in Hannoverischen Diensten stehende Baron Grotheus **seynd** in dieser Woche aus Corsica zurück gelanget, allwo sie 3. Tage bey dem General Paoli zubrachten, sodann giengen sie nacher Bastia, und empfiengen an beyden Orten sehr viele Ehren, letztere zwey **sind** nacher Florenz abgereißet. (*Wienerisches Diarium* 1769: col 13, my emphasis)

> The gentlemen Wood, an English cavalier, Conte Carletti from Monte Pulciano, and Baron Grotheus, who is in Hanoverian services, [have] arrived from Corsica this week, where they had spent 3 days with General Paoli, after that they went to Bastia and received many honours in both places, the latter two [have] departed to Florence.

It is difficult to find plausible explanations for this variation, but this example clearly shows that both variants were still in use in 1769.

4.4.4 Conclusion: Analysis of newspaper issues

The results above indicate that the language use differed between individual articles, which means that newspapers have to be seen as a compilation of texts rather

---

185 Today, too, the spirantization of [k] to [x] is uncommon in the south (cf. Elspaß & Möller (2003), http://www.atlas-alltagssprache.de/runde-1/f15a-b/ [accessed 26.04.2017]).

than one homogenous text. Nevertheless, certain overall trends can be detected in a quantitative diachronic analysis of newspaper issues. The *e*-apocope in feminine and plural nouns was clearly avoided in the *Wienerisches Diarium* by 1744, while the ending *-e* is dominant. In this regard, the ECG norm was introduced to the *Wienerisches Diarium* prior to the publication of Gottsched's grammar in 1748 and the introduction of the school reform in 1774. Thus the language use in newspapers may have strengthened the implementation of the ECG norms through the model character of printed texts. Instances of *e*-apocope in strong masculine and neuter nouns in the dative case, on the other hand, can be found throughout the period under investigation, with the *e*-apocope clearly dominating until 1764. Thereafter, the dative *-e* gained ground in the newspaper issues, i.e. a general trend away from the *e*-apocope can be observed. The qualitative analysis of newspaper issues revealed that individual correspondents preferred either dative *-e* or forms without final *-e*, with a few correspondents employing morpho-syntactic principles (e.g. *e*-apocope in dative constructions introduced with the preposition *mit*). With regard to the dative *-e*, it is certainly plausible to suggest that the grammarians discussed in chapter 3 influenced the language use in newspapers, whereas this is less likely in the case of final *-e* in feminine and plural nouns, which had been adopted to a large extent by 1744.

A comparison between these findings and Rössler's (2005: 267) results, which suggest that the prescription of 18th-century grammarians (particularly Gottsched) led to a drastic language change between 1720 and 1765, demonstrates the importance of fine-grained analyses. While the use of final *-e* clearly increased between 1720 and 1765 in Rössler's texts, the analysis of the newspaper corpus reveals that this change occurred before 1744 in feminine and plural nouns, i.e. before Gottsched's grammar was published. Durrell (2016), too, categorizes texts into long periods of time (50 years), which does not allow for detailed comparisons. However, Durrell's analysis of newspapers suggests that the *e*-apocope in plural nouns significantly decreased in the first half of the 18th century. He found 19 instances of *e*-apocope in plural forms in the first period (1650–1700), nine in the second (1701–1750) and two in the third (1751–1800). Durrell's findings generally match the results from the analysis of the *Wienerisches Diarium/Wiener Zeitung* more closely than the findings presented by Rössler (2005), who included different text types in his analyses.[186] In Rössler's texts, the percentage of *e*-apocope in feminine nouns was higher around 1765 (40 %) than in dative constructions (27 %) and plural forms (26 %), whereas the dative *-e* was introduced significantly later and less consistently than the final *-e* in feminine and plural nouns in the *Wienerisches Diarium/Wiener*

---

186 It should, however, be pointed out that the percentage of dative *-e* in the East Upper German newspapers analysed by Durrell (2016: 227) is considerably higher (71 %) in the third period (1751–1800) than in the same time frame in the *Wienerische Diarium/Wiener Zeitung* (52 %).

Zeitung. This suggests that the implementation of ECG norms developed differently in different text types, with newspapers leading the change regarding the final -*e* in feminine and plural nouns.

UG variants of past participles without the prefix *ge*- appear very rarely in the newspaper corpus and are completely invisible from 1789 onwards. The four instances that do occur (*vorgeben, worden* [2], *geessen*) were not marked as 'incorrect' by Antesperg (1747) and the verbs *geben* and *worden* are also attested in Rössler's (2005: 307) corpus of 18th-century texts. Rössler (ibid. 303) points out that variation between past participles with and without the prefix *ge*- only occurs in a small group of verbs and the verbs found in the newspaper corpus belong to this group. Generally, however, the use of past participles without the prefix *ge*- was clearly avoided, and the ECG norm (past participles with *ge*-) was certainly the more dominant one in the whole period under investigation. In other words, the ECG norm had largely been adopted in the *Wienerisches Diarium* before the publication of Gottsched's grammar and subsequent normative works.

Considerably more variation can be found in regular past participle endings, with a clear trend towards the ending -*t* in the newspaper corpus (from 17 % in 1744 to 76 % in 1834). Variation between the two variants (-*t* versus -*et*) can be found in every newspaper issue and mainly depended on phonetic but also (in a few cases) lexical and morphological factors. Furthermore, certain correspondents showed preferences for one particular past participle ending, indicating that a particular newspaper issue cannot be considered to be one homogeneous text.

Rössler's (2005: 297) analyses revealed that the ending -*t* was dominant in texts printed around 1690 (62 %). The use of the ending -*t* then decreased to 31 % in 1720 and 21 % in 1765 (ibid.). The latter percentage is in line with the results of the analysis of the newspaper issues printed in 1754 (21 %) and 1764 (18 %). After that, however, the use of the ending -*t* clearly increases in the newspaper corpus. This illustrates that the development of regular past participle endings was not completed by the beginning of the 19th century, with both variants co-occurring in the whole period under investigation.

As Rössler (2005: 300) points out, it was Adelung (1781) who restored the oral usage of the ending -*t* in regular past participles as a benchmark for the written norm. Adelung – in contrast to Gottsched and other 18th-century grammarians – prescribed the ending -*t* for verbs in active indicative (but not passive or subjunctive). Interestingly, the analysis of the newspaper corpus showed that the ending -*t* was already dominant (76 %) in the issue published in 1779, i.e. two years prior to the publication of Adelung's *Deutsche Sprachlehre* in 1781. This may indicate that Adelung merely codified the language use common in newspapers and other 'model texts', i.e. he described rather than prescribed the use of regular past participle endings. Instead of Adelung influencing the use of past participle endings in the *Wienerisches Diarium/Wiener Zeitung*, his grammar may have been based on newspaper texts to some extent. It should also be noted that the ending -*et* was widely used in newspapers as well as in Rössler's corpus before it was prescribed by Gottsched and subsequent grammarians. It can, therefore, be concluded that the grammarians discussed in chapter 3 did not have a significant influence on the language use in the *Wienerisches Diarium/Wiener Zeitung* when it comes to regular past participle endings.

With regard to the variant *wir/sie seynd*, which appears relatively often in newspaper issues printed before 1760 but disappears from the *Wienerisches Diarium* in 1774, it is more likely that grammarians influenced the language used by correspondents. These results are in line with Rössler's (2005: 220f.) findings, which reveal that the UG variant was dominant until 1750 but decreased significantly by 1765, especially in texts printed in Austria but less so in texts printed in Bavaria. This indicates that the use of *wir/sie seynd* was regionally determined, which was also observed in the newspaper issues, with the UG variant being used more frequently in local than in supra-regional news. Rössler's (2005: 221) suggestion that Maria Theresa's language reform contributed to the consistent implementation of the ECG variant *wir/sie sind* is certainly plausible and verified by the analysis of the newspaper corpus. The following section will discuss to what extent these developments can be observed in the corpus of petitions.

4.5 Language use in petitionary letters

Similar to the previous sections, the results of the analysis of petitionary letters are first provided in tables, which are described and discussed. In contrast to the results of the analysis of the reading primers and newspaper issues, the figures in this section illustrate absolute numbers (not percentages) due to the low number of variants occurring within a single petition. In order to achieve greater comparability between individual petitionary letters, some of which differ considerably in length, the frequency of the variants was normalised (per 1,000 words) and illustrated in a second figure. This allows for a more accurate comparison of the language use in petitionary letters. Furthermore, a polynomial trend line was added in this second figure, resulting in a clearer picture of the development.[187] As in the previous sections, the findings of *e*-apocope in nouns will be discussed first, followed by past participles and alternative forms of *wir/sie sind*.

---

187 In order to prevent any distortions in the data, only petitions with occurrences of the features under investigation were included in the second figure. This means that, for example, the petition written in 1755, in which no nouns that can end in -*e* appear, is not presented in the second figure. The first figure, on the other hand, illustrates every single petition.

4.5.1 *e*-apocope in nouns

The overall results for *e*-apocope in nouns show a clear trend towards using the final
-*e* in nouns (see table and figures below). The first instance of final -*e* in nouns can
be observed in the petitionary letter written in 1749 (*Güte*). In the three petitions
submitted before 1749 (1744, 1746, and 1747), the ending -*e* is never used for the
nouns under investigation, while the *e*-apocope occurs 13 times altogether in these
three letters. The *e*-apocope is dominant in all petitionary letters written before 1773,
except in the petition submitted in 1764, in which just one occurrence of *e*-apocope
and two instances of final -*e* can be found. In the majority of petitionary letters (7
out of 10) written between 1773 and 1782, a preference for *e*-apocope can still be
observed, with 43 instances of *e*-apocope (i.e. 70 %) and 18 occurrences of final -*e*
(i.e. 30 %) in these 10 petitions.

Tab. 43: *e*-apocope versus using the ending -*e* in petitionary letters: overall (absolute numbers)

Petitionary letter	Year	Number of words	*e*-apocope	ending -*e*
STLA_1744w_Lamberg	1744	339	6	0
STLA_1746w_Lamberg	1746	266	2	0
STLA_1747r_Lamberg	1747	335	5	0
OOLA_1749r_Neuhaus	1749	290	4	1
OOLA_1751r_a_Weinberg	1751	332	3	0
OOLA_1751r_b_Weinberg	1751	354	5	1
OOLA_1752r_Weinberg	1752	289	4	0
STLA_1752p_Lamberg	1752	349	5	2
STLA_1754p_Saurau	1754	244	4	0
STLA_1754r_Donnersbach	1754	384	6	0
STLA_1755w_Saurau	1755	211	0	0
STLA_1757p_Saurau	1757	235	7	2
STLA_1758p_Saurau	1758	236	7	0
STLA_1760r_Rothenfels	1760	362	7	2
OOLA_1763w_Schwertberg_M	1763	230	2	0
OOLA_1764w_Schwertberg	1764	127	1	2
STLA_1766p_Rothenfels	1766	215	10	0
OOLA_1768p_Waldenfels	1768	362	5	0
OOLA_1769r_Weinberg	1769	338	2	0
OOLA_1771w_Weinberg	1771	531	11	8
OOLA_1772r_Weinberg	1772	349	5	0

Petitionary letter	Year	Number of words	*e*-apocope	ending -*e*
OOLA_1773r_a_Weinberg	1773	285	3	0
OOLA_1773r_b_Weinberg	1773	367	3	0
OOLA_1773w_Weinberg	1773	285	1	2
OOLA_1775r_Weinberg	1775	286	1	3
OOLA_1776r_Weinberg	1776	263	6	0
OOLA_1777r_Zunftarchivalien	1777	381	5	2
OOLA_1778r_Weinberg	1778	546	11	5
OOLA_1781r_a_Weinberg	1781	386	5	6
OOLA_1781r_b_Weinberg	1781	320	3	0
STLA_1782r_Lamberg	1782	439	5	0
STLA_1783w_St. Lambrecht	1783	211	1	1
OOLA_1784w_Weinberg	1784	298	0	5
OOLA_1786w_Weinberg	1786	138	1	4
STLA_1786w_Lamberg_M	1786	224	1	1
STLA_1787w_Rothenfels	1787	189	0	3
STLA_1788w_a_Lamberg	1788	108	2	3
STLA_1788w_b_Lamberg	1788	208	0	0
STLA_1792w_Rothenfels	1792	255	0	3
OOLA_1792w_Obernberg	1792	230	1	5
STLA_1796w_Lamberg	1796	389	7	6
STLA_1797w_Saurau	1797	147	2	2
STLA_1801w_Oberradkersburg	1801	286	2	5
STLA_1801w_Pflindsberg	1801	228	3	2
STLA_1802w_Pflindsberg	1802	272	7	9
STLA_1803w_Pflindsberg	1803	115	0	1
STLA_1804w_Oberradkersburg	1804	149	0	1
STLA_1806w_Pflindsberg	1806	164	4	5
STLA_1810w_Oberradkersburg_M	1810	280	4	5
STLA_1811w_Oberradkersburg_M	1811	536	9	8
OOLA_1812w_Vöcklabruck_M	1812	412	3	17
STLA_1820w_Rothenfels	1820	353	3	7
OOLA_1822w_a_Neuhaus	1822	216	3	4
OOLA_1822w_b_Neuhaus	1822	564	7	24
OOLA_1824w_Vöcklabruck_M	1824	489	1	15
OOLA_1824w_Vöcklabruck	1824	671	1	17
OOLA_1825w_Neuhaus_M	1825	628	3	18
STLA_1828w_Pflindsberg	1828	156	1	2

Petitionary letter	Year	Number of words	e-apocope	ending -e
STLA_1829w_Pflindsberg_M	1829	358	2	8
OOLA_1830p_Ort	1830	168	0	8

From 1784 onwards, the final -e is used more frequently than in earlier petitions. Indeed, the final -e occurs more often than the e-apocope in 22 out of 27 petitionary letters submitted between 1784 and 1830.[188] While the preference for the ending -e becomes particularly obvious from 1812 onwards, the e-apocope is not completely invisible in these petitions – it still appears in 9 out of 10 petitionary letters written between 1812 and 1830.

The figures below illustrate the general trend away from the e-apocope. The first figure shows the absolute number of nouns without final -e (black column) and with final -e (grey column) for each petitionary letter. The second figure provides the normalised frequency (per 1,000 words) of the occurrences of e-apocope (red diamond) and nouns with the ending -e (blue square) as well as a polynomial trend line, which indicates the decrease of e-apocope (red line) and increase of the ending -e (blue line) between 1744 and 1830.

Both figures suggest a shift in language use in the mid 1780s – from 1784 onwards, the writers of the petitionary letters seem to generally prefer the ending -e in nouns. Nevertheless, the e-apocope was not completely dismissed by the majority of writers. It still appears in 21 out of 27 petitions. The significant decrease of e-apocope sets in about 35 years after the publication of the first edition of Gottsched's successful grammar in 1748 and just ten years after the introduction of the school reform (1774). Given that the first instance of the ending -e appears in 1749, i.e. after the publication of Gottsched's grammar, and that a considerable shift from the e-apocope to the ending -e can be observed around 1784, i.e. at a time when various grammars were on the market, it is plausible that the grammarians discussed in chapter 3 had an influence on the language use in petitionary letters in 18th-century Austria. The school reform introduced in 1774 may have also contributed to this development, leading to a further increase in the use of the ending -e.

---

188 Petitions without any of the two variants, i.e. STLA_1788w_b_Lamberg in this case, were not included in this and similar counts.

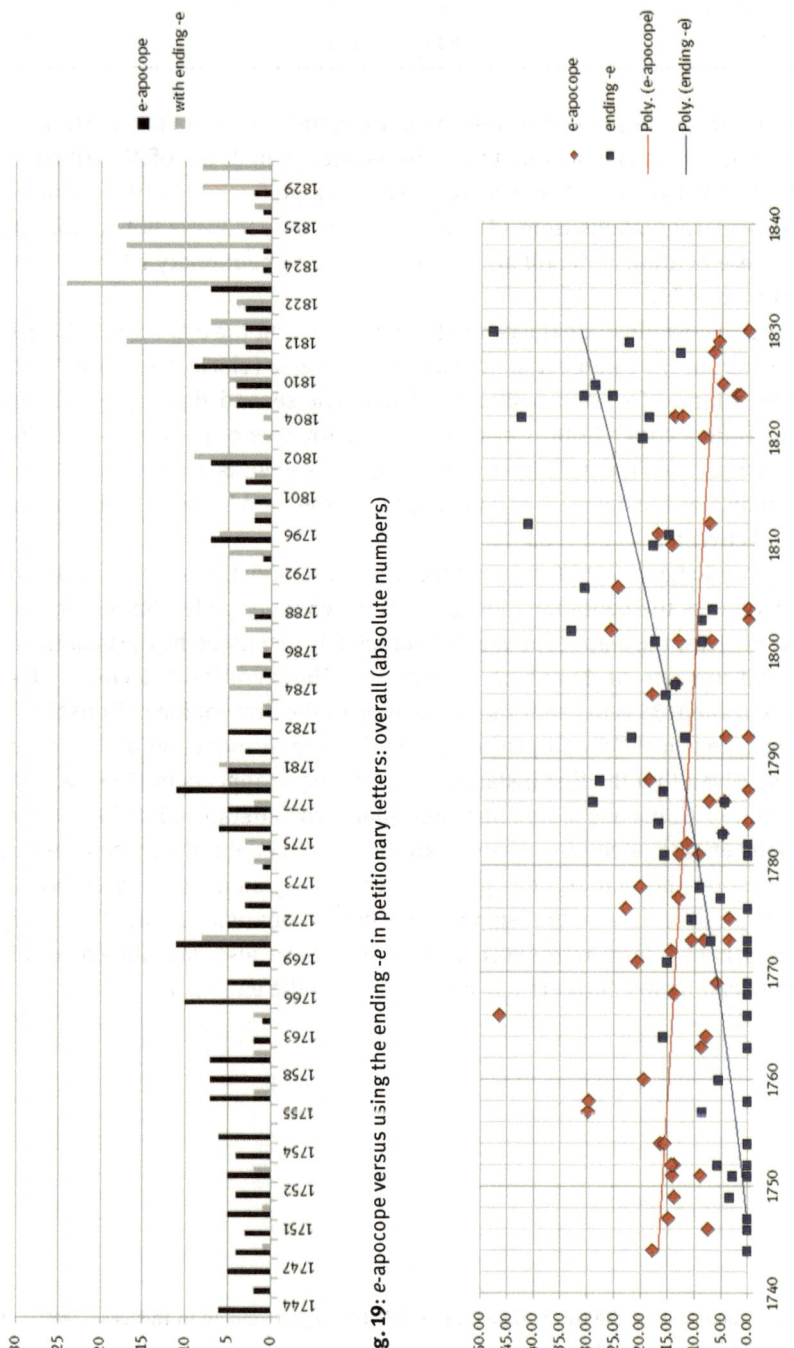

Fig. 19: *e*-apocope versus using the ending -*e* in petitionary letters: overall (absolute numbers)

Fig. 20: *e*-apocope versus using the ending -*e* in petitionary letters: overall (normalised frequency: per 1,000 words)

In order to assess the influence of 18th-century grammarians and the school reform of 1774 more accurately, the development of *e*-apocope in feminine nouns, strong masculine and neuter nouns in the dative singular form, and plural nouns has to be investigated separately.

The development of *e*-apocope in feminine nouns resembles the overall trend described above (see table and figures below). As mentioned before, the first feminine noun ending in -*e* (*Güte*) appears in the petition submitted in 1749, in which two feminine nouns are spelled without final -*e* (*Gnad, Mild*). Until 1772, the *e*-apocope appears more frequently than the ending -*e* in feminine nouns in the majority of petitions (i.e. in 16 out of 19 petitionary letters). Between 1773 and 1783, the use of both variants is fairly balanced, with individual writers either using both variants (1773w, 1775, 1777, 1778, 1783) or one of the variants exclusively (*e*-apocope: 1773r_a, 1776, 1781r_b, 1782; ending -*e*: 1781r_a).

Tab. 44: *e*-apocope versus using the ending -*e* in petitionary letters: feminine nouns (absolute numbers)

Petitionary letter	Year	Number of words	*e*-apocope	ending -*e*
STLA_1744w_Lamberg	1744	339	2	0
STLA_1746w_Lamberg	1746	266	2	0
STLA_1747r_Lamberg	1747	335	4	0
OOLA_1749r_Neuhaus	1749	290	2	1
OOLA_1751r_a_Weinberg	1751	332	2	0
OOLA_1751r_b_Weinberg	1751	354	0	1
OOLA_1752r_Weinberg	1752	289	1	0
STLA_1752p_Lamberg	1752	349	4	2
STLA_1754p_Saurau	1754	244	0	0
STLA_1754r_Donnersbach	1754	384	4	0
STLA_1755w_Saurau	1755	211	0	0
STLA_1757p_Saurau	1757	235	5	2
STLA_1758p_Saurau	1758	236	3	0
STLA_1760r_Rothenfels	1760	362	1	2
OOLA_1763w_Schwertberg_M	1763	230	1	0
OOLA_1764w_Schwertberg	1764	127	1	1
STLA_1766p_Rothenfels	1766	215	2	0
OOLA_1768p_Waldenfels	1768	362	1	0
OOLA_1769r_Weinberg	1769	338	1	0
OOLA_1771w_Weinberg	1771	531	7	4

Petitionary letter	Year	Number of words	*e*-apocope	ending -*e*
OOLA_1772r_Weinberg	1772	349	2	0
OOLA_1773r_a_Weinberg	1773	285	2	0
OOLA_1773r_b_Weinberg	1773	367	0	0
OOLA_1773w_Weinberg	1773	285	1	2
OOLA_1775r_Weinberg	1775	286	1	2
OOLA_1776r_Weinberg	1776	263	2	0
OOLA_1777r_Zunftarchivalien	1777	381	2	2
OOLA_1778r_Weinberg	1778	546	2	4
OOLA_1781r_a_Weinberg	1781	386	0	4
OOLA_1781r_b_Weinberg	1781	320	1	0
STLA_1782r_Lamberg	1782	439	4	0
STLA_1783w_St. Lambrecht	1783	211	1	1
OOLA_1784w_Weinberg	1784	298	0	5
OOLA_1786w_Weinberg	1786	138	0	1
STLA_1786w_Lamberg_M	1786	224	0	1
STLA_1787w_Rothenfels	1787	189	0	1
STLA_1788w_a_Lamberg	1788	108	0	3
STLA_1788w_b_Lamberg	1788	208	0	0
STLA_1792w_Rothenfels	1792	255	0	3
OOLA_1792w_Obernberg	1792	230	1	2
STLA_1796w_Lamberg	1796	389	2	5
STLA_1797w_Saurau	1797	147	0	1
STLA_1801w_Oberradkersburg	1801	286	1	1
STLA_1801w_Pflindsberg	1801	228	0	2
STLA_1802w_Pflindsberg	1802	272	2	4
STLA_1803w_Pflindsberg	1803	115	0	1
STLA_1804w_Oberradkersburg	1804	149	0	0
STLA_1806w_Pflindsberg	1806	164	1	4
STLA_1810w_Oberradkersburg_M	1810	280	0	0
STLA_1811w_Oberradkersburg_M	1811	536	2	4
OOLA_1812w_Vöcklabruck_M	1812	412	0	8
STLA_1820w_Rothenfels	1820	353	0	4
OOLA_1822w_a_Neuhaus	1822	216	3	4
OOLA_1822w_b_Neuhaus	1822	564	3	9
OOLA_1824w_Vöcklabruck_M	1824	489	0	5
OOLA_1824w_Vöcklabruck	1824	671	0	7
OOLA_1825w_Neuhaus_M	1825	628	1	6

Petitionary letter	Year	Number of words	e-apocope	ending -e
STLA_1828w_Pflindsberg	1828	156	0	1
STLA_1829w_Pflindsberg_M	1829	358	0	5
OOLA_1830p_Ort	1830	168	0	4

From 1784 onwards, the use of final -e in feminine nouns is clearly dominant in the petitionary letters. In the petitions submitted between 1784 and 1792, no instances of e-apocope in feminine nouns can be found and in the period from 1784 to 1830, the ECG variant is used exclusively in 16 out of 25 petitions. The UG e-apocope, by contrast, only appears in nine petitionary letters submitted between 1784 and 1830, in eight of which it is used less frequently than the ending -e.

The figures below, which show the absolute numbers (first figure) and the normalised frequency (second figure) of both variants in the petitionary letters, illustrate the findings of the quantitative analysis described above. The first figure suggests a shift in language use at around 1784, when the ECG variant became dominant and the UG e-apocope was only used sporadically by nine writers thereafter. The ending -e was, however, used in feminine nouns from 1749 onwards and was used consistently by two writers before 1784. The polynomial trend line in the second figure indicates that the use of e-apocope and final -e in feminine nouns was fairly balanced in the 1770s, with the ending -e steadily increasing over time. Both figures show that the UG e-apocope in feminine nouns did not disappear completely from petitionary letters until 1828. Nevertheless, the decrease of e-apocope in feminine nouns is obvious in the period under investigation, with the ending -e becoming the preferred variant after the mid-1770s.

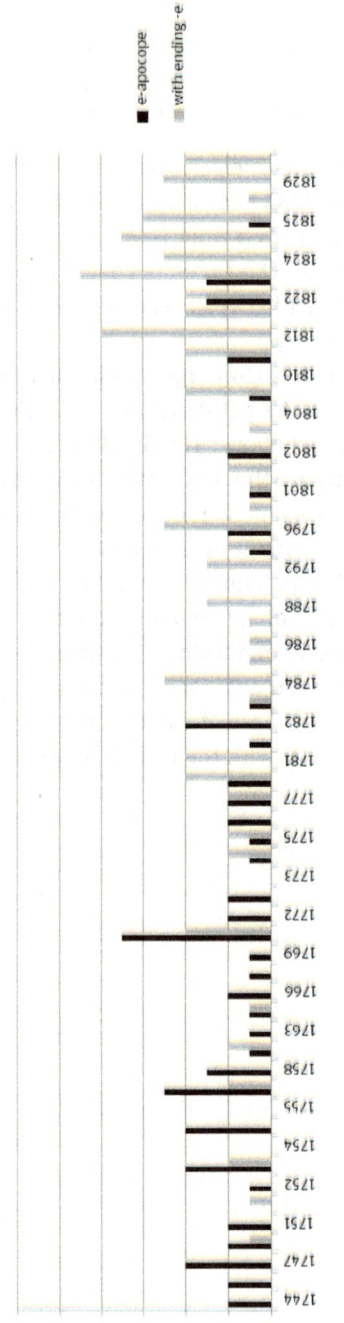

Fig. 22: *e*-apocope versus using the ending *-e* in petitionary letters: feminine nouns (absolute numbers)

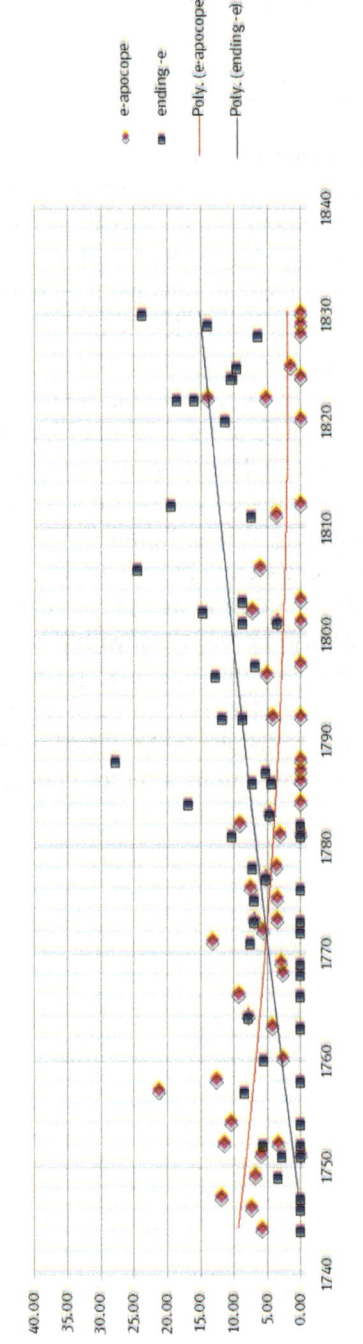

Fig. 21: e-apocope versus using the ending -e in petitionary letters: feminine nouns (normalised frequency: per 1,000 words)

Variation between both variants occurs in 20 out of the 54 petitionary letters. In order to determine whether the use of the variants is lexically determined, the occurrences in these 20 petitions are listed in the table below, with the number of instances provided in square brackets, if exceeding 1.

Tab. 45: Variation between *e*-apocope and final *-e* in feminine nouns

Petitionary letter	e-apocope	ending -e
OOLA_1749r_Neuhaus	Gnad, Mild	Güte
STLA_1752p_Lamberg	Buß, Pfarr, Schand [2]	Gnade, Sache
STLA_1757p_Saurau	Bitt [2], Gnad [3]	Gnade, Milde
STLA_1760r_Rothenfels	Sach	Hälfte [2]
OOLA_1764w_Schwertberg	Beihilf	Gnade
OOLA_1771w_Weinberg	Altmühl [3], Beihilf, Hilf [2], Hilf[leistung]	Behörde, Mühe, Mühle, Weile
OOLA_1773w_Weinberg	Gnad	Güte, Milde
OOLA_1775r_Weinberg	Hilf	Gnade, Milde
OOLA_1777r_Zunftarchivalien	Mühl, Ursach	Anfrage, Schleiffe
OOLA_1778r_Weinberg	Herberg, Reis	Gnade, Hilfe [2], Mühe
STLA_1783w_St. Lambrecht	Klass	Hilfe
OOLA_1792w_Obernberg	Bitt	Anzeige, Gnade
STLA_1796w_Lamberg	Pfarr, Unruh[stifter]	Behörde, Beschwerde, Gemeinde, Güte, Weide
STLA_1801w_Oberradkersburg	Pfarr	Zusage
STLA_1802w_Pflindsberg	Pfann [2]	Bitte [2], Holzlege, Stube
STLA_1806w_Pflindsberg	Frey	Freye [2], Gemeinde, Hilfe
STLA_1811w_Oberradkersburg_M	Thür, Übergab	Kasse, Lage [2], Zusage
OOLA_1822w_a_Neuhaus	Saag, Sag[mühle] [2]	Bitte, Mühle, [Sag]mühle [2]
OOLA_1822w_b_Neuhaus	Saag, Sag, Säg	Anzeige, Ehe, Hilfe, Mühle [3], Sorge, Urkunde [2]
OOLA_1825w_Neuhaus_M	Feldenpfarr	Bittwoche, Dirne, Rede, Sache, Stalldirne, Treue

The table above shows that variation of the same word can only be detected in two petitionary letters. In the petitionary letter submitted in 1757, *Gnad* occurs three times and *Gnade* once. This variation even appears within the same constructions: *die Hoche gnade* versus *die hoche gnad*. This example indicates that the writer of this petition was certainly aware of the ending *-e* but s/he did not use it consistently. In the petition written in 1806, both variants *Frey* and *Freye* appear in identical constructions: *beym Grundlsee befindlichen Freÿe* versus *beim Grundlsee befindliche*

Freÿ. This indicates that both variants were acceptable for the writer of this petition. Generally, the different spelling (once with and once without final -*e*) of the same word within one petitionary letter is rare. This means that individual writers had preferences for writing a certain word with or without final -*e*. In order to determine whether these preferences were shared by different writers and whether they changed over time, the following table lists all feminine nouns that occur in the petitionary letters alphabetically, categorized into two periods (pre 1784 and post 1784), with the number of instances provided in square brackets, if exceeding 1.

Tab. 46: *e*-apocope versus ending -*e* in feminine nouns in petitionary letters (pre and post 1784)

Periods	*e*-apocope	ending -*e*
pre 1784	Altmühl [3], Beihilf [5], Beylag, Bitt [9], Buß [2], Gnad [18], Herberg, Hilf [4], Hilf[leistung], Hoffmühl, Klass, Mild, Mühl [6], Pfarr, Reis, Sach [3], Schand [2], Ursach	Anfrage, Behörde, Ehe, Feuchte, Gnade [5], Güte [2], Hälfte, Hilfe [3], Hitze, Milde [3], Mühe [3], Mühle [2], Sache, Schleiffe, Weile, Weise
post 1784	Bitt, Feldenpfarr, Frey, Pfann [2], Pfarr [2], Sag[mühle] [2], Sag [4], Thür, Übergab, Unruh[stifter]	Anlage, Anzeige [3], Behörde [4], Beihilfe [2], Beilage [2], Berchtesgadnerwaare, Beschwerde, Bitte [17], Bittwoche, Dirne, Ehe, Einnahme, Feile [2], Freye [2], Gemeinde [5], Gnade [2], Grenze, Güte, Hilfe [2], Hofstelle, Holzlege, Holzwaare, Kasse, Lage [2], Lehre, Milde, Mühle [4], Oberamtsbehörde, Quelle, Rede, Reise, Reise[bewilligung] [2], Reise[einschaltung], Sache, [Sag]mühle [2], Seite, Sorge [2], Stalldirne, Strafe [3], Streitsache, Stube, Tatsache, Treue [2], Unkunde, Urkunde [2], Waare, Weide, Zusage [2]

The table above reveals that *Behörde*, *Ehe*, and *Güte* are always spelled with final -*e*, both pre and post 1784. In these nouns, the *e*-apocope seems to have been perceived as unacceptable across time, in contrast to *Bitt* and *Pfarr*, which appear without final -*e* in both periods. While *Bitt* is more frequently spelled with final -*e* from 1784 onwards, the UG variant without final -*e* occurs more often before 1784. The noun *Pfarr*, on the other hand, consistently displays *e*-apocope in the whole petitionary letter corpus, appearing once pre 1784 and three times (including *Feldenpfarr*) post 1784 (in different petitionary letters). Indeed, the noun *Feldenpfarr* in the petition written in 1825 is the last instance of *e*-apocope in feminine nouns in the corpus of petitionary letters. This indicates that the *e*-apocope was accepted in the noun *Pfarr* in Austria, even in the first half of the 19th century, despite Adelung's prescription of final -*e* in *Pfarre* (see section 3.6.1).[189] From 1828 onwards, however, the *e*-apocope in feminine nouns is invisible in the handwritten petitions.

The general development from the *e*-apocope to the ending -*e* in petitionary letters in the period under investigation can be exemplified with certain lexical items. The UG variant *Gnad*, for example, is used significantly more often than *Gnade* (18 versus 5 times) before 1784. From 1784 onwards, only the latter form occurs in petitionary letters. The feminine noun *Bitte*, on the other hand, is still spelled without final -*e* once after 1784 (in OOLA_1792w_Obernberg) but the variant with final -*e* is certainly more common (used 17 times). Before 1784, only the UG variant *Bitt* is used in petitionary letters. Similarly, the variant *Mühl* is used more frequently than *Mühle* (6 times versus twice) before 1784. After 1784, only the latter variant occurs in petitionary letters (altogether 6 times, including *[Sag]mühle*). The development of these lexical items can thus serve as an example for the general trend away from the *e*-apocope as described above.

The development of *e*-apocope in strong masculine and neuter nouns in the dative singular form differs significantly from feminine nouns. From 1749 to 1768, the dative -*e* never occurs in the corpus of petitions. The first two instances of dative -*e* occur in the petitionary letter written in 1771 (*auf diesem Mühlwerke, zum Raube*), in which, however, the *e*-apocope is still dominant with four occurrences (*mit Todt, am Fest, mit einem Mühlwerk, meinem Hausstock*).[190] Indeed, the *e*-apocope remains dominant in all petitionary letters submitted before 1801, with the dative -*e* appearing in only two petitions: OOLA_1771w_Weinberg (two instances, see above) and OOLA_1781r_a_Weinberg (one instance: *dem bevorstehenden Elende*). In the latter petition, the *e*-apocope occurs three times in nouns in the dative singular form (*dem so trocknen Frühjahr, zum Brod, auf dem Haunschild Haus*). In total, dative -*e* appears in the corpus of petitions only three times before the end of the 18th century (1797) while the *e*-apocope occurs 66 times until then (see table below).

---

189 It is debatable whether it is appropriate to use the term 'e-apocope' for nouns that are always spelled without final -*e* in one of my corpora. Since 18th-century grammarians prescribed the form with final -*e* (see chapter 3), it can be argued that *Pfarr* constitutes an example of *e*-apocope, i.e. a noun, in which the final -*e* is absent (in comparison to the norm prescribed by grammarians).
190 It is striking that the writer of this petitionary letter does not use the dative -*e* after the prepositions *mit* and *an* but after *auf* and *zu*, which may suggest that the variation in this petition is morphologically determined.

Tab. 47: *e*-apocope versus using the ending *-e* in petitionary letters: strong masculine and neuter nouns in the dative singular form (absolute numbers)

Petitionary letter	Year	Number of words	*e*-apocope	ending *-e*
STLA_1744w_Lamberg	1744	339	0	0
STLA_1746w_Lamberg	1746	266	0	0
STLA_1747r_Lamberg	1747	335	0	0
OOLA_1749r_Neuhaus	1749	290	1	0
OOLA_1751r_a_Weinberg	1751	332	1	0
OOLA_1751r_b_Weinberg	1751	354	0	0
OOLA_1752r_Weinberg	1752	289	0	0
STLA_1752p_Lamberg	1752	349	1	0
STLA_1754p_Saurau	1754	244	1	0
STLA_1754r_Donnersbach	1754	384	2	0
STLA_1755w_Saurau	1755	211	0	0
STLA_1757p_Saurau	1757	235	2	0
STLA_1758p_Saurau	1758	236	1	0
STLA_1760r_Rothenfels	1760	362	6	0
OOLA_1763w_Schwertberg_M	1763	230	1	0
OOLA_1764w_Schwertberg	1764	127	0	0
STLA_1766p_Rothenfels	1766	215	8	0
OOLA_1768p_Waldenfels	1768	362	3	0
OOLA_1769r_Weinberg	1769	338	0	0
OOLA_1771w_Weinberg	1771	531	4	2
OOLA_1772r_Weinberg	1772	349	1	0
OOLA_1773r_a_Weinberg	1773	285	1	0
OOLA_1773r_b_Weinberg	1773	367	3	0
OOLA_1773w_Weinberg	1773	285	0	0
OOLA_1775r_Weinberg	1775	286	0	0
OOLA_1776r_Weinberg	1776	263	4	0
OOLA_1777r_Zunftarchivalien	1777	381	3	0
OOLA_1778r_Weinberg	1778	546	8	0
OOLA_1781r_a_Weinberg	1781	386	3	1
OOLA_1781r_b_Weinberg	1781	320	2	0
STLA_1782r_Lamberg	1782	439	0	0
STLA_1783w_St. Lambrecht	1783	211	0	0
OOLA_1784w_Weinberg	1784	298	0	0
OOLA_1786w_Weinberg	1786	138	1	0

Petitionary letter	Year	Number of words	e-apocope	ending -e
STLA_1786w_Lamberg_M	1786	224	1	0
STLA_1787w_Rothenfels	1787	189	0	0
STLA_1788w_a_Lamberg	1788	108	2	0
STLA_1788w_b_Lamberg	1788	208	0	0
STLA_1792w_Rothenfels	1792	255	0	0
OOLA_1792w_Obernberg	1792	230	0	0
STLA_1796w_Lamberg	1796	389	5	0
STLA_1797w_Saurau	1797	147	1	0
STLA_1801w_Oberradkersburg	1801	286	1	4
STLA_1801w_Pflindsberg	1801	228	2	0
STLA_1802w_Pflindsberg	1802	272	3	2
STLA_1803w_Pflindsberg	1803	115	0	0
STLA_1804w_Oberradkersburg	1804	149	0	1
STLA_1806w_Pflindsberg	1806	164	3	0
STLA_1810w_Oberradkersburg_M	1810	280	2	0
STLA_1811w_Oberradkersburg_M	1811	536	7	1
OOLA_1812w_Vöcklabruck_M	1812	412	3	2
STLA_1820w_Rothenfels	1820	353	0	2
OOLA_1822w_a_Neuhaus	1822	216	0	0
OOLA_1822w_b_Neuhaus	1822	564	4	4
OOLA_1824w_Vöcklabruck_M	1824	489	1	1
OOLA_1824w_Vöcklabruck	1824	671	1	3
OOLA_1825w_Neuhaus_M	1825	628	1	11
STLA_1828w_Pflindsberg	1828	156	1	0
STLA_1829w_Pflindsberg_M	1829	358	2	2
OOLA_1830p_Ort	1830	168	0	4

In 1801, we find the first petition in which the dative -e occurs more often in strong masculine and neuter nouns than the e-apocope (STLA_1801w_Oberradkersburg: *im Jahr* versus *am Zisserhofe* [3], *im Amte*). However, the e-apocope appears more frequently than the dative -e in the majority of petitions (6 out of 8) submitted between 1801 and 1812. After 1820, the use of e-apocope versus final -e in strong masculine and neuter nouns in the dative singular form is balanced in three petitions (OOLA_1822w_b_Neuhaus, OOLA_1824w_Vöcklabruck_M, and STLA_1829w_ Pflindsberg_M). While the dative -e is dominant in four petitions (STLA_1820w_ Rothenfels, OOLA_1824w_Vöcklabruck, OOLA_1825w_Neuhaus_M, OOLA_1830p_

Ort) between 1820 and 1830, its use is clearly not as common as the use of final -e in feminine nouns.

Nevertheless, a trend towards the use of dative -e can be observed from the beginning of the 19th century in the corpus of petitionary letters. The two figures below – showing the absolute number and normalised frequency (per 1,000 words) of e-apocope versus dative -e in the petitions – illustrate that the dative -e becomes more widely used by the writers of petitions in the 19th century. However, the e-apocope still appears frequently in dative constructions and is visible in petitions right to the end of the period under investigation, with the last instances of e-apocope in strong masculine and neuter nouns in the dative singular form being found in the petition written in 1829. It is only from the 1820s onwards that the dative -e is used more frequently than the e-apocope in dative constructions (see polynomial trend line in the second figure below).

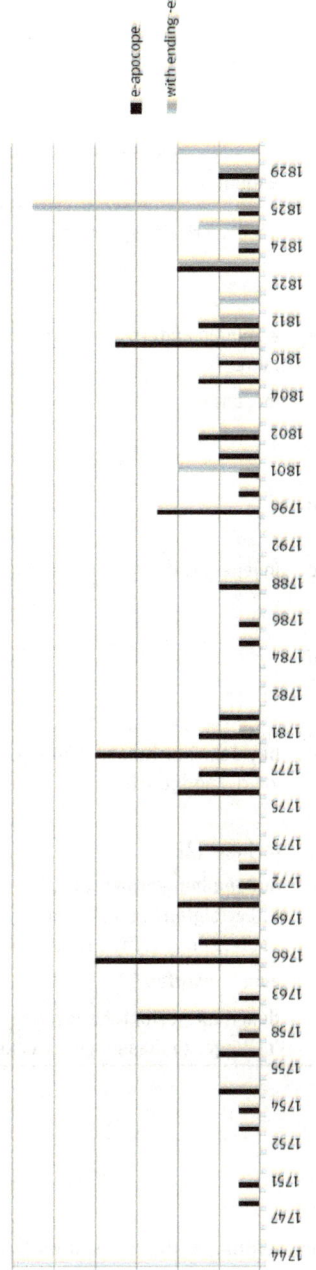

Fig. 24: *e*-apocope versus using the ending *-e* in petitionary letters: strong masculine and neuter nouns in the dative singular form (absolute numbers) *e*-apocope

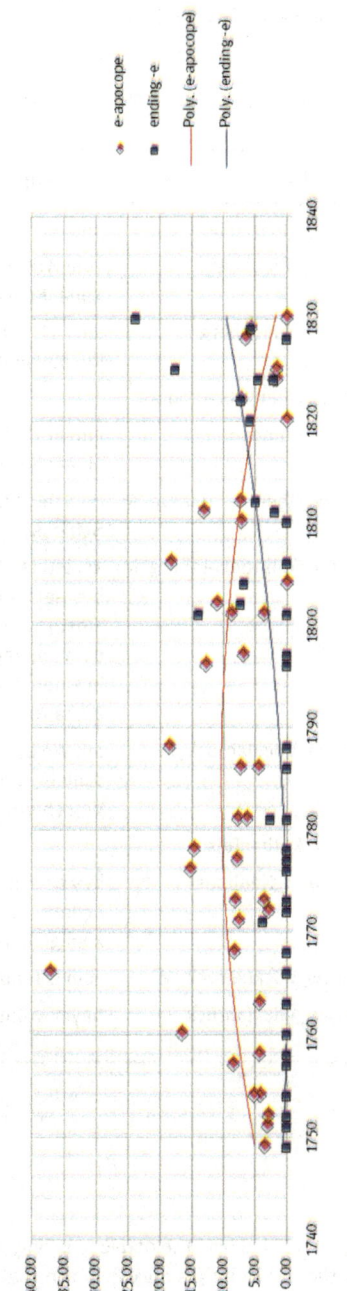

Fig. 23: *e*-apocope versus using the ending *-e* in petitionary letters: strong masculine and neuter nouns in the dative singular form (normalised frequency: per 1,000 words)

In order to find out whether there are any morphological patterns behind the use of dative *-e* in the 19th-century petitions[191], the following table lists all instances of *e*-apocope versus ending *-e* in strong masculine and neuter nouns in the dative singular form in alphabetical order, with the number of occurrences being provided in square brackets, if exceeding 1.

Tab. 48: Dative *-e* variation in 19th-century petitionary letters

Petitionary letter	e-apocope	ending -e
STLA_1801w_Oberradkersburg	im Jahr	am Zisserhofe [3], im Amte
STLA_1801w_Pflindsberg	vom Wirt, von einem Löbl: Kaisl: Konigl. Halloberamt	
STLA_1802w_Pflindsberg	am <gap/>berg, samt seinem Weib, von dem Salzoberamt	an einem andern Orte, von Jahre
STLA_1804w_Oberradkersburg		im Lande
STLA_1806w_Pflindsberg	einem Theil, mit Stein, von einem Salzoberamt	
STLA_1810w_Oberradkersburg_M	im Schloss, in dem Hochgräfl. Schloss	
STLA_1811w_Oberradkersburg_M	am letzten Jahrstag, am Wald, bey dem Abschluß, dem Einsturz, im Verhältnis, in dem anliegenden Verzeichniß, in einem mittel-mässigen Zustand	in jenem Falle
OOLA_1812w_Vöcklabruck_M	mit Weib, zum öffentl. Verschleiß, zum selbst Verschleiß	bey dem Eintritte, zum königl. kaÿrl. Landgerichte
STLA_1820w_Rothenfels		im Jahre [2]
OOLA_1822w_b_Neuhaus	bey deßen mäßigen Betrag, im Jahr, seit der Eltern Tod, zum gleichen sechsten Teill	außer allem Verhältnüße, bey [...] erfolgten Todte, beym Todte, zum gleichen Teille
OOLA_1824w_Vöcklabruck_M	vom Eisenblech	zum Vorwurfe
OOLA_1824w_Vöcklabruck	beym wohllöbl: kk. Kr Amt	dem Kupferschmidhandwerke, im Wege, zu diesem Endzwecke

---

191 As mentioned above, the dative *-e* is only used in two petitions written in the 18th century (see above for the particular instances). Given that variation between *e*-apocope and dative *-e* mainly occurs in the 19th century, the following table focuses on the period between 1801 and 1830.

Petitionary letter	*e*-apocope	ending *-e*
OOLA_1825w_Neuhaus_M	zum ganz jährlichen Liedlohn	am Abende, am Lichtmesstage, am Montage, mit dem Auftrage, mit einem Verweise, nach geredeten Gottesdienste, von dem gewis gerechten [...] Commissariate, von dem sogenanten [...] Anbirdgelde, von [...] Liedlohne, von Lohne, zum jährlichen Liedlohne
STLA_1828w_Pflindsberg	in seines Brudersfeld	
STLA_1829w_Pflindsberg_M	auf seinem [...] eigenthuml. Grund, mit Weib	im guten [...] Stande, im Walde
OOLA_1830p_Ort		auf dem Gesuche, bey dem Löbl: Magistrate, im Dienste, in dem [...] Wanderbuche

As the table above shows, the writers of four petitionary letters (STLA_1801w_Pflindsberg, STLA_1806w_Pflindsberg, STLA_1810w_Oberradkersburg_M, and STLA_1828w_Pflindsberg) consistently used the *e*-apocope in strong masculine and neuter nouns in the dative singular form. The dative *-e*, on the other hand, is used consistently in three out of the 16 petitions (STLA_1804w_Oberradkersburg, STLA_1820w_Rothenfels, and OOLA_1830p_Ort). This means that variation occurs in nine petitionary letters. The variation between *e*-apocope and dative *-e* does not seem to be morphologically determined since both variants are often used after the same preposition. The writer of the 1801w_Oberradkersburg petition, for example, does not use the dative *-e* in *im Jahr* but in *im Amte*. In the 1822 petition, the constructions *zum gleichen sechsten Teill* and *zum gleichen Teille* occur. Also the writer of the 1825 petition uses the dative *-e* only once in two very similar constructions: *zum ganz jährlichen Liedlohn* and *zum jährlichen Liedlohne*. In the 1829 petition, on the other hand, the use of dative *-e* may depend on the preposition, with the *e*-apocope occurring after the prepositions *auf* and *mit* but not after *im* (see table above).

Overall, however, no consistent principles with regard to the use of dative *-e* that are followed by more than one writer can be found. In general, it can, therefore, be argued that variation between *e*-apocope and dative *-e* was the norm in petitions submitted at the beginning of the 19th century. Indeed, the dative *-e* is only used consistently in three petitionary letters in the whole corpus (1804, 1820, and 1830). Nevertheless, an increase in the use of dative *-e* can be observed in the whole period of investigation (see figures above). The dative *-e* never occurs before 1771 and the *e*-apocope remains clearly dominant in dative constructions until the beginning of the 19th century. While the use of dative *-e* increases in the 19th century, the *e*-apocope in strong masculine and neuter nouns does not disappear completely from petitionary letters.

In summary, the development towards the dative -e in masculine and neuter nouns began significantly later than the move towards final -e in feminine nouns in the corpus of petitions, with the first instance of dative -e occurring in 1771 while the first instance of the ending -e in feminine nouns can be observed in 1749. The use of final -e in feminine nouns is clearly dominant after 1784, but the dative -e was less common than the e-apocope in dative constructions until 1820. It can, therefore, be concluded that the prescription of compulsory final -e in feminine nouns was implemented more consistently and quickly than the prescription of dative -e in petitionary letters. The development of e-apocope in plural nouns resembles that of e-apocope in feminine nouns more closely, as the following analysis shows.

Despite the low number of instances of nouns in plural in the corpus of petitionary letters (see table and figures below), some tentative conclusions can be drawn from the results of the analysis. Firstly, it is striking that the plural is never marked with a final -e in the petitions written before the 1760s. The first instance of final -e in a plural noun can be found in the petition written in 1764 (*Gäste*). Between 1764 and 1782, the occurrences of e-apocope versus the suffix -e are fairly balanced across the petitionary letters. In seven out of nine petitions with plural forms written between 1764 and 1782, the writers either mark (in three petitions) or do not mark (in four petitions) the plural forms with a final -e. This means that variation occurs in two of these nine petitionary letters. From 1786 onwards, the marking of plural forms with the suffix -e can be observed in every petitionary letter, which contains plural forms, apart from the STLA_1801w_Pflindsberg petition, which only contains the noun *Quardier* without plural marking. Furthermore, there is just one petition (STLA_1820w_Rothenfels) in which the frequency of e-apocope is higher than the frequency of plural -e (3 versus 1 instances) in the period from 1786 to 1830. By contrast, using the final -e for plural marking is dominant in 14 petitionary letters submitted in this period of time, with variation between marked and unmarked forms occurring in only two of these 14 petitions (see STLA_1802w_Pflindsberg and STLA_1810w_Oberradkersburg_M). Generally, it can be said that plural forms are more frequently marked than unmarked by the majority of writers from 1786 onwards.

Tab. 49: *e*-apocope versus using the ending -*e* in petitionary letters: plural (absolute numbers)

Petitionary letter	Year	Number of words	*e*-apocope	ending -*e*
STLA_1744w_Lamberg	1744	339	4	0
STLA_1746w_Lamberg	1746	266	0	0

Petitionary letter	Year	Number of words	e-apocope	ending -e
STLA_1747r_Lamberg	1747	335	1	0
OOLA_1749r_Neuhaus	1749	290	1	0
OOLA_1751r_a_Weinberg	1751	332	0	0
OOLA_1751r_b_Weinberg	1751	354	5	0
OOLA_1752r_Weinberg	1752	289	3	0
STLA_1752p_Lamberg	1752	349	0	0
STLA_1754p_Saurau	1754	244	3	0
STLA_1754r_Donnersbach	1754	384	0	0
STLA_1755w_Saurau	1755	211	0	0
STLA_1757p_Saurau	1757	235	0	0
STLA_1758p_Saurau	1758	236	3	0
STLA_1760r_Rothenfels	1760	362	0	0
OOLA_1763w_Schwertberg_M	1763	230	0	0
OOLA_1764w_Schwertberg	1764	127	0	1
STLA_1766p_Rothenfels	1766	215	0	0
OOLA_1768p_Waldenfels	1768	362	1	0
OOLA_1769r_Weinberg	1769	338	1	0
OOLA_1771w_Weinberg	1771	531	0	2
OOLA_1772r_Weinberg	1772	349	2	0
OOLA_1773r_a_Weinberg	1773	285	0	0
OOLA_1773r_b_Weinberg	1773	367	0	0
OOLA_1773w_Weinberg	1773	285	0	0
OOLA_1775r_Weinberg	1775	286	0	1
OOLA_1776r_Weinberg	1776	263	0	0
OOLA_1777r_Zunftarchivalien	1777	381	0	0
OOLA_1778r_Weinberg	1778	546	1	1
OOLA_1781r_a_Weinberg	1781	386	2	1
OOLA_1781r_b_Weinberg	1781	320	0	0
STLA_1782r_Lamberg	1782	439	1	0
STLA_1783w_St. Lambrecht	1783	211	0	0
OOLA_1784w_Weinberg	1784	298	0	0
OOLA_1786w_Weinberg	1786	138	0	3
STLA_1786w_Lamberg_M	1786	224	0	0
STLA_1787w_Rothenfels	1787	189	0	2
STLA_1788w_a_Lamberg	1788	108	0	0
STLA_1788w_b_Lamberg	1788	208	0	0
STLA_1792w_Rothenfels	1792	255	0	0

Petitionary letter	Year	Number of words	e-apocope	ending -e
OOLA_1792w_Obernberg	1792	230	0	3
STLA_1796w_Lamberg	1796	389	0	1
STLA_1797w_Saurau	1797	147	1	1
STLA_1801w_Oberradkersburg	1801	286	0	0
STLA_1801w_Pflindsberg	1801	228	1	0
STLA_1802w_Pflindsberg	1802	272	2	3
STLA_1803w_Pflindsberg	1803	115	0	0
STLA_1804w_Oberradkersburg	1804	149	0	0
STLA_1806w_Pflindsberg	1806	164	0	1
STLA_1810w_Oberradkersburg_M	1810	280	2	5
STLA_1811w_Oberradkersburg_M	1811	536	0	3
OOLA_1812w_Vöcklabruck_M	1812	412	0	7
STLA_1820w_Rothenfels	1820	353	3	1
OOLA_1822w_a_Neuhaus	1822	216	0	0
OOLA_1822w_b_Neuhaus	1822	564	0	11
OOLA_1824w_Vöcklabruck_M	1824	489	0	9
OOLA_1824w_Vöcklabruck	1824	671	0	7
OOLA_1825w_Neuhaus_M	1825	628	1	1
STLA_1828w_Pflindsberg	1828	156	0	1
STLA_1829w_Pflindsberg_M	1829	358	0	1
OOLA_1830p_Ort	1830	168	0	0

The analysis of petitionary letters thus shows a trend away from the *e*-apocope towards marking plural forms with final -*e*. The figures below, which show the absolute number and normalised frequency (per 1,000 words) of marked and unmarked plural forms, illustrate that plural nouns are not marked with final -*e* in the petitions submitted between 1744 and 1758. From 1764 onwards, instances of marked plural forms can be found. Individual writers seem to have preferences for either marked or unmarked plural forms, with variation occurring in only 7 out of 27 petitions submitted between 1764 and 1830. The first figure illustrates that the marking of plural forms with final -*e* becomes generally more wide-spread in the corpus of petitionary letters from 1786 onwards. The trend away from the *e*-apocope in plural nouns can, however, already be observed before then, with the marking of plural forms beginning to outweigh the unmarking of nouns in plural in the 1770s (see polynomial trend line in the second figure). Instances of *e*-apocope can still be found in the 19th century, with the last occurrence appearing in the petition written in 1825 (*1.5 Jahr*). In other words, the *e*-apocope decreases in the period under investigation but is not completely invisible in the corpus of petitionary letters until 1828.

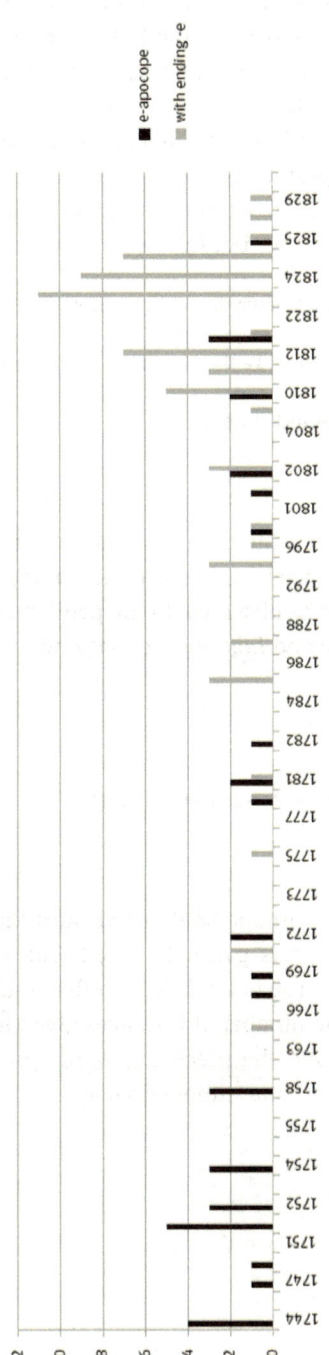

Fig. 26: *e*-apocope versus using the ending -*e* in petitionary letters: plural (absolute numbers)

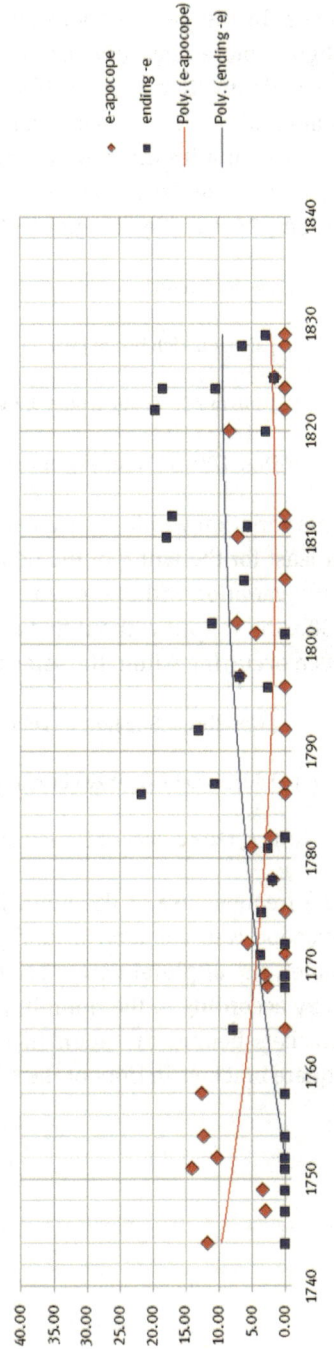

Fig. 25: *e*-apocope versus using the ending -*e* in petitionary letters: plural (normalised frequency: per 1,000 words)

As mentioned above, the noun that remains unmarked in its plural form in the 1825 petition is *Jahr*. This noun is always unmarked in the petitions submitted before the 1760s (13 times), and the unmarked form is more common than the variant with final -*e* between 1768 and 1782, with *Jahr* appearing seven times and *Jahre* occurring four times. In the petitions written between 1786 and 1820, the latter variant appears slightly more often (five or rather six times, including the noun *Lebensjahre*) than the variant with *e*-apocope (four times). After 1820, the variant with final -*e* is clearly dominant, with *Jahr* occurring just once while *Jahre* appears six times. This noun thus exemplifies the move towards marking plural forms with final -*e*. Furthermore, *Jahr(e)* is the only noun that displays variation within the same document. In OOLA_1781r_a_Weinberg, the plural is marked once but *Jahr* occurs twice:

[...] wenn ich nicht die zwey verflossene **Jahre** gänzlich um die Feldfrucht gekom̃en wäre

[...] also, daß ich beede **Jahr** das Getreyde sowohl in ds. Felde als zum Brod erkauffen muste

[...] daß mir 30 K: auf 2. oder 3. **Jahr** mögen vorgestrecket werden

(OOLA_1781r_a_Weinberg, my emphasis)

This variation within the same petition indicates that both variants were acceptable, at least for the writer of the petitionary letter. Even at the beginning of the 19th century, variation within the same document can be observed. In the petition written in 1802, the variant without final -*e* occurs twice and *Jahr* appears once, with variation even occurring within the same sentence:

[...] woselbst er 8 ½ **Jahr** zu gebracht

[...] durch volle 16 **Jahre** einschlüßlich der in Bannat abwesenden 8 ½ **Jahr**

(STLA_1802w_Pflindsberg, my emphasis)

The frequent use of the noun *Jahr* in plural without final -*e* indicates that the *e*-apocope was common in and acceptable for this particular word. The following table lists all plural nouns occurring in the corpus of petitions, ordered alphabetically according to the noun in plural with the number of instances given in square brackets behind the noun (if exceeding 1) and the preceding words provided in square brackets in front of the nouns for the variants without final -*e*.

Tab. 50: *e*-apocope versus ending *-e* in plural nouns in petitionary letters

Petitionary letter	*e*-apocope	ending *-e*
STLA_1744w_Lamberg	[38] Jahr, ‹unclear›so lang‹/unclear› Jahr, [7] Täg, [die] Wein	
STLA_1747r_Lamberg	[alle] Jahr	
OOLA_1749r_Neuhaus	[3] Jahr	
OOLA_1751r_b_Weinberg	[7] Jahr, [15] Jahr, [22] Jahr, [24] Jahr, [28] Jahr	
OOLA_1752r_Weinberg	[10] Jahr, [56] Jahr, [21] Monat	
STLA_1754p_Saurau	Händt, [27] Jahr, [lange] Jahr	
STLA_1758p_Saurau	Kueh, [so viel] Ort, [3] Stuckh	
OOLA_1764w_Schwertberg		Gäste
OOLA_1768p_Waldenfels	[die wenigste] Jahr	
OOLA_1769r_Weinberg	[5] Jahr	
OOLA_1771w_Weinberg		Jahre [2]
OOLA_1772r_Weinberg	[3] Jahr, [23] Jahr	
OOLA_1775r_Weinberg		Jahre
OOLA_1778r_Weinberg	[die schlechtesten] Schmachtworth	Kräfte
OOLA_1781r_a_Weinberg	[3] Jahr, [beede] Jahr	Jahre
STLA_1782r_Lamberg	[23] Jahr	
OOLA_1786w_Weinberg		Jahre [2], Lebensjahre
STLA_1787w_Rothenfels		Dienste, Geschäfte
OOLA_1792w_Obernberg		Feinde, Gesundheitszustände, Umstände
STLA_1796w_Lamberg		Grundstücke
STLA_1797w_Saurau	[20] Jahr	Gründe
STLA_1801w_Pflindsberg	[die] Quardier	
STLA_1802w_Pflindsberg	[8.5] Jahr [2]	Befehle, Gründe, Jahre
STLA_1806w_Pflindsberg		Gründe
STLA_1810w_Oberradkersburg_M	[8] Kamin, [diese] Kamin	Jahre, Rauchfänge, Verdienste [3]
STLA_1811w_Oberradkersburg_M		Geschäfte [2], Hände
OOLA_1812w_Vöcklabruck_M		Kinderspielwerke, Märkte [2], Unfälle, Wochenmärkte [3]

Petitionary letter	*e*-apocope	ending -*e*
STLA_1820w_Rothenfels	[4] Jahr, [die H:] Offizier, [die] Offizier Pferd	Jahre
OOLA_1822w_b_Neuhaus		Aufwände, Bedürfnüße, Jahre [4], Pfleglinge [4], Vorteile
OOLA_1824w_Vöcklabruck_M		Eingriffe, Fensterbeschläge, Fenstervorhänge, Gesetze, Gründe, Jahre, Ofenfüße, Rechte, Schmide
OOLA_1824w_Vöcklabruck		Gewerbe, Gründe [2], Kupferschmide, Schmide, Werkzeuge [2]
OOLA_1825w_Neuhaus_M	[1.5] Jahr	Einlösungsscheine
STLA_1828w_Pflindsberg		Schafe
STLA_1829w_Pflindsberg_M		Jahre

Similar to the newspaper issues discussed in the previous section, it is mainly nouns denoting periods of time (*Jahr, Monat, Täg*) as well as loan words (*Kamin, Offizier, Quardier*) which are unmarked in their plural forms. Apart from these instances, also the nouns *Händt, Kueh, Ort, Pferd, Schmachtworth, Stuckh,* and *Wein* appear without final -*e* in plural. With regard to the first noun in this list, it can be argued that the plural is marked by the umlaut and the final -*e* is thus superfluous. On the other hand, the plural nouns *Gäste* and *Kräfte*, which are also marked by the umlaut, are written with final -*e* in 1764 and 1778 respectively. Another notable plural form is *Stuckh*, which is not necessarily marked with final -*e* in plural in modern standard German, depending on the context. If *Stück* denotes parts of a whole or mass object it does not have to be marked with final -*e* in plural according to the *Duden*, e.g. *zwei Stück/Stücke Kuchen essen, 5 Stück Zucker.*[192] This is, however, not the case in the instance found in the petitionary letter submitted in 1758:

> Vnterfange mich Treÿ stuckh Vnthl: Vor dero gnedig augen zu legen (STLA_1758p_Saurau)

In this case, *Stück* would be marked with a final -*e* in modern standard German, according to the *Duden*.

In summary, the *e*-apocope in plural nouns disappeared in the period under investigation, with plural nouns not being marked with final -*e* before 1764 and the *e*-apocope almost being invisible by 1822. This process resembles that of *e*-apocope in

---

192 Cf. examples in section 1b provided in the online version of the *Duden* (http://www.duden.de/rechtschreibung/Stueck [accessed 26.04.2017]) as well as the 24th edition of the *Duden* (2006: 980).

feminine nouns, which also decreased significantly in the corpus of petitions. The shift towards dative -*e*, by contrast, was slower and less consistent.

4.5.2 Past participles

Only six out of 117 past participles are spelled without the prefix *ge-* in the corpus of petitions. All of these instances occur in five petitionary letters written in the 18th century (see table below).

Tab. 51: Past participles without the prefix *ge-* in the corpus of petitionary letters

Petitionary letter	without *ge-*	with *ge-*
STLA_1746w_Lamberg	aufzeichnet, geben	
OOLA_1772r_Weinberg	abgangen	gebeten
OOLA_1773r_a_Weinberg	kommen	gekostet
OOLA_1781r_b_Weinberg	kommen	
STLA_1792w_Rothenfels	angebnen	angekleidet, angekündet, ange- tragenen, aufgebrochen, getrieben, gezwungen

In two of these petitionary letters (1746w and 1781r_b), there is no variation between past participles with and without the prefix *ge-*, meaning that the UG form is used in 100 % of the cases. This might, however, be due to the limited number of past participles that can drop the prefix. The 100 % use of UG variants, therefore, may be rather incidental. In the other three petitionary letters, variation between past participles with and without the prefix can be observed, with a 1:1 distribution in the petitions submitted in 1772 and 1773 and a 1:6 distribution in 1792. In other words, past participles with the prefix *ge-* are clearly more dominant in the latter petition.

As discussed in section 3.2.2, Antesperg accepted the UG variant without the prefix *ge-* for the verb *geben*. With regard to *gehen* and *kommen*, however, he only lists the past participle variant with *ge-*. It can, therefore, not be argued that the writers of the petitions (apart from the author of the 1792 petition) followed Antesperg's prescriptions. The verbs *kommen* and *gehen* do occur as past participles without the prefix *ge-* in Rössler's (2005) corpus until around 1765. As Rössler (2005: 303) suggests, variants without the prefix *ge-* were restricted to a few high frequency lexical items.

Generally, however, the ECG variants with the prefix *ge-* were dominant in the whole period under investigation. The ECG form of the verbs *geben*, *gehen*, and *kommen* also occur more frequently in the whole corpus of petitions than the variants without the prefix *ge-*.[193] Even in the first petitionary letter of the corpus (1744), three past participles occur with the prefix *ge-* (*gebracht, gezeugt, geblieben*) while there are no instances without the prefix *ge-*. This indicates that the ECG norm had been introduced to and accepted in formal writing in the south of the German-speaking area by 1744 and that the grammarians discussed in chapter 3 were not influential with regard to the introduction of this feature.

As regards regular past participle endings, the use of *-t* versus *-et* seems to depend on individual writers, which results in a rather 'messy' picture (see table and figures below). Nevertheless, the findings of the analysis of past participle endings in petitionary letters do reveal a wave-like trend (see figures below), similar to the one found in reading primers. Three out of four petitions submitted in the 1740s show a preference for the ending *-t* in regular past participles. In five out of eight petitions written in the 1750s, on the other hand, the ending *-et* is used more frequently than the ending *-t*. Overall, the preference for the ending *-et* seems to prevail until the beginning of the 19th century. Between 1760 and 1801, the ending *-t* appears more frequently than the ending *-et* in only five out of 26 petitions. The ending *-et*, by contrast, is used more frequently than *-t* in 19 petitions, with 14 writers using the ending *-et* exclusively.

Tab. 52: Regular past participle ending in *-t* versus *-et* in petitionary letters (absolute numbers)

Petitionary letter	Year	Number of words	ending *-t*	ending *-et*
STLA_1744w_Lamberg	1744	339	6	2
STLA_1746w_Lamberg	1746	266	7	1
STLA_1747r_Lamberg	1747	335	2	1
OOLA_1749r_Neuhaus	1749	290	0	1
OOLA_1751r_a_Weinberg	1751	332	1	0
OOLA_1751r_b_Weinberg	1751	354	1	5
OOLA_1752r_Weinberg	1752	289	0	2
STLA_1752p_Lamberg	1752	349	1	4
STLA_1754p_Saurau	1754	244	0	3
STLA_1754r_Donnersbach	1754	384	1	4
STLA_1755w_Saurau	1755	211	3	2
STLA_1757p_Saurau	1757	235	0	0
STLA_1758p_Saurau	1758	236	3	0

---

193 *Gegeben* and *gekommen* appear six times each, *gegangen* occurs twice in the whole corpus of petitions.

Petitionary letter	Year	Number of words	ending -t	ending -et
STLA_1760r_Rothenfels	1760	362	1	1
OOLA_1763w_Schwertberg_M	1763	230	0	2
OOLA_1764w_Schwertberg	1764	127	0	0
STLA_1766p_Rothenfels	1766	215	0	0
OOLA_1768p_Waldenfels	1768	362	3	2
OOLA_1769r_Weinberg	1769	338	0	2
OOLA_1771w_Weinberg	1771	531	2	9
OOLA_1772r_Weinberg	1772	349	4	0
OOLA_1773r_a_Weinberg	1773	285	0	1
OOLA_1773r_b_Weinberg	1773	367	0	2
OOLA_1773w_Weinberg	1773	285	2	0
OOLA_1775r_Weinberg	1775	286	0	1
OOLA_1776r_Weinberg	1776	263	0	2
OOLA_1777r_Zunftarchivalien	1777	381	1	7
OOLA_1778r_Weinberg	1778	546	0	4
OOLA_1781r_a_Weinberg	1781	386	2	5
OOLA_1781r_b_Weinberg	1781	320	3	1
STLA_1782r_Lamberg	1782	439	0	5
STLA_1783w_St. Lambrecht	1783	211	0	1
OOLA_1784w_Weinberg	1784	298	0	4
OOLA_1786w_Weinberg	1786	138	0	0
STLA_1786w_Lamberg_M	1786	224	2	0
STLA_1787w_Rothenfels	1787	189	0	2
STLA_1788w_a_Lamberg	1788	108	0	0
STLA_1788w_b_Lamberg	1788	208	0	3
STLA_1792w_Rothenfels	1792	255	0	7
OOLA_1792w_Obernberg	1792	230	1	1
STLA_1796w_Lamberg	1796	389	3	5
STLA_1797w_Saurau	1797	147	0	0
STLA_1801w_Oberradkersburg	1801	286	3	5
STLA_1801w_Pflindsberg	1801	228	0	1
STLA_1802w_Pflindsberg	1802	272	1	1
STLA_1803w_Pflindsberg	1803	115	1	1
STLA_1804w_Oberradkersburg	1804	149	1	3
STLA_1806w_Pflindsberg	1806	164	2	1
STLA_1810w_Oberradkersburg_M	1810	280	7	0
STLA_1811w_Oberradkersburg_M	1811	536	1	1

Petitionary letter	Year	Number of words	ending -t	ending -et
OOLA_1812w_Vöcklabruck_M	1812	412	3	1
STLA_1820w_Rothenfels	1820	353	0	4
OOLA_1822w_a_Neuhaus	1822	216	1	0
OOLA_1822w_b_Neuhaus	1822	564	6	3
OOLA_1824w_Vöcklabruck_M	1824	489	3	3
OOLA_1824w_Vöcklabruck	1824	671	10	6
OOLA_1825w_Neuhaus_M	1825	628	1	3
STLA_1828w_Pflindsberg	1828	156	0	2
STLA_1829w_Pflindsberg_M	1829	358	0	1
OOLA_1830p_Ort	1830	168	1	0

After 1801, the ending -t seems to become more popular again. The first figure below, which shows the absolute number for each variant in every petitionary letter, illustrates that the ending -t is used more frequently than the ending -et in seven out of 16 petitions and the use of both variants is balanced in four petitions. This means that the ending -et is used more often than the ending -t by five writers, i.e. fewer writers prefer the ending -et in the period between 1802 and 1830.

Despite the preferences of individual writers, a trend away from the ending -t can be observed in the second half of the 18th century, with the use of the ending -t increasing again in the 19th century. The polynomial trend line in the second figure below, which shows the normalized frequency (per 1,000 words) for each variant in the petitions, illustrates this wave-like development.

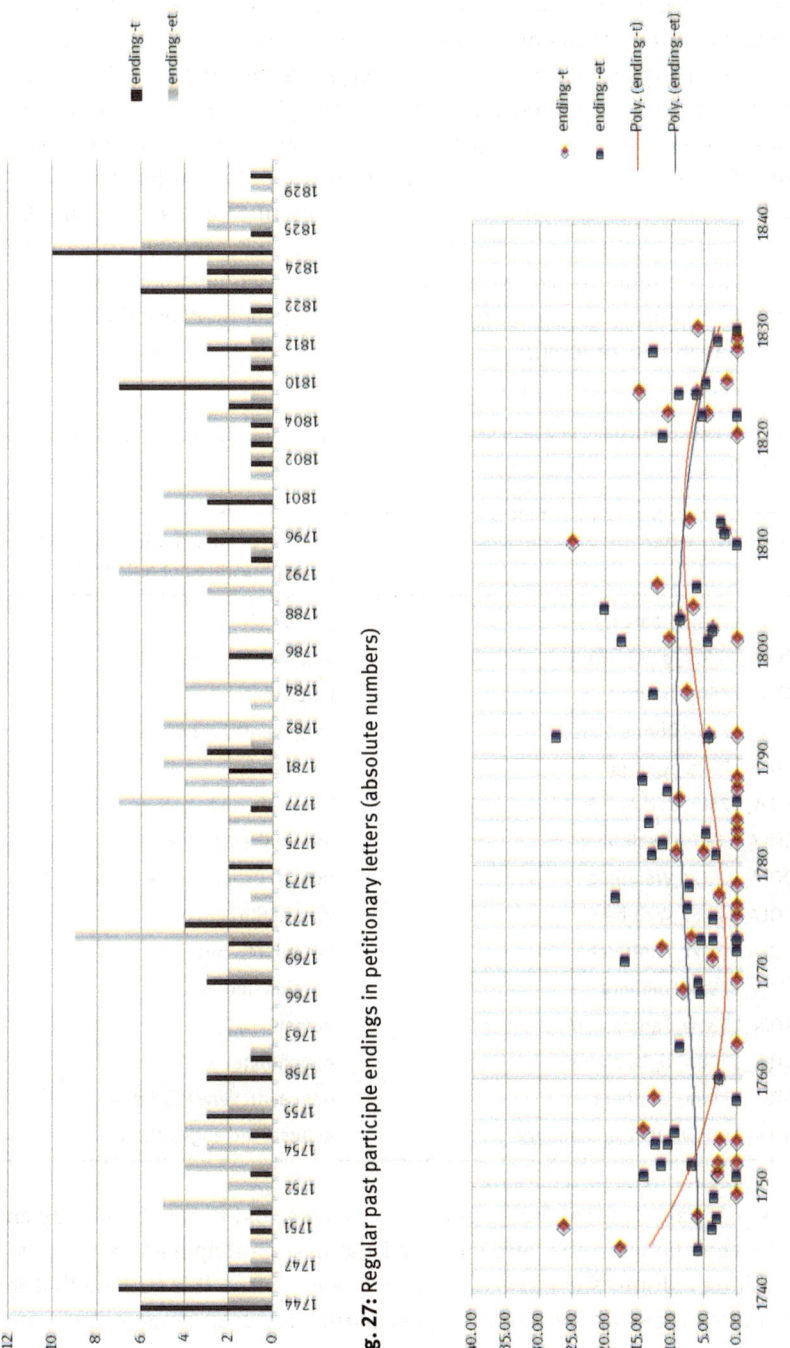

Fig. 27: Regular past participle endings in petitionary letters (absolute numbers)

Fig. 28: Regular past participle endings in petitionary letters (normalised frequency: per 1,000 words)

In the majority of petitionary letters, variation between the endings -*t* and -*et* occur. As mentioned before, this variation is partly due to morpho-phonological reasons, with the ending -*t* being used if the verb stem ends in -*el* or -*er*, and the ending -*et* if the verb stem ends in -*d*/-*t* or a fricative/plosive plus a nasal sound. In the petition written in 1746, for example, the ending -*t* is used consistently, with the ending -*et* only occurring in the past participle of *aufzeichnen*. Similarly, the writer of the 1811 petition uses the ending -*t* for the past participle of *hindern* and in all past participles used as adjectives, with the exception of one adjective ending in -*t* (*gepachtete*) and the past participle of *versetzen*. In other words, the large majority of writers follow the morpho-phonological principles described above but a number of exceptions can be found until the beginning of the 19th century. These exceptions are listed in the table below, with past participles used as adjectives being marked in grey and the number of occurrences given in square brackets, if exceeding 1. The list is alphabetically ordered.

Tab. 53: Past participles in which morpho-phonological principles were not followed in the corpus of petitions

Petitionary letter	Past participles in which morpho-phonological principles were not followed
STLA_1744w_Lamberg	gericht [2]
OOLA_1751r_b_Weinberg	abgeforderet, invermeldt
STLA_1754p_Saurau	geleisten
STLA_1754r_Donnersbach	aufgerichten, obbemelten
STLA_1757p_Saurau	gemelte [2]
STLA_1760r_Rothenfels	obermelt, obgemelten
OOLA_1771w_Weinberg	erheirathen, gesteuret
OOLA_1772r_Weinberg	behaft, bemelt, ermelt, ohneracht
OOLA_1776r_Weinberg	invermelte
OOLA_1777r_Zunftarchivalien	beförderet, beschweret
STLA_1782r_Lamberg	geschmähleret
STLA_1786w_Lamberg_M	gemelt
STLA_1788w_b_Lamberg	behandlete
STLA_1796w_Lamberg	ungeacht, verwechsleten
STLA_1801w_Oberradkersburg	geäusseret, zugesicheret

The past participles of the verbs *achten*, *melden*, and *richten* frequently end in -*t*, i.e. *e*-syncope between the verb stem and the past participle ending can be observed, resulting in forms such as *geacht*, *gemelt*, and *gericht*. It is striking that the majority of these cases can be found in past participles used as adjectives. Indeed, past participles that are used as adjectives are usually spelled with -*t* in the corpus of petitionary letters, even if the verb stem ends in -*d* or -*t*. If the verb stem ends in a fricative/plosive plus a nasal sound, on the other hand, the ending -*et* is consistently used, also in past participles used as adjectives. This means that the latter morpho-phonological principle was applied more consistently. The ending -*et* also appears in a few past participles with verb stems ending in -*er* (e.g. *beförderet*) or -*(e)l*: *behandlete* (1788w_b) and *verwechsleten* (1796w).

Because of the low number of past participles within one petitionary letter, it is difficult to establish if the writers chose to use a particular past participle ending according to lexical or morphological principles. It is, however, striking that the variant *gemacht*, which was dominant in the corpus of reading primers and newspaper issues, is also used more frequently than *gemachet* in the corpus of petitions (*gemacht* appears four times, while *gemachet* occurs twice). Furthermore, in the 1752p petition, *gemacht* is the only past participle spelled with the ending -*t* (apart from one other past participle that is used as an adjective: *bedrängten*). All other past participles (*geschützet*; *gesetzet*, which occurs twice; and *ausgestrecket*), on the other hand, are consistently spelled with the ending -*et* in this particular petition. It can, therefore, be argued that the writer of this petition treated the past participle of *machen* as an exception to the otherwise consistent use of the ending -*et*. In other words, the lexical item itself seems to determine the use of the past participle ending in some cases. The writers of the two petitions with the form *gemachet*, on the other hand, did not treat the verb *machen* as an exception. In their petition, the ending -*et* is either clearly dominant (OOLA_1771w_Weinberg) or used consistently (STLA_1792w_Rothenfels).

In other petitions, some morphological patterns can be observed. In the petitionary letter written in 1755, for example, the ending -*t* is used in passive structures, while the ending -*et* occurs in active constructions:

> [...] vor 10. Tägen meine Mutter beÿ hoch dero herrn *Secretario* in gräz sich deme *repetendo* **erkundiget**.[2] in andworth **replilirt** worden: wie daß *quohtionirter* u: mir untert²gst erbettener *pahs* schon anhero **geschikht** worden seÿe; gleichwie aber *dato* nichts Empfang: habe mich dahero zu hl:ⁿ: landtgericht Verwald<unclear>a</unclear> in Doñerspach umbständlich zu <unclear>*Inhinuiren*</unclear> **verfüeget**, [...] (STLA_1755w_Saurau, my emphasis)

The writer of this petition may have deliberately chosen the endings according to their morphological context. In fact, the use of the past participle endings are in line with Popowitsch's (1754a: 86–97) prescriptions of using the ending -*et* in the active voice, while using the ending -*t* in the passive voice formed with *sein* (e.g. *ich bin gelobt*). The writer of the 1755 petition dropped the auxiliary verbs for the first two past participles (*erkundiget* [*hat*] and [*ist*] *replilirt worden*) but followed Popowitsch prescriptions. Given the low number of past participles and that neither any instances of *e*-apocope nor final -*e* in nouns occur in this petition, it would stretch rather too far to suggest that this writer studied Popowitsch's grammar and followed the rules prescribed in it. It can, however, be concluded that the variation between the ending -*t* and -*et*, which occurred in 21 petitionary letters[194], was not necessarily random but due to phonological, lexical, and morphological factors.

Generally, it can be argued that the use of the past participle endings depends on the preferences of individual writers. Nevertheless, the quantitative analysis reveals a wave-like development of the ending -*t* in petitionary letters, as shown in the figures above. While the ending -*t* is dominant in the petitions written in the 1740s, the ending -*et* is used significantly more often in the second half of the 18th century. After 1801, on the other hand, an increase of the ending -*t* can be observed. This development is striking since it can be linked to the increasing influence of grammarians in the second half of the 18th century. Gottsched and Felbiger, especially, prescribed the use of the ending -*et* in regular past participles. These prescriptions seemed to have an influence on a number of writers in the second half of the 18th century, many of which used the ending -*et* consistently in their petitions. However, in order to verify the influence of grammarians on the language use in petitionary letters, a larger corpus of texts would have to be analysed since the rather low number of past participles in the corpus of petitions does not allow for definite conclusions in this regard.

4.5.3 Alternative forms of *wir/sie sind*

The low number of occurrences is even more problematic with regard to variants of the verb *to be* in the 1st and 3rd person plural indicative present active. In the whole corpus, there are only three instances for *wir/sie seyn(d)*, all of which appear in petitions submitted before 1778, and 12 instances of *wir/sie sind*, with the first occurrence in the petitionary letter submitted in 1768 (see table below). Variation between the UG and ECG variants cannot be observed within one text, i.e. the writers either used the UG or the ECG form.

Tab. 54: *wir/sie seynd* versus *wir/sie sind* in petitionary letters (absolute numbers)

Petitionary letter	wir/sie seyn/d	wir/sie sind
STLA_1754p_Saurau	1	0
STLA_1760r_Rothenfels	1	0
OOLA_1768p_Waldenfels	0	1
OOLA_1771w_Weinberg	0	1

---

194 This count excludes past participles used as adjectives and four petitions, in which the variation is solely morpho-phonologically determined.

Petitionary letter	*wir/sie seyn/d*	*wir/sie sind*
OOLA_1777r_Zunftarchivalien	1	0
STLA_1787w_Rothenfels	0	1
STLA_1801w_Pflindsberg	0	1
STLA_1806w_Pflindsberg	0	1
STLA_1810w_Oberradkersburg_M	0	2
OOLA_1822w_b_Neuhaus	0	1
OOLA_1824w_Vöcklabruck	0	4

Despite the low number of occurrences, the results of the analysis of the verb *to be* reveal that UG variants (*wir seyn* in 1754 and *sie seynd* in 1768 and 1777) were used in handwritten petitions until at least 1777. From 1787 onwards, only the ECG variant *wir/sie sind*, which first occurs in 1768, is used in petitionary letters. This means that the UG variants are invisible from at least 1787 onwards in the corpus of petitions. The period between 1768 and 1777 seems to be a time when both variants were in use, while the UG form was more common in 1754 and 1760.

Given that the UG variant was still used in 1777, it cannot be argued that the prescriptions of Gottsched and Popowitsch affected the use of *wir/sie seynd* in petitionary letters immediately. However, their grammars may have contributed – with a delay of 14 to 20 years – to the introduction of the ECG form *wir/sie sind* in 1768. Felbiger's approved textbooks and Adelung's grammar may have been more influential with regard to this feature. After all, the UG form is invisible from 1787 onwards. With the low numbers of instances, it is, however, difficult to reach any definite conclusions with regard to this feature.

4.5.4 Conclusion: Analysis of petitionary letters

The corpus I compiled provides a first indication of the language use in petitionary letters and overall trends can certainly be observed. However, a much larger corpus is necessary to reach definite and more reliable results with regard to certain features.

With regard to the *e*-apocope, the findings are relatively clear, with a trend towards the ending -*e* being observable in the period under investigation. The development differs, however, between feminine, strong masculine and neuter nouns in the singular dative case, and plural nouns. In feminine and plural nouns the ending -*e* becomes dominant after the mid-1770s, whereas the dative -*e* only starts to be more commonly used at the beginning of the 19th century. It is only from 1812 onwards that the dative -*e* is used as or more frequently than the *e*-apocope in strong masculine and neuter nouns by the majority of writers. By contrast, the *e*-

apocope in feminine nouns is used very rarely from 1784 onwards, and the majority of writers mark plural forms with final -e after 1786, with just the noun *Jahr* being unmarked in plural in the petition written in 1825. Therefore, it can be concluded that the ECG ending -e was implemented more quickly and consistently in feminine and plural nouns than in strong masculine and neuter nouns in the dative singular form.

The grammarians discussed in chapter 3 may have influenced this development. It is striking that the first feminine noun with final -e can be found in the petition submitted in 1749, i.e. one year after the publication of Gottsched's *Grundlegung einer deutschen Sprachkunst* (1748). In most of the petitions written between 1744 and 1773, the e-apocope in feminine nouns is, however, still dominant. From 1773 onwards, a more consistent implementation of final -e in feminine nouns can be observed and from 1784 onwards, the final -e is clearly dominant. It can, therefore, be argued that Felbiger's grammar (1775) as well as the approved textbooks (published from 1775 onwards) and Adelung's *Deutsche Sprachkunst* (1781) had a more significant effect on the language used in petitionary letters with regard to the final -e in feminine nouns. The grammarians discussed in chapter 3 may have also contributed to the significant decrease of e-apocope in plural nouns in the 18th and 19th century. With regard to the dative -e, the results indicate that the grammarians did not have an immediate effect on the language use in petitions since a considerable increase of dative -e can only be observed at the beginning of the 19th century.

In comparison to Rössler's (2005) and Durrell's (2016) results, the trend away from the e-apocope seems to be slower and less consistent in the petitionary letters than in the corpora analysed by Rössler and Durrell. Rössler (2005: 254) states that the percentage of e-apocope in feminine nouns had dropped to 40 % around 1765 in his corpus, while the e-apocope in petitions is dominant until 1773. Similarly, Rössler's (2005: 266) analysis revealed that the percentage of e-apocope in plural nouns had decreased to 26 % around 1765. In comparison, the percentage of plural nouns that are not marked with final -e in the petitions I analysed is 57 % (on average) between 1764 and 1782. The greatest difference between the findings of Rössler (2005) and the results gained from the analysis of the petitionary letters appears in nouns with dative -e. While Rössler (2005: 261) found that 27 % of nouns were spelled without dative -e around 1765, the first instance of dative -e can be found in the petition written in 1771. Between 1771 and 1797, the percentage of e-apocope in dative constructions is still 96 % (on average) in the corpus of petitionary letters. This indicates that there is a significant difference between the language use in printed and handwritten texts and highlights the importance of analysing a variety of text types. Durrell's (2016) research also suggests that – especially with regard to the dative -e – differences in language use between different text types can be detected.

The results of the prefix *ge-* in past participles, on the other hand, resemble those of Rössler (2005: 306f.) who states that the percentage of past participles with the prefix *ge-* had increased to 86 % at around 1765. This ECG variant was clearly dominant by 1744 in the petitions I analysed while past participles without the prefix *ge-* were almost invisible in the whole period under investigation. In total, only six out of 117 past participles are written without the prefix *ge-*. All of these six instances occur in the 18th century, with the last occurrence found in a petition written in 1792. In other words, the UG variant was not used in petitions after the end of the 18th century. Given that the ECG variant was dominant by 1744, it can be argued that the grammarians discussed in chapter 3 did not have a significant influence on the writing practice of petitionary letters with regard to this feature. The ECG variant was clearly introduced in the south German-speaking area before the publication of Antesperg's and Gottsched's grammar. This does, however, not exclude other grammarians, who had published their work before 1744, from introducing the ECG variant to the UG language area. Indeed, Solms & Wegera (1993: 237) state that the consistent use of the prefix *ge-* in past participles becomes fixed during the 18th century and has to be seen in connection with the prescriptions by grammarians:

> Der konsequente Gebrauch des *ge-* als Teil des Part. Prät.-Flexivs wird in vielen Fällen erst im Verlauf des 18. Jhs. fest und muß im Zusammenhang der normativen Bemühungen der zeitgenössischen Grammatiker gesehen werden. (Solms & Wegera 1993: 237)

> The consistent use of the prefix *ge-* in past participles only becomes fixed during the 18th century in many cases, and has to be seen in connection with the normative efforts of the contemporary grammarians.

While Solms & Wegera (1993: 237) do not provide the names of specific grammarians, the results of the corpus of petitions suggests that it was grammarians before Gottsched, Felbiger, Adelung and others who contributed to the decrease of the UG variant and the implementation of the ECG norm.

With regard to regular past participle endings, on the other hand, a connection between the publication of grammars after 1747 and the language use in petitionary letters is more likely. The wave-like development that can be observed in the whole period under investigation – with the dominance of *-t* in the 1740s, followed by a period of preference for the ending *-et* in the second half of the 18th century, and an increase in the use of the ending *-t* in the first 30 years of the 19th century – can be linked to the prescriptions by 18th-century grammarians, particularly Gottsched and Felbiger. However, a much larger corpus of petitions needs to be analysed in order to reach any definite conclusion about the influence of grammarians with regard to this feature. Generally, it seems that the use of either *-t* or *-et* at the end of regular past participles is due to the preferences of individual writers and morpho-phonological factors. In some cases, also lexical (e.g. *gemacht*) and morphological (active versus passive) patterns can be detected. Overall, a trend away from the ending *-t* in the second half of the 18th century can be observed, which seems to be reversed in the 19th century, with the ending *-et* decreasing again. It can, therefore, be concluded that the development of this feature had not ended by 1830 and requires further investigation.

Rössler's (2005: 295–297) findings, by contrast, show that the ending *-et* was already dominant (69 %) around 1720 in his corpus, with another increase around 1765 to 79 %. Such a gradual development was not observed in the petitionary letters, with significant differences between relatively short periods of time, e.g. within the ten years between 1744 and 1754. This is mainly due to the fine-grained nature of my analysis. The findings presented here thus stress the importance of such fine-grained research, and the analysis of the regular past participle endings indicate that further analysis in the 19th century is necessary to achieve a full understanding of the development of this feature.

The development of the implementation of the ECG form *wir/sie sind*, on the other hand, was completed by about 1780 in petitionary letters. In 1777, the last UG variant (*sie seynd*) can be found in the corpus of petitions, while the first instance of the ECG variant occurs in 1768. The grammarians discussed in chapter 3 may have contributed to the invisibilisation of *wir/sie seyn(d)* in the second half of the 18th century. While the number of instances of this feature in the petitionary letter corpus is too low to reach any final conclusions, Rössler's (2005: 212–221) research suggests that the language reform in 18th-century Austria was the decisive factor for the disappearance of UG *wir/sie seyn(d)* in formal written discourse.

In summary, the findings from the corpus of petitions indicate that the 18th-century grammarians discussed in chapter 3 had an influence on the language use in formal handwritten texts. This influence was, however, restricted to certain features (*e*-apocope in feminine and plural nouns, regular past participle endings, and *wir/sie seynd*) and cannot be generalised. The following section compares these findings with the results from the analysis of reading primers and newspaper issues in order to reveal to what extent the language use in these text types differed.

4.6 Comparison of results

This section compares the results of the three corpora described above in order to establish whether there are any significant differences in the language use in different text types. Two of these text types are printed (reading primers and newspaper issues), while one of them is handwritten. Furthermore, they differ with regard to other aspects, especially the intended readership.

Reading primers were designed for a large proportion of the general population – the textbooks for school use printed after the introduction of the school reform in 1774 were specifically written for children, while other reading primers addressed anyone who wanted to learn to read, i.e. also adults. Nevertheless, the content of the latter reading primers, too, was adapted to children, which becomes apparent in the content of stories and the illustrations added to individual words.

Newspaper issues, by contrast, addressed largely only educated people in the period under investigation. As mentioned in section 4.1.2, newspapers did not become a wide-spread reading material for the masses before the 1830s (Hosokawa 2014: 24). Instead, the readership belonged to the nobility and the bourgeoisie before relatively cheap tabloids began to appear from the 1830s onwards (ibid. 24, 39). The peasant population in the countryside did not read newspapers until the beginning of the 19th century (ibid. 40). The readership of newspapers in the second half of the 18th century was, therefore, rather restricted. Furthermore, at that time newspapers were a compilation of reports from different correspondents, which were minimally edited, as the analysis in section 4.4 revealed. It is, therefore, problematic to consider them as one homogenous text type. Despite the heterogeneous nature of newspapers, some general trends in 18th- and early 19th-century language use were revealed through the analysis of newspaper issues, which will be compared to the overall findings from reading primers and petitionary letters below.

The petitionary letters, in contrast to the reading primers and the newspapers, are addressed to individual recipients and contain personal information. The address, layout and structure of these petitions clearly indicate that they belong to a formal text type. The writers of these petitions aimed at writing what they considered 'standard' or 'sophisticated' German. While the petitions are not necessarily conceptually closer to orality (cf. Koch & Oesterreicher 1985, 1994) than the other text types I analysed, they do present ego-documents (cf. Dekker 2002), i.e. they contain personal information about the petitioner. Furthermore, each petition was written by one individual (in contrast to the issues of the *Wienerisches Diarium/Wiener Zeitung*) and did not undergo rigorous editing (in contrast to reading primers) before it was submitted.

Despite the fact that all three corpora are compiled of formal texts, significant differences in the language use in these corpora were observed. These differences are described in detail in this section, discussing the *e*-apocope in nouns first, then the past participles, and finally, alternative forms of *wir/sie sind*.

Where the differences between the three corpora are particularly striking, which is the case for *e*-apocope in nouns as well as regular past participle endings, figures are used to illustrate these differences. In these figures, the overall period under investigation is divided into six sub-periods, with five intervals spanning 15 years and one period of 16 years (1759–1774). These intervals were chosen in line with the overall period under investigation (91 years) as well as the results obtained from the three corpora. The findings in the corpus of reading primers resulted in one period of 16 years (1759–1774) since the introduction of Felbiger's school policy in December 1774 had a significant effect on the language use in the reading primers. Each of the six intervals contains at least two reading primers, three newspaper issues, and four petitionary letters. The following table lists the exact distribution of texts in each period.

Tab. 55: Time periods and the distribution of texts for the comparison of results

Periods	Number of reading primers (RP)	Number of newspaper issues (NI)	Number of petitionary letters (PL)
1744–1758	2	3	13
1759–1774	2	4	11
1775–1789	5	3	14
1790–1804	2	3	9
1805–1819	2	3	4
1820–1834	2	3	9

For each text, the percentage of *e*-apocope and the past participle ending -*t* was calculated and the mean value of these percentages was then formed for each period.[195] In other words, the percentages provided in the figures below depict how often the *e*-apocope and the ending -*t* appeared on average in the six periods. In the figures, the blue line represents reading primers (abbreviated as RP), the red line shows the results of the newspaper issues (NI), and the green line illustrates the findings from the analysis of petitionary letters (PL).

4.6.1 *e*-apocope in nouns

The figure below shows that the development of the UG *e*-apocope in feminine nouns differed considerably between the different text types. Firstly, the *e*-apocope was clearly dominant in the petitionary letters (green line) in the first two periods (1744–1774), while it had been almost completely replaced by the ECG variant by 1744 in the newspaper issues (red line). In reading primers (blue line), too, the percentage of *e*-apocope in feminine nouns is considerably lower than in petitionary letters between 1744 and 1758. The final -*e* is dominant in this period of time, which includes Antesperg's *Josephinische Erzherzogliche A.B.C.* (1744) and the *Teutsches Namen- oder Lehrbüchl* (c. 1750), with Antesperg's book containing significantly fewer instances of *e*-apocope than the other primer. The sharp increase in the number of *e*-apocope in feminine nouns in the second period (1759–1774) is due to the high percentage of *e*-apocope in the two subsequent reading primers (printed in c. 1770 and 1774). This peak in the number of feminine nouns displaying *e*-apocope equals the percentage in petitionary letters in the same period at 78 %. The subsequent sharp decrease of *e*-apocope in reading primers can be linked to the introduc-

---

195 In the corpus of petitionary letters, this mean value excludes texts without any instances of the variable under investigation.

tion of the school reform in 1774. From 1775 onwards, the *e*-apocope in feminine nouns is almost invisible in the reading primers and completely disappears in newspaper issues.

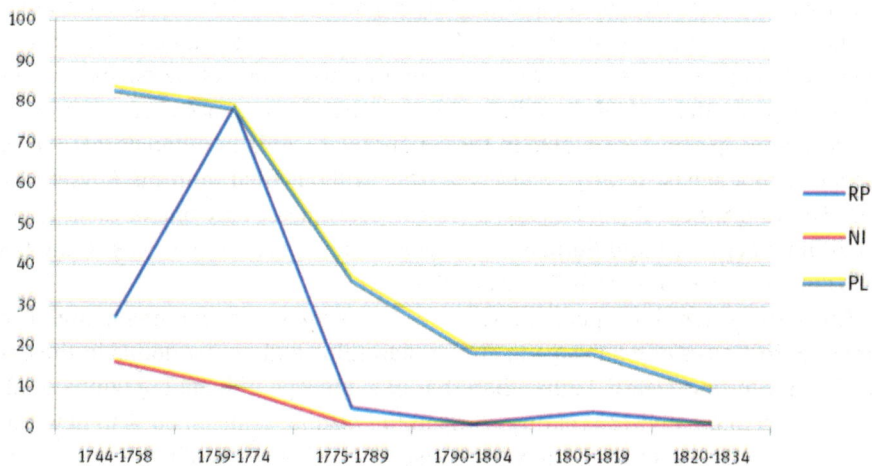

Fig. 29: Development of *e*-apocope in feminine nouns in the three corpora (in percentages)

While the introduction of Felbiger's school policy led to a consistently lower number of instances of *e*-apocope in feminine nouns in reading primers printed after 1774, the development is more gradual in newspaper issues and petitionary letters. In the *Wienerisches Diarium*, the *e*-apocope in feminine nouns had almost disappeared by 1744, i.e. before the introduction of the school reform and the publication of the grammars discussed in chapter 3, and further decreases between 1759 and 1774. From 1775 onwards, not a single instance of *e*-apocope in feminine nouns can be found in the corpus of newspaper issues. In the petitionary letters, by contrast, the *e*-apocope in feminine nouns remains dominant until at least 1774 and is still frequently used between 1775 and 1789 (36 % on average). In petitionary letters, too, the UG variant decreases further but the average number of instances remains at 9 % between 1820 and 1834, in contrast to the reading primers (1 %) and the newspaper issues (0 %).

Certain feminine words are spelled without final -*e* in more than one corpus. The noun *Hilf/Hülf* even appears in all three corpora: in the reading primer printed around 1750, in the newspaper issue published on 4 July 1759, and in the petitions submitted in 1771, 1775, and 1782.[196] This is particularly interesting since *Hilf* is the only feminine noun that Felbiger spells without final -*e* in his *Anleitung zur deutschen Sprachlehre* (1775). Feminine nouns without final -*e* that appear in both, the reading primer and the newspaper corpus are *Freud*, *Sonn*, *Sprach*, and *Stund*. In the corpus of petitionary letters and reading primers, too, a few of the same feminine nouns are spelled without final -*e*: *Bitt*, *Gnad*, *Herberg*, *Sach*, and *Schand*. The following feminine nouns displayed *e*-apocope in the corpus of newspaper issues and petitionary letters: *Mühl*, *Reis*, *Ruh*, *Thür*, *Ursach*. These co-occurrences indicate that the *e*-apocope was acceptable in these particular words in different text types. Antesperg, too, spells *Herberg*, *Mühl*, and *Thür* without final -*e* in his *Kayserliche Deutsche Grammatick* (1747). Despite these co-occurrences, only one of them is accepted in modern standard German: *Thür* (see section 4.4.1). In most cases, the UG forms did not prevail over their ECG equivalents.

The dative -*e* develops quite differently from the final -*e* in feminine nouns. The number of instances of *e*-apocope in strong masculine and neuter nouns in the dative singular form is clearly higher than that of *e*-apocope in feminine nouns in all three corpora in the mid-18th century: 74 % in the reading primers, 86 % in newspaper issues, and 100 % in petitionary letters (see figure below). While the dative -*e* is never used in the petitions between 1744 and 1758, it had found its way into Antesperg's reading primer and into newspaper issues by 1744. In other words, the dative -*e* was introduced earlier in the latter two text types, and before the introduction of the school reform and the publication of the grammars discussed in chapter 3. The dative -*e* was also implemented in a few petitionary letters before 1774 but the *e*-apocope in dative constructions remains dominant until 1820 in this corpus. In newspaper issues, on the other hand, the *e*-apocope decreases steadily between 1759 and 1789. This decrease is less drastic, i.e. more gradual, than the sharp fall of the percentage of *e*-apocope in reading primers. In the *[N]utzliches Stimmen-Büchlein* (c. 1770) and in the *Catholisches Namen-Büchl* (1774), the dative -*e* is never used, while it is dominant in the textbooks printed after the introduction of Felbiger's school reform in December 1774.

---

196 Furthermore, the noun *Beihilf* occurs without final -*e* in five petitions that were submitted between 1751 and 1773.

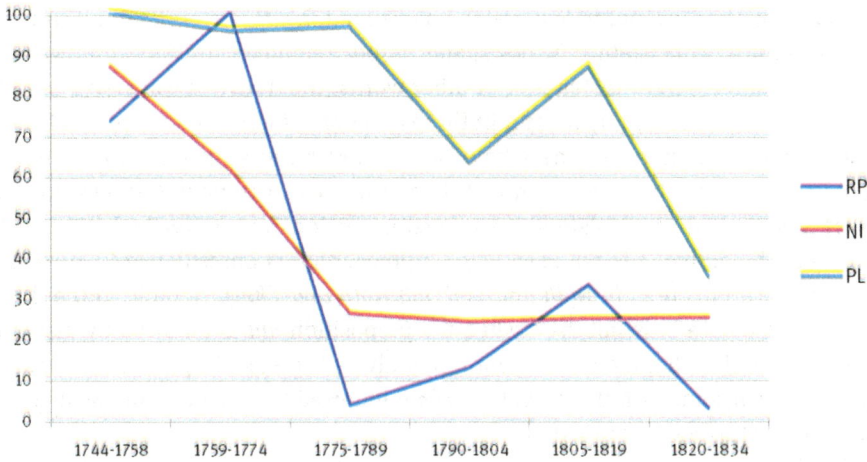

Fig. 30: Development of *e*-apocope in strong masculine and neuter nouns in the dative singular form in the three corpora (in percentages)

In the corpus of reading primers, it was also observed that the dative -*e* appears less often in primers that were not designed for school use than in Felbiger's approved textbooks, which explains the increase of *e*-apocope in dative constructions between 1805 and 1819 since this period contains two primers for home use.[197] In the *Wienerisches Diarium/Wiener Zeitung*, on the other hand, the percentage of *e*-apocope in strong masculine and neuter nouns in the dative singular form remains at about 25 % from 1775 onwards. Since the use of dative -*e* depended on the preference of individual correspondents, the dative -*e* is not used consistently in any newspaper issue. Between 1820 and 1834, the percentage of *e*-apocope in dative constructions is still relatively high in newspaper issues (25 %) and petitions (35 %) compared to reading primers (3 %). It can, therefore, be argued that the prescriptions of grammarians (Gottsched, Popowitsch, Felbiger, and Adelung) for dative -*e* were not implemented completely in the *Wiener Zeitung*, petitions, and in reading primers for home use by the early 19th century.

In the previous sections (4.3.1, 4.4.1, 4.5.1), a number of morphological patterns were detected, with the dative -*e* being used after certain prepositions. While these morphological patterns were dependent on the authors of particular texts, one pattern that emerged in more than one reading primer was the *e*-apocope after the preposition *mit* if it was immediately followed by a noun, i.e. without an article or

---

197 The increase of *e*-apocope in petitionary letters submitted between the same period of time (1805–1819) may not be representative for the development of language use in petitions since this period only contains four petitionary letters (see table above).

pronoun (e.g. *mit Fleiß* or *mit Sauerteig*). It is striking that this morphological principle was applied consistently in newspaper issues (eighteen instances) as well as petitionary letters (eight instances). In other words, the dative *-e* was never used if *mit* was directly followed by a noun in these corpora, which were compiled of texts by a variety of authors, in the whole period under investigation (from 1744 to 1834).[198] This poses the question how this morphological principle developed and why it was applied so consistently. As noted in section 3.3.1, Gottsched (1752: 493) states that the dative *-e* is not used when a preposition is immediately followed by two or more nouns (e.g. *in Noth und Tod, mit Rath und That*). Notably in the three corpora, the dative *-e* is not used when the preposition *mit* is followed by just one noun. It is striking that the prescriptions on dative *-e* were not implemented consistently in the corpora, with the exception of *mit* followed by one noun being an issue that deserves further investigation.

The final *-e* in plural nouns was implemented more consistently and quicker than the dative *-e* across all three corpora.[199] Striking differences between the text types can, however, be observed at the beginning of the period under investigation (see figure below). Plural nouns are never marked with final *-e* in petitions submitted between 1744 and 1758, while the percentage of *e*-apocope in newspaper issues and reading primers is below 10 % during this period of time. In newspaper issues, the *e*-apocope in plural nouns further decreases and is almost invisible from 1759 onwards. The trend away from the *e*-apocope in petitions starts before the introduction of the school reform (1774) but the final *-e* is not implemented as quickly and as consistently as in the reading primers printed after 1775. Before then, an increase of *e*-apocope in plural nouns can be observed in the *[N]utzliches Stimmen-Büchlein* (c. 1770) and in the *Catholisches Namen-Büchl* (1774), which – as mentioned before – generally contain more cases of *e*-apocope. From 1775 onwards, the *e*-apocope in plural nouns is hardly visible in reading primers, while it still occurs frequently in petitionary letters until the beginning of the 19th century. Even between 1820 and 1834, the percentage of *e*-apocope in plural forms is 18 % on average in petitions while it is completely invisible in the corpus of reading primers and newspaper issues during this period of time.

---

198 In combination with other prepositions, such as *zu*, the dative *-e* is used in similar constructions (e.g. *zu Pferde*).

199 This observation was also made by Nübling et al. (2013: 53), who state that the plural *-e* was reintroduced much more consistently than the dative *-e* in Early New High German. In other words, indicating the plural took priority over indicating the case (ibid.).

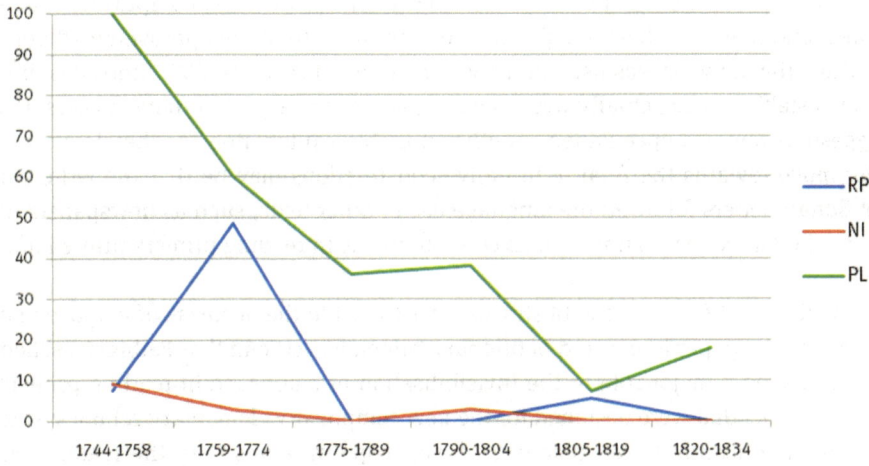

Fig. 31: Development of *e*-apocope in plural nouns in the three corpora (in percentages)

A few similarities between the three corpora can be found when investigating the instances of *e*-apocope in plural nouns. In all three corpora, nouns denoting periods of time, such as *Tag* and *Jahr*, are frequently not marked with a final -*e* in plural. Additionally, loan words without plural marking appear in the corpus of newspaper issues as well as petitionary letters. It seems that the *e*-apocope was acceptable in these particular words before it disappeared completely in writing.

In summary, it can be concluded that the *e*-apocope in feminine and plural nouns was first avoided in the *Wienerisches Diarium* as well as Antesperg's reading primer, which contains considerably fewer instances of *e*-apocope than the three subsequent reading primers. With the school reform (1774), the prescriptions for the final -*e* in feminine and plural nouns as well as in dative constructions proposed by Felbiger, who based his grammar on Gottsched's and Popowitsch's work, were implemented quickly in reading primers, while the development of dative -*e* was more gradual in newspaper issues. After the introduction of Felbiger's school policy, the final -*e* in feminine and plural nouns also became dominant in petitionary letters. A trend away from the *e*-apocope can, however, already be observed before 1774. It can, therefore, be argued that the school policy was not the initiator of the move towards the final -*e* in feminine and plural nouns. The writers of petitions who used the ending -*e* in these nouns before 1774 either studied the grammars discussed in chapter 3 or read other texts, such as newspapers, in which the final -*e* was used in feminine and plural nouns. Nevertheless, the introduction of the school reform may have contributed to the decrease of *e*-apocope in these nouns. An influence on the language use in petitions by the school reform is more likely in the development of dative -*e*, which only became more commonly used in the 19th century. By that time, some of the writers of the petitions may have attended the new, compulsory school system and may have been taught to read with the help of the approved textbooks, in which the dative -e was used in the vast majority of cases by 1777. Since it is difficult to establish who actually wrote a particular petitionary letter in most cases, this suggestion remains speculative. Another possible explanation for the slower and later move towards the final -e in dative constructions may be that the writers of petitionary letters followed the language use in other texts, such as newspapers, in which the dative -e was not used as consistently as in reading primers printed after 1775.

While it is difficult to establish what exactly led to the decrease of e-apocope in nouns in newspaper issues and petitionary letters, it is certain that Felbiger's school reform played a major role in the invisibilisation of e-apocope in reading primers. The textbooks that were designed for the new compulsory elementary school system contain significantly fewer instances of e-apocope in nouns than the reading primers printed before 1775, with Antesperg's primer (1744) appearing more 'modern' than the reading primers printed in c. 1750, c. 1770, and 1774. The school reform also had an effect on reading primers created for private use and, overall, only little linguistic variation can be found between individual reading primers printed after 1774. More generally, the disappearance of e-apocope can clearly be observed in all three corpora in the second half of the 18th and the early 19th century.

4.6.2 Past participles

With regard to the prefix ge- in past participles, by contrast, the development of the implementation of the ECG norm, i.e. past participles with the prefix ge-, had been largely implemented before the second half of the 18th century. Not a single past participle without the prefix ge- was found in the corpus of reading primers. The number of instances of past participles without the prefix ge- was also very low in the newspaper corpus, with just four out of 527 past participles occurring without ge- (geessen, vorgeben, worden [2]). This equates to merely 0.76 % and all instances appear before 1785. The percentage of the UG variant is slightly higher but still negligible in the corpus of petitions: 5.13 %, i.e. six out of 117 past participles are written without the prefix ge- (abgangen, angebnen, aufzeichnet, geben, kommen [2]), with the last occurrence being found in 1792. From the end of the 18th century, the UG variant is completely invisible in the corpora. The low number of instances in the second half of the 18th century indicates that the ECG norm had been implemented to a very large extent by 1744, i.e. before the publication of the grammars discussed in chapter 3. It can, therefore, be concluded that neither Gottsched or any subsequent grammarian nor the school reform initiated the replacement of the UG variant by the ECG form in written texts. The UG form was clearly avoided in all three corpora before the appearance of these language-external factors.

The development of the regular past participle ending -*t* is more complicated. Due to morpho-phonological principles, variation between the ending -*t* and the ending -*et* can be found in every reading primer, newspaper issue and in many petitionary letters. Nevertheless, certain trends emerged through the analyses of the three corpora. In the corpus of reading primers, the ending -*et* is clearly dominant in Antesperg's primer and in all textbooks prescribed by Felbiger's school policy (1774). In the other primers, the use of the ending -*t* and -*et* is fairly balanced, with the ending -*t* being clearly dominant in only one reading primer designed for home use (1818). Generally, it seems that the ending -*t* becomes more widely used in the 19th century in reading primers. This trend can also be observed in newspapers, where the ending -*et* is replaced by the ending -*t* during the second half of the 18th century. By the end of the 18th century, the ending -*t* is dominant in every newspaper issue. Also in the corpus of petitions, the ending -*t* is used more frequently than -*et* between 1805 and 1819. While, however, the ending -*t* develops in a wave-like manner in the corpus of petitions as well as reading primers, the development in the newspaper issues is more gradual: starting with the dominance of the ending -*et* and moving towards the ending -*t* (see figure below).

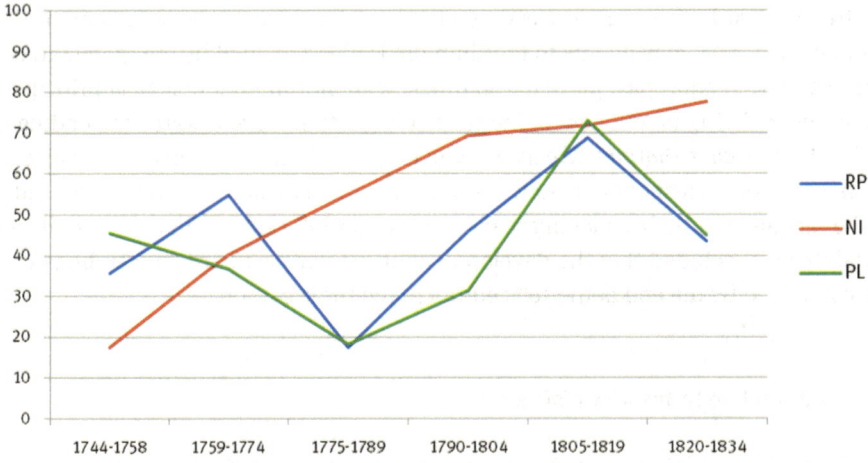

Fig. 32: The development of the regular past participle ending -*t* in the three corpora (in percentages)

While it was difficult to establish morphological patterns for the use of a particular past participle ending that were applied across the three corpora, certain lexically determined spellings were detected. The most striking of these is the use of the ending -*t* in the past participle of the verb *machen,* with *gemacht* appearing 74 times[200], while *gemachet* only occurs four times[201]. While Gottsched (1752) and Felbiger (1775) generally prescribe the ending -*et* for regular past participles (see sections 3.3.2 and 3.5.2), also the ending -*t* is used for the past participle of *machen* in their grammars. Popowitsch (1754a, 1754b) and Adelung (1781), by contrast, use the ending -*t* consistently for the past participle of *machen.* In other words, the lexical pattern that emerged from the analyses of the three corpora can also be observed in the grammars discussed in chapter 3. In the particular case of *machen,* the grammarians seem to follow the trend established in other text types, especially in newspaper issues.

In turn, language-external factors influencing the language use in the three corpora can be detected in the corpus of reading primers, with a decrease of the ending -*t* after the introduction of Felbiger's school policy in 1774. The development of the ending -*t* in petitionary letters, too, can be linked to the normative works of 18th-century grammarians, especially Gottsched and Felbiger (see section 4.5.2). However, the ending -*et* was certainly used before the publication of Gottsched's grammar in 1748 and the subsequent grammars that prescribed the ending -*et,* which means that the grammarians discussed in chapter 3 did not introduce the ending -*et* in any of the three corpora. In the *Wienerisches Diarium/Wiener Zeitung,* the trend towards the ending -*t* even seems to go against the prescriptions of the grammarians. This may be due to the simplified rules provided by the grammarians with regard to regular past participle endings, with morpho-phonological principles generally not being mentioned.[202] The relatively gradual move towards the ending -*t* in the *Wienerisches Diarium/Wiener Zeitung* may also indicate a conscious choice of the newspaper correspondents to write in a less sophisticated style and thus adjust to the language of their widening readership in the 19th century. In any case, it can certainly be concluded that the development of regular past participle endings was not completed by the end of the 18th century in the three corpora.

4.6.3 Alternative forms of *wir/sie sind*

The UG variant *wir/sie seyn(d)* disappears at about the same time in each corpus. In reading primers, the ECG form *wir/sie sind* is used exclusively from 1777 onwards, in the newspaper issues from 1774 onwards, and in the corpus of petitions the last

---

200 The variant *gemacht* occurs 27 times in the corpus of reading primers, 43 times in the corpus of newspaper issues, and four times in the corpus of petitionary letters.
201 The form *gemachet* appears twice in the corpus of reading primers and petitionary letters.
202 Adelung is the only grammarian discussed in chapter 3 who does mention that the past participles of verbs with stems ending in -*eln* and -*ern* usually end in -*t* (see section 3.6.2).

instance of *wir/sie seynd* can be found in 1777. Before the mid-1770s, both variants occur in each corpus, with the first instance of *wir/sie sind* appearing in 1744 in Antesperg's reading primer and in the newspaper issue printed in that year. In the corpus of petitions, the first instance of the ECG form occurs in 1768, i.e. before the introduction of the school reform. With regard to reading primers, Felbiger's school policy may have led to the consistent implementation of the ECG form. The disappearance of the UG variant in newspaper issues and in petitionary letters can also be linked to the normative work by 18th-century grammarians. With the low number of instances of this feature it is difficult to reach any final conclusion as to who or what exactly caused the replacement of the UG form. The analysis of the three corpora revealed, however, that the UG variant was invisibilised in the second half of the 18th century and does not appear in any written text from 1778 onwards.

While there are only minimal differences between the three corpora with regard to this feature, significant differences can be observed in the development of *e-*apocope in nouns and the regular past participle ending *-t*. The wider implications of these results will now be discussed in the conclusion.

5 Conclusion

My research has investigated the disappearance of UG features in Austrian writing (i.e. reading primers, newspaper issues, and petitionary letters) in the 18th and early 19th century. It has examined to what extent this disappearance was caused by a process of invisibilisation, i.e. the conscious and deliberate stigmatisation of linguistic features (cf. Langer & Havinga 2015). In particular, the role of 18th-century grammarians and the school reform advocated by Empress Maria Theresa in the disappearance of UG features was assessed.

The research literature ascribes a considerable influence on the standardisation process of German to 17th- and 18th-century grammarians (cf. Rössler 2005, Wiesinger 2008). Grammarians codified certain variants and thus – implicitly or explicitly – dismissed other variants as 'incorrect'. While the success of these prescriptions differed between certain features and did not necessarily affect spoken language use (cf. Konopka 1996, Takada 1998, Langer 2001, McLelland 2011), the instructions given by grammarians were often adhered to in formal writing.

One of the major challenges that historical linguists face is that the available sources were all written before devices for sound recording and reproduction were invented, i.e. before the late 19th century. It has to be kept in mind that these written sources do not represent spoken language use. Instead, they only present a fragment of how language was used at a particular point in time, with the language used in everyday or spoken discourse usually remaining invisible to modern-day researchers. 18th-century grammarians contributed to the invisibilisation of variants and varieties by stigmatising them implicitly (i.e. not mentioning them at all) or explicitly (i.e. by describing them as 'wrong' or 'bad'). In other words, their stigmatisations prevented certain variants and varieties from being written down.

This, however, does not mean that the stigmatised forms and constructions ceased to exist in language use overall. The features I analysed (*e*-apocope in nouns, the absence of the prefix *ge*- in past participles, the ending -*t* in regular past participles, and alternative forms of *wir/sie sind*) are all still typical for the language use in the UG area in spoken and informal written contexts. Indeed, the ending -*t* (rather than -*et*) not only survives in spoken UG but also became the default form for regular past participles in modern standard German everywhere. The other features, however, are neither codified in grammars nor used in formal writing today – they were invisibilised.

In this monograph, the process of invisibilisation of Austrian German features has been investigated in its 18th-century socio-political context. Empress Maria Theresa, who believed in a close connection between language and the ability to advance in socio-economic fields, advocated the 18th-century language reform and introduced compulsory elementary education in December 1774. The analysis of 18th- and early 19th-century reading primers revealed that this new school policy,

DOI 10.1515/9783110547047-005

written by the educationist Johann Ignaz Felbiger, certainly influenced the language use in reading primers. The uniform textbooks introduced by Felbiger contained significantly fewer UG features than the reading primers printed before December 1774. Pupils attending elementary school, which became compulsory with the introduction of the school reform in December 1774, were taught how to read with the help of these uniform textbooks that were adjusted to the ECG norm. Thus Felbiger, who wrote or edited these textbooks and who followed Gottsched's and Popowitsch's prescriptions to a large extent, played a major role in the dissemination of the ECG norms in schools. The influence of the grammarians discussed in chapter 3 (Antesperg, Gottsched, Popowitsch, Felbiger, and Adelung) can also be observed in petitionary letters, and – to a far lesser extent – in newspaper issues. The ECG norm appears to have been adopted in the *Wienerisches Diarium/Wiener Zeitung* before the publication of grammars in the second half of the 18th century and the introduction of the school reform in 1774. A notable exception is the significant increase of dative -*e* after 1764, which, however, was never implemented consistently in the newspaper issues. With regard to petitionary letters, which generally contain more UG forms than the other two text types, it cannot be determined for certain whether the writers of petitions adjusted their language use according to grammars or other model texts, such as newspapers. Also the school reform may have had an effect on the language used in petitionary letters. Particularly in the early 19th century, it is likely that at least some of the writers of petitions had attended the compulsory elementary schools introduced by Empress Maria Theresa and had been taught with Felbiger's textbooks.

While the influence of Gottsched and other 18th-century grammarians can be observed with regard to some features and specific text types, a number of ECG forms were already used before the publication of the reputedly influential grammars discussed in chapter 3. This is particularly obvious in the newspaper issues, which may have played a more significant role in the introduction of ECG forms in 18th-century Austria than previously anticipated. A reason for the early introduction of ECG features in newspaper issues is probably the nature of newspaper writing in the 18th century, with international correspondents sending their articles, which were usually not – or only minimally – changed by editors. While the readership of 18th-century newspapers was certainly restricted, they were read by people in powerful positions, i.e. the nobility and the bourgeoisie, and may have served as model texts.

In summary, the quantitative analyses of these three corpora revealed a trend away from the UG forms during the 18th and early 19th century. These developments reflect processes of invisibilisation rather than morphological language change. While the UG variants were replaced by their ECG equivalents in writing, the UG forms are still widely used in Austria today. In other words, they disappeared from written contexts but not from the actual language use. As discussed above, there was certainly not one factor alone that led to the invisibilisation of UG variants in 18th- and early 19th-century Austria. It is far more likely that a number of factors –

Empress Maria Theresa's appeal for a language reform, the normative work of 18th-century grammarians, Felbiger's school policy, and the early introduction of ECG variants in newspaper issues – contributed to this development. This conclusion partly disproves previous research findings.

The general development towards the ECG norms in 18th-century Austria has been described in recent research literature, particularly Rössler (2005) and Wiesinger (2008). Rössler's (2005) results of the features I discussed suggest that Maria Theresa's language reform and 18th-century grammarians (especially Gottsched) were the decisive factors for this development. While the language reform 'from above' and grammarians certainly played a major role in the dissemination of the ECG norms in 18th-century Austria, the more fine-grained analysis I employed revealed that some of the ECG features (ending -e in feminine and plural nouns, past participles with *ge-*) had been adopted in 18th-century texts, especially in the *Wienerisches Diarium*, by 1744, i.e. *before* the publication of Gottsched's grammar. This is particularly obvious in past participles without the prefix *ge-*, which were avoided in all three corpora by 1744. Rössler's (2005: 307) suggestion that the clear increase of past participles with the prefix *ge-* after the mid-18th century indicates an increasing influence of the grammarians, therefore, could not be confirmed by the analysis I carried out. In other cases (dative -e, *wir/sie sind*), it is more likely that the grammarians discussed in chapter 3 had an influence on the language use. Furthermore, Gottsched may have influenced the language used in 18th-century writing prior to the publication of his grammar through language societies and their publications, such as the *Beyträge zur Critischen Historie der Deutschen Sprache, Poesie und Beredsamkeit* (*Contributions to the critical history of the German language, poetry and eloquence*) (1732–1744) (see section 2.1 and 3.3). As mentioned in section 3.2, Gottsched recommended linguistic adjustments to the variety used by the *Deutsche Gesellschaft*, i.e. ECG, when Antesperg asked him for suggestions of improvement in 1734. In order to investigate Gottsched's influence on the language use before 1744, further text analyses have to be carried out.

While the findings described above certainly widen our knowledge of the standardisation process of written German in Austria, there are still a number of open questions that could and should be addressed in further research. Firstly, similar analyses, including further features on all linguistic levels (such as the use of definite articles in front of proper nouns, e.g. **Die** Laura war da.), should be carried out on a range of text types. Given that I have identified significant differences in the language use between reading primers, newspaper issues, and petitionary letters, i.e. formal text types, it can be assumed that similar observations can be made when analysing more informal texts, such as private letters or diaries. Including a variety of sources in corpus linguistic analyses would certainly widen our understanding of language use in the past. The analysis of private and informal texts, especially, may uncover variants that remain completely invisible in the text types I analysed since personal texts are conceptually closer to spoken language (cf. Koch & Oesterreicher 1985, 1994).

There is scope for further research on the role of education in the standardisation of German. The results of the analysis of reading primers indicate that Felbiger's school policy (1774) had a considerable effect on the language use in schoolbooks. This does not, however, mean that the variants printed in schoolbooks were used by the teachers. School inspection reports may prove revealing in determining whether there were any discrepancies between the language in textbooks and the language of instruction. The work by pupils themselves, too, would constitute a very valuable source since any hypercorrections and transfer interferences would provide insights into the actual language use of students. Locating such work will, however, be difficult, given that pupils usually wrote their work on slates in school, which were wiped off.

Besides the role of education, the role of historical newspapers in the dissemination of certain language norms needs to be examined in more detail. The analysis of the *Wienerisches Diarium/Wiener Zeitung* revealed that this newspaper had largely adjusted its language use to the ECG norm by 1744. Despite the rather limited readership, the *Wienerisches Diarium/Wiener Zeitung* may have served as a distributor of what the readers considered 'model texts'. In other words, the readers may have adjusted their language use to the varieties and variants used in the newspaper. With a widening readership in the 19th century, the influence of newspapers on the writing practice of its readers may have played a major role in the final stages of the standardisation of written German.

My research showed that fine-grained diachronic analyses set within contemporary socio-political contexts can expose factors that influenced the standardisation of languages and led to processes of invisibilisation or actual language change. The findings presented in this monograph will hopefully serve as an initiator for further research in this field.

Appendix

Timetables

Tab. 56: Timetable for the *Normalschule* (*Allgemeine Schulordnung* 1774: Lit. A)

	The 1st teacher teaches the following in the 1st classroom	The 2nd teacher teaches the following in the 2nd room	The 3rd teacher teaches the following in the 3rd room	The 4th teacher teaches the following in the 4th room
7.30–8.00	All children (except for the youngest in the winter) attend Mass			
8.00–9.00	Instruction for the teachers-to-be by the headmaster	Husbandry (in the 1st term) and natural science (in the 2nd term)	Orthography	Reading
9.00–10.00	Arts (taught by an artist)	Arithmetic (beginners)	Writing	Spelling
10.00–11.00	Latin	Religion and lesson about the benefit of learning		
11.00–12.00	Geography and history	Nothing	Nothing	Nothing
13.00–14.00	Nothing	Geometry (in the 1st term), architecture & mechanics (in the 2nd term)	Writing (beginners)	Spelling
14.00–15.00	Instruction for the teachers-to-be by the headmaster	Arithmetic	Writing	Reading
15.00–16.00	German grammar (in the 1st term), letter writing or exercises for written compositions (in the 2nd term)	Ethics, Biblical religious history, decency as well as explanations of the Epistles and the Gospel on varying days.		

DOI 10.1515/9783110547047-006

Tab. 57: Timetable for the *Hauptschule* (*Allgemeine Schulordnung* 1774: Lit. B)

	The 1st teacher teaches the following in the 1st classroom	The 2nd teacher teaches the following in the 2nd room	The 3rd teacher teaches the following in the 3rd room
7.30–8.00	All children (except for the youngest in the winter) attend Mass		
8.00–9.00	Arithmetic	Writing	Reading
9.00–10.00	Arithmetic (beginners)	Husbandry (in the 1st term) and natural science (in the 2nd term)	Spelling
10.00–11.00	The catechist teaches ...	Mondays: Lower catechism class (3rd room) Tuesdays: Geography (1st room) Wednesdays: Lower catechism class (3rd room) Thursdays: History (1st room) Fridays: Biblical religious history (2nd room) Saturdays: Explanation of the Epistles (2nd room)	
13.00–14.00	German grammar (in the 1st term) and letter writing (in the 2nd term)	Writing (beginners)	Spelling
14.00–15.00	Latin taught by the catechist	Writing	Reading
15.00–16.00	The catechist in the 1st classroom teaches ...	Mondays: Ethics Tuesdays: Introductory lesson and the 2nd reading book in table form Wednesdays: Upper catechism class Thursdays: Recreation Fridays: Rules of decency Saturdays: Explanation of the Gospel	

Categorization of the pupils in a *Hauptschule* into 4 classes (*Allgemeine Schulordnung* 1774: Lit. B).

The first class.

These are the smallest children, who study the following every day.

9.00–10.00	Spelling
10.00–11.00	Religion (only on Mondays and Wednesdays)
13.00–14.00	Spelling

All in the 3rd room.

The second class.

Slightly older children.

8.00–9.00	Reading (in the 3rd room)
9.00–10.00	Spelling (in the 3rd room)
10.00–11.00	Religion (only Mondays and Wednesdays in the 3rd room)
13.00–14.00	Writing (beginners, in the 2nd room)
14.00–15.00	Reading (in the 3rd room)

The third class.

Still older children.

8.00–9.00	Writing (in the 2nd room)
9.00–10.00	Arithmetic (beginners, in the 1st room)
10.00–11.00	Mondays and Wednesdays: Religion (in the 3rd room)
	Fridays: Biblical history (in the 2nd room)
	Saturdays: Explanation of the Epistles (in the 2nd room)
13.00–14.00	Writing (in the 2nd room)
14.00–15.00	Reading (in the 3rd room)
15.00–16.00	Mondays: Ethics
	Tuesdays: Introductory lesson, and the 2nd reading book in table form

Wednesdays: Religion

Thursdays: Recreation

Fridays: Rules of decency

Saturdays: Explanation of the Gospel

All in the 1st room.

The fourth class.

Attended by the oldest pupils.

8.00–9.00	Arithmetic (in the 1st room)
9.00–10.00	Natural science or Husbandry (in the 2nd room)
10.00–11.00	Tuesdays: Geography (in the 1st room)
	Thursdays: History (in the 1st room)
	Fridays: Biblical history (in the 2nd room)
	Saturdays: Explanation of the Epistles (in the 2nd room)
13.00–14.00	German grammar or letter writing (in the 1st room)
14.00–15.00	Latin (in the 1st room)
	Those who do not learn Latin, attend the writing class in the 2nd room.
15.00–16.00	Mondays: Ethics
	Tuesdays: Virtues
	Wednesdays: Religion
	Thursdays: Recreation
	Fridays: Decency
	Saturdays: Explanation of the Gospel

All in the first room.

Tab. 58: Timetable for the *Trivialschulen* in towns (*Allgemeine Schulordnung* 1774: Lit. C)

	The 1st teacher teaches the following in the 1st classroom	The 2nd teacher teaches the following in the 2nd room
7.30–8.00 or 11.00–12.00	Mass	
8.00–9.00	Lower Arithmetic	Upper Arithmetic
9.00–10.00	Spelling	Reading
10.00–11.00	The catechist teaches ...	Mondays: Biblical history Tuesdays: Lower catechism class Wednesdays: History Thursdays: Lower catechism class Fridays: Upper catechism class Saturdays: Explanation of the Epistles
13.00–14.00	Reading (beginners)	Upper writing class and orthography
14.00–15.00	Lower writing class	Written compositions
15.00–16.00	The catechist teaches ...	Mondays: Ethics Tuesdays: Decency Wednesdays: Geography Thursdays: Recreation Fridays: Introductory lessons, and the 2nd reading book in table form Saturdays: Explanation of the Gospel

Tab. 59: Timetable for the *Trivialschulen* in small towns and in the countryside (*Allgemeine Schulordnung* 1774: Lit. D)

8.00–9.00	Arithmetic
9.00–9.45	Spelling
9.45–10.30	Reading
10.30–11.00	Orthography (for the bigger or older pupils), exercise in copying written compositions and writing of dictation
Twice a week from	
10.00 to 11.00	Catechism (once with the smaller, once with the bigger children)
13.00–14.00	Writing
14.00–15.00	Spelling and reading
15.00–16.00	Reading of the Epistle and the Gospel (the latter only on Saturdays, without forming their own interpretations)
Once a week (on Wednesday or Thursday afternoon) there is time for recreation.	

List of prescribed textbooks

Lit. E.

Verzeichniß

Der Bücher, deren man sich beym Lehren und Lernen in den deutschen Schulen der kaiserl. königl. Erblande bedienen soll.

I. Das Methodenbuch für Lehrer der deutschen Schulen in den kaiserlich = königlichen Erblanden, darinn nicht allein ausführlich gewiesen wird, wie die in der Schulverordnung bestimmte Lehrart überhaupt, sondern auch wie sie bey jedem Gegenstande, der zu lehren befohlen ist, soll beschaffen seyn, nebst der genauen Bestimmung wie sich die Lehrer der Schulen in allen Theilen ihres Amtes zu bezeugen haben, um der Schulordnung das gehörige Genügen zu leisten.

II. Anweisung für Privatlehrer oder Hausinstruktores.

III. Das Namenbüchel oder A B C nebst dem dazu gehörigen Täflein zum Buchstaben kennen, und der großen Buchstabiertabelle.

IV. Das aus 4. Stücken bestehende Lesebuch für Schüler über Gegenstände welche die Religion betreffen.

V. Eben diese 4. Stücke tabellarisch für Lehrer, und katechetisch, das ist in Fragen und Antworten für Eltern, die ihre Kinder selbst prüfen wollen.

VI. Der erläuterte und erwiesene Katechismus.

VII. Das Evangelium nebst den Episteln.

VIII. Das Buch für Schüler der deutschen Schulen in den kaiserlich = königlichen Erblanden; es enthält die Anleitung zu allen Gegenständen, welche für alle 3. Arten der deutschen Schulen sind vorgeschrieben worden.

Wie aber nicht alle Gegenstände weder für jeden Schüler, noch für jeden Lehrer gehören, so soll das zu jedem Lehrgegenstande Gehörige besonders abgedruckt, und sowohl einzeln als alles zusammen zu haben seyn.

Dieß Buch besteht aus der

Anleitung zum Schönschreiben nebst Vorschriften.

An.

Fig. 33: List of prescribed textbooks, page 1 (*Allgemeine Schulordnung* 1774: Lit. E.)

Anleitung zum Rechnen.

a.) überhaupt für Schüler aller Art,

b.) besonders für die, welche in Städten weiter gebracht werden.

Anleitung zur Rechtschreibung.

Anleitung zur deutschen Sprache.

Anleitung zum Verfassen schriftlicher Aufsätze.

Anleitung zum Lateinischen.

Anleitung zur Rechtschaffenheit, Sittsamkeit, Haushaltungskunst, und dem was für einen guten Bürger gehöret, nebst einer historischen Nachricht von Künsten und Handwerken.

Anleitung zur Erkenntniß der nützlichsten physikalischen Wahrheiten.

Anleitung zur Landwirthschaft.

Anleitung zur Erdbeschreibung und Geschichte.

Anleitung zum Zeichnen.

Anleitung zur Geometrie, bürgerlichen Baukunst und Mechanik.

Fig. 34: List of prescribed textbooks, page 2 (*Allgemeine Schulordnung* 1774: Lit. E.)

Bibliography

Primary sources

ABC oder Buchstabirbüchlein zum Gebrauche der Landschulen in den kaiserlich-königlichen Staaten. 1777. Prag: Verlag der k. k. Normalschulbuchdruckerey. BMB: JH 369.

ABC oder Namenbüchlein zum Gebrauche der Landschulen in den kaiserlich-königlichen Staaten. 1783. Wien: Verlagsgewölbe der deutschen Schulanstalt bei St. Anna. BMB: JH 361.

ABC oder Namenbüchlein zum Gebrauche der Oesterreichischen Normalschule. 1782. Wien: Verlag der Normalschule. BMB: JH 360.

ABC oder Namenbüchlein zum Gebrauche der Schulen in den kaiserlich-königlichen Staaten. 1778. Laibach: Johann Friedrich Eger. BMB: JH 335.

ABC oder Namenbüchlein zum Gebrauche der Schulen in den kaiserlich-königlichen Staaten. 1779. Prag: k. k. Normalschulbuchdruckerey. BMB: JH 358.

ABC und Buchstabierbüchlein nebst Leseübungen für Anfänger. 1809. Botzen: Karl Joseph Weiß. BMB: JH 343.

Adelung, Johann Christoph. 1774–1786. Versuch eines vollständigen grammatisch-kritischen Wörterbuches der Hochdeutschen Mundart, mit beständiger Vergleichung der übrigen Mundarten, besonders aber der oberdeutschen. 5 Bände. Leipzig: Bernhard Christoph Breitkopf und Sohn.

Adelung, Johann Christoph. 1781. *Deutsche Sprachlehre. Zum Gebrauche der Schulen in den Königl. Preuß. Landen.* Berlin: Christian Friedrich Voß und Sohn. Available at: https://books.google.co.uk/books?id=3iJWAAAAYAAJ&printsec=frontcover#v=onepage&q&f=false [accessed 26.04.2017].

Adelung, Johann Christoph. 1782. Umständliches Lehrgebäude der Deutschen Sprache, zur Erläuterung der Deutschen Sprachlehre für Schulen. Leipzig: Johann Gottlob Immanuel Breitkopf. Available at: https://books.google.co.uk/books?id=HjVGAAAAcAAJ&printsec=frontcover#v=onepage&q&f=false [accessed 26.04.2017].

Adelung, Johann Christoph. 1806–1817. Mithridates oder allgemeine Sprachenkunde mit dem Vater Unser als Sprachprobe in bey nahe fünfhundert Sprachen und Mundarten. 1. Theil. Berlin. Nachdruck. Hildesheim, New York 1970.

Aichinger, Carl Friedrich. 1753. Versuch einer teutschen Sprachlehre, anfänglich nur zu eignem Gebrauche unternommen, endlich aber, um den Gelehrten zu fernerer Untersuchung Anlaß zu geben. Frankfurt und Leipzig.

Allgemeine Schulordnung, für die deutschen Normal- Haupt- und Trivialschulen in sämmtlichen Kaiserl. Königl. Erbländern d. d. Wien den 6ten December 1774. Wien: Johann Thomas Edlen von Trattner. Österreichisches Staatsarchiv: AVA Unterricht StHK Teil 1, K. 87.

ANNO – AustriaN Newspapers Online. 2011. http://anno.onb.ac.at/ [accessed 26.04. 2017].

Antesperg, Johann Balthasar. [1734]. Kayserliche deutsche Sprachtabelle zur Verbesserung der deutschen Sprache und zum einhellig nutzlichen Gebrauch des ganzen Deutschlands (mit zum Schreiben an den Kaiser umgewandelter Einführung). Wien: Maria Theresia Voigtin.

Antesperg, Johann Balthasar von. 1744. Das Josephinische Erzherzogliche A.B.C. Oder Namenbüchlein In Zweyerley Schriften, Mit vielen angenehmen, zur Unterweisung dienlichen Figuren und Vorschriften, Wodurch sowohl junge, als auch erwachsene Leute auf eine vernünftige Weise in kurzer Zeit das Buchstabieren und Lesen in zweyerley Schriften ganz leicht lernen, und anbey zum Schreiben, Rechnen, und Christlichen Sitten mit geringer Mühe und Unkosten sonderbar geschickt werden können. Wien: Johann Ignatz Heyinger. Nachdruck

DOI 10.1515/9783110547047-007

des Widmungsexemplars von 1741 [1744] im Landesmuseum Joanneum in Graz, 1980. Dortmund: Harenberg.

Antesperg, Johann Balthasar von. [1747]. Die Kayserliche Deutsche Grammatick. Oder Kunst, die deutsche Sprache recht zu reden, Und ohne Fehler zu schreiben. Wien: Johann Ignatz Heyinger. Available at: https://books.google.co.uk/books?id=mQ1NAAAAcAAJ&printsec=frontcover#v=onepage&q&f=false [accessed 26.04.2017].

Anweisung die deutsche Sprache richtig zu sprechen, zu lesen und zu schreiben. Nebst Beispielen von Briefen und andern schriftlichen Aufsätzen. Zum Gebrauche der Trivial=Schulen in den k. k. Staaten. 1794. Graz: Verlag der sämtlichen bürgerlichen Buchbinder. Available at: https://books.google.co.uk/books?id=z1dZAAAAcAAJ&printsec=frontcover#v=onepage&q&f=false [accessed 26.04.2017].

Beyträge zur Critischen Historie der Deutschen Sprache, Poesie und Beredsamkeit, herausgegeben von einigen Liebhabern der deutschen Litteratur. 1732–1744. Leipzig: Bernhard Christoph Breitkopf.

Bodmer, Johann Jakob & Johann Jacob Breitinger. 1746. *Der Mahler Der Sitten.* [...]. Der erste Band. Zürich. Reprographischer Nachdruck. Hildesheim, New York 1972.

Brauser, Wolffgang. 1687. Der Hurtige Briefsteller. Das ist: Ausführlich=deutliche Anweisung / in allerhand Zeit / Freud / Leid / Streit=Fällen und Begebenheiten / einen zierlichen Brief / ohne allzulanges Nachsinnen / zu Papier zu bringen / und dardurch sein Vorhaben nachdenklichst auszudrücken / damit man den ihme vorgestellten Zweck / bey Hohen und Niedern desto füglicher erlangen möge. Allen / in dieser Materie / theils mittelmässig=Erfahrnen / theils noch ganz Ungeübten zu reiffem Nutzen / auf reine Hochteutsche heut zu Tage übliche Schreib=Art / solcher Gestalt eingerichtet / und statt eines Secretarii mitgetheilet. Nürnberg: Martin Endters. Available at: https://books.google.co.uk/books?id=KCZEAQAAMAAJ&printsec=frontcover#v=onepage&q&f=false [accessed 26.04.2017].

Catholisches Namen-Büchl. Das ist: Ein sehr sonderbarer kurzer Weg / bald und leicht lesen zu lernen / sowohl für alte als junge Personen / welche nicht Zeit haben / lang gemeine Schulen zu besuchen. Mit schönen Bildnussen gezieret / und aufs Neue übersehen. 1774. Linz: Johann Adam Auinger. BMB: JH 41.

Der kleine Abc-Schüler. Ein Geschenk für Kinder, welche bald zu lesen und das Gelesene zu verstehen wünschen. Zehnte Auflage. 1818. Salzburg: Xav. Duyle. BMB: JH 365.

Deutsche Sprachlehre. Zum Gebrauche der deutschen Normal- und Hauptschulen in den k. k. Staaten. 1798. Wien: Verlagsgewölbe der deutschen Schulanstalt. BMB: JH 69.

Duden. 2006. Die deutsche Rechtschreibung. Mannheim: Dudenverlag.

Duden (online). http://www.duden.de/ [accessed 26.04.2017].

Ein sehr nutzliches Stimmen-Büchlein / Welches sowohl für die Lehr- als Lernende im Schreiben / und Buchstabiren nach der reinen Rechtschreibung mit allem Fleiß zusammen getragen worden; auch mit Schönen Catholischen Gebethlein / Morgens und Abends / vor= und nach dem Essen in allen verbessert. c. 1770. Graz: Widmanstätteris. Erben. BMB: JH 357.

Elspaß, Stephan & Robert Möller. 2003. *Atlas zur deutschen Alltagssprache.* http://www.atlas-alltagssprache.de/ [accessed 26.04.2017].

Entwurf zur Instruction der Schul Commissionen in den Kayserl. Königlichen Erblanden. 1775. Österreichisches Staatsarchiv: AVA Unterricht StHK Teil 1, K. 87.

[Felbiger, Johann Ignaz]. 1774. Anleitung zur deutschen Rechtschreibung. Zum Gebrauche der deutschen Schulen in den kaiserlich-königlichen Staaten. Wien: Deutsche Schulanstalt bey St. Anna.

[Felbiger, Johann Ignaz]. 1775. Anleitung zur deutschen Sprachlehre. Zum Gebrauche der Schulen in den kaiserlich-königlichen Staaten. Wien: Deutsche Schulanstalt bey St. Anna.

Fulda, Friedrich Carl. 1774. 'Über die beiden Hauptdialecte der Teutschen Sprache [...].' In: Johann Christoph Adelung. Versuch eines vollständigen grammatisch-kritischen Wörterbuches der Hochdeutschen Mundart, mit beständiger Vergleichung der übrigen Mundarten, besonders aber der oberdeutschen. Erster Theil. Leipzig, 1–60.

Gerlach, Friedrich Wilhelm. 1758. Kurzgefasste Deutsche Sprachlehre, welche die allgemeinen Gründe, samt einem Verzeichnisse der Stammwörter, und vieler abstammenden und zusammengesetzten Wörter der deutschen Sprache in sich enthält; und aus Hochachtung der Muttersprache und der Wissenschaften herausgegeben worden [...]. Wien: Eva Maria Schilgin.

Gesner, Conrad. 1555. Mithridates de differentis linguis.

Gottsched, Johann Christoph. 1748. Grundlegung einer Deutschen Sprachkunst. Nach den Mustern der besten Schriftsteller des vorigen und jetzigen Jahrhunderts abgefasset. Leipzig: Bernhard Christoph Breitkopf.

Gottsched, Johann Christoph. 1752. Grundlegung einer Deutschen Sprachkunst. Nach den Mustern der besten Schriftsteller des vorigen und jetzigen Jahrhunderts abgefasset, und bey dieser dritten Auflage merklich vermehret. Leipzig: Bernhard Christoph Breitkopf. Available at: https://books.google.co.uk/books?id=5n4HAAAAQAAJ&printsec=frontcover#v=onepage&q&f=false [accessed 26.04.2017].

Gottsched, Johann Christoph. 1753. *Kern der Deutschen Sprachkunst aus der ausführlichen Sprachkunst*. Leipzig: Bernhard Christoph Breitkopf.

Gottsched, Johann Christoph. 1762. Vollständigere und Neuerläuterte Deutsche Sprachkunst. Nach den Mustern der besten Schriftsteller des vorigen und itzigen Jahrhunderts abgefasset, und bei dieser fünften Auflage merklich verbessert. Leipzig: Bernhard Christoph Breitkopf und Sohn. Available at: https://books.google.co.uk/books?id=2M4CAAAAYAAJ&printsec=frontcover#v=onepage&q&f=false [accessed 26.04.2017].

Grimm, Jacob & Wilhelm Grimm. 1854–1961. *Deutsches Wörterbuch*. Leipzig. Available at: http://woerterbuchnetz.de/DWB/ [accesses 26.04.2017].

Heynatz, Johann Friedrich. 1771. *Briefe, die deutsche Sprache betreffend*. Erster Theil. Berlin: August Mylius. Available at: http://reader.digitale-sammlungen.de/de/fs1/object/display/bsb10583795_00002.html? [accessed 26.04.2017].

Imperial Chancellery (Böhmische und Österreichische Hofkanzlei). *Vortrag über den Zustand der Normal-Schulen in den gesammten Kayl: Königl^{en}: Erbländern*. An die Majestät. Wien, 15. April 1775. Österreichisches Staatsarchiv: AVA Unterricht StHK Teil 1, K. 87.

Justi, Johann Heinrich Gottlob. 1750. Abhandlung von dem Zusammenhang der Vollkommenheit der Sprache mit dem Blühenden Zustand der Wissenschaften. Wien: Joh. Thomas Trattner. Available at: https://books.google.co.uk/books?id=gBNRAAAAcAAJ&pg=PT8&dq#v=onepage&q&f=false [accessed 26.04.2017].

Justi, Johann Heinrich Gottlob. 1755. Anweisung zu einer guten deutschen Schreibart, und allen in Geschäften und Rechtssachen vorfallenden Ausarbeitungen. Leipzig.

Kirchmayr, Laur[entius]. 1828. Syllabier-Büchlein. Stufenweise geordnete und zum Lesenlernen hinreichende Buchstabier- und Syllabier-Übungen zum Privatgebrauche. Wien: Leopold Grund. BMB: JH 339.

Leibniz, Gottfried Wilhelm von. 1697. Unvorgreifliche Gedanken, betreffend die Ausübung und Verbesserung der Deutschen Sprache. Ein Handbuch für Deutsche Jünglinge. Nachdruck, 1831. Dessau: Christian Georg Ackermann. Available at:

https://books.google.co.uk/books?id=kZAOAQAAMAAJ&printsec=frontcover#v=onepage&q&f
=false [accessed 26.04.2017].

Lizel, Georg (= Megalissus). 1731. Der Undeutsche Catholik Oder Historischer Bericht Von der allzu
grossen Nachläßigkeit der Römisch-Catholischen, insonderheit unter der Clerisey der Jesuiten,
In Verbesserung der deutschen Sprache und Poesie. Jena: Joh. Friedrich Rittern. Available at:
http://reader.digitale-sammlungen.de/en/fs1/object/display/bsb10584041_00002.html [ac-
cessed 26.04.2017].

Moritz, Karl Philipp. 1832. Allgemeiner deutscher Briefsteller, welcher enthält: Grundsätze der
Rechtschreibung und Interpunktion; Lehre vom Unterschied des Accusativs und Dativs, von
den Präpositionen und den unregelmäßigen Zeitwörtern; Hauptregeln des Styls im
allgemeinen und des Briefstyls insbesondere; Anweisung zum richtigen Gebrauch der
Titulaturen; Beispielsammlung von Vorstellungen und Briefen; nicht minder Belehrung über
Begriff und Abfassung der Wechsel, Anweisungen, Schuldverschreibungen, Cessionen,
Rechnungen, Quittungen, Frachtbriefe, Zeugnisse und der durch die öffentlichen Blätter zu
erlassenden Anzeigen. 10. gänzlich umgearbeitete Aufl. Berlin: August Rücker. Available at:
https://books.google.co.uk/books?id=02YHAAAAQAAJ&printsec=frontcover#v=onepage&q&f
=false [accessed 26.04.2017].

Nahmenbüchlein für Stadtschulen in den kaiserl. königl. Staaten. 1833. Linz: Jos. Feichtinger's, sel.,
Witwe. BMB: JH 367.

Nahmenbüchlein zum Gebrauche der Stadtschulen in den kaiserl. königl. Staaten. 1804. Graz:
Verlag der sämmtlichen bürgerlichen Buchbinder, und gedruckt mit Leykam'schen Schriften.
BMB: JH 364.

Nast, Johannes (ed.). 1777. Der teütsche Sprachforscher. Allen Liebhabern ihrer Mutersprache zur
Prüfung vorgelegt. Erster Teil. Stutgart: Johann Benedict Mezler. Available at:
http://digi.ub.uni-heidelberg.de/diglit/teutsche_sprachforscher1777/0001 [accessed 26.04.
2017].

Neuestes ABC-Buch, oder Uebungen im Syllabiren oder Buchstabiren und im Lesen; sie bestehen
aus Denk- und Sittensprüchen, aus moralischen Erzählungen und Schilderungen, Fabeln,
Gebethen und Liedern. 1802. Wien: In der Camesinaischen Buchhandlung. BMB: JH 363.

Österreichisches Wörterbuch. 1979. 35th edition. Wien: Österreichischer Bundesverlag.

Österreichisches Wörterbuch. 2012. 42nd edition. Wien: Österreichischer Bundesverlag.

Petitionary letter. 1744. Signed: Annä Mariä Diewaltin. Ref.: STLA_1744w_Lamberg, Fam. K. 319 H.
1390.

Petitionary letter. 1746. Signed: Maria Rettin. Ref.: STLA_1746w_Lamberg, Fam. K. 320, H. 1393.

Petitionary letter. 1747. Signed: Larenz Dakhl. Ref.: STLA_1747r_Lamberg, Fam. K. 320, H. 1393.

Petitionary letter. 1749. Signed: Wolfgang Stainparzer. Ref.: OOLA_1749r_Neuhaus, Herrsch. Nr.
149, VI, 18.

Petitionary letter. 1751. Signed: Nicolaus Hollaus. Ref.: OOLA_1751r_a_Weinberg, Herrsch. Sch.
1061, B70.

Petitionary letter. 1751. Signed: Maria Anna Liebin. Ref.: OOLA_1751r_b_Weinberg, Herrsch. Sch.
1061, B70.

Petitionary letter. 1752. Signed: Johann Michael Liechtenauer. Ref.: OOLA_1752r_Weinberg, Herrsch.
Sch. 1061, B70.

Petitionary letter. 1752. Signed: Maria Hausenstukhin. Ref.: STLA_1752p_Lamberg, Fam. K. 329, H.
1428.

Petitionary letter. 1754. Signed: Elisabetha Millerin. Ref.: STLA_1754p_Saurau, Fam. K. 154, H. 1479.

Petitionary letter. 1754. Signed: Johännes Stenizer. Ref.: STLA_1754r_Donnersbach, Herrsch. K. 41,
H. 154.

Petitionary letter. 1755. Signed: Johann Perwein. Ref.: STLA_1755w_Saurau, Fam. K. 56, H. 928.

Petitionary letter. 1757. Signed: Elisabeth Fridrichin. Ref.: STLA_1757p_Saurau, Fam. K. 154, H. 1479.

Petitionary letter. 1758. Signed: Martin Hammer. Ref.: STLA_1758p_Saurau, Fam. K. 188, H. 1860.

Petitionary letter. 1760. Signed: Andree Stöller. Ref.: STLA_1760r_Rothenfels, Herrsch. K. 211 H. 730.

Petitionary letter. 1763. Signed: Engelbert Probst. Ref.: OOLA_1763w_Schwertberg, Herrsch. Sch. 134_M.

Petitionary letter. 1764. Signed: Mathias Grohsniger. Ref.: OOLA_1764w_Schwertberg, Herrsch. Sch. 134.

Petitionary letter. 1766. Signed: Frantz Lechner. Ref.: STLA_1766p_Rothenfels, Herrsch. K. 211, H. 730.

Petitionary letter. 1768. Signed: Thomas Wilmauer. Ref.: OOLA_1768p_Waldenfels, Herrsch. Sch. 330, 4.

Petitionary letter. 1769. Signed: Michael Seÿrl. Ref.: OOLA_1769r_Weinberg, Herrsch. Sch. 1061, B70.

Petitionary letter. 1771. Signed: Franz Adam. Ref.: OOLA_1771w_Weinberg, Herrsch. Sch. 1061, B70.

Petitionary letter. 1772. Signed: Catharina Pichlerin. Ref.: OOLA_1772r_Weinberg, Herrsch. Sch. 1061, B70.

Petitionary letter. 1773. Signed: Geörg Saneckhmillner. Ref.: OOLA_1773r_a_Weinberg, Herrsch. Sch. 1061, B70.

Petitionary letter. 1773. Signed: Magdalena Hollausin. Ref.: OOLA_1773r_b_Weinberg, Herrsch. Sch. 1061, B70.

Petitionary letter. 1773. Signed: Thereßia Stüffingerin. Ref.: OOLA_1773w_Weinberg, Herrsch. Sch. 1061, B70.

Petitionary letter. 1775. Signed: Anna Maria Grinauerin. Ref.: OOLA_1775r_Weinberg, Herrsch. Sch. 1061, B70.

Petitionary letter. 1776. Signed: Katharina Buchhueberin. Ref.: OOLA_1776r_Weinberg, Herrsch. Sch. 1061, B70.

Petitionary letter. 1777. Signed: Johann georg Bainhakel. Ref.: OOLA_1777r_Zunftarchivalien, Sch. 68.

Petitionary letter. 1778. Signed: Catharina Marböckin. Ref.: OOLA_1778r_Weinberg, Herrsch. Sch. 1061, B70.

Petitionary letter. 1781. Signed: Georg Weningeder. Ref.: OOLA_1781r_a_Weinberg, Herrsch. Sch. 1061, B70.

Petitionary letter. 1781. Signed: Franz Wissinger. Ref.: OOLA_1781r_b_Weinberg, Herrsch. Sch. 1061, B70.

Petitionary letter. 1782. Signed: Johann Wagner. Ref.: STLA_1782r_Lamberg, Fam. K. 177, H. 764.

Petitionary letter. 1783. Signed: Martin Neuer. Ref.: STLA_1783w_St. Lambrecht, Stiftsarchiv, K. 149 H. 70.

Petitionary letter. 1784. Signed: Rosalia Hofstetterin. Ref.: OOLA_1784w_Weinberg, Herrsch. Sch. 1061, B70.

Petitionary letter. 1786. Signed: Adam Wascherbauer. Ref.: OOLA_1786w_Weinberg, Herrsch. Sch. 1061, B70.

Petitionary letter. 1786. Signed: Johann Georg Zowalt. Ref.: STLA_1786w_Lamberg, Fam. K. 177, H. 764_M.

Petitionary letter. 1787. Signed: Joseph Würthenstetter. Ref.: STLA_1787w_Rothenfels, Herrsch. K. 211, H. 730.

Petitionary letter. 1788. Signed: Lorenz Berghamer. Ref.: STLA_1788w_a_Lamberg, Fam. K. 177, H. 764.

Petitionary letter. 1788. Signed: Franz Karl Nigauer. Ref.: STLA_1788w_b_Lamberg, Fam. K. 177 H. 764.

Petitionary letter. 1792. Signed: Franz Wisbaur. Ref.: OOLA_1792w_Obernberg, Herrsch. Nr. 878, XX, 55.

Petitionary letter. 1792. Signed: Martin <gap quantity="1" unit="words"/>. Ref.: STLA_1792w_Rothenfels, Herrsch. K. 211, H. 730.

Petitionary letter. 1796. Signed: Johann Stampler. Ref.: STLA_1796w_Lamberg, Fam. K. 192, H. 823.

Petitionary letter. 1797. Signed: Fiman Judt. Ref.: STLA_1797w_Saurau, Fam. K. 154, H. 1479.

Petitionary letter. 1801. Signed: Patritz Leitner. Ref.: STLA_1801w_Oberradkersburg, Herrsch. K. 150, H. 564.

Petitionary letter. 1801. Signed: Ingnaz Grishoffer. Ref.: STLA_1801w_Pflindsberg, Herrsch. K. 25, H. 167.

Petitionary letter. 1802. Signed: Johann Gandl. Ref.: STLA_1802w_Pflindsberg, Herrsch. K. 25, H. 161.

Petitionary letter. 1803. Signed: Mathias Gaiswinkler. Ref.: STLA_1803w_Pflindsberg, Herrsch. K. 25, H. 159.

Petitionary letter. 1804. Signed: Gregor Reich. Ref.: STLA_1804w_Oberradkersburg, Herrsch. K. 150, H. 564.

Petitionary letter. 1806. Signed: Michl Hessenberger. Ref.: STLA_1806w_Pflindsberg, Herrsch. K. 25, H. 173.

Petitionary letter. 1810. Signed: Georg Bellän. Ref.: STLA_1810w_Oberradkersburg, Herrsch. K. 150, H. 564_M.

Petitionary letter. 1811. Signed: Andree Neuhold. Ref.: STLA_1811w_Oberradkersburg, Herrsch. K. 150, H. 564_M.

Petitionary letter. 1812. Signed: Michael Stadler. Ref.: OOLA_1812w_Vöcklabruck, Stadtarchiv Sch. 29, Nr. 15_M.

Petitionary letter. 1820. Signed: Joh. Ebner. Ref.: STLA_1820w_Rothenfels, Herrsch. K. 211, H. 730.

Petitionary letter. 1822. Signed: Joseph and Theresia Bruckmüller. Ref.: OOLA_1822w_a_Neuhaus, Herrsch. Nr. 149, VI.

Petitionary letter. 1822. Signed: Joseph und Theresia Bruckmühler. Ref.: OOLA_1822w_b_Neuhaus, Herrsch. Nr. 149, VI.

Petitionary letter. 1824. Signed: Mathäus Meizner. Ref.: OOLA_1824w_Vöcklabruck, Stadtarchiv Sch. 29, Nr. 29_M.

Petitionary letter. 1824. Signed: Michael Kuttner. Ref.: OOLA_1824w_Vöcklabruck, Stadtarchiv Sch. 29, Nr. 29.

Petitionary letter. 1825. Signed: Franz Schachiger. Ref.: OOLA_1825w_Neuhaus, Herrsch. Nr. 149, VI, 19_M.

Petitionary letter. 1828. Signed: Johann Freÿsmuth. Ref.: STLA_1828w_Pflindsberg, Herrsch. K. 24, H. 155.

Petitionary letter. 1829. Signed: Stephan Baumgartner. Ref.: STLA_1829w_Pflindsberg, Herrsch. K. 24, H. 141_M.

Petitionary letter. 1830. Signed: Johann Pfifferling. Ref.: OOLA_1830p_Ort, Herrsch. Sch. 85 VI.

[Popowitsch, Johann Siegmund Valentin]. 1750. Untersuchungen vom Meere, die auf Veranlassung einer Schrift, DE COLVMNIS HERCVLIS, welche der hochberühmte Professor in Altorf, Herr Christ. Gottl. Schwarz, herausgegeben, nebst andern zu derselben gehörigen Anmerkungen, von einem Liebhaber der Naturlehre und der Philologie, vorgetragen werden. Frankfurt und Leipzig. Available at: https://books.google.co.uk/books?id=L5A_AAAAcAAJ&printsec=frontcover#v=onepage&q&f=false [accessed 26.04.2017].

Popowitsch, Johann Siegmund Valentin. 1754a. Die nothwendigsten Anfangsgründe der Teutschen Sprachkunst zum Gebrauche der Österreichischen Schulen herausgegeben. Wien: Zwei Brüder Grundt. [short version]. Available at: https://books.google.co.uk/books?id=Dd5IAAAAcAAJ&printsec=frontcover#v=onepage&q&f=false [accessed 26.04.2017].

Popowitsch, Johann Siegmund Valentin. 1754b. Die nothwendigsten Anfangsgründe der Teutschen Sprachkunst zum Gebrauche der Österreichischen Schulen auf allerhöchsten Befehl ausgefertiget. Wien: Zwei Brüder Grundt. [extended version]. Available at: https://books.google.co.uk/books?id=3g1NAAAAcAAJ&pg=PA1&dq#v=onepage&q&f=false [accessed 26.04.2017].

Popowitsch, Johann Siegmund Valentin. 1780. Versuch einer Vereinigung der Mundarten von Teutschland als eine Einleitung zu einem vollständigen Teutschen Wörterbuche mit Bestimmungen der Wörter und beträchtlichen Beiträgen zur Naturgeschichte aus den hinterlassenen Schriften des berühmten Herrn Prof. Joh. Siegm. Val. Popowitsch. Wien: Joseph Edlen von Kurzböck. Available at: https://books.google.co.uk/books?id=KN5IAAAAcAAJ&printsec=frontcover#v=onepage&q&f=false [accessed 26.04.2017].

Sonnenfels, Joseph von. 1761. Ankündigung einer deutschen Gesellschaft in Wien. In der ersten feyerlichen Versammlung den 2. Jäner 1761 abgelesen. Wien: Joseph Kurzböcken. Available at: https://books.google.co.uk/books?id=Q-ZOAAAAcAAJ&pg=PA1&dq#v=onepage&q&f=false [accessed 26.04.2017].

Sonnenfels, Joseph von. 1784. Über den Geschäftsstil. Die ersten Grundlinien für angehende österreichische Kanzleybeamten. Wien: Joseph Edler von Kurzbek. Available at: https://books.google.co.uk/books?id=Y8tOAAAAcAAJ&printsec=frontcover#v=onepage&q&f=false [accessed 26.04.2017].

Soria, Paul Graf Amor von. 1772. 'Abhandlung Von den Hauptfehlern der österreichischen Mundart.' In: *Jugendfrüchte des k. k. Theresianums*. Band 1. Wien: Joseph Kurzböck, 227–236.

TEI Consortium. 2017. *TEI P5: Guidelines for Electronic Text Encoding and Interchange*. Available at: http://www.tei-c.org/Guidelines/P5/ [accessed 26.04.2017].

Teutsches Namen- oder Lehrbüchl. Der Lieben Jugend zum Besten auf solche Art eingerichtet / daß hierdurch im ersten Theil sie zum richtigen Grund des Buchstabiren / oder Sylben-theilen / recht aussprechen / und lesen: Im anderē aber zur Rechtschreib- und Wörterforschung angewiesen werden kan. c. 1750. Wien: Maria Eva Schilgin. BMB: JH 39.

Über den gegenwärtigen Zustand des deutschen Schulwesens in den deutschen Erblanden [...], nebst Bemerkungen, was noch zu tun wäre, um das Schulwesen [...] in vollkommenen Stand zu setzen. 1777. Österreichisches Staatsarchiv: AVA Unterricht StHK Teil 1, K. 87.

Wiennerisches Diarium. Enthaltend Alles Denkwürdige / so von Tag zu Tag so wohl in dieser Käyserlichen Residentz=Stadt Wienn selbsten sich zugetragen / als auch von andern Orthen auß der gantzen Welt allda nachrichtlich eingeloffen / Mit diesem besondern Anhang / Daß auch alle die jenige Persohnen / welche wochentlich allhier gestorben / hingegen was von Vornehmen gebohren / dann copuliret worden / ferner anhero und von dannen verreiset / darinnen befindlich. 08.08.1703. Wien: [Schönwetter]. Available at: http://anno.onb.ac.at/cgi-content/anno?aid=wrz&datum=17030808&seite=1&zoom=33 [accessed 26.04.2017].

Wienerisches Diarium. 30.04.1729. Wien: Johann Peter v. Ghelen. Available at: http://anno.onb.ac.at/cgi-content/anno?aid=wrz&datum=17290430&zoom=33 [accessed 26.04.2017].

Wienerisches Diarium. 01.07.1744. Wien: Joh. Peter v. Ghelen. Available at: http://anno.onb.ac.at/cgi-content/anno?aid=wrz&datum=17440701&zoom=33 [accessed 26.04.2017].

Wienerisches Diarium. 02.07.1749. Wien: Joh. Peter v. Ghelen. Available at:
http://anno.onb.ac.at/cgi-content/anno?aid=wrz&datum=17490702&zoom=33 [accessed
26.04.2017].

Wienerisches Diarium. 03.07.1754. Wien: Joh. Peter v. Ghelen. Available at:
http://anno.onb.ac.at/cgi-content/anno?aid=wrz&datum=17540703&zoom=33 [accessed
26.04.2017].

Wienerisches Diarium. 04.07.1759. Wien: von Ghelen. Available at: http://anno.onb.ac.at/cgi-
content/anno?aid=wrz&datum=17590704&zoom=33 [accessed 26.04.2017].

Wienerisches Diarium. 04.07.1764. Wien: von Ghelen. Available at: http://anno.onb.ac.at/cgi-
content/anno?aid=wrz&datum=17640704&zoom=33 [accessed 26.04.2017].

Wienerisches Diarium. 01.07.1769. Wien: von Ghelischen Erben. Available at:
http://anno.onb.ac.at/cgi-content/anno?aid=wrz&datum=17690701&zoom=33 [accessed
26.04.2017].

Wienerisches Diarium. 02.07.1774. Wien: von Ghelenschen Erben. Available at:
http://anno.onb.ac.at/cgi-content/anno?aid=wrz&datum=17740702&zoom=33 [accessed
26.04.2017].

Wienerisches Diarium. 03.07.1779. Wien: von Ghelenschen Erben. Available at:
http://anno.onb.ac.at/cgi-content/anno?aid=wrz&datum=17790703&zoom=33 [accessed
26.04.2017].

Wiener Zeitung. 03.07.1784. Wien: von Ghelenschen Erben. Available at: http://anno.onb.ac.at/cgi-
content/anno?aid=wrz&datum=17840703&zoom=33 [accessed 26.04.2017].

Wiener Zeitung. 01.07.1789. Wien: von Ghelenschen Erben. Available at: http://anno.onb.ac.at/cgi-
content/anno?aid=wrz&datum=17890701&zoom=33 [accessed 26.04.2017].

Wiener Zeitung. 02.07.1794. Wien: von Ghelenschen Erben. Available at: http://anno.onb.ac.at/cgi-
content/anno?aid=wrz&datum=17940702&zoom=33 [accessed 26.04.2017].

Wiener Zeitung. 03.07.1799. Wien: von Ghelenschen Erben. Available at: http://anno.onb.ac.at/cgi-
content/anno?aid=wrz&datum=17990703&zoom=33 [accessed 26.04.2017].

Wiener Zeitung. 04.07.1804. Wien: von Ghelenschen Erben. Available at: http://anno.onb.ac.at/cgi-
content/anno?aid=wrz&datum=18040704&zoom=33 [accessed 26.04.2017].

Wiener Zeitung. 01.07.1809. Wien: von Ghelenschen Erben. Available at: http://anno.onb.ac.at/cgi-
content/anno?aid=wrz&datum=18090701&zoom=33 [accessed 26.04.2017].

Wiener Zeitung. 03.07.1809. Wien: von Ghelenschen Erben. Available at: http://anno.onb.ac.at/cgi-
content/anno?aid=wrz&datum=18090703&zoom=33 [accessed 26.04.2017].

Wiener Zeitung. 01.07.1814. Wien: von Ghelenschen Erben. Available at: http://anno.onb.ac.at/cgi-
content/anno?aid=wrz&datum=18140701&zoom=33 [accessed 26.04.2017].

Wiener Zeitung. 01.07.1819. Wien: von Ghelenschen Erben. Available at: http://anno.onb.ac.at/cgi-
content/anno?aid=wrz&datum=18190701&zoom=33 [accessed 26.04.2017].

Wiener Zeitung. 01.07.1824. Wien: von Ghelenschen Erben. Available at: http://anno.onb.ac.at/cgi-
content/anno?aid=wrz&datum=18240701&zoom=33 [accessed 26.04.2017].

Wiener Zeitung. 01.07.1829. Wien: von Ghelenschen Erben. Available at: http://anno.onb.ac.at/cgi-
content/anno?aid=wrz&datum=18290701&zoom=33 [accessed 26.04.2017].

Wiener Zeitung. 01.07.1834. Wien: von Ghelenschen Erben. Available at: http://anno.onb.ac.at/cgi-
content/anno?aid=wrz&datum=18340701&zoom=33 [accessed 26.04.2017].

Zöllner, Johann Friedrich. 1796. 'Über die Deutsche Aussprache.' In: *Beiträge zur deutschen
Sprachkunde. Vorgelesen in der königlichen Akademie der Wissenschaften zu Berlin.* Zweyte
Sammlung. Berlin, 204–216.

Secondary sources

Ágel, Vilmos & Mathilde Hennig (eds). 2006a. Grammatik aus Nähe und Distanz. Theorie und Praxis am Beispiel von Nähetexten 1650–2000. Tübingen: Niemeyer.

Ágel, Vilmos & Mathilde Hennig. 2006b. 'Theorie des Nähe- und Distanzsprechens.' In: Vilmos Ágel & Mathilde Hennig (eds), *Grammatik aus Nähe und Distanz. Theorie und Praxis am Beispiel von Nähetexten 1650–2000*. Tübingen: Niemeyer, 3–32.

Ágel, Vilmos & Mathilde Hennig. 2006c. 'Praxis des Nähe- und Distanzsprechens.' In: Vilmos Ágel & Mathilde Hennig (eds), *Grammatik aus Nähe und Distanz. Theorie und Praxis am Beispiel von Nähetexten 1650–2000*. Tübingen: Niemeyer, 33–74.

Ammon, Ulrich. 2003. 'On the Social Forces that Determine what is Standard in a Language and on Conditions of Successful Implementation.' In: *Sociolinguistica* 17, 1–10.

Barton, David & Nigel Hall. 1999. 'Introduction.' In: David Barton & Nigel Hall (eds), *Letter Writing as a Social Practice*. (Studies in Written Language and Literacy 9). Amsterdam: John Benjamins, 1–14.

Besch, Werner. 1983. 'Dialekt, Schreibdialekt, Schriftsprache, Standardsprache. Exemplarische Skizze ihrer historischen Ausprägung im Deutschen.' In: Werner Besch, Ulrich Knoop, Wolfgang Putschke, Herbert E. Wiegand (eds), *Dialektologie. Ein Handbuch zur deutschen und allgemeinen Dialektforschung*. 2. Halbband. (HSK 1/2). Berlin: De Gruyter, 961–990.

Besch, Werner. 1987. *Die Entstehung der deutschen Schriftsprache: Bisherige Erklärungsmodelle – neuester Forschungsstand.* (Vorträge / Rheinisch-Westfälische Akademie der Wissenschaften: Geisteswissenschaften G 290). Opladen: Westdeutscher Verlag.

Boyer, Ludwig. 2002. 'Johann Ignaz Felbigers Fibeln und ihr Beitrag zur Alphabetisierung in Österreich.' In: Arnold Grömminger (ed.), *Geschichte der Fibel*. (Beiträge zur Geschichte des Deutschunterrichts 50). Frankfurt am Main: Peter Lang, 251–271.

Boyer, Ludwig. 2004. Das Prunk ABC Buch für Maximilian I. Österreich älteste Fibel (um 1466). Eine pädagogisch-didaktische Studie. Wien: öbv & hpt.

Brüggemann, Theodor. 1975. 'ABC-Buch.' In: Klaus Doderer (ed.), *Lexikon der Kinder- und Jugendliteratur*. Band 1. Basel: Beltz, 1–7.

Büttner, Peter O. 2015. *Schreiben lehren um 1800.* Hannover: Wehrhahn Verlag.

Czeike, Felix. 1992–1997. *Historisches Lexikon Wien*. Band 5. Wien: Kremayr & Scheriau. Available at: http://www.digital.wienbibliothek.at/wbrobv/content/pageview/1115553 [accessed 26.04. 2017].

Davies, Winifred & Nils Langer. 2014. 'Die Sprachnormfrage im Deutschunterricht: das Dilemma der Lehrenden.' In: Albrecht Plewnia & Andreas Witt (eds), *Sprachverfall? Dynamik – Wandel – Variation*. (IDS Jahrbuch 2013). Berlin: De Gruyter, 299–321.

Dekker, Rudolf. 2002. 'Introduction.' In: Rudolf Dekker (ed.), *Egodocuments and History. Autobiographical writing in its social context since the Middle Ages*. (Publicaties van de Faculteit der Historische en Kunstwetenschappen Maatschappijgeschiedenis 38). Hilversum: Verloren, 7–20.

Deumert, Ana & Wim Vandenbussche (eds). 2003. *Germanic standardizations: past to present.* (Impact: Studies in language and society 18). Amsterdam: John Benjamins.

Döring, Detlef. 2002. Die Geschichte der Deutschen Gesellschaft in Leipzig. Von der Gründung bis in die ersten Jahre des Seniorats Johann Christoph Gottscheds. (Frühe Neuzeit 70). Tübingen: May Niemeyer.

Durrell, Martin, Astrid Ensslin & Paul Bennett. 2008. 'Zeitungen und Sprachausgleich im 17. und 18. Jahrhundert.' In: *Zeitschrift für deutsche Philologie* 127, Sonderheft, 263–279.

Durrell, Martin. 2016. 'Textsortenspezifische und regionale Unterschiede bei der Standardisierung der deutschen Sprache.' In: Sarah Kwekkeboom & Sandra Waldenberger (eds),

PerspektivWechsel oder: Die Wiederentdeckung der Philologie. Band 1. Berlin: Schmidt, 211–232.

Durrell, Martin. forthcoming. 'Zeitungssprache und Literatursprache bei der Ausbildung standardsprachlicher Normen im Deutschen im 17. und 18. Jahrhundert. Ein Vergleich anhand eines repräsentativen Korpus.' In: Oliver Pfefferkorn, Jörg Riecke & Britt-Marie Schuster (eds), *Die Zeitung als Medium in der neueren Sprachgeschichte: Korpora – Analyse – Wirkung*. (Lingua Historica Germanica 15). Berlin: De Gruyter.

Elspaß, Stephan. 2002. 'Standard German in the 19th century? (Counter-) evidence from the private correspondence of 'ordinary people'.' In: Andrew R. Linn & Nicola McLelland (eds), *Standardization. Studies from the Germanic languages*. (Current Issues in Linguistic Theory 235). Amsterdam: John Benjamins, 43–65.

Elspaß, Stephan. 2005. Sprachgeschichte von unten. Untersuchungen zum geschriebenen Alltagsdeutsch im 19. Jahrhundert. (Germanistische Linguistik 263). Tübingen: Max Niemeyer.

Elspaß, Stephan, Nils Langer, Joachim Scharloth, Wim Vandenbussche (eds). 2007. *Germanic Language Histories 'from Below' (1700–2000)*. (Studia Linguistica Germanica 86). Berlin: De Gruyter.

Elspaß, Stephan. 2007. 'A twofold view 'from below': New perspectives on language histories and language historiographies.' In: Stephan Elspaß, Nils Langer, Joachim Scharloth, Wim Vandenbussche (eds), *Germanic language histories 'from below' (1700–2000)*. (Studia Linguistica Germanica 86). Berlin: De Gruyter, 3–9.

Elspaß, Stephan. 2012. 'The use of private letters and diaries in sociolinguistic investigation.' In: Juan Manuel Hernández-Campoy & Juan Camilo Conde-Silvestre (eds), *The Handbook of Historical Sociolinguistics*. Oxford: Wiley-Blackwell, 156–169.

Engelbrecht, Helmut. 1984. Geschichte des österreichischen Bildungswesens. Erziehung und Unterricht auf dem Boden Österreichs. Band 3: Von der frühen Aufklärung bis zum Vormärz. Wien: ÖBV.

Fairman, Tony. 1999. 'English Pauper Letters 1800–34, and the English Language.' In: David Barton & Nigel Hall (eds), *Letter Writing as a Social Practice*. (Studies in Written Language and Literacy 9). Amsterdam: John Benjamins, 63–82.

Fairman, Tony. 2003. 'Letters of the English labouring classes and the English language, 1800–34.' In: Marina Dossena & Charles Jones (eds), *Insights into Late Modern English*. (Linguistic Insights: Studies in Language and Communication 7). Bern: Peter Lang, 265–282.

Fairman, Tony. 2007. ''Lower-order' letters, schooling, and the English language, 1795 to 1834.' In: Stephan Elspaß, Nils Langer, Joachim Scharloth, Wim Vandenbussche (eds), *Germanic language histories 'from below' (1700–2000)*. (Studia Linguistica Germanica 86). Berlin: De Gruyter 31–43.

Faninger, Kurt. 1996. *Johann Siegmund Valentin Popowitsch. Ein österreichischer Grammatiker des 18. Jahrhunderts*. (Schriften zur deutschen Sprache in Österreich 18). Frankfurt am Main: Peter Lang.

Faulstich, Katja. 2008. *Konzepte des Hochdeutschen. Der Sprachnormierungsdiskurs im 18. Jahrhundert*. (Studia Linguistica Germanica 91). Berlin: De Gruyter.

Fries, Udo, Hans Martin Lehmann, Beni Ruef, Peter Schnieder, Patrick Studer, Caren auf dem Keller, Beat Nietlispach, Sandra Engler, Sabine Hensel & Franziska Zeller. 2004. *Zen: Zurich English Newspaper Corpus, Version 1.0*. Zürich: University of Zürich. Available at: http://www.es.uzh.ch/en/Subsites/Projects/zencorpus.html [accessed 26.04.2017].

Frühmann, Norbert. 2010. ''Die Schule nimmt uns unsere Kinder weg." Maria Theresias mutiger Schritt zur schulischen Bildung des Volkes.' In: *Fleißbild, Rohrstab, Eselsbank. Eine Zeitreise durch 400 Jahre Schulgeschichte im OÖ. Schulmuseum Bad Leonfelden*. Bad Leonfelden: Eigenverlag, 21–25.

Gardt, Andreas. 1994. *Sprachreflexion in Barock und Frühaufklärung. Entwürfe von Böhme bis Leibniz*. (Quellen und Forschungen zur Sprach- und Kulturgeschichte der germanischen Völker N.F. 108). Berlin: De Gruyter.

Gardt, Andreas. 1999. Geschichte der Sprachwissenschaft in Deutschland. Vom Mittelalter bis ins 20. Jahrhundert. (De Gruyter Studienbuch). Berlin: De Gruyter.

GerManC, 1650–1800. Compiled by Martin Durrell, Paul Bennett, Silke Scheible & Richard J. Whitt. 2008–2012. School of Languages, Linguistics and Cultures in the University of Manchester. Available at: http://www.llc.manchester.ac.uk/research/projects/germanc/files/ [accessed 26.04. 2017].

Graser, Helmut & B. Ann Tlusty. 2012. 'Sixteenth-Century Street Songs and Language History 'From Below'.' In: Nils Langer, Steffan Davies & Wim Vandenbussche (eds), *Language and History, Linguistics and Historiography. Interdisciplinary Approaches*. (Studies in Historical Linguistics 9). Bern: Peter Lang, 363–388.

Grateau, Philippe. 2001. *Les Cahiers de doléances, une relecture culturelle*. Rennes: Presses Universitaires de Rennes.

Grosse, Siegfried. 1989. 'Vorbemerkung.' In: Siegfried Grosse, Martin Grimberg, Thomas Hölscher, Jörg Karweick, "Denn das Schreiben gehört nicht zu meiner täglichen Beschäftigung." Der Alltag kleiner Leute in Bittschriften, Briefen und Berichten aus dem 19. Jahrhundert. Ein Lesebuch. Bonn: J.H.W. Dietz Nachf., 9–15.

Habermann, Mechthild. 1997. 'Das sogenannte 'Lutherische e'. Zum Streit um einen armen Buchstaben.' In: *Sprachwissenschaft* 22, 435–477.

Haugen, Einar. 1966. 'Dialect, Language, Nation.' In: *American Anthropologist* 68/4, 922–935.

Haugen, Einar. 1994. 'Standardization.' In: R. E. Asher & J. M. Y. Simpson (eds), *The Encyclopedia of Language and Linguistics*. Vol. 8. Oxford: Pergamon Press, 4340–4342.

Havinga, Anna D. & Nils Langer (eds). 2015. *Invisible Languages in the Nineteenth Century*. (Historical Sociolinguistics 2). Bern: Peter Lang.

Havinga, Anna D. 2015. 'Germanising Austria: The Invisibilisation of East Upper German in Eighteenth- and Nineteenth-Century Austria.' In: Anna D. Havinga & Nils Langer (eds), *Invisible Languages in the Nineteenth Century*. (Historical Sociolinguistics 2). Bern: Peter Lang, 257–279.

Hosokawa, Hirofumi. 2014. *Zeitungssprache und Mündlichkeit. Soziopragmatische Untersuchungen zur Sprache in Zeitungen um 1850*. (Kieler Forschungen zur Sprachwissenschaft 4). Frankfurt am Main: Peter Lang.

Jaklin, Ingeborg. 2003. Das österreichische Schulbuch im 18. Jahrhundert. Aus dem Wiener Verlag Trattner und dem Schulbuchverlag. (Buchforschung. Beiträge zum Buchwesen in Österreich 3). Wien: Praesens.

Jakob, Kurt. 2003. *Lexikon der Salzwirtschaft*. Available at: http://members.kabsi.at/seeau/Encyclopaedia/Kompendien/Lexikon-Salzwirtschaft.htm#S [accessed 26.04.2017].

Janda, Richard D. & Brian D. Joseph. 2003. 'On language, change, and language change – or, of history, linguistics, and historical linguistics.' In: Brian D. Joseph & Richard D. Janda (eds), *The Handbook of Historical Linguistics*. Oxford: Blackwell, 2–180.

Jellinek, Max Hermann. 1913. *Geschichte der neuhochdeutschen Grammatik. Von den Anfängen bis auf Adelung*. (Germanische Bibliothek. Untersuchungen und Texte 7). Band 1. Heidelberg: Winter.

Joseph, Brian D. 2012. 'Historical Linguistics and Sociolinguistics: Strange Bedfellows or Natural Friends?' In: Nils Langer, Steffan Davies & Wim Vandenbussche (eds), *Language and History, Linguistics and Historiography. Interdisciplinary Approaches*. (Studies in Historical Linguistics 9). Bern: Peter Lang, 67–88.

Josten, Dirk. 1976. Sprachvorbild und Sprachnorm im Urteil des 16. und 17. Jahrhunderts. Sprachlandschaftliche Prioritäten, Sprachautoritäten, sprachimmanente Argumentationen. (Arbeiten zur mittleren deutschen Literatur und Sprache 3). Bern: Peter Lang.

Karweick, Jörg. 1989. '"Vertröste mich hochgeneigter Willfahrung." Bittschriften.' In: Siegfried Grosse, Martin Grimberg, Thomas Hölscher, Jörg Karweick, *"Denn das Schreiben gehört nicht zu meiner täglichen Beschäftigung." Der Alltag kleiner Leute in Bittschriften, Briefen und Berichten aus dem 19. Jahrhundert. Ein Lesebuch.* Bonn: J.H.W. Dietz Nachf., 25–68.

Klenk, Marion. 1997. Sprache im Kontext sozialer Lebenswelt. Eine Untersuchung zur Arbeiterschriftsprache im 19. Jahrhundert. (Germanistische Linguistik 181). Tübingen: Niemeyer.

Klippel, Diethelm. 1999. 'Reasonable Aims of Civil Society: Concerns of the State in German Political Theory in the Eighteenth and Early Nineteenth Centuries.' In: John Brewer & Eckhart Hellmuth (eds), *Rethinking Leviathan. The Eighteenth-Century State in Britain and Germany.* (Studies of the German Historical Institute London). Oxford: Oxford University Press, 71–98.

Koch, Peter & Wulf Oesterreicher. 1985. 'Sprache der Nähe – Sprache der Distanz. Mündlichkeit und Schriftlichkeit im Spannungsfeld von Sprachtheorie und Sprachgeschichte.' In: *Romanistisches Jahrbuch* 36/85, 15–43.

Koch, Peter & Wulf Oesterreicher. 1994. 'Schriftlichkeit und Sprache.' In: Hartmut Günther & Otto Ludwig (eds), *Schrift und Schriftlichkeit. Ein interdisziplinäres Handbuch internationaler Forschung.* (Handbücher zur Sprach- und Kommunikationswissenschaft 10). Berlin: De Gruyter, 587–604.

König, Werner. 1978. dtv-Atlas zur deutschen Sprache. Tafeln und Texte. Mit Mundartkarten. München: dtv.

Konopka, Marek. 1996. *Strittige Erscheinungen der deutschen Syntax im 18. Jahrhundert.* (Germanistische Linguistik 173). Tübingen: Max Niemeyer.

Labov, William. 1994. *Principles of Linguistic Change.* Vol. 1: *Internal factors.* (Language in Society 20). Oxford: Blackwell.

Langer, Nils. 2001. Linguistic Purism in Action. How auxiliary tun was stigmatized in Early New High German. (Studia Linguistica Germanica 60). Berlin: De Gruyter.

Langer, Nils. 2012. 'Finding non-dominant languages in the nineteenth century – problems and potentials from historical sociolinguistics.' In: Rudolf Muhr (ed.), *Non-dominant varieties of pluricentric languages. Getting the picture.* In memory of Michael Clyne. In Collaboration with Catrin Norrby, Leo Kretzenbacher, Carla Amorós. (Österreichisches Deutsch – Sprache der Gegenwart 14). Wien: Peter Lang, 83–106.

Langer, Nils & Anna D. Havinga. 2015. 'Invisible Languages in Historical Sociolinguistics: A Conceptual Outline, With Examples from the German-Danish Borderlands.' In: Anna D. Havinga & Nils Langer (eds), *Invisible Languages in the Nineteenth Century.* (Historical Sociolinguistics 2). Bern: Peter Lang, 1–34.

Leweling, Beate. 2005. Reichtum, Reinigkeit und Glanz – Sprachkritische Konzeptionen in der Sprachreflexion des 18. Jahrhunderts. Ein Beitrag zur Sprachbewusstseinsgeschichte. (Germanistische Arbeiten zu Sprache und Kulturgeschichte 46). Frankfurt am Main: Peter Lang.

Lodge, Anthony R. 2004. *A Sociolinguistic History of Parisian French.* Cambridge: Cambridge University Press.

Macha, Jürgen. 2014. Der konfessionelle Faktor in der deutschen Sprachgeschichte der Frühen Neuzeit. (Religion und Politik 6). Würzburg: Ergon.

Mannheimer Korpus für Historische Zeitungen und Zeitschriften. Compiled by IDS-Mannheim. 2013. Available at: http://repos.ids-mannheim.de/fedora/objects/clarin-ids:mkhz1.00000/datastreams/CMDI/content [accessed 26.04.2017].

Mattheier, Klaus J. 1988. 'Nationalsprachenentwicklung, Sprachenstandardisierung und Historische Soziolinguistik.' In: *Sociolinguistica* 2, 1–9.

Mattheier, Klaus J. 1991. ''Gemeines Deutsch' – ein Sinnbild der sprachlichen Einigung.' In: Eijiro Iwasaki & Yoshinori Shichiji (eds), *Begegnungen mit dem 'Fremden'. Grenzen – Traditionen – Vergleiche*. Akten des VIII. Internationalen Germanisten-Kongresses Tokyo 1990. Band 3. *Sprachgeschichte. Sprachkontakte im germanischen Sprachraum*. München: Iudicium, 39–48.

Mattheier, Klaus J. 2003. 'German.' In: Ana Deumert & Wim Vandenbussche (eds), *Germanic Standardizations. Past to Present*. (Impact: Studies in language and society 18). Amsterdam: John Benjamins, 211–244.

Mauthe, Gabriele. 2008. 'Abecedarium, ABC-Bücher, Buchstabierbüchlien – Wie und womit Kinder lesen lernten. Kostbare Beispiele aus der Österreichischen Nationalbibliothek.' In: Ernst Seibert & Susanne Blumesberger (eds), *Kinderliteratur als kulturelles Gedächtnis. Beiträge zur historischen Schulbuch-, Kinder- und Jugendliteraturforschung I*. (Kinder- und Jugendliteraturforschung in Österreich 11). Wien: Praesens, 177–191.

McLelland, Nicola. 2011. *J.G. Schottelius's* Ausführliche Arbeit von der Teutschen HaubtSprache (1663) *and its place in early modern European vernacular language study*. (Publications of the Philological Society 44). Oxford: Wiley-Blackwell.

Messerli, Alfred. 2002. Lesen und Schreiben 1700 bis 1900. Untersuchungen zur Durchsetzung der Literalität in der Schweiz. (Germanistische Linguistik 229). Tübingen: Max Niemeyer.

Mihm, Arend. 1998. 'Arbeitersprache und gesprochene Sprache im 19. Jahrhundert.' In: Dieter Cherubim, Klaus J. Mattheier & Siegfried Grosse (eds), *Sprache und Bürgerliche Nation. Beiträge zur deutschen und europäischen Sprachgeschichte des 19. Jahrhunderts*. Berlin: De Gruyter, 282–316.

Moosmüller, Sylvia. 1995. 'Evaluation of Language Use in Public Discourse: Language Attitudes in Austria.' In: Patrick Stevenson (ed.), *The German Language and the Real World. Sociolinguistic, Cultural, and Pragmatic Perspectives on Contemporary German*. Oxford: Clarendon Press, 259–280.

Mraz, Gerda. 1980. 'Nachwort.' In: Johann Balthasar von Antesperg, *Das Josephinische Erzherzogliche A.B.C. Oder Namenbüchlein*. Wien: Johann Ignatz Heyinger. Nachdruck des Widmungsexemplars von 1741 [1744] im Landesmuseum Joanneum in Graz. Dortmund: Harenberg, 55–88.

Nevalainen, Terttu & Helena Raumolin-Brunberg. 2012. 'Historical Sociolinguistics: Origins, Motivations, and Paradigms.' In: Juan Manuel Hernández-Campoy & Juan Camilo Conde-Silvestre (eds), *The Handbook of Historical Sociolinguistics*. Oxford: Wiley-Blackwell, 22–40.

Nobels, Judith. 2013. (Extra)Ordinary letters. A view from below on seventeenth-century Dutch. Utrecht: LOT.

Nübling, Damaris, Antje Dammel, Janet Duke & Renata Szczepaniak. 2013. Historische Sprachwissenschaft des Deutschen. Eine Einführung in die Prinzipien des Sprachwandels. Tübingen: Narr.

Nubola, Cecilia. 2005. 'Die ''via supplicationis'' in den italienischen Staaten der frühen Neuzeit (15.–18. Jahrhundert).' In: Cecilia Nubola & Andreas Würgler (eds), *Bittschriften und Gravamina. Politik, Verwaltung und Justiz in Europa (14.–18. Jahrhundert)*. (Schriften des Italienisch-Deutschen Historischen Instituts in Trient 19). Berlin: Duncker & Humblot, 53–92.

Piirainen, Ilpo Tapani. 1980. 'Deutsche Standardsprache des 17./18. Jahrhunderts.' In: Hans Peter Althaus, Helmut Henne & Herbert Ernst Wiegand (eds), *Lexikon der germanistischen Linguistik*. Tübingen: Max Niemeyer, 598–603.

Polenz, Peter von. 1978. *Geschichte der deutschen Sprache*. Berlin: De Gruyter.

Polenz, Peter von. 1994. Deutsche Sprachgeschichte vom Spätmittelalter bis zur Gegenwart. Band 2: 17. und 18. Jahrhundert. Berlin: De Gruyter.

Reichmann, Oskar, unter Mitwirkung von Christiane Burgi, Martin Kaufhold & Claudia Schäfer. 1988. 'Zur Vertikalisierung des Varietätenspektrums in der jüngeren Sprachgeschichte des Deutschen.' In: Horst H. Munske, Peter von Polenz, Oskar Reichmann, Reiner Hildebrandt (eds), *Deutscher Wortschatz. Lexikologische Studien. Ludwig Erich Schmitt zum 80. Geburtstag von seinen Marburger Schülern.* Berlin: De Gruyter, 151–180.

Reichmann, Oskar & Klaus-Peter Wegera. 1993. 'Schreibung und Lautung.' In: Oskar Reichmann & Klaus-Peter Wegera (eds), *Frühneuhochdeutsche Grammatik.* (Sammlung kurzer Grammatiken germanischer Dialekte 12). Tübingen: Niemeyer, 13–163.

Reiffenstein, Ingo (ed.). 2005. Fort mit Dir nach Paris! Mozart und seine Mutter auf der Reise nach Paris. Salzburg: Jung & Jung.

Romaine, Suzanne. 1988. 'Historical sociolinguistics. Problems and methodology.' In: Ulrich Ammon, Norbert Dittmar, Klaus J. Mattheier & Peter Trudgill (eds), *Sociolinguistics. An International Handbook of the Science of Language and Society.* Vol. 2. (Handbücher zur Sprach- und Kommunikationswissenschaft 3/2). Berlin: De Gruyter, 1452–1469.

Rössler, Paul. 1995. 'Sprache zur Erziehung – Erziehung zur Sprache. Felbigers Grammatiken und die schriftsprachliche Reform in Österreich in der zweiten Hälfte des 18. Jahrhunderts.' In: *Das achtzehnte Jahrhundert und Österreich. Jahrbuch der österreichischen Gesellschaft zur Erforschung des achtzehnten Jahrhunderts.* Band 10. Wien: WUV-Universitätsverlag, 55–72.

Rössler, Paul. 1997. Die deutschen Grammatiken der zweiten Hälfte des 18. Jahrhunderts in Österreich. Ein Beitrag zur Reform der deutschen Schriftsprache. (Schriften zur deutschen Sprache in Österreich 21). Frankfurt am Main: Peter Lang.

Rössler, Paul. 2005. Schreibvariation – Sprachregion – Konfession. Graphematik und Morphologie in österreichischen und bayerischen Drucken vom 16. bis ins 18. Jahrhundert. (Schriften zur deutschen Sprache in Österreich 35). Frankfurt am Main: Peter Lang.

Rudolph, Harriet. 2005. '"Sich der höchsten Gnade würdig zu machen". Das frühneuzeitliche Supplikenwesen als Instrument symbolischer Interaktion zwischen Untertanen und Obrigkeit.' In: Cecilia Nubola & Andreas Würgler (eds), *Bittschriften und Gravamina. Politik, Verwaltung und Justiz in Europa (14.–18. Jahrhundert).* (Schriften des Italienisch-Deutschen Historischen Instituts in Trient 19). Berlin: Duncker & Humblot, 421–449.

Salmons, Joseph. 2012. A History of German: What the past reveals about today's language. Oxford: Oxford University Press.

Schennach, Martin Paul. 2004. 'Supplikationen.' In: Josef Pauser, Martin Scheutz & Thomas Winkelbauer (eds), *Quellenkunde der Habsburgermonarchie (16.–18. Jahrhundert). Ein exemplarisches Handbuch.* (Mitteilungen des Instituts für Österreichische Geschichtsforschung Ergänzungsband 44). Wien: Oldenbourg, 572–584.

Schiegg, Markus. 2015. 'The Invisible Language of Patients from Psychiatric Hospitals.' In: Anna D. Havinga & Nils Langer (eds), *Invisible Languages in the Nineteenth Century.* (Historical Sociolinguistics 2). Oxford: Peter Lang, 71–94.

Schiegg, Markus. 2016. 'Code-Switching in Lower-Class Writing: Autobiographies by Patients from Southern German Psychiatric Hospitals (1852–1931).' In: *Journal of Historical Sociolinguistics* 2(1), 47–81.

Schneider, Edgar W. 2002. 'Investigating variation and change in written documents.' In: J. K. Chambers, Peter Trudgill & Natalie Schilling-Estes (eds), *The Handbook of Language Variation and Change.* Oxford: Blackwell, 67–96.

Schrimpf, Hans Joachim. 1980. *Karl Philipp Moritz.* (Realien zur Literatur, Sammlung Metzler Band 195). Stuttgart: Metzler.

Skutnabb-Kangas, Tove. 2000. Linguistic genocide in education – or worldwide diversity and human rights? Mahwah, New Jersey: Erlbaum.

Sokoll, Thomas. 1996. 'Selbstverständliche Armut. Armenbriefe in England 1750–1834.' In: Winfried Schulze (ed.), *Ego-Dokumente. Annäherung an den Menschen in der Geschichte?* (Selbstzeugnisse der Neuzeit 2). Berlin: Akademie, 227–271.

Sokoll, Thomas (ed.). 2001. *Essex Pauper Letters. 1731–1837*. Oxford: Oxford University Press.

Solms, Hans-Joachim & Klaus-Peter Wegera. 1993. 'Flexionsmorphologie.' In: Reichmann, Oskar & Klaus-Peter Wegera (eds), *Frühneuhochdeutsche Grammatik*. (Sammlung kurzer Grammatiken germanischer Dialekte 12). Tübingen: Niemeyer, 164–312.

Sroka, Wendelin. 2013. '"Milchrahm instead of Obers!" – on the long-term fate of vocabulary-related norms in primers of the Habsburg Monarchy.' In: *Reading Primers International* 9, 11–17.

Takada, Hiroyuki. 1998. Grammatik und Sprachwirklichkeit von 1640–1700. Zur Rolle deutscher Grammatiker im schriftsprachlichen Ausgleichsprozeß. (Germanistische Linguistik 203). Tübingen: Niemeyer.

Topalović, Elvira. 2003. Sprachwahl – Textsorte – Dialogstruktur. Zu Verhörprotokollen aus Hexenprozessen des 17. Jahrhunderts. Trier: Wissenschaftlicher Verlag Trier.

Ulbrich, Claudia. 1996. 'Zeuginnen und Bittstellerinnen. Überlegungen zur Bedeutung von Ego-Dokumenten für die Erforschung weiblicher Selbstwahrnehmung in der ländlichen Gesellschaft des 18. Jahrhunderts.' In: Winfried Schulze (ed.), *Ego-Dokumente. Annäherung an den Menschen in der Geschichte?* (Selbstzeugnisse der Neuzeit 2). Berlin: Akademie, 207–226.

Ulbricht, Otto. 1996. 'Supplikationen als Ego-Dokumente. Bittschriften von Leibeigenen aus der ersten Hälfte des 17. Jahrhunderts als Beispiel.' In: Winfried Schulze (ed.), *Ego-Dokumente. Annäherung an den Menschen in der Geschichte?* (Selbstzeugnisse der Neuzeit 2). Berlin: Akademie, 149–174.

Universiteit Leiden. *Letters as Loot*. Available at: http://www.hum.leiden.edu/research/letters-as-loot/ [accessed 26.04.2017].

Valentinitsch, Helfried. 1983. 'Advokaten, Winkelschreiber und Bauernprokuratoren in Innerösterreich in der frühen Neuzeit.' In: Winfried Schulze (ed.), *Aufstände, Revolten, Prozesse*. (Geschichte und Gesellschaft 27). Stuttgart: Klett-Cotta, 188–201.

Vandenbussche, Wim. 1999. ''Arbeitersprache' in Bruges during the 19th century.' In: Helga Bister-Broosen (ed.), *Beiträge zur historischen Stadtsprachenforschung*. (Schriften zur diachronen Sprachwissenschaft 8). Wien: Praesens, 21–47.

Vandenbussche, Wim. 2007. ''Lower-class language' in 19th century Flanders.' In: *Multilingua* 26, 277–288.

Voeste, Anja. 2008. *Orthographie und Innovation. Die Segmentierung des Wortes im 16. Jahrhundert*. (Germanistische Linguistik – Monographien 22). Hildesheim: Olms.

Voss, Lex Heerma van (ed.). 2002. *Petitions in Social History*. Cambridge: Cambridge University Press.

Wal, Marijke van der. 2006. *Onvoltooid verleden tijd. Witte vlekken in de taalgeschiedenis*. Amsterdam: Koninklijke Nederlandse Akademie van Wetenschappen.

Watts, Richard & Peter Trudgill (eds). 2002. *Alternative Histories of English*. London: Routledge.

Wegera, Klaus-Peter. 2013. 'Language data exploitation. Design and analysis of historical language corpora.' In: Paul Bennett, Martin Durrell, Silke Scheible & Richard J. Whitt (eds), *New Methods in Historical Corpora*. (Korpuslinguistik und interdisziplinäre Perspektiven auf Sprache 3). Tübingen: Narr, 55–73.

Weißenböck, Franz. 2010. 'Vom Dorfschulmeister zum Oberlehrer.' In: Fleißbild, Rohrstab, Eselsbank. Eine Zeitreise durch 400 Jahre Schulgeschichte im OÖ. Schulmuseum Bad Leonfelden. Bad Leonfelden: Eigenverlag, 34–40.

Wiesinger, Peter. 1995. 'Die sprachlichen Verhältnisse und der Weg zur allgemeinen deutschen Schriftsprache in Österreich im 18. und frühen 19. Jahrhundert.' In: Andreas Gardt, Klaus J.

Mattheier & Oskar Reichmann (eds), *Sprachgeschichte des Neuhochdeutschen. Gegenstände, Methoden, Theorien.* (Germanistische Linguistik 156). Tübingen: Niemeyer, 319–367.

Wiesinger, Peter. 1997. 'Die theoretischen Grundlagen der österreichischen Sprachreform des 18. Jahrhunderts.' In: Michael Benedikt & Reinhold Knoll (eds), *Verdrängter Humanismus – Verzögerte Aufklärung.* Band 1, Teilband 2: *Die Philosophie in Österreich zwischen Reformation und Aufklärung (1650–1750). Die Stärke des Barock.* Klausen-Leopoldsdorf: Editura Triade, 723–758.

Wiesinger, Peter. 2000. 'Die Entwicklung der deutschen Schriftsprache vom 16. bis 18. Jahrhundert unter dem Einfluß der Konfessionen.' In: *Zeitschrift der Germanisten Rumäniens* 9, 155–161.

Wiesinger, Peter. 2008. *Das österreichische Deutsch in Gegenwart und Geschichte.* (Austria: Forschung und Wissenschaft. Literatur- und Sprachwissenschaft 2). Wien: LIT.

Wiesinger, Peter. 2010. 'Johann Balthasar von Antespergs "Deutsches Kayserliches Schul- und Canzeley-Wörterbuch" von 1738.' In: Hubert Bergmann, Manfred Michael Glauninger, Eveline Wandl-Vogt & Stefan Winterstein (eds), *Fokus Dialekt. Analysieren – Dokumentieren – Kommunizieren. Festschrift für Ingeborg Geyer zum 60. Geburtstag.* (Germanistische Linguistik 199-201). Hildesheim: Olms, 481–502.

Wild, Reiner. 1990. 'Aufklärung.' In: Reiner Wild (ed.), *Geschichte der deutschen Kinder- und Jugendliteratur.* Stuttgart: Metzler, 45–98.

Würgler, Andreas. 2005. 'Bitten und Begehren. Suppliken und Gravamina in der deutschsprachigen Frühneuzeitforschung.' In: Cecilia Nubola & Andreas Würgler (eds), *Bittschriften und Gravamina. Politik, Verwaltung und Justiz in Europa (14.–18. Jahrhundert).* (Schriften des Italienisch-Deutschen Historischen Instituts in Trient 19). Berlin: Duncker & Humblot, 17–52.

Yonan, Michael. 2011. *Empress Maria Theresa and the Politics of Habsburg Imperial Art.* University Park: Pennsylvania State University Press.

Zenker, Ernst Victor. 1903. 'Die Geschichte der Wiener Zeitung in ihrem Verhältnisse zur Staatsverwaltung.' In: *Zur Geschichte der Kaiserlichen Wiener Zeitung. 8. August 1703–1903.* Wien: Selbstverlag der kaiserlichen Wiener Zeitung, 1–44. Available at: https://archive.org/details/zurgeschichteder00wienuoft [accessed 26.04. 2017].

Index

DOI 10.1515/9783110547047-008